# Federalism and European U the Building of Europe, 195

A revisionist interpretation of the post-war evolution of European integration and the European Union (EU), this book attempts to reappraise and reassess conventional explanations of European integration. It adopts a federalist approach which supplements state-based arguments with federal political ideas, influences and strategies. By exploring the philosophical and historical origins of federal ideas and tracing their influence throughout the whole of the EU's evolution, the book makes a significant contribution to the scholarly debate about the nature and development of the EU.

In order to reinstate federalism as a major influence upon both the origins and evolution of the EU, the book looks at federal ideas stretching back to the sixteenth century and demonstrates their fundamental continuity to contemporary European integration. It situates these ideas in the broad context of post-war Western Europe and underlines their practical relevance in the activities of Jean Monnet and Altiero Spinelli. Post-war empirical developments are explored from a federalist perspective, revealing an enduring persistence of federal ideas which have been either ignored or overlooked in conventional interpretations. The book challenges traditional conceptions of the post-war and contemporary evolution of the European Union, to reassert and reinstate federalism in theory and practice at the very core of European integration.

This challenging and thought-provoking volume is essential reading for all those interested in the history and philosophy of European federalism, European politics and the history of the EU.

**Michael Burgess** is Reader in Politics, Director of the Centre for European Union Studies (CEUS) and holds a Jean Monnet Chair in European Integration at the University of Hull. He has published widely on federalism and the European Union, British federal ideas, Canadian constitutional politics and comparative federalism. His current research interests include federalism in theory and practice and Canada–EU relations.

# Federalism and European Union: the Building of Europe, 1950–2000

Michael Burgess

London and New York

First published 2000
by Routledge
11 New Fetter Lane, London EC4P 4EE

Simultaneously published in the USA and Canada
by Routledge
29 West 35th Street, New York, NY 10001

*Routledge is an imprint of the Taylor & Francis Group*

Typeset in Baskerville by Wearset, Boldon, Tyne and Wear
Printed and bound in Great Britain by TJ International Ltd,
Padstow, Cornwall

*British Library Cataloguing in Publication Data*
A catalogue record for this book is available from the British Library

*Library of Congress Cataloging in Publication Data*

Burgess, Michael, 1949–
    Federalism and European union: the building of Europe,
    1950–2000/Michael Burgess
        p.   cm.
    Includes bibliographical references and index.
    ISBN 0–415–22646–5 (HB) – ISBN 0–415–22647–3 (PB)
    1. Federal government–European Union countries. 2. European
    federation–History–20th century. 3. European Union–History. 4.
    National state. 1. Title.

    JN30.B89 2000
    341.242'2'09–dc21                                99–053300

**For Adam**

# Contents

# Acknowledgements

The idea for this book did not emerge from many years of research on European integration. Indeed, I cannot claim paternity for it at all. It arose from a suggestion by an anonymous reviewer as an alternative to my original, rather unimaginative proposal for a successor volume to my earlier study, *Federalism and European Union: political ideas, influences and strategies in the European Community, 1972–87*, published by Routledge in 1989.

The previous study of federalism and European union, while now clearly outstripped by subsequent events and developments in European integration, has nonetheless been instrumental in enabling me to write a revisionist history of the post-war years since 1950. During this time, the evolution of the European idea came increasingly to resemble the federal idea. I have, therefore, drawn upon some material from the earlier study when it proved appropriate to do so, while not in any sense reproducing that book. Since 1989, I have become even more convinced about the significance of federalism in the building of Europe. At that time it was a risky business for an academic in the United Kingdom (UK) to make almost any claim for federalism in the progress and evolution of European integration. There was much hostility towards the federal idea and those who espoused it. My own task was to restore its reputation as a perfectly plausible and rational subject to reinstate in the building of Europe by detaching it from its unfortunate propagandist associations. Since then, it is fair to say that federalism as a political idea, influence and strategy has been taken much more seriously even by its earlier detractors.

Today the research community on European integration in the UK is much more inclined to accept the resilience and relevance of federalism than it has ever been. It is no longer a subject that generates more heat than light. The reasons for this are many and contentious but the empirical reality of the European Union (EU) itself is certainly a key factor. The EU exhibits so many federal and confederal elements in its constitutional, legal, economic and political make-up that only the most ill-intentioned, not to say perverse, observers would attempt to deny it. But their hostility to a federal Europe is based upon a fundamental misunderstanding of federalism itself.

A book like this is long overdue. Scholarly research requires that we consider many different approaches to the study of European integration and revisionist history should be welcomed in the continuing search for convincing explanations based upon empirically valid analyses and interpretations. I hope that this book will be received in this spirit.

# Introduction

This is a book about history, but history of a particular kind. My purpose is to re-examine and reappraise the post-war history of European integration with the intention of restoring the importance of federalism to the building of Europe. I intend to reinstate the federal idea as a perfectly feasible and empirically valid component in the overall explanation of the European construction.

It has long been my belief that it is dangerous to leave the study of history to historians. Political scientists have an important contribution to make to the study of post-war west European history which looks not only for the origins and development of political ideas but also for persistent patterns of human behaviour. Political ideas take root in specific social contexts and these contexts in turn facilitate particular kinds of human responses and reactions. At its most basic level, the germination and gestation of political ideas in the context of the building of Europe suggest that federalism merits detailed investigation as a distinct idea which harbours a particular vision of the evolving European reality. The history of post-war Western Europe, then, requires revision if this vision is to become a tangible reality. When the federal idea coincides with reality it has the possibility to be translated into practical action.

For too long the federal idea has been construed by its opponents as something which can be recognised and tolerated but which ultimately is either hopelessly impractical or downright Utopian. Indeed, for some hostile critics, it would be a real dystopia. Why has federalism provoked such an obviously irrational human response and why does it continue today to upset even well-informed observers of the evolving European Union (EU)? Put simply, the answer would seem to lie in context. The federalists' adversaries look upon the federal idea in the EU much less favourably than they do in its national context in federations like Switzerland, Germany or the United States. This is largely because they understandably construe the federal experience in these countries as part of the complex historical processes of state-building and national integration which have yielded new national states. Federalism has, therefore, become inextricably intertwined with the dual ideas of building both a new 'nation' and a new 'state'. Transposed to the EU level, it requires little imagination to comprehend the nightmare scenarios that can be conjured up as the price which would have to be paid for building Europe.

The equation of a federal Europe with the disappearance of the national state is of course over-simplified and chimerical. But the fear persists among some groups throughout Europe. It has acquired a strong grip in important sections of the populations of member states like Denmark, Sweden, France and the United Kingdom (UK) and it continues to be the source of much confusion and misunderstanding about Europe's ultimate destination. One purpose of this book is to help quell these fears and to clarify the nature and meaning of a federal Europe. Part of the problem lies in the use and abuse of conventional language and terminology to describe the building of Europe. Familiar words and phrases, like 'sovereignty', 'independence' and 'national identity', have invariably been couched in emotive terms deliberately intended to mislead people into thinking in zero-sum terms which result in fatuous conclusions. The building of Europe and the survival of the national state, as Alan Milward's historical research has shown, are perfectly compatible. Indeed, they are, in his view, two sides of the same coin.

The structure of this book is designed to explain, expose and underline federal ideas and influences in the post-war building of Europe in a chronological sequence so that their continuity, relevance and resilience is firmly established. Once the long intellectual journey of the European idea is explored and clarified in Chapter 1 and the theoretical discourse of federalism and federation are analysed in Chapter 2, the book follows a fairly simple, straightforward revisionist route intended to investigate, uncover and examine federal ideas, influences and strategies as they appear in the political history of the European adventure during 1950–2000. But, while the revisionist path was certainly intended to challenge the dominant realist or intergovernmentalist interpretation of European integration, it was not expected either to remove or replace it. My purpose was much less ambitious. In seeking to reinstate the federal idea and restore its significance to the post-war building of Europe, I merely wanted to put the record straight. I wanted to supplement rather than to replace existing explanations of European integration.

To pretend that the building of Europe can be understood solely in terms of the activities of the so-called founding fathers of European integration like Jean Monnet, Robert Schuman, Paul-Henri Spaak and Johan Willem Beyen has always been fanciful. No federalist has ever believed this. But this is not to say that elite political leadership, whether in a national or a supra-national context, has been irrelevant to major progress in European integration. As this study suggests, elite political leadership and institutional context have combined with skilful political strategies to devastating effect in the opportunities to move forward in both European cooperation and integration. Progress in these areas has never been mutually exclusive.

In my determination to emphasize the significance of federal ideas, influences and strategies in the development of post-war European integration, I have also noted the recent intellectual *rapprochement* between history and theory. In this book, I have tried to situate these two seemingly contradictory phenomena in a relationship which serves to point up the strength of the federalists' case. In other words, I have attempted throughout the book to demonstrate the empirical validity of federal ideas, influences and strategies in specific historical examples and episodes, and to relate them later to integration theory. Often the standard intergovernmentalist interpretation of a given set of historical events needs to be challenged from a federalist perspective in order to furnish a valid alternative explanation having its own empirical verifiability. As we know only too well, intergovernmental approaches to explaining European integration, with their exclusive emphasis upon the role of states and governmental elites, effectively close off and shut out rival perspectives. This is just one example of how competing historical interpretations can have important theoretical implications. The capacity of historical analysis to explain the course of European integration, as Milward has astutely argued, should not be underestimated but it depends ultimately upon who decides what constitute 'historical facts' and whether or not they are decisive.

The book is intended to be a modest contribution to both the history and theory of post-war European integration. As such, its revisionist thrust has theoretical implications which are implicit throughout but are made explicit only in Chapters 8 and 9. These implications can be summarized in the assertion that federalism must in future be firmly incorporated in current theories, models and approaches to European integration. Those who continue to dispute this must explain why it is that the EU has assumed the largely confederal shape that it has. It is time to turn to the first chapter which introduces us to the historical and philosophical origins of the European idea as a federal idea, and prepares the ground for a survey of the theoretical discourse on federalism and federation in Western Europe that follows it.

# 1 Federalism, the state and the European idea

At the end of the twentieth century, we continue to live in a world of states whose historical origins stretch back to sixteenth-century Europe. Europe was both the harbinger and the birthplace of the modern state. Its early evolution can be explained by the gradual breakdown of the feudal system and the increasing incidence of war. Indeed, there is plenty of historical and philosophical evidence which construes the early modern state simply as a war machine driven by the fundamental imperatives of princely power and territorial aggrandizement. The rise of the modern state in Renaissance Europe during the sixteenth and early seventeenth centuries went hand in hand with the emergence of sovereignty as a conceptual instrument for the organization of power in the state. The modern state, then, is an historical phenomenon but it is also, analytically, a distinct political institution developed by society; it is a particular means of organizing political power. In this chapter, I intend to explore the conceptual, philosophical and historical aspects to the relationship between federalism, the state and the European idea in order to furnish the basis for an initial understanding of what is implied by a 'federal' Europe. In the course of this exploration, we will establish two quite distinct traditions of federalism, namely, the 'Continental European' and the 'Anglo-American', and we will address the key distinction between *intrastate* and *interstate* federalism. But first, let us begin with a short survey of the modern state.

Through its evolution, the state came to be seen as 'public' power while society was equated with 'private' activities related to the ordinary day-to-day business of living. The seventeenth and eighteenth centuries witnessed the gradual development and consolidation of the modern territorial state as the sole legitimate source of public order and political authority. And the state was 'sovereign' in the sense that it admitted no rival or competing authority within its own territorially demarcated boundaries. The modern territorial sovereign national state was predicated upon the assumption that there was a final and absolute political authority in the political community. In Weber's terms, it possessed the legitimate monopoly of the means of physical coercion in a given territory. And it had two faces. The internal face of sovereignty was understood to be the source of the legal sanctions governing the use of physical coercion while the external face of sovereignty – international relations – confronted a world of similarly sovereign states where elite actors recognised no authority higher than their own except for treaty commitments which they could always revoke. In the absence of any overarching international authority which might attempt to monitor the behaviour of states and arbitrate between them in incidences of conflict, there was, therefore, an implicit 'anarchy' of international relations.

It is in this sense that Francis H. Hinsley referred to the origins and history of the state and sovereignty as indissolubly connected. The origin and history of sovereignty are intimately linked to the origin, nature and history of the modern state.[1] In the turbulence of sixteenth-century Europe, in an era of sustained dynastic and civil wars, religious schisms and a Holy Roman Empire in decay, the case for 'sovereignty' was made most forcibly and cogently by the French scholar, Jean Bodin. His *Les Six Livres de la République* was first published in 1576 and became the classic rationalization of the unitary monarchical state.[2] Bodin constructed his major work principally as a prescription for the achievement of order, stability and security for France in a dangerously uncertain world, but his recommendations also served the established interests of the hereditary nobility and medieval constitutional authorities. *La République* distilled the need for an undisputed sovereign authority into a simple formula: first, the authority of the state should be absolute, centralized and indivisible; and, secondly, the supreme sovereign power should reside in a monarch answerable only to God and natural law. Unless royal authority was endowed with supreme and indivisible authority, anarchy and civil war would result. Particular interests were elevated to universal prescription. However, it is also true that Bodin was addressing something much more profound than mere political expediency. *La République* stood as a bridge between the medieval, feudal period and the early modern epoch in the extent to which it recognised the existence of a natural order of things together with the new requirement that authority must henceforth be based upon legitimacy and consent. This reflected the shift from the divine rule of God to the notion of human will – the idea that human beings 'will' authority into existence via consent.

The Bodinian conception of the state and sovereignty was extremely rigid. The equation of order and stability with centralized, indivisible and unlimited power yielded a strict hierarchical structure – a single, basic pyramid of command and obedience. But if the triumph of the secular monarchical sovereign nation state – the state in which there was only one master – became the dominant political reality of this historical epoch, it was not without its critics from the very beginning. Indeed, the fundamental principles of political authority and the true attributes of sovereignty established by Bodin gave rise to much philosophical argument and speculation. The challenge to the Bodinian state began almost immediately he had formulated and disseminated his ideas about political authority.

The significance of Bodin for the emergence of federal ideas about the organization of the state resided in the imperative to refute his rigid conception of the state and sovereignty. By defining the state in such an exclusivist manner, he compelled his critics to come to terms either with his formulation of the concept or its application to particular cases. As S. Rufus Davis observed, it might initially seem paradoxical to include Bodin in a study of federal ideas but to omit him would be 'a grave error' for:

> whether by the force of repulsion or resistance, his catalytic influence on federal theory cannot be ignored ... other jurists could no more evade Bodin than successive generations of political jurists could free themselves from the questions – who commands, and how many masters can there be in a stable state, one, two, three, or more?[3]

Bodin's legacy was enduring. In the following two centuries after *La République*, the debate about the nature of the state and sovereignty continued to shape the philosophical climate. In the great pantheon of British political thinkers who helped to mould this new philosophical environment, the names of Thomas Hobbes, Algernon Sydney, John Locke and David Hume loom large. Hobbes's *Leviathan* (1651) stands in a direct line of descent to Bodin's *La République* as a theory of sovereignty. But Hobbes, who in a sense continued the work that Bodin had begun, must also be set in the context of 'social contract' theory which 'opened the door to a restatement of the classical notion of the popular basis of sovereignty'.[4] Along with Locke's *Treatise on Civil Government* (1690), the idea of the social contract epitomized the shift from absolutism and the divine right of kings to the subversive ideas of consent – the notion of a compact or contract (or even covenant) freely entered into – and limited government. Whereas Hobbes was agnostic about where the sovereign power should logically reside (though his own sneaking preference was for monarchy), Locke's reasoning catapulted him in the direction of the rights of man and representative parliamentary government.

It is important to note that neither Hobbes nor Locke donated anything directly to the modern federal idea, but in helping to shape a climate of intense political speculation and debate in which the old encrusted ideas and assumptions about authority and obligation were gradually discredited, they contributed the fundamental philosophical basis to it. Political theorists trace a fairly consistent line of thought grounded in social contract, natural rights, popular consent, the justification of resistance to authority, and utilitarianism, which brings into question the very essence of sovereign power. And the same observation may be made regarding the particular contributions of Rousseau and Montesquieu which reflected secular liberal Enlightenment thinking. Montesquieu's *Esprit des Lois* (1748) and Rousseau's *Contrat Social* (1762) both addressed philosophical questions which were germane to a political climate in which notions of popular sovereignty, individual liberty, limited government and the separation of powers could flourish. However, the main intellectual inspiration for the Continental European tradition of federalism did not derive from this broad philosophical source. Scholars of federalism are well-acquainted with the mainly political–theological, collectivist, corporatist identity of mainstream European federalism which derives from both Roman Catholic social theory and Protestant reformism, and begins with the German Calvinist intellectual, Johannes Althusius.[5] They are also familiar with the much later and very different secular anarchist–socialist intellectual strand of European federalism which is most closely associated with the French philosopher, Pierre-Joseph Proudhon.[6] However, if we wish to be more specific about federalism, the state and the European idea, we must investigate a much less well-known philosophical dimension to our subject, which can be traced back to the age of Bodin.

Recent research on the Anglo-American tradition of federalism has revealed the existence of a strand of federal thought unknown to most scholars of federalism until now. It is a source of European federalism which is quite different from the modern secular liberal Enlightenment thinking derived from Hobbes, Locke and Montesquieu, and it is located in what is called 'covenant' theory. As we shall see, this investigation brings the existence of two quite distinct political traditions of federalism into sharp focus. And, by bringing them closer together, it also furnishes the basis for some comparative reflections which serve to deepen and enrich our historical and philosophical understanding of a 'federal' Europe.

In 1991, two American academic specialists in theology, Charles McCoy and J. Wayne Baker, published their revisionist monograph entitled *Fountainhead of Federalism: Heinrich Bullinger and the Covenantal Tradition*.[7] This essay identified a hitherto unknown dimension of Anglo-American federalism best described as the Biblical–Reformed–Puritan–ethical religious strand of federal thought. The intellectual origins of this strand stretch back to Heinrich Bullinger, a Swiss theologian–philosopher of the sixteenth century. This revealing survey of Bullinger's own intellectual contribution to federal theory underlines how far this theological–political strand of federal thought antedates that of the conventional western liberal individualism of Hobbes, Locke and Montesquieu. But it is also of great significance for both the Continental European and the Anglo-American federal political traditions. We will take a closer look at the particular intellectual contribution of Bullinger to both of these traditions, but first let us address the idea of the covenantal tradition.

In modern times, covenantal theory is most closely associated with the American contributions to federal scholarship of Vincent Ostrom and Daniel Elazar. It is, above all, a biblical perspective of federalism.

According to this perspective, the concept of covenantal federalism embodies a set of normative principles which bind partners together in a moral contract or agreement of trust. The act of coming together remains a 'political bargain' but it is much more than just this; it is also based upon mutual recognition, tolerance, respect, obligation and responsibility. Indeed, Elazar refers to the genesis of such an arrangement in the original relationship between God and man which derives from the Bible. In a recent research paper, Michael Stein has underlined this:

> In the religious compact there is supposed to be a set of tacit moral obligations mutually accepted by the Deity and those who adopt his code of law and its moral precepts. The same covenant is supposed to commit the individual members of the covenanting group to appropriate moral behaviour in their relations with each other.[8]

Elazar's own research on American federalism arrived at the conclusion that a major source of the covenantal idea was both the Federalist Papers of Hamilton, Jay and Madison and the American Constitution (1789) itself.[9] The journey to this destination was assisted by Ostrom's pioneering work on the interpretation of late-eighteenth-century American political debates and constitutional negotiations in terms of these normative and convenantal principles.[10] This scholarship has, therefore, firmly established the link between federal theology and federal politics. Covenantal theory is clearly central to a particular perspective of and approach to the study of modern federalism and modern federal political systems.

If we now turn to examine the intellectual contribution of Heinrich Bullinger to two distinct federal political traditions, we can begin to understand why it is that McCoy and Baker are able to corroborate the evidence assembled earlier by Elazar and Ostrom. Indeed, McCoy and Baker are unequivocal in their belief that 'the terms "federal" and "covenantal" are closely related and, when carefully examined, virtually interchangeable.'[11] This argument, of course, is not restricted solely to American intellectual debate. In 1978, the Australian scholar of federalism, S. Rufus Davis, acknowledged precisely the same point:

> ... somewhere near the beginning of it all is the idea of 'foedus' ... And the lexicographic association of foedus with covenant, and of its cognate 'fides' with faith and trust, provide us with the first crucial clue. Because in the idea of covenant, and the synonymous ideas of promise, commitment, undertaking, or obligation, vowing, and plighting one's word to a course of conduct in relation to others, we come upon a vital bonding device of civilization ... the idea of covenant ... involves the idea of cooperation, reciprocity, mutuality, and it implies the recognition of entities – whether it be persons, a people, or a divine being.[12]

To McCoy and Baker, then, 'federal' derives from the Latin 'foedus' which means covenant. A covenantal order is federal. A federal order is covenantal.[13]

But what role does Bullinger play in the unfolding revelation of both European and Anglo-American federalism? The key to understanding Bullinger's contribution to these two quite distinct federal political traditions is to realise that academic specialization has separated the terms 'federal' and 'covenantal'. McCoy and Baker claim that what has been forgotten as academic disciplines have tended to isolate themselves from one another is that 'federal terminology is used by theological and political writers, as also is the language of covenant, compact and contract':

> In the sixteenth, seventeenth and eighteenth centuries, the era when the institutions of the modern world were taking shape, federal theologians dealt with political as well as ecclesiastical issues and political philosophers concerned with societal covenants dealt also with religious issues.[14]

Bullinger's 1534 treatise entitled *The One and Eternal Testament or Covenant of God*, according to these commentators, is the fountainhead of federalism in the specific sense that it is a basic source of federal thought among theologians, political philosophers and practising leaders in church and state. Bullinger was the leader of the Reformed Church of Zurich during 1531 and 1575 so that the *Testament* became a major theological and political influence upon the Reformed tradition in the sixteenth century. McCoy and Baker claim that the *Testament* is important for three principal reasons: first, because its influence was 'direct in the century following its publication and indirect during later times'; second, because in both theological and philosophical terms it established the formal link between federalism and covenant; and, third, because it recognised the significance of primary social entities – such as families, congregations, occupational guilds and commercial organizations – and their relationships as essentially 'federal'.[15] Additional reasons for its continuing significance are the emphasis (long before Montesquieu) upon the division of powers, the need to construe federalism in dynamic terms as a pattern of changing relations and, finally, the belief in humanity and history as both developmental and progressive.

In the *Testament*, Bullinger regarded the covenant as the divine framework for human life, both religious and civil. The Scripture in its entirety taught the covenant and its conditions; the moral law was a restatement of these conditions, and the magistrate had been designated to enforce the covenant's conditions among God's people. In short, the divine covenant between God and his people was to be replicated on earth as the very essence of human organization and civil society. Bullinger's *Testament*, therefore, became a hallmark of the Reformed tradition in continental

Europe, and in England and Scotland by the end of the sixteenth century. McCoy and Baker claim that, at this time, federal theology and political philosophy were 'evolving into the forms that permeate modern democratic societies' and that it was 'this federal tradition, with explicit theological, ethical and political dimensions, that was taken to the new world by the Puritans and used as a model for the colonies of New England'.[16]

Bullinger's *Testament* has now been rescued from obscurity and stands as a distinct branch of the larger Reformed tradition which has tended to be equated solely with Calvinism and thus over-simplified. This recent research reminds us that it is difficult, if not impossible, completely to disengage theological from political federalism in the sixteenth century. It is only later, in the seventeenth century, that the two elements can in practice be separated. But if, for the purposes of academic convenience, we do disconnect the development of theological federalism from the evolution of political federalism, it becomes clear how the first fully developed, systematic articulation of modern federal political philosophy emerged in 1603 in the form of *Politica Methodice Digesta* written by Johannes Althusius.

Althusius was a German Calvinist intellectual and political magistrate who emerged out of the Reformist tradition and built a political philosophy based upon the covenant theology already outlined above.[17] His conception of federalism grew out of a particular view of the polity, one that construed it basically as a compound political organization ranging from private associations composed of small groups, families and voluntary corporations to public associations and territorial units such as the local community, the province, the canton, and later, by implication, the national state. His was essentially an organic notion of society in which the integrity of the component parts was guaranteed by being built up from below:

> The result was a purely natural structure of society, in which the family, the vocational association, the commune and the province are all necessary and organic members intermediate between the individual and the state, and the wide union is always consolidated in the first place from the corporative unities of the narrower unions and obtains its members by this means. In this structure of society every narrow union as a real and original community creates for itself a distinct common life and a legal sphere of its own, and gives up to the higher union only so much thereof as the higher union absolutely needs for the attainment of its specific purpose.[18]

The political ideas and assumptions embedded in this classic work include the following: a fundamentally organic conception of society and the structures which comprised it, delineated by the principles of corporatism and subsidiarity; a recognition of both functional and territorial bases of representation; the belief in 'foedus' as a normative and ethical principle of human organization rather than as a mere empirical and/or instrumental meaning; and an acknowledgement of the complex interaction between individuals, groups and societies which characterized the fundamental interdependence of human life. The Althusian compound state, in contrast to the Bodinian centralized state, is therefore an amalgam of political associations based upon consent and built up from below, in which power is dispersed both territorially and functionally. Federation thus emerges as a political order which seeks to accommodate the greatest possible number of communities and societies, primary and intermediate, without destroying them. It is a living, pluralist, organic order which builds itself from the ground upwards, constructing its tiers of authority and decision-making according to the principle of subsidiarity.

Clearly it is important to situate Althusius's federalism in the context of the Reformed tradition: 'Althusius is immersed in Reformed faith, in the political thought of the Reformed communities, and in the biblical and theological scholarship of the Reformed tradition'.[19] This suggests that Althusius must continue to be regarded as the first great European theorist of modern federalism but that his own intellectual development was shaped and moulded by a religious, political and philosophical climate which already expressed, admittedly embryonic, elements of a federal tradition. Bullinger's *Testament* of 1534 therefore provided the philosophical assumptions and moral imperatives essential for the crystallization of Althusius's own federal political ideas. It was the intellectual backdrop essential to their early evolution.

But the impact of Bullinger's *Testament* should not be confined solely to a focus upon Althusius. It is also important to emphasize the intellectual links which were made across the generations in different countries. The transmission of Bullinger's 'theological–political' federalism appears to have been pervasive. According to McCoy and Baker, federal political thought spread rapidly during the seventeenth and eighteenth centuries and was brought to America by early settlers in the British colonies: the Anglicans in Virginia, the Puritans in New England in particular, and later the Presbyterians in the Middle Colonies. Furthermore, it was taught in the colonial colleges, one of the most striking examples being John Witherspoon, a Scottish federal theologian and political philosopher at the College of New Jersey, who taught James Madison. Small wonder that the federal tradition of the early American colonies should have influenced the formation of colonial charters and, later, the state constitutions. As Donald S. Lutz has already acknowledged, 'most state constitutions can be seen as reflecting a direct link with religious covenants traced through the compacts written by colonists during the seventeenth century'.[20] Hence, the major sources of federalism in America were 'the federal theology, the federal political philosophy, and the federal practice in societal institutions brought by groups coming from Europe to establish colonies and developed in distinctive ways in the 180 years from Jamestown to

Philadelphia'.[21] In this remarkably circuitous manner, a distinct Anglo-American tradition of federal political thought emerged during the seventeenth and eighteenth centuries which was highly complex and variegated. It drew upon a veritable myriad of continental European, British and indigenous American historical, philosophical and practical sources.[22]

The Anglo-American tradition of federalism, then, is much more distinctive and complex than might previously have been appreciated by scholars of modern federalism. It has usually been loosely referred to as pragmatic, instrumental and based largely upon Lockean notions of western liberal individualism. However, this general perception of its origins must now give way to the recognition of a much more normative, communitarian and pluralistic conception of federalism. Indeed, this view brings it much closer to the Continental European federal tradition than might originally have been anticipated. Given the relatively recent research focus upon the links between Bullinger and Althusius, it is now clear that these two intellectual pioneers of early modern federal political thought have had a pervasive influence upon both Anglo-American and European federal political traditions.

Daniel Elazar has observed that Althusius had the misfortune of publishing his great work at the very beginning of the seventeenth century, just at the time when his contemporaries were already turning towards Bodinian statism:

> In the struggle over the direction of European state-building in the seventeenth century, the Althusian view, which called for the building of states on federal principles – as compound political associations – lost out to the view of Jean Bodin and the statists who called for the establishment of reified centralized states where all powers were lodged in a divinely ordained king at the top of the power pyramid or in a sovereign center.[23]

Accordingly, Althusian thought gradually faded by the end of the seventeenth century and had to await the interest of a school of German thinkers, led by the jurist and legal historian, Otto von Gierke, in the late nineteenth century before it was rediscovered and rescued from relative obscurity. By then, of course, the Americans had invented modern federalism on the basis of an individualism which conformed to western liberal Enlightenment thinking and overshadowed the sort of convenantal, communitarian and pluralistic federal ideas originally derived from Bullinger and Althusius. However, there has also been a twentieth-century revival of interest in the political thought of Althusius spearheaded in 1932 by Carl Joachim Friedrich who republished the 1614 edition of the *Politics* in its original Latin language with an extensive introduction. This renewed academic interest in Althusius carried over into the post-World War Two era with various scholars researching into different aspects of Althusian federal political thought.[24] Althusius has therefore enjoyed something of a philosophical revival and restoration for those scholars who study federalism.

Coincident with this revival of interest in Althusius and his political thought has been a renewed interest in two further philosophical sources of the Continental European tradition of federalism. These are the nineteenth-century French socialist-anarchist philosopher, Pierre-Joseph Proudhon, and late nineteenth- and early twentieth-century Catholic social theory and personalist thought. We will not investigate these separate but related strands of European federalist thought in detail here, but it is nonetheless important to furnish a brief summary of their content because, together, they convey the great complexity of the European federal political tradition and help us to understand what is meant by the expression a 'federal' Europe.

Proudhon is probably best known as the father of anarchism and libertarian socialism. However, he is also part and parcel of the Continental European tradition of federalism. His major work on this subject, published in 1863, was *Du principe fédératif* in which he recommended a model of the state and society composed of autonomous communities which federated on the basis of contracts freely entered into.[25] His conception of the state–society relationship was, like that of Althusius, very much an organic view based upon corporatism and subsidiarity. Accordingly, power should be divided in order to be as close as possible to the level of the problems to be solved. But the focus of Proudhon's corporatist structure placed greater stress upon economic production. The Proudhonian society was concerned with the liberty and justice of men and women principally in their economic relations. For Proudhon, the free economic association of workers or producers in their local communities, workshops and small factories was the departure point for what he called a 'mutualist' society. This mutualism found its main expression in the desire to limit and regulate conflicts by balanced contracts between autonomous groups. Conflict was accepted as a given, but it would be regulated and contained in a federal structure. In this conception, then, federalism was about liberty and justice via autonomy and democratic self-management.

The similarities with Althusian federalism are quite striking. Apart from his emphasis upon corporatism and subsidiarity, Proudhon's mutualism was predicated upon the recognition of society as essentially multi-layered. It began with the individual and was built up from below via families, groups, economic units and local communities, and extended beyond even the state into an all-embracing transnational federation. And, like Althusius, his highly normative conception of federalism construed human beings as both social and moral persons rather than as mere isolated, atomistic individuals; they were 'whole' persons in the sense that their liberty and autonomy were achieved only by their interaction with and responsibility to other humans. And real personal relations could only succeed in a civilization of participation. We can appreciate from this brief outline of Proudhon's conception of federalism how 'personalism' – sometimes referred to as 'integral' federalism – first emerged in France during the 1930s.[26] The philosophy was developed and expounded in the two organizations known as 'L'Ordre Nouveau' and 'Esprit' which also published reviews by the same name. The personalists were originally led by a small group of highly influential philosophers among whom Alexander Marc, Robert Aron, Emmanuel Mounier, Daniel Rops and Denis de Rougemont were the most important.[27] They were joined, after the end of the Second World War, by Henri Brugmans, whose own wartime experience in the Resistance had converted him to personalism. We will return to this strain of federalism in the next chapter which looks in greater detail at the theoretical discourse on federalism, but for the moment it will suffice to emphasize once again the philosophical continuity evident here.

The other dimension to the Continental European tradition of federalism which we must consider briefly in this chapter is Catholic social theory. This dates from the late nineteenth century and is properly located in 'political Catholicism' which existed to defend both the spiritual and material interests of the Church. Catholic social thought was spelled out in a series of important papal encyclicals which spanned the years between the 1880s and the 1930s. For our purposes, the key encyclicals are *Rerum Novarum* enunciated in 1891 and *Quadragesimo Anno* which appeared in 1931.[28] Together, these doctrinal pronouncements constituted a philosophy of man and society which was rooted in pluralism, personalism, solidarism and subsidiarity. The Church did not formally address itself to federalism per se in these papal encyclicals, but in propounding a peculiarly organic view of society and its ethical–religious implications, it gave ecclesiastical authority to the central concepts which formed the basis of federal thought and action. The papal encyclicals, therefore, incorporated a set of assumptions and principles about man, the state and society which yielded a particular brand of Continental European federalism to be firmly integrated into the later Christian Democratic conception of European Union.[29]

Our short survey of Proudhonian federalism and Catholic social thought gives us the essential context for a much better understanding and appreciation of the richness and complexity of the Continental European tradition of federalism. We have not surveyed the whole philosophical literature on European federalism but our sketch outline of the key contributors to this tradition suggests that together Bullinger, Althusius, Proudhon, the Protestant Reformed tradition and the Roman Catholic papal encyclicals provide us with the contours of a continuous, unbroken political tradition which retains its direct relevance to the overall evolution of the European idea. It remains for us to demonstrate this continuing relevance. We will begin by identifying the important connecting links within this distinct political tradition and then relate them to the problems of a contemporary Europe where the national state has become increasingly embattled in its struggle to remain the sole legitimate public power and authority in relation to its mass population. The European tradition of federalism, traced back to its origins in Bullinger and Althusius, must be reconnected to the main contemporary concerns of power, authority, legitimation, identity, autonomy and sovereignty which continue to characterize the public debate about European Union. It is in this particular sense that Europe can return to itself.

In his research on Althusius, Elazar urges us to look closely at this philosopher not only in historical perspective as a transitional figure from medieval corporatism to modern federalism, but also as a source of ideas and models for what he calls a 'post-modern' federalism.[30] He bases this plea upon the distinction between 'premodern' and 'modern' federalism:

> Premodern federalism had a strong tribal or corporatist foundation, one in which individuals were inevitably defined as members of permanent, multi-generational groups and whose rights and obligations derived entirely or principally from group membership. Modern federalism broke away from this model to emphasize polities built strictly or principally on the basis of individuals and their rights, allowing little or no space for recognition or legitimation of intergenerational groups.[31]

Elazar claims that Althusius speaks to this philosophical rift by offering us a new synthesis, a way to reconcile the two diverging pathways. A 'post-modern' federalism would recognise the need for individuals in civil society to be secure in their individual rights while simultaneously acknowledging group identities as also having real, legitimate collective rights reflected in an appropriate constitutional or political status. This is a response which goes to the very heart of one of the major philosophical problems of the contemporary state and society, but it is obvious that the political ideas of Althusius cannot be literally transposed whole into what Elazar calls the 'post-modern epoch' at the end of the twentieth century. Nonetheless, he claims that 'much of his system, its ideas, and even its terminology, may be adaptable or at least form the basis for a post-modern federalism'.[32] We will return to the notion of 'post-modern' federalism at the end of the chapter. For the moment, let us consider the implications of our brief examination of the Continental European tradition of federalism for European integration.

We have already established the significance of Bullinger, Althusius and the covenantal dimension to both the Anglo-American and the Continental European federal traditions. Let us turn now to an examination of the key characteristics of the European tradition of federalism which remain fundamental to the idea of a 'federal' Europe. It is important to clarify these basic assumptions and features of European federalism at the outset because they help us to understand the imperatives which drive 'federalists' to want to build a 'federal' Europe. It should be added that they also help us to appreciate the real fears and anxieties of those who oppose this conception of Europe. Unfortunately, many critics of federalism either genuinely misunderstand the federal conception or deliberately seek to distort it for their own purposes. In the following sketch outline of the basic features of modern federalism and their implications for the building of Europe, then, we must tread very carefully in order to avoid such confusion and misunderstanding while at the same time acknowledging that we cannot prevent determined critics from deliberate distortion.

Before we go into detail, let us recapitulate what should be understood by federalism. Since it is a word which derives from the Latin root 'foedus', we must begin with its original meaning which has already been identified above by S. Rufus Davis. Foedus means agreement, bargain, covenant, compact or contract. But as such it is no ordinary agreement. Foedus also means 'fides' which is faith or trust. The implication of these terms for contemporary meaning is that a 'federal' pact or agreement is a union which must be voluntary and must be based upon mutual recognition and respect. The consequent rules and obligations freely entered into form a special relationship or covenant, namely a union which is binding and whose bonds are founded upon a moral contract, an agreement of trust. In summary, the act of coming together remains, as William Riker famously argued, a 'political bargain', but it is more than just this.[33] The act itself changes the contracting parties. Each participating state places itself within a new totality. And in addition to mutual recognition and respect, the new undertaking is also based upon toleration, cooperation, compromise, bargaining, negotiation, reciprocity, obligation and responsibility. These constitute, in a nutshell, its moral imperatives.

This summary conveys the sense in which federalism should be understood. Theoretically it may seem untidy and imprecise, but this is because in its broadest sense it seeks to explain the very essence of political activity and experience, namely, specific forms of human association. Federalism is an organizing concept; it is concerned with how human relations are best organized in order to accommodate, preserve and promote distinct interests and identities. The hallmark of foedus or federalism is the simultaneous combination of 'union' and 'autonomy'. And this combination can apply to what we have already identified as the 'external' face of the state, or international relations, as well as to the 'internal' face of the state, or domestic politics. In the world of states, that which we call international relations, this suggests a particular type of federal union. Traditionally it refers to a form of limited union, a partnership or association of states to which the label 'confederation' has typically been attached. In its simplest sense, this form of union is one in which the participating states maintain their integrity or identity as states. We will examine the nature and meaning of confederation in the next chapter. For the moment, let us continue with this line of analysis. If we descend from the world of relations *between* states – interstate relations – to the level of the state itself and relations *within* the state, we would focus narrowly upon intrastate relations. This would bring us into the conceptually more precise world of the federal state or federation, and our attention would be riveted upon the sort of intrastate issues, like Bund-lander relations in Germany or fiscal federalism in Switzerland, which would typically characterize federation. Since Chapter 8 looks in some considerable detail at how far these conventional classifications apply to the European Union (EU), we will look instead at what the Continental European tradition of federalism suggests about the building of Europe on the threshold of the twenty-first century.

What, then, does our brief survey of the European tradition of federalism tell us about a 'federal' Europe today? And how far does it help us to conceptualize and clarify the 'European idea'? Clearly the contributions of Bullinger, Althusius and Proudhon to federal theory point to a Europe in which different forms of groups, associations and identities should be organized both horizontally and vertically. The EU must, therefore, be more like the compound union of Althusius rather than the centralized, hierarchical political authority of Bodin. Decisions must be taken as closely as possible to the citizenry in whatever associations or organizations correspond to their ordinary, routine practice of life. In other words, it should be federal rather than unitary. The reality and resilience of the modern state is, of course, self-evident and it is likely to remain the key building block of the EU for the foreseeable future. But it is not the only actor in the process of European integration. Both the internal and the external environment of the state have changed significantly since the end of the Second World War. It can no longer shape and determine its future alone. Only by entering into new economic and political relationships can it hope to enhance its own autonomy, security and general well-being in a much more complex and competitive world. New threats and challenges call for adjustment and adaptability to change. They call for new ways of structuring and organizing human relations both within and without the state.

The European federal tradition suggests that the EU should be a union of states and citizens in which the limits to central authority are clearly identified. However, this would suggest a shift from the language of treaty to the language of constitution. Its implication is a fully-fledged, federal constitution in which powers and competences are divided and shared between the EU, its constituent member states and, in turn, their component regional units. Only in this way can the limits to central authority really be firmly entrenched. The principle of subsidiarity, by which basic social functions can be carried out at primary or lower levels of associational life with performance criteria determining which functions should be managed at a higher level, has been inserted into the EU but in a somewhat confused and confusing context. It remains subject to a variety of conflicting interpretations and, as we will see in Chapter 7, it has no necessary implications for the internal structures of the member states.

The question of the internal structures of the constituent units of the EU, however, is interesting from an Althusian perspective. His own conception of the European reality, as Elazar has remarked, was one which accommodated four or five arenas of territorial governance instead of two or three which is the usual number in modern federations.[34] There are now three established federations in the EU, namely, Germany, Austria and Belgium, with Spain widely recognised to be federal in all but name. This means that for these member states, which already have three or four arenas of territorial governance, the EU represents a fourth or a fifth level. In such a creative, imaginative way is the complexity of late modernity effectively managed.

Finally, the European federal tradition helps us to understand and finally to come to terms with the contentious question of sovereignty. Neither Althusius nor Proudhon construed sovereignty as particularly problematical. Since they did not accept the notion of indivisible sovereignty extolled by Bodin, they were able to conceive of sovereign power as both shared and divided. For Althusius, the polity was founded upon the natural tendency for human beings to interact and communicate (in the sense of sharing) so that its members were 'symbiotes'. Sovereignty was, therefore, embodied in symbiotically organized associations rather than in the individual citizen. Moreover, Althusius constructed a federal polity which was territorial, functional and consociational. This meant that the constituent power of the people, or popular sovereignty, was also vested in a *consociatio consociationum* which enabled the people to delegate the exercise of sovereign power to different bodies. And the principle of corporate representation of state and societal structures reflected a non-territorial, functional basis to the polity. The overall consequence was a conception of sovereignty which was much more flexible than that bequeathed by Bodin. Clearly the European federal tradition suggests that we should not let the frequently emotive issue of sovereignty obscure the debate about the building of Europe. As a political concept, sovereignty has long been emptied of substance. The character of the state and relations between states have changed so much that the conceptual coherence of sovereignty has been shattered. Sovereignty is neither final nor absolute; it is simply irrelevant. Bodin has been effectively superseded. As Elazar has observed, 'even where the principle is not challenged, the practical exercise of absolute sovereignty is no longer possible'. Where it survives, sovereignty has been vested in constitutions.[35] Today it is much more accurate to refer to the 'autonomy' of the modern state – its capacity to determine itself – than it is to speak of what is now an outmoded sovereignty.

This discussion of the relevance of the European tradition of federalism to a 'federal' Europe brings us back full circle to the European idea itself. What, then, do we mean by the 'European idea'? At first glance it seems to be nothing more than an abstract, Utopian notion incapable of being translated into reality. This would be true if we were to construe it in the nonsensical terms that Mrs Thatcher used in her infamous Bruges Speech of September 1988 when she railed against an imagined 'Identikit European Personality'.[36] The pursuit of a single European identity is clearly chimerical. However, there is no necessary antipathy between the national state and European integration. Nor is there a fundamental contradiction or incompatibility between the national state and a 'federal' Europe. Indeed, it is perfectly possible to claim with considerable conviction that the very salvation of the national state lies in the construction of an EU which is based upon federal principles. There is already an established school of thought which argues that the progress of European integration, though not federalism, has actually strengthened rather than weakened the national state since 1945.[37]

Much has been written about the 'European idea' and it has been conceptualized in several different ways. A recent collection of essays on the subject has claimed that it is embedded in a mix of three interrelated concepts: first, the claim that there is something specific called 'Europe'; second, that there is a European 'self-identity' which is perceived by Europeans themselves; and, third, that history has revealed various political schemes for European unity.[38] History, of course, has often been pressed into the service of a particular cause and that of European unity is no exception. When necessary, a selective interpretation of history – European history – has been adopted in order to highlight fundamental continuities which help to support a particular vision of the future. And there is no doubt that the so-called 'European idea' has been idealistic. It has been used often to refer back to an imagined 'Golden Age' of Europe just as it has been invoked to engage the perceived crises of the twentieth century.

Before we clarify what we take the 'European idea' to mean in this book, it is appropriate first to call attention to a paradox which lies at the root of this question. The essence of the paradox lies in the empirical origins of both the national state and the 'European idea'. They appear to have emerged simultaneously. The emergence of a 'distinct, self-reflective idea of a Europe with a history and meaning of its own' only emerged with the French Revolution.[39] And 'the idea of the nation-state, to which all citizens feel committed, much as they once did to their family, or local community or church' was also a product of the French Revolution so that it was the nineteenth century which witnessed 'the emergence of the nation-state system we today view as natural and eternal'.[40] This confirms the view that there is no necessary contradiction between the European idea and the idea of the national state. Indeed they coexist quite comfortably.

For our purposes in this chapter, we will take the 'European idea' to be a political idea. It is the vehicle for the political union of Europe based upon federal principles. We have already drawn upon Europe's rich federal heritage in order to legitimize this goal and we have addressed some of the genuine fears and objections to this conception of Europe. A 'federal' Europe is not about a unitary centralized state. Nor is it 'imperium', a new form of empire. Indeed, it is the exact opposite. And, put simply, European integration today is an attempt by the modern state to accommodate and adjust to unprecedented changes in the global political economy. Change, however, generates new problems. But the response of the state is a recognition that many of the new problems are common problems which can be resolved only by novel forms of concerted action requiring more complex levels of institutionalization. The expression 'European idea' conveys the sense of a 'unity in diversity'. It acknowledges the need to attempt to solve new problems in a context which is radically different from conventional international relations. It has gone beyond this familiar mode of interstate relations towards a much more binding and integrated political union, one which is clearly much more than a mere free trade area or common market but which is less than a state. The most significant feature of this evolving union based upon federal principles is that it continues to recognise the fundamental integrity and autonomy of its constituent parts. This is a federal conception and it has the distinct advantage that it is in direct contact with Europe's history, philosophy and contemporary constitutional and political realities. Let us now conclude the chapter by reflecting broadly upon some of the linkages made in our survey of federalism, the state and the European idea.

This chapter suggests that federalism, the state and the European idea are interrelated in a highly complex manner. The complexity is underlined by a series of novel historical and philosophical paradoxes which are as surprising as they are perplexing. Ironically the very emergence and evolution of the modern state, which might have been expected to render the federal idea obsolete, actually made it a real practical possibility. The historical and philosophical development of the state has revealed a quite remarkable capacity to adjust and adapt in order to endure. And this conceptual and empirical flexibility has meant that the state has never been imprisoned by the language and conventions of one particular era or generation. The story is similar with history. Popular acceptance of the European idea does not depend upon how far we can present it as a logical historical extension of the nineteenth-century national state. The attempt to explain the European idea in terms of conventional processes of nation-building is plainly misleading. Federalists do not wish to create a 'European nation-state' of the sort alluded to by Mrs Thatcher. To paraphrase Jeremy Bentham, this would indeed be 'nonsense on stilts'. It would be inaccurate, absurd and disingenuous. Rather the European idea is much

more civic and much less exclusivist than the national state. It is not condemned to succeed and there is no blueprint for its success. Its future
progress will depend upon how far it can successfully reflect contemporary
European realities. At the end of the twentieth century, these realities
compel it to focus upon the representation of western liberal democratic
constitutionalism suffused with specific national cultures and particular,
selective historical memories. This is the only way that the European idea
can be compatible with the established sense of national identity in
Europe. As one writer has recently remarked, 'it is possible that the nature
of European political identity is more in tune with post-modern patterns
of identification' which involve 'multiple identities'.[41] This observation
brings us back conveniently to Elazar's notion of a 'post-modern' federalism which we mentioned above. Since it has interesting implications for
the European idea, we will bring the chapter to a close by looking briefly
at it.

In a sense, Elazar's 'post-modern' thesis brings us full circle to the
beginning of the chapter when we first referred to a world of states. The
premise of his thesis is that in the late twentieth century we are 'in the
midst of a paradigm shift from a world of states, modeled after the ideal of
the nation-state developed at the beginning of the modern epoch in the
seventeenth century, to a world of diminished state sovereignty and
increased interstate linkages of a constitutionalized federal character'.[42]
The origins of the paradigm shift are located at the end of the Second
World War, but Elazar claims that its extensive and decisive character was
not fully recognised until the disintegration of the Soviet Union during
1989–93. Indeed, even to most informed observers, it seemed to have
'crept up unawares'.[43] The reality of this momentous change is not that
states are disappearing but that the state system is 'acquiring a new dimension' which is now beginning 'to overlay and, at least in some respects, to
supersede the system that prevailed throughout the modern epoch'.
Accordingly, the implications are enormous:

> Whereas before, every state strove for self-sufficiency, homogeneity,
> and, with a few exceptions, concentration of authority and power in a
> single center, under the new paradigm, all states have to recognize as
> well their interdependence, heterogeneity, and the fact that their
> centers, if they ever existed, are no longer single centers but parts of a
> multi-centered network that is increasingly noncentralized, and that
> all of this is necessary in order to survive in the new world.[44]

Elazar's conception is global and he construes this network of complex
interactions as compelling states into 'various combinations of self-rule
and shared rule', his own shorthand definition of modern federalism.[45]
This 'federalist revolution', however, is not confined to modern federation
but includes a variety of looser federal arrangements designed to

accommodate internal divisions. It also explains the emergence and evolution of the EU which has developed into a 'new-style confederation ... designed to fit European realities'.[46]

This allusion to a 'post-modern' federalism has obvious implications for the EU which is the latest stage in the evolution of the European idea as a constitutional and political idea. However, it also has important theoretical implications for the study of federalism itself, especially the assertion that the term 'federation' is now far too restrictive and confining to assist us in explaining what is happening in the contemporary world of states. With this suggestion in mind, we will turn in the next chapter to examine the theoretical discourse on federalism and federation in Western Europe in order principally to explain its continuing relevance to the post-war evolution of European integration.

## NOTES

1  F.H. Hinsley, *Sovereignty*, London: C.A. Watts, 1966.
2  See M.J. Tooley (ed.), *Six books of the commonwealth*, Oxford: Basil Blackwell, 1955.
3  S.R. Davis, *The federal principle: a journey through time in quest of a meaning*, London: University of California Press, 1978, pp. 46–47.
4  S. Lakoff, 'Between either/or and more or less: sovereignty versus autonomy', *Publius*, 24(1), p. 68, 1994.
5  See F.S. Carney, *The politics of Johannes Althusius*, London: Eyre & Spottiswoode, 1964.
6  See R. Vernon, *The principle of federation by P.-J. Proudhon*, Toronto: University of Toronto Press, 1979.
7  C.S. McCoy and J.W. Baker, *Fountainhead of federalism: Heinrich Bullinger and the covenantal tradition*, Louisville, Kentucky: Westminster/John Knox Press, 1991.
8  M. Stein, 'Changing concepts of federalism since World War II: Anglo-American and Continental European traditions', paper presented to the International Committee for the Study of the Development of Political Science, Mexico City, Mexico, 1994.
9  See J. Kincaid and D.J. Elazar (eds), *The covenant connection: federal theology and the origins of modern politics*, Durham, N.C.: Carolina Academic Press, 1985; and D.J. Elazar, *Exploring federalism*, Tuscaloosa, AL, University of Alabama Press, 1987.
10  V. Ostrom, *The political theory of a compound republic: designing the American experiment*, Lincoln and London: University of Nebraska Press, 1987.
11  C.S. McCoy and J.W. Baker, *Fountainhead of federalism*, p. 11.
12  S.R. Davis, *The federal principle*, p. 3.
13  C.S. McCoy and J.W. Baker, *Fountainhead of federalism*, pp. 11–12.
14  C.S. McCoy and J.W. Baker, *Fountainhead of federalism*, p. 12.
15  C.S. McCoy and J.W. Baker, *Fountainhead of federalism*, pp. 12–14.
16  C.S. McCoy and J.W. Baker, *Fountainhead of federalism*, p. 21.
17  See F.S. Carney, *The politics of Johannes Althusius*.

18  S. Mogi, *The problem of federalism: a study in the history of political theory*, vol. II, London: Allen & Unwin, 1931, pp. 1073–74.

19  C.S. McCoy and J.W. Baker, *Fountainhead of federalism*, p. 53.

20  D.S. Lutz, 'From covenant to constitution in American political thought', *Publius*, 10(4), p. 128, 1980.

21  C.S. McCoy and J.W. Baker, *Fountainhead of federalism*, p. 89.

22  See M. Burgess, 'Federalism in Anglo-American political thought during the seventeenth and eighteenth centuries', paper presented to the International Symposium on Federalism and Civil Societies, German Institute for Federal Studies, Hanover, Germany, 1996.

23  D.J. Elazar, 'Federal-type solutions and European integration, in C.L. Brown-John (ed.), *Federal-type solutions and European integration*, p. 444, Lanham, Md.: University Press of America, 1995.

24  C.J. Friedrich, *The politica methodice digesta of Johannes Althusius*, Cambridge, Mass.: Harvard University Press, 1932; see also F.S. Carney, *The politics of Johannes Althusius*, 1964; P. Riley, 'Three seventeenth century German theorists of federalism', *Publius*, 6(3), pp. 7–41, 1976; and T.O. Hueglin, 'Johannes Althusius: medieval constitutionalist or modern federalist?', *Publius*, 9(4), pp. 9–41, 1979.

25  R. Vernon, 'Introduction' in *The principle of federation by P.-J. Proudhon*, pp. xxxvii–xxxix, Toronto: University of Toronto Press, 1979.

26  See R. Nelson, 'The federal idea in French political thought', *Publius*, 5(3), pp. 9–62, 1976; F. Kinsky, 'Personalism and federalism', *Publius*, 9(4), pp. 131–56, 1979; L. Roemheld, *Integral federalism*, New York: Verlag Peter Lang, 1990; and G.L. Ulmer, 'What is integral federalism?', *Telos*, 91(2), pp. 135–49, 1992.

27  A comprehensive bibliography of writings on integral federalism can be found in L. Roemheld, *Integral federalism*, 1990.

28  A. Fremantle (ed.), *The papal encyclicals in their historical context*, London: Mentor-Omega, 1963.

29  See M. Burgess, 'The European tradition of federalism: christian democracy and federalism', in M. Burgess and A.-G. Gagnon (eds), *Comparative federalism and federation: competing traditions and future directions*, pp. 138–53, Hemel Hempstead: Harvester Wheatsheaf, 1993.

30  D.J. Elazar, 'Federal-type solutions and European integration', pp. 447–48.

31  D.J. Elazar, 'Federal-type solutions and European integration', p. 447.

32  D.J. Elazar, 'Federal-type solutions and European integration', p. 448.

33  W.H. Riker, *Federalism: origin, operation, significance*, Boston: Little Brown, 1964.

34  D.J. Elazar, 'Federal-type solutions and European integration', p. 444.

35  D.J. Elazar, 'Federal-type solutions and European integration', p. 449.

36  M. Thatcher, 'Britain and Europe: the Bruges speech, 20 September 1988', London: Conservative Political Centre, 1988.

37  A. Milward, *The European rescue of the nation-state*, London: Routledge, 1994 and S. Hoffman, *The European sisyphus: essays on Europe, 1964–1994*, Oxford: Westview Press, 1995, are representative examples of this school of thought.

38  K. Wilson and J. van der Dussen (eds), *What is Europe?: the history of the idea of Europe*, London: Routledge, 1995, p. 9.

39  K. Wilson and J. van der Dussen (eds), *What is Europe?*, p. 10.

40  M. Horsman and A. Marshall, *After the nation-state: citizens, tribalism and the new world disorder*, London: HarperCollins Publishers, 1995, p. 10.

41  O. Waever, 'Europe since 1945: crisis to renewal', in K. Wilson and J. van der Dussen (eds), *What is Europe?: the history of the idea of Europe*, p. 207.

42  D.J. Elazar, 'From statism to federalism: a paradigm shift', *Publius*, 25(2), p. 5, 1995.

43  D.J. Elazar, 'From statism to federalism', p. 6.
44  D.J. Elazar, 'From statism to federalism', p. 7.
45  See D.J. Elazar, *Exploring federalism*, p. 5.
46  D.J. Elazar, 'Federal-type solutions and European integration', p. 441.

# 2 Federalism and federation in Western Europe
## The theoretical discourse

We have already demonstrated how far federalism in its historical and philosophical dimensions has been woven into the fabric of the European idea. It has criss-crossed into both the Anglo-American and the Continental European political traditions, yielding a highly flexible, versatile amalgam of social, economic and political ideas which relate directly to different forms of human association and the organization of power at different levels. These received ideas about how human beings organize human relations in order to achieve order and stability in the polity have important theoretical implications for both contemporary intrastate and interstate relations. In other words, they have become part and parcel of the theoretical discourse on the structure and organization of the state and on the relations between states. For our purposes in this book, the subject of European integration is a convenient bridge which spans these two separate but intimately interconnected worlds. Put simply, federalism operates at the level of the domestic West European state – in Germany, Austria, Switzerland and Belgium – and simultaneously at the level of so-called 'intergovernmental relations' between the member states in the European Union (EU). In this chapter, I intend to examine the nature of the relationship between federalism and European integration. In order to do this, it is first necessary to distinguish between 'federalism' and 'federation' as key political concepts. This conceptual distinction will inform the analysis which follows, and is intended primarily to provide a convenient entry point into what is a complicated relationship with many twists and turns, and not a little controversy. We will also briefly examine the federal political ideas of Jean Monnet and Altiero Spinelli since it has been their activities which have been largely responsible for the peculiar evolution of European integration. Finally, the changing research agenda for federalism and European integration will be addressed in an effort to point up some of the intellectual trends in the theoretical discourse. But let us begin with a brief discussion of the basic concepts involved, together with a look at the terminological implications of our definitions.

## Federalism, federation and the European Union

Federalism and federation are two terms which have usually been used synonymously by scholars. This compression of terms is largely the legacy of K.C. Wheare whose enormously influential *Federal Government* was first published in 1946.[1] Wheare's approach to the subject reflected a long intellectual lineage, rooted in nineteenth-century English liberal constitutional and political ideas about the state, government and the citizen, which stretched back at least to E.A. Freeman, Regius Professor of Modern History at Oxford, whose own *History of Federal Government in Greece and Italy* first appeared in 1863.[2] This legacy presented the study of federation and federal government in essentially historical, constitutional and juridical terms. It was a very static interpretation of the subject which understandably reflected the political science scholarship of the age. Since then, however, studies of federation, federal political systems and federal government have progressed and expanded *pari passu* with the overall advances made in political science itself. The so-called 'behavioural revolution' in the post-war social sciences exposed the narrow, rigid and legalistic view of the subject and brought it under the intellectual influences of economics, sociology and psychology, resulting in a much wider, more inclusive, scholarly ambit.

One consequence of this intellectual evolution was that a new conceptual distinction gradually, almost imperceptibly, appeared, albeit in an implicit sense. W.S. Livingston implicitly acknowledged the distinction in his provocative and influential article, 'A note on the nature of federalism', first published in 1952.[3] C.J. Friedrich also recognised the distinction and its validity in his own *Trends of Federalism in Theory and Practice*, first published in 1968.[4] However, the implicit became explicit in 1982 when Preston King's study, *Federalism and Federation*, was published, calling attention to federalism as an avowedly ideological and/or philosophical position.[5] My own book as editor, *Federalism and Federation In Western Europe*, appeared in 1986 and another, jointly edited, contribution to the subject, *Comparative Federalism and Federation*, was published in 1993.[6] Moreover, the International Political Science Association (IPSA) also acknowledged the validity of the distinction by confirming the existence of the Comparative Federalism and Federation Research Committee which continues to promote and publish research founded largely but not entirely upon this conceptual distinction.[7]

It is important to note, however, that this conceptual distinction between federalism and federation has not replaced earlier approaches to the study of the subject. It has simply added another perspective to the continuing intellectual debate about federations and federal governments. Some scholars still use the terms 'federalism' and 'federation' interchangeably to refer to both a process and a terminal end-point. For them, the legacy of Wheare has endured. Indeed, King observed in 1982 that many, perhaps most, writers 'continue to make no distinction at all' between the terms.[8] Consequently, these terms might be used to describe the process of 'federalizing' whereby two or more states come together to form a new union of states, namely, a federal union or confederation. Or, if the new union was more binding and included both states and citizens, they might equally be used to refer to the logical outcome of this process, namely, a federal state or federation. At first glance, this may seem a harmless indulgence. However, the problem with this kind of terminological imprecision is that it produces both confusion and genuine misunderstanding, especially when we relate it directly to European integration. For example, it is not clear precisely how the term 'federal' should be applied to the EU without either misleading people or making the study of the EU itself intellectually unintelligible. Yet we know that there are some aspects of the EU which are decidedly 'federal' or are referred to as 'federal-type'. How, then, do we use the terms 'federalism' and 'federation' in order to bring clarity to our subject? We will return to this conundrum later in the chapter. For the moment let us define our terms and refine our basic concepts.

Since 'federation' is a long-standing term with which political scientists are familiar, we will begin by defining it. According to King, federation is defined as 'an institutional arrangement, taking the form of a sovereign state, and distinguished from other such states solely by the fact that its central government incorporates regional units in its decision procedure on some constitutionally entrenched basis'.[9] This definition is perfectly acceptable because it recognizes the cardinal feature of federation, namely, the institutionalization of diversity in a state or, to put it bluntly, the institutionalization of those relationships in a state which have political salience. This accords well with the essentially moral thrust evident in the federal political thought of both Bullinger and Althusius, sketched out in the previous chapter. Federation exists precisely because it formally acknowledges the sorts of identities and diversities which constitute that sense of difference so essential to a living, breathing, pluralist social and political order. But diversity takes many forms and political science is concerned chiefly with those diversities which have the capacity for political mobilization. Federation is not and cannot be the appropriate political expression for every form of diversity that exists. It is not a universal panacea for the politics of difference. On the contrary, it is one direct response to those diversities which can determine the very legitimacy and stability of the state itself.

Following this reasoning, federation is a specific organizational form which includes structures, institutions, procedures and techniques. It is a tangible institutional reality. And it can be distinguished from other forms of state relatively clearly. King is unequivocal about its distinguishing hallmark: it is the accommodation of the constituent units of the union in the decision-making procedure of the central government 'on some

constitutionally entrenched basis'. In so far as this is achieved, the federation 'is to be viewed as non-absolutist, as constitutional, in this sense as a
democracy'. It is 'a case of corporate self-rule, which is to say as some form
of democratic or constitutional government'.[10] There are, however, many
forms of democratic and constitutional rule, and federation is only one of
these.

It is important to note that the gist of recent scholarly analyses of federation regarding their constitutionality is that it is constitutional autonomy
which matters rather than the particular division of powers between
central and local governments.[11] A variety of ways exist of affording special
or entrenched constitutional representation in the decision-making procedure of the central government. Constitutionality rests upon both autonomy and representation. In the context of European integration, it is
particularly significant to remember that the constituent units of a federation are not mere local authorities subordinate to a dominant, overarching central power of the kind we would expect to find in a unitary state
like the United Kingdom or France. On the contrary, they themselves 'are'
states, with states' rights. The very essence of federation as a particular
form of union is, in Daniel Elazar's words, 'self-rule plus shared rule'.[12] In
short, the constituent units in a federation have the constitutionally-
endowed right of existence together with the right to an area of legislative
and administrative autonomy. Constitutional entrenchment is, therefore,
the key to their political, economic and cultural self-preservation. Indeed,
it is the guarantee of their very survival as states within a larger state.

Our discussion of federation demonstrates that – at least in western
liberal democracies – there is a distinctive organizational form or institutional fact which exists to accommodate the constituent units of a union in
the decision-making procedure of the central government by means of
constitutional entrenchment. The genius of federation lies in its infinite
capacity to accommodate and reconcile the competing and sometimes
conflicting array of diversities having political salience within a state. Tolerance, respect, compromise, bargaining and mutual recognition are its
watchwords and 'union' combined simultaneously with 'autonomy' is its
hallmark. Some conceptual problems with federation, such as the related
debate about constitutionalism, remain to be fully resolved but for our
purposes it has been defined and, as King would put it, it has been given
'some reliable and fairly fixed sense'.[13] Its conceptual application to European integration and its empirical utilization in the EU will be explored
later in the chapter. For the moment, let us turn our attention to federalism and examine its distinctive features in order to assess the utility of our
conceptual distinction.

Federalism informs federation and vice versa. It is essentially a symbiotic
relationship. Federalism can be taken to mean ideological position, philosophical statement and empirical fact. Mindful of our conceptual distinction between federalism and federation, let us here take federalism to

mean the recommendation and (sometimes) the active promotion of support for federation. It is ideological in the sense that it can take the form of an overtly prescriptive guide to action, and it is philosophical to the extent that it is a normative judgement upon the ideal organization of human relations and conduct. It can also be viewed as empirical fact in its recognition of diversity – broadly conceived in its social, economic, cultural and political contexts – as a living reality, something which exists independent of ideological and philosophical perceptions. This is what is meant when some federalists claim that social life is by nature 'federal'. The way people live their lives and organize themselves naturally, without state intervention, is intrinsically federal; it is a natural social reality expressive of overlapping multiple roles, aims and identities. In this regard we are driven back to Althusius, whose theory of society, based upon natural law, construed individuals as freely organizing themselves into associations, both religious and secular, which were the fundamental elements of the state. These associations or intermediate bodies, we are reminded, were a complex amalgam of religious groups, guilds, communes, corporations, leagues of towns, merchant associations and many other organizations which antedated the modern state and owed nothing to it for their existence. They constituted the living practice of society. And in the emergent federal political thought of Althusius, the family, the association, the commune, the province and the state represented a kind of rising hierarchical nexus of complex social institutions which together created the state, were incorporated within it and effectively intervened between it and the individual. This, then, is what is meant by federalism as empirical reality.

Whichever perspective of federalism is adopted – and each is both highly contentious and contestable – the concept is anchored in the belief that political authority should be organized, as far as possible, in a manner which accurately reflects natural socio-economic diversities. This means that in practice, authority should be divided and power dispersed among and between different groups and organizations in society. But if we are to fully understand and appreciate its significance, federalism must be viewed through conceptual lenses which are sensitized to different political cultures. Only when we consider its application to specific cultural and historical milieux can we begin to fill out the concept with particular meaning. Like federation, federalism is rooted in its context, and meaning derives from context. We must therefore locate the concept in its own distinct setting: historical, cultural, intellectual, social, economic, philosophical and ideological. In this way we can begin to appreciate its huge multidimensional complexities. King summarized the phenomenon succinctly and, in so doing, drew attention to the subtle and complex relationships between federalism and federation when, in a provocative essay, he observed: 'Federation might best be understood in terms of the problems to which it has constituted a set of historically varying answers. If we understand the problems, the understanding of structure more clearly follows'.[14]

Having defined and examined the twin concepts of federalism and federation, it is time to return to the thorny question of how the term 'federalism' should be applied to European integration in general and to the EU in particular. Let us begin by resorting to the simple distinction which we have already made in the previous chapter between the sort of federalism associated with national state government and politics and that which operates beyond the state. The former refers to relations 'within' the state or intrastate relations while the latter has its focus on the world of relations 'between' states or inter-state relations. Intrastate relations would bring us into the realm of the federal state or federation where in the EU we might study the politics and government of Austria, Germany or Belgium. But a focus upon inter-state relations – commonly associated with international relations – would compel us to examine the nature of intergovernmental relations as they exist within the EU's central institutions. The point is that federal principles of organization operate at both levels of government and administration in these examples. In short, federal thought and practice cut across the established boundaries of the state and the EU.

In order to make plain how the distinction between federalism and federation is useful in the specific context of the EU, let us refer to a statement made by King which aptly summarizes the position: 'Although there may be federalism without federation, there can be no federation without some matching variety of federalism'.[15] It is perfectly possible, then, to have federalism without federation. And this surely is an important way to look at the evolving EU. Federal ideas and influences constantly permeate its institutional framework and policy-making processes; they flow through many channels both within and without the EU. Supra-national elites in the European Commission, member state leaders in the European Council, elite activists elected to the European Parliament (EP), judges in the European Court of Justice (ECJ) and a whole host of European interest and public relations groups and organizations combine to promote an alternative conception of Europe which extends beyond mere intergovernmentalism. Many of these federal ideas, influences and strategies are difficult to identify and quantify but they have helped to alter political atmospheres, environments and contexts in a manner which has shaped and reshaped people's perceptions of what already exists and what might conceivably exist in significant ways.[16]

Federalism, then, has been – and continues to be – an important alternative conception of Europe. Those who champion this particular idea are engaged in a political strategy designed to achieve a federal goal, but they also construe federalism in the EU as a 'process' of building Europe. In the context of European integration, federalism is both a dynamic process and a goal to be attained. Indeed it has many faces: political idea, strategy, influence, process and goal. Federalism is all of these things. However, it is not necessarily the case that every 'federalism' will always lead to 'federation' in the sense that Europe will simply be like Germany or Switzerland writ large – a new putative national state. Nor will it replicate the United States of America, although it does already exhibit many of the traits of the American Confederation during 1781–89. The EU of course is not a federation; it does not fit the established criteria by which we conventionally define such a state. Logically, then, we have a classic case of federalism without federation. But this is not unique to the EU. The case of Spain is also an appropriate example where federal instalments have been added cumulatively to the evolving Spanish constitution. Spain is not yet a fully-fledged federation but it has such strong federal elements that it is a federation in virtually everything but name.[17]

Whatever the EU is, it is not yet a state. But it has to be acknowledged that it does have several institutional features and policy-making characteristics of an established federation. The increasingly complex decision-making procedures, involving co-operation and co-decision, between intergovernmental and supra-national institutions are similar in many respects to those of a working federation. The dominant decision-making triad of Commission, Council and EP acting as the EU's legislature, serves to represent the combined interests of the member states, their respective electorates and the overall integrity of the Union as a union of states and peoples. The directly-elected EP also fits into a conventional federal category representing the electors of the EU as both peoples and citizens. The purported absence of a single European people or 'Demos' is not as important as some critics and observers would have us believe. It is simply the product of the building of Europe via concrete economic means without fully engaging the problem of constitutionalism. And it only becomes a significant question once efforts are finally focused, as they now are, upon the building of a constitutional and political Europe. The ECJ is another central institution which clearly conforms to a federal character in the extent to which it acts as overseer of European laws which override national laws and operate directly upon the citizens of the union. Indeed, the very notion of citizenship itself, albeit still in an embryonic form, is also indicative of an evolving array of individual rights, duties and obligations which suggests a federal relationship. These, then, are some pertinent examples of how and why the EU is often perceived by some commentators as approximating to a 'federal' Europe. The EU does seem in many important respects to be evolving gradually in a federal direction. There is much substance to this public perception.

It is clear, then, that the source of public fears and anxieties about the idea of a federal Europe derives from a fundamental misunderstanding about the meaning and implications of the word 'federal'. Our conceptual analysis and brief empirical investigation into the public perception of a federal EU makes it perfectly clear that people sense in it a direct threat to the national state. More precisely, they detect a loss of autonomy which seems both pervasive and irreversible. Power and decision-making have drifted gradually upwards to Brussels and mass publics are not convinced that this accords with their own perception of their national interest. They construe even the current limited centralization of power in the Brussels institutions as a zero-sum relationship: what Europe gains the national state loses. The obvious over-simplification inherent in this narrow-minded perspective is not so obvious to them. The EU's central institutions quickly become objects of scorn in being portrayed as bureaucratic, remote, unaccountable and lacking in legitimacy. In these difficult circumstances, where mass publics strive desperately to come to terms with their perceived loss of national self-determination, federalism rapidly becomes a scapegoat. The temptation to resort to scaremongering for many hostile critics of the EU is irresistible. But the consequence is something of a paradox: what is in reality a perfectly rational response to an increasingly hostile and competitive global environment can easily become a source of contempt and derision. Put simply, mass publics confuse the cause with the effect. Federalism – as a function of the imperative to readjust national priorities – is just one organizational and structural response to the inescapable circumstances of international change.

The thrust of this chapter began with the purpose of defining the twin concepts of federalism and federation in order subsequently to demonstrate the value of this conceptual distinction when applied to the EU in particular and European integration in general. This is useful as a conceptual groundclearing exercise because it enables us to focus clearly upon the idea of a reciprocal, mutually interdependent relationship between the national state and its offspring – the evolving EU. These two worlds, however, should not always be depicted as antithetical, with discrete interests which continually collide with each other. Conflict, after all, is predicated upon a fundamental consensus about the need to have Europe. In reality, the two worlds are complementary: their interests overlap and intermingle. We are also encouraged to construe the EU not as a federation in the making but rather as a constitutional hybrid, albeit with an evolving constitutional personality, whose destiny is not predetermined. The presence of federal ideas and principles does not mean that the EU's constitutional future is a foregone conclusion. How far it travels down the joint federal–confederal path remains to be seen; it is a goal towards which federalists have been struggling since the early post-war years.

Our short survey of federalism and federation in the context of the EU provides a simple analytical framework which helps us to clarify our understanding of what is meant by a 'federal' Europe. However, it appears to be of only limited usefulness in helping us to understand the larger, more complex, relationship between federalism and European integration. In order to examine this relationship in more detail, we must look closely at how the process of European integration has evolved since the end of the

Second World War. Our route into this early post-war world is a relatively unusual one, but in furnishing us with a unique insight into the relationship between federalism and European integration it fulfils an important requirement. Consequently we shall investigate the political ideas and strategies of Jean Monnet and Altiero Spinelli, two pioneers of European integration, in order to identify the principal motives and driving-forces behind the goal of 'an ever closer union of European peoples'.

## Monnet and Spinelli: the two faces of federalism

Mindful of our principal purpose to examine the relationship between federalism and European integration, let us concentrate upon the history and development of federalist thought and practice as it evolved in the respective careers of Monnet and Spinelli. Here it is worth pointing out that we will not be providing a detailed analysis of the political careers of these two rival protagonists of European integration, since this has already been published elsewhere.[18] Instead we shall focus narrowly upon those assumptions and concepts which combined to form the basis of their respective ideas about what constituted a federal Europe. However, since their rival approaches to European unification continue today to serve as the source of lively controversy about the future of the European project, it is necessary to sketch out briefly some background information about their lives before we enter their world of federalist thought and practice.

Monnet and Spinelli have usually been depicted as opposing forces in the quest for closer union yet, although their paths did diverge en route, in their separate journeys they travelled towards the same destination. Monnet was born in Cognac in 1888 while Spinelli's birth in Rome occurred in 1906. Both, therefore, belonged to an age far older than the EU and both played an active role in the strengthening of its institutions, Monnet as President of the High Authority of the European Coal and Steel Community (ECSC) during 1952–55 and Spinelli as a European Commissioner during 1970–76 and a member of the EP in the years between 1976–86, the year of his death. Furthermore, many of their basic views about history, the dangers of nationalism, the anachronistic nature of the state, the importance of common solutions to common problems, the role of new institutions and the need for lasting peace in Europe were identical. Their ultimate goal, it should be noted, was also the same: namely, a European federation.

Today we do not regard Monnet as having been a champion of the federal cause in Europe. His own particular method of uniting Europe primarily by economic integration has compelled political scientists to be cautious when attaching a label to him. Whereas Spinelli was without question the leading European federalist of the contemporary era, Monnet has been described predominantly as the foremost 'functionalist' and only occasionally as an 'incremental federalist'.[19] Spinelli's own persistent criticisms of Monnet's 'method' have undoubtedly contributed to this somewhat blurred image but it is also due to the various theoretical controversies which continue to surround the idea of shifting from functionalism to constitutionalism or, as Spinelli put it, to assert the political element. Let us turn now to examine in more detail the evolution of their political ideas and strategies. We will begin by looking first at Monnet's approach to Europe.

Monnet's political ideas are both easy and difficult to define. They are simple in the sense that they were forged out of practical experience and yet at the same time elusive to the extent that they defy a precise ideological classification. In his *Memoirs*, Monnet confessed to a 'distrust' of 'general ideas' which were never allowed to lead him 'far away from practical things'. His purpose was 'very practical'. It was 'collective action' – 'the product of circumstances as they arose' – designed to be 'useful beyond the experience of one individual'.[20] These autobiographical reflections furnish a clue to the intellectual and practical influences which drove him to champion the cause of Europe. If we look a little closer at the fundamental principles which guided his indomitable energies over three generations from the First World War until his retirement from the Action Committee for the United States of Europe in 1975, we can obtain a sense of what lay behind his activities. François Duchene alluded to his two qualities of 'imagination and realism' which produced 'an existential style' that was intellectual yet 'owed little to theory and books'. And he also referred to Monnet's 'fusion of idealism and the pragmatic approach' which produced an idea 'usually action-oriented'.[21] The following extract from Monnet's *Memoirs* is worth more than a moment's reflection:

> The essential thing is to hold fast to a few fixed principles that have guided us since the beginning; gradually to create among Europeans the broadest common interest, served by common democratic institutions to which the necessary sovereignty has been delegated. This is the dynamic that has never ceased to operate.[22]

What, then, was the basis to this intellectual, existential style which owed so little to theory and books? What were these few 'fixed principles' upon which Monnet sought to construct Europe?

Writing thirty years ago on the role of Monnet, Richard Mayne claimed that 'Monnet's own written words, oddly enough, are relatively unrevealing: they have the strength but also the limpidity of pure spirit. Fined and pared away until they achieve a stark simplicity', they conceal more than they reveal and their very clarity may make them 'seem banal'.[23] However, in 1978, when Monnet's *Memoirs* were first published in English, the stark simplicity of his political ideas seemed far from banal.[24] The bare bones of his thinking were fleshed out to reveal a substantive body of consistent and connected themes and beliefs which together place him in a long tradition of political thought about European unity stretching back several centuries. The overarching aim was peace but, in order to achieve it, Monnet sought to change the nature of international relations by altering the relations between peoples: 'to unite men, to solve the problems that divide them, and to persuade them to see their common interest'. And the need to forge direct links between people did not stop with Europe. Monnet was convinced that 'the union of Europe was not only important for the Europeans themselves: it was valuable as an example for others, and this was a further reason for bringing it about'. To his mind, this enterprise had implications for the whole of civilization: it would 'allow men to develop their potential within communities freely chosen and built'.[25] These goals, of course, are rooted in the age-old pursuit of international pacification and it is easy to see how they are linked to classical federal theory.

Monnet believed that in every set of circumstances which might conceivably generate conflict there lurked a common interest. It was not something which had to be invented; it was something which merely had to be discovered and revealed. The fundamental problem for Monnet always remained the same: 'How can people be persuaded to approach the problem in the same way, and to see that their interests are the same, when men and nations are divided?' He arrived at his conclusion in piecemeal, cumulative fashion. He intended to change men's attitudes by 'transforming the very reasons for their rivalry' which meant a radical transformation of the political context in which the conflicts were traditionally set.[26] Particular attitudes, perceptions and values were legitimate only according to specific contexts. Change the context and the problems themselves are changed. Monnet summarised this method succinctly in his *Memoirs* when recalling the events of 1950 which prompted him to take the initiative over the Schuman Plan:

> It was at that time, undoubtedly, and on that precise problem, that I realised the full possibilities of an approach which had long been familiar to me, and which I had applied empirically in trying to overcome difficulties of all kinds. I had come to see that it was often useless to make a frontal attack on problems, since they have not arisen by themselves, but are the product of circumstances. Only by modifying the circumstances – 'lateral thinking' – can one disperse the difficulties that they create. So, instead of wearing myself out on the hard core of resistance, I had become accustomed to seeking out and trying to change whatever element in its environment was causing the block.[27]

Having elaborated the idea of changing the context within which conventional problems between states were customarily located, Monnet was compelled to give that context a solid form. Institutional innovation answered the call for new habits of thought and action. Monnet's faith in the value of new rules and institutions was, like that of Spinelli, peculiar and deep-rooted. His remarks about them are couched in uncharacteristically philosophical terms:

> Nothing is possible without men: nothing is lasting without institutions ... The union of Europe cannot be based on goodwill alone. Rules are needed. The tragic events we have lived through and are still witnessing may have made us wiser. But men pass away; others will take their place. We cannot bequeath them our personal experience. That will die with us. But we can leave them institutions. The life of institutions is longer than that of men: if they are well built, they can accumulate and hand on the wisdom of succeeding generations.[28]

Clearly, the assumptions which shaped Monnet's approach to European integration were: the obsolescence of the state; the danger of nationalism; the imperative to change the context of problems; and the need for new institutions with which to anchor the common interest. He also believed in what he called 'a certain disorder' for national elites to be ready to make the sort of compromises that they would not usually make under normal circumstances. In his quest to build Europe, Monnet repeated his basic axiom: 'people only accept change when they are faced with necessity and only recognise necessity when a crisis is upon them'. The notion of 'crisis' was pivotal for Monnet: 'I have always believed that Europe would be built through crises and that it would be the sum of their solutions'.[29]

But if these basic assumptions and concepts help to explain his approach to integration, how did federalism fit into his political strategy? After all, Monnet seems to have been an advocate of federation without ever having been a federalist. What, then, was its significance to the building of Europe? The key to understanding the relationship between federalism and European integration lies in Monnet's consistent approach to federation which remains the source of continuing controversy today: namely, the belief that by forging specific functional links between states in a way that does not directly challenge national sovereignty, the door to federation will gradually be opened. These so-called 'functional' links were primarily economic activities and they were perfectly expressed in the ECSC initiative. This new form of sectoral 'supra-national' organization would be the foundation of the European federation which would evolve only slowly to engage national elites in a process of mutual economic interest. These concrete benefits would gradually form that crucial solidarity – the common interest – which Monnet believed indispensable for the removal of physical and mental barriers.

If we glance at a preliminary sketch outline of what became the Schuman Plan, this continuity in Monnet's thinking is quite striking. Since

Franco-German union could not be achieved at once, a start would be made by 'the establishment of common bases for economic development'. The goal of a federal Europe would be attained via Franco-German union which would itself be realised 'through the interplay of economics and institutions' necessitating 'new structures on a European scale'. The approach to federation, which Monnet called 'the ECSC method' of establishing 'the greatest solidarity among peoples', implied that 'gradually' other tasks and other people would become subject to the same common rules and institutions – or perhaps to new institutions – and this experience would 'gradually spread by osmosis'. No time limits were imposed on what was clearly deemed to be a long, slow, almost organic, process of economic and political integration:

> We believed in starting with limited achievements, establishing *de facto* solidarity, from which a federation would gradually emerge. I have never believed that one fine day Europe would be created by some great political mutation, and I thought it wrong to consult the peoples of Europe about the structure of a Community of which they had no practical experience. It was another matter, however, to ensure that in their limited field the new institutions were thoroughly democratic; and in this direction there was still progress to be made ... the pragmatic method we had adopted would ... lead to a federation validated by the people's vote; but that federation would be the culmination of an existing economic and political reality, already put to the test ... it was bringing together men and practical matters.[30]

This exceptionally lucid explanation of how Monnet viewed the path to federation contains the essence of what later came to be the major theoretical controversy about federalism and European integration. Monnet's own method of piecemeal, cumulative building whereby 'political' Europe would be the 'culminating point of a gradual process' contained the huge assumption that at some future undefined point a qualitative change would occur in the political and constitutional relations between states and peoples. But he believed that this would happen only when 'the force of necessity' made it 'seem natural in the eyes of Europeans'.[31] In short, Monnet's approach to federation rendered constitutionalism – political Europe – contingent upon cumulative functional achievements. At this point we can anticipate certain criticisms of his self-styled 'method' of integration. First, his particular functional approach to the building of Europe smacked far too much of economic determinism in the extent to which it subordinated political to economic factors. Its causal, unidimensional conception might also easily place Europe in a straitjacket, unable to grow and augment its corporative personality. Monnet's critics, especially federalists, could also claim that he misunderstood and thereby oversimplified the very nature of the integration process itself. Indeed, to many of his opponents, Monnet's conception of integration seemed almost like an act of blind faith.

It was precisely at this juncture – in the interaction between economics and politics – that Altiero Spinelli entered the theoretical debate. What lay at the root of Spinelli's conceptual differences with Monnet? After all, both men envisaged a federal Europe. The mistake which Spinelli attributed to Monnet was inherent in the functional approach which neglected to deal with 'the organization of political power at the European level'.[32] This meant that the political centre remained weak and impotent, lacking the capacity to go much beyond what already existed and unable to adapt to new forces and problems encountered at the European level. Here the focus shifted to the role of the European institutions. For Monnet, institutions were crucial but his conception differed somewhat from Spinelli's in the extent to which he viewed their development as akin to organic growth arising directly out of functional performance. Spinelli, however, had a much more positive conception of institutions. As the bedrock of political integration they had to be solid. He believed that Europe could not afford the 'wait and see' policy of Monnet: what was urgently required if Europe was not to suffer political immobilism and stagnation was institutional reform.

Spinelli's verdict on Monnet's conception of Europe can be succinctly summarized like this: it failed by its own terms of reference. It did not possess that inherent sustaining dynamic which Monnet believed, at least initially, would evolve inexorably towards a union among peoples. The predicted shift from quantity to quality did not occur precisely because of Monnet's excessive reliance upon functionalist logic. His confidence in it was misplaced because he failed to confront the realities of organized political power. Only strong independent central political institutions could provide European solutions to European problems; otherwise, national answers would prevail over European solutions.[33] Spinelli acknowledged that Monnet had made the first steps easier to achieve but he had also made the later steps more difficult. The building of 'political' Europe based upon economic performance criteria would not necessarily follow according to Monnet's logic. Europe might very well remain as little more than a 'Common Market'. Let us now focus our attention more firmly upon the connection between federalism and European integration in order to clarify what is sometimes a confused and confusing conceptual relationship.

## Federalism and European integration

What does this brief survey of the two faces of federalism tell us about the relationship between federalism and European integration and what are its implications for the building of Europe on the threshold of the twenty-first century? There appears to be an emerging consensus among commentators on the EU that we have now reached the limits of Monnet's conception of European integration. The EU – the current expression of the European project – has reached a new crossroads in its economic and political evolution. It is time to confront the political implications of Monnet's Europe and engage the difficult and controversial task of building 'political' Europe. We will return to this assertion later in this section of the chapter. For the moment let us examine briefly the relationship between federalism and European integration from the perspective of conventional integration theories.

The term 'integration' is a homonym. It is a word which means different things to different people and can be used in a variety of different contexts. Let us consider what Charles Pentland referred to as 'the lowest common denominator' and define integration as:

> a process whereby a group of people, organized initially in two or more independent nation-states, come to constitute a political whole which can in some sense be described as a community.[34]

This minimal definition exists at an admittedly high level of generality and begs many questions at the very outset. However, it is a convenient working definition which conveys the sense of a coming together of previously separate parts to form a new whole, a new totality of relations between states and peoples. Whether or not this new totality involves the creation of a single people – a new body politic – depends ultimately upon which approach to integration is adopted. Some theories, like that of neo-functionalism, identify a 'community-model' which points to some form of supra-nationality while others, like federalism, are 'state-centric' and have traditionally construed the new totality created as a new state with a single people. But there are enormous variations both within and between contemporary theories and some of them are open-ended about the destination or terminal end-point of integration.

Given this broad sense of what is involved when we refer to integration as a dynamic process, it is obvious that it is a highly complex phenomenon which can be approached and understood in several different ways. We are concerned with political integration but there are also many different dimensions to investigate within one single theory. And some dimensions are more important for one theory than they are for another. In the case of European integration, it is clear that the economic dimension to integration has been of paramount importance compared to social or political culture aspects of the process. As we have just seen, this is due largely to Monnet's own particular approach to the building of Europe. The attention paid to constitutional arrangements was minimal, as was the idea of a social or a 'peoples'' Europe.

Many conceptual problems with integration remain to be resolved but for our limited purposes here it has been defined and given some fairly fixed sense. At a high level of generality, and despite its inherent ambiguity, there is a significant degree of agreement among scholars about what 'integration' means. It need not detain us any further. Instead, we need to remember that it is vitally important to make a firm distinction between normative and empirical integration theories. This means that we must be aware of those normative theories which are prescriptive and actively recommend particular goals and strategies to be pursued compared to empirical theories which purport to explain what is happening and make predictions, under given circumstances, about what is likely to occur. In reality, of course, most integration theories combine both prescriptive and empirical elements in their explanations of the building of Europe.

Mindful of these preliminary observations about integration theories, what do the two faces of federalism tell us about European integration? First, let us acknowledge that, although what Monnet initially proposed and helped to implement in Western Europe was 'economic integration', it was driven by a political imperative and his long-term goal was a European federation. In a prescient essay entitled 'The relevance of federalism to Western European economic integration', published in 1955, William Diebold confirmed this, observing that the ECSC was 'a major federal measure of economic integration' and that at the basis of the Schuman Plan was 'a series of truly federal equations, concerning the relations of the parts to one another and of each to the federal agency'.[35] And the ECSC reality was not simply 'economic means to achieve political results'. Rather, political and economic elements were 'inextricably mingled' in the Schuman Plan.[36]

Secondly, by 'transforming the basic facts' this approach to the building of Europe was unprecedented. Changing the context of international relations in order to identify the elusive common interest between states ensured that their energies were diverted from the old channels of power politics into new areas of unity and cooperation which transcended the state. The EC/EU has introduced a rule of law into relations between European countries which, as Duchene remarked, has 'cut off a whole dimension of destructive expectations in the minds of policy-makers'. It has effectively domesticated the balance of power so that the power politics of the so-called 'realist' school of international relations has been replaced by 'aspirations that come nearer to the "rights" and responsibilities which reign in domestic politics'.[37] This was a major breakthrough in European inter-state relations which must not be underestimated.

Nonetheless, in seeking to build a federal Europe principally by a series of economic steps, Monnet was attempting something which had no historical precedent. Indeed the EU has evolved in the opposite way to any of its supposed models. To the extent that it has developed by the gradual 'aggregation' of previously separate political units, it is similar to the process by which the United States of America was consolidated during 1787–89. But here the similarity ends. Past federations have been constructed as a result of treaty-like political negotiations which created a new federal constitution and government. There is no historical precedent for the creation of a multinational, multicultural and multilingual federation composed of 15 to 20 established national states – some of which are *ancien régimes* – with mature social, economic, political and legal systems.

In summary, it is clear that both 'federalism' and 'integration' are concepts which can be construed essentially as processes of international change. Federalism, then, is a form of political integration. In the context of European integration, however, federalism has been characterized by piecemeal incremental steps, or federal elements, which have been added in cumulative fashion to produce an EU in which supra-national, federal and intergovernmental features co-exist in an uneasy and incomplete union. As Duchene has put it, the European Communities were 'steps to a federation that might have to operate indefinitely in intermediate zones. It was federal minimalism confined to certain economic areas'.[38]

## Federalism and Europe: the changing research agenda

We have now reached the point where we can address some of the issues which we raised in the previous chapter. These were the questions concerning personalism and federalism, confederation and Elazar's post-modern federalism. However, we will also look at those aspects of federalism and federation whose application to European integration suggest theoretical implications. Together, these two sets of concerns constitute our changing research agenda.

First let us concentrate upon the issue of personalism. This is less an approach to the study of federalism than a particular perception of human relations. Indeed, for many personalists, it is part and parcel of federalism itself. But it must be noted that there are several distinct philosophical strands within personalism which make it extremely complex and here we will convey its meaning in only the broadest sense. Derived mainly from the philosophical writings of Alexander Marc, Robert Aron, Emmanuel Mounier, Daniel Rops, Denis de Rougemont and Henri Brugmans, the principles of personalism – often referred to as 'integral' or Proudhonian federalism – are based upon a set of underlying assumptions which revolve around the dignity of the human person. These principles are premised upon a searching critique of the modern capitalist state whose mass society, in cutting man off from his family, his neighbours and his local associations, has reduced him to the isolation of anonymity in a monist world where he finds himself confronted directly by global society. As an isolated individual, man is ultimately cut off from himself. Put simply, personalism seeks to restore man as a whole person who is in close touch with his own social life and with himself. Logically, then, personalism is a perception of the world which is societal rather than state based and is concerned to bring political authority back to human beings as complex, responsible members of society.

It is easy to appreciate from this summary of personalism precisely how it combines with federalism. Local autonomy can be restored by 'a real decentralization of decision-making power to the grassroots or, better, by the creation of new communities with human dimension'.[39] And since the principle of autonomy is based not upon the individual but upon the person, political authority and laws derive first from personal differences, then local, then regional differences and ever onwards and upwards in a pluralist spiral until they engage the central federal authority. But since all federated bodies participate in the common interest which is entrusted to the federal authority there is a rock solid guarantee to respect the autonomy of the constituent communities. Consequently 'it is the principle of participation which constitutes the real transcendental act of the person in society'.[40] Extended to the EU, this personalist perspective seeks not merely to support the goal of a European federation but it also supports 'a federal society'.[41]

The relationship between personalism and federalism is equally simple and complex. Personalism is the sort of philosophy and ideology of federalism to which it is easy to relate. We can recognise many familiar problems in its diagnosis of what is wrong with modern capitalist states and societies, and we can also empathize with certain aspects of the personalist remedy without accepting every premise and recommendation. Nonetheless, it suffers *inter alia* from the problem of how precisely to translate these ideas into practical action. It is true that it is perfectly possible to achieve practical progress in the pursuit of constitutional change in the EU by operating through its existing intergovernmental and supranational institutional channels of decision-making. However, it is very difficult to secure 'a radical change in attitudes, in mentalities, through the training and education of activists aware of what is at stake' even if they would be acting 'on the structures "regulated" by the personalist tendencies which already exist in our society'.[42]

It is easy to understand why many federalists describe the personalists as 'Utopian' federalists. The goal of an integral federalist society does seem hopelessly impractical. But their political ideas should not be peremptorily dismissed. Their claim that many personalist traits and principles, such as respect for and recognition of local cultures, already exist as human practice in European societies is a valid one. With very little effort they can be detected in every contemporary federation. Nor should the political influence of the personalists in Europe be underestimated. They were enormously influential in the early years of the EC, and they remain well connected in the contemporary EU. Indeed, they continue to flourish as one of the many 'educational' pressure groups in the member states but accept that their ideas can succeed only after a process of long-term evolution. Their respectable intellectual heritage together with their single-minded vision of an integrated Europe suggest that they should be neither forgotten nor ignored when we reassess the changing research agenda for federalism and Europe. The recent research focus on the emergence of a European identity might conceivably renew interest in personalism and the Utopian federalists.[43]

Our second issue for consideration is that of confederation. This question will not be explored in great detail here because it is examined further in Chapter 8. However, it is appropriate to convey the nature and meaning of confederation albeit in a very brief manner, not least because it relates directly to the third question which follows. In his *Unions of states: the theory and practice of confederation*, published in 1981, Murray Forsyth defined confederation as a 'federal union' which constituted 'the spectrum between inter-state and intrastate relations'. It was, he argued, the 'intermediary stage between normal inter-state relations and normal intrastate relations'. It was not a state because it was 'not a union of individuals in a body politic, but a union of states in a body politic'. He summarized it as 'the process by which a number of separate states raise themselves by contract to the threshold of being one state, rather than the organisation that exists once this threshold has been crossed'; it occupied 'the intermediary ground between the inter-state and the state worlds, of going beyond the one but of not unequivocally reaching the other'.[44]

These views were expressed in 1981, long before the Single European Act (SEA) of 1987, the Treaty on European Union (TEU) of 1993 and the Treaty of Amsterdam (TA) of 1997 had been agreed. His conclusion then was that the EEC was an 'economic confederation' which was clear 'from both its content and its form'.[45] More recently, however, he has been compelled to revise this judgement to take account of the recent changes to the institutional and policy-making bases of the EU. Now he concedes that there is good reason to 'place a much greater emphasis on the federal–constitutional approach to integration, and to apply it more openly and thoroughly than has been done in the past'.[46] This sounds remarkably like a plea for the building of 'political' Europe and conforms more readily to the strategic position of Spinelli; it is time to confront the legacy of Monnet's Europe.

If, as Forsyth concludes, the current EU is 'confused and incoherent', what does this suggest about the changing nature and meaning of confederation? Clearly the EU remains a union of states in a body politic but the recent changes to its form and character are of such constitutional and political significance that we may justifiably question the adequacy of the label 'economic confederation'. In this book, I wish to argue that the EU represents something distinctly new in the world of both inter-state and intrastate relations. It is not yet a union of *individuals* in a body politic but it is more than merely a union of *states* in a body politic. It is not a federation but it is also more than a confederation understood in the classical sense. It exists, then, in a kind of conceptual limbo, a twilight zone where the firm boundaries that once defined it have been gradually eroded, reducing many of its distinct features to a blurred and indistinct union which has no name. The nature of its origins and development have combined to shape a peculiar, unique form of union the like of which we have never seen before. History is of only limited assistance. However, if it has no historical precedent how are we supposed to classify it? Without resorting to a neologism it remains the task of political science to address the ever-present problem of classification. In these circumstances we are compelled to rely upon the conventional language of political science. This is why I have chosen to describe the EU as a species of 'new' confederation, thus acknowledging the basic form out of which it has grown but beyond which it has evolved. We will return to this subject in a much more detailed analysis in Chapter 8. Let us turn now to address the third issue which we mentioned at the beginning of the section.

This concerns Daniel Elazar's post-modern federalism. As we have already seen from the previous chapter, Elazar's concept of post-modern federalism is not concerned with the much broader philosophy of post-modernism which we commonly associate with moral and political philosophers like Jean-François Lyotard, Jacques Derrida and Michel Foucault. It has nothing in common with their fields of inquiry. Its focus of attention, instead, is upon the specific issue of fundamental change in the international states system. In this sense it is of crucial significance to the changing research agenda and chimes conveniently with our own reappraisal of confederation in this book. Elazar's basic thesis, that we have already embarked upon a paradigm shift in the world of states, suggests that the EU might actually be at the forefront of this recent post-war development because it was the West European states which first began to pursue 'what they called functional rather than federal solutions to their problems of union'. However, these activities 'slowly evolved into confederal arrangements to take the lead in bringing about the paradigm shift'.[47]

The theoretical implications of this thesis are far-reaching. At the very least it implies that the established concept of federation may no longer be helpful and that the federation–confederation antithesis may prove to be completely misleading. Elazar's diagnosis of post-war international change is clearly rooted in what he sees as the contemporary challenge to statism. The future does not lie in an outmoded state sovereignty but in a new theory of association which reflects this fundamental structural change occurring in international relations. But in this new era of global change it is not only sovereignty which is outmoded. The established concept of federation has also been challenged because it is simply too constricting and is unable to encapsulate the complex realities which now exist. It cannot explain the world of states on the threshold of the new millennium. The theoretical implication is obvious: we have to expand our conceptual categories or we will simply fail to grasp and accommodate global empirical change.

Elazar's conception of a new paradigm also has implications for the age-old distinction between the study of international relations and other forms of political science. It suggests that the intellectual boundaries between international relations and other rival approaches, like comparative political science, have *ipso facto* become much more blurred. The intellectual division between them has not completely disappeared, but it has diminished significantly. The EU is indicative of this change. It represents a new, expanded form of confederal arrangements which operates at the intersection of the inter-state and intrastate worlds. Elazar's belief that the EU model has finally replaced the much-vaunted American model as a means of economic and political integration illustrates further the increasing obsolescence of this conceptual and theoretical gap between confederation and federation – or between international relations and comparative political science. The EU seems to point the way forward to a much more imaginative, flexible accommodation of organized local, regional, national, supra-national and international interests than the United States of America. As a model of economic and political integration, its unitary thrust has been held in check, it is a much less centralized polity and its statist features are counterbalanced by rival sources of political authority and legitimacy. One conclusion to be drawn from this analysis of Elazar's new world is somewhat ironic. This is that our reappraisal of federation has unintentionally propelled us into re-thinking and re-assessing the nature of confederation. We are, in effect, recycling old concepts but they have the merit of being familiar to us. Finally, it is worth noting that Elazar construes the EU in the 1990s as being part of a vast and expanding global network of different kinds of federal arrangements. These include federations, federacies, associated states and regional free trade areas as well as the new confederations, and their variety reflects the several dimensions of the paradigm shift.

In keeping with Elazar's reasoning about the conflation of international relations studies and other forms of political science, it is appropriate here to pay some limited attention to conventional international relations (IR) theory. What relevance does IR theory have for our changing research agenda on federalism and European integration? How does it help us to understand the nature and meaning of the EU? IR theorists typically view the EU as an international organization or an international regime. Since the dominant theoretical debate is in one form or another between the so-called 'realists' and/or 'neorealists' and the 'liberal institutionalists' and/or the 'neoliberal institutionalists', the emergence and development of the EU has been situated primarily in the context of the debate about international co-operation, the capacity of such institutions to be able to achieve it and the conditions under which it can best be promoted. In this labyrinthine setting, the major conclusions to be drawn about the EU relate directly to its standing and significance as an international organization in world politics. The EU is, therefore, of interest only to the extent that it supports the basic assumptions of either one or other of these two main theoretical positions.[48]

Where IR theory is of particular interest and value to those working in other areas of political science is in what the neo-liberal institutionalists refer to as different degrees and levels of institutionalization and of changing patterns and variations of institutionalization.[49] One of the leading neoliberal institutionalists, Robert Keohane, asserted the importance of international institutions, without denigrating the role of state power, in unequivocal terms which are of particular relevance to the EU:

> Institutions may ... affect the understandings that leaders of states have of the roles they should play and their assumptions about others' motivations and perceived self-interests. That is, international institutions have constitutive as well as regulative aspects: they help define how interests are defined and how actions are interpreted.[50]

From an IR standpoint, we can understand and appreciate the intensity of the theoretical differences between the neorealist and the neoliberal institutionalist schools of thought. However, if Keohane is encouraged to bring this intellectual baggage into the theoretical debate about European integration and the EU, the value of his contribution remains highly questionable. As he and Stanley Hoffman have candidly admitted, they are 'students of world politics based in North America whose primary research interests have not been in the subject of European integration'.[51] This is true of most IR theorists and reflects the narrow compartmentalization of the disciplines of IR and comparative political science which we have just observed. Consequently it should hardly be surprising if in 1990 the main conclusion of Keohane and Hoffman concerning recent EU developments was that progress in European economic and political integration depended largely upon the changing global political economy and member state governments which promoted spillover via intergovernmental bargaining. They did, however, concede that spillover pressures would be subject to 'the vagaries of domestic politics, the diverse pressures of the external environment, and the health of the economies of Western Europe, as well as on the individuals leading European governments, and the Commission, at that time'.[52] Later, in 1991, they concluded tentatively that the explanation for institutional change in the 1980s was due to a combination of factors which were closely interrelated and conformed happily with regime theory: changes in the world political economy, spillover and intergovernmental bargains made possible by the convergence of preferences of the major EU member states.[53]

From the specific standpoint of federalism and European integration, this short survey of the two broad tendencies which exist in IR theory does not seem to lead us very far. On this admittedly brief reading, IR theory tells us little about the nature of the relationship between federalism and

European integration. We are inevitably pulled into the conceptually narrow world of statism, multilevel governance, liberal intergovernmentalism and the intermittent congruent preferences of EU member states.[54] It is difficult to see what is new about all of this. The statist intergovernmental focus is clearly accurate as far as it goes. But this is the problem: it does not go far enough. In its overriding concern to stress the dominance of states and governments in the integration process, it is uni-dimensional and blind to the existence of other actors, pressures and influences which also help to shape policy outcomes. Consequently the theoretical implications of this recent literature on European integration seem disappointing.

Finally, let us look at a very different approach to the relationship between federalism and European integration which does seem to furnish some interesting theoretical implications. This is what, in 1986, John Pinder labelled 'neo-federalism' and refers to 'the process of incremental federalism'.[55] The main thrust of Pinder's argument is that federalist theory needs to incorporate the notion of a series of steps critical to the building of a federal Europe. He claimed:

> The tendency to identify federalism with a great leap to a federation with military and coercive power inhibits practical thought about the prospects for taking further steps in a federal direction, whether in the form of a system of majority voting to complete the internal market, developing the EMS in the direction of monetary union, an increase in the powers of the European Parliament, or a package of such reforms that could deserve to be called European Union. Such thought would be helped by systematic study of the specific steps that could be taken and of the conditions that favour or impede them.[56]

In 1993, he developed this argument further when he stated that a step towards federation can be identified when 'a federal element is put in place or strengthened, provided that it can be held to pave the way for further steps, or at least not to present an obstacle to them'.[57] This was what he called 'the method of the new European federalism' and is an interesting focus for what it suggests about the relationship between federalism and European integration, especially when we recall Spinelli's claim that Monnet made the first steps easier but the later steps much more difficult to achieve. Pinder acknowledged that it will not be possible to know for sure whether the progress of the EU so far has included steps towards federation or not. As Spinelli put it, we will know only at the end, not at the beginning. However, the longer that European integration evolves with stronger, more visible, federal elements added in cumulative fashion, the greater the validity of the federalists' claims that 'incremental federalism' works. The history of the EC/EU itself can be used to demonstrate precisely how far the steps that have been taken to date have usually been successful enough to generate support for more. There is, then, sufficient empirical evidence for federalists to assume that a way of dealing with practical problems that has worked already is likely to work again.[58] Provided that the steps taken do not lead to a countervailing intergovernmental backlash, Pinder's analysis of the EC/EU suggests that graduated federalism can lead ultimately to federation. It is, at the very least, a theoretical possibility and one which has much historical evidence to support it.

We have reflected only briefly upon the changing research agenda for the study of federalism and European integration but this cursory survey has taken us into several interesting areas of investigation which invite further contemplation and analysis. Operating at the intersection between classical international relations and classical state relations, the study of federalism and federation points in many directions when we focus upon European integration. And this is as it should be. It merely reflects the untidy complexity of the relationship. It is now time to conclude the chapter with a few remarks about the nature of the theoretical discourse on federalism, federation, European integration and the EU.

## Conclusion: theory and practice

Theorizing about European integration in the 1990s has been a hazardous enterprise. That this should be so is hardly surprising when we contemplate the magnitude of contemporary change which has been brought to bear on the integration process. The combined impact of intra- and extra-European events and circumstances have yielded both centrifugal and centripetal pressures on European integration. Theorists approach the subject with justified caution. There does appear to be an emerging consensus about the futility of persisting with the old neofunctionalism–intergovernmentalism antithesis, but recent theoretical contributions to European integration seem, nonetheless, to have contributed little to what we already know about the process.[59]

Recent theoretical debates have been concerned mainly with the juxtaposition of a set of key dependent and independent variables which purport to explain integration. These variables include the following: domestic policy-making and policy-makers; inter-state bargaining and negotiations; the potential convergence of national preferences; issue linkage; transaction costs; the power and influence of the national state; and the 'passive' role of the EC/EU central institutions and actors.[60] Rather like IR theory which we mentioned briefly above, this so-called new 'liberal intergovernmentalism' becomes a self-fulfilling prophecy which results in the predictable conclusion that European integration is explained largely by intergovernmentalism. But any theory whose focus is confined to domestic coalitions, the relative power of national states, and heads of state and government in single-minded pursuit of elevated domestic policy interests, is bound to arrive at a narrow statist destination.

The broad but not unanimous academic consensus about the value of this particular approach to explaining European integration is symptomatic of the desire to bridge the domestic–international cleavage. This in itself is perfectly valid, but in downgrading the importance of supra-national institutions and actors, ignoring the pivotal ideas and influences of particular national elite figures and overlooking the possibility of autonomous EC/EU-centred preferences and pressures, it fails to recognise non-statist influences in the integration process.[61]

The recent literature on European integration has, however, made some limited progress in its focus upon specific case studies of economic and political integration, such as the Single European Act (SEA) and Economic and Monetary Union (EMU), but their relationship to the larger integration process remains unclear.[62] Perhaps, like Pinder's federal 'steps', this might be the most theoretically-productive way forward in the extent to which such studies could gradually accumulate a solid body of empirical evidence about actors, issues, policies and timing which might form the basis of genuine comparative analysis. Nevertheless, it has to be acknowledged that the relatively recent shift of focus in favour of case studies is indicative of a broad intellectual trend which has much lower theoretical expectations than previously, and which derives from two main sources: first, it is itself symptomatic of the move away from old-style, all-embracing grand theories and towards partial theories concerned with different aspects of the integration process; and, second, it recognises the need for less normative, more empirically valid, explanations of European integration. This is why commentators today offer much lower level theoretical perspectives – like multilevel governance, policy networks and communities, and decision-making processes – which have an empirical focus and rivet attention on the actual mechanics of the EC/EU.

In view of these contemporary theoretical trends, where, then, does federalism stand as a particular form of European integration? In a recent contribution to the debate about the future of the EC/EU, Alberta Sbragia recommended the study of federalism, and in particular comparative federalism, as a useful benchmark for identifying various pathways for the building of Europe.[63] She implicitly accepted the conceptual distinction between federalism and federation when she noted that 'one can have what might be called segmented federalism, that is, treaty-based federal arrangements in certain policy-arenas, without having a formal, constitutionally based federation'. Or again, 'a federal-type organization could evolve without becoming a constitutionally based federation in the traditional sense'. This makes 'the study of federations useful in thinking about the Community's future'.[64] Moving from the theoretical study of comparative federalism and federation to consideration of the EC/EU itself as a federation, William Wallace returned in 1994 to the scene of his own earlier conceptual exploits when he observed that:

the European Community is a constitutional system which has some state attributes, but which most – or all – of its constituent governments do not wish to develop into a state, even while expecting it to deliver outcomes which are hard to envisage outside the framework of an entity which we would recognize as a (federal) state.[65]

The paradox for Wallace was that, even while the EC/EU had not become a federation, it nevertheless retained 'a constitutional agenda which implied the need for a federal–state framework'.[66] We can easily understand why academics remain perplexed by the construction of Europe; it is not a federation but it does incorporate strong federal and confederal elements.

In the 1990s, there is a clear recognition that none of the old established grand theories of integration can either explain or predict what Philippe Schmitter calls 'the emerging Euro-polity'.[67] For the moment, let us concentrate upon his recent contribution to the debate about the future of the EC/EU. He claims that all of the prevailing theories of integration focus on 'process, not outcome', and that even if each of them does presuppose that it will lead to 'some kind of stable institutionalized equilibrium' it will be 'some time before we can discover for sure what type of polity it is going to become'.[68] As with the theories that he rejects, then, Schmitter takes evasive action regarding the outcome of the integration process, but argues that whatever it will become the EC/EU cannot be confined to the status of a 'confederation' because it is already 'well on its way to becoming something new'.[69] He does, however, concede that the closest approximation in practice to an integrated Europe is the 'co-operative federalism' of Germany and Switzerland, thus implicitly acknowledging the validity of comparative federalism and federation as an approach to studying the EC/EU. And his passing reference to the conceptual inadequacy of classic confederation as an appropriate label for the EC/EU is correct. This is precisely why we have introduced the appellation 'new' confederation which reflects the need for a reconceptualization of an old category. It renders the need for Schmitter's neo-logisms, and even a new lexicon, superfluous.

It is abundantly clear from our concluding survey of federalism and federation in the context of the EC/EU that most academics remain uncomfortable with this relationship. As Sbragia has emphasized, 'many analysts do not feel that using concepts drawn from federalism is appropriate in analyzing Community activities'.[70] They are unable to make the mental leap from national state analogies. This remains the awkward predicament for federalism both as theory and practice. Accordingly, federalism as a form of European integration can result in 'federal-type' structures and 'federal-type' decision-making processes, but it must not, in the minds of its critics, lead inexorably to federation. This particular dilemma has been inherent in the building of Europe ever since the Schuman Declaration of 1950. But the meaning of concepts change and much of the problem with the study of federalism and European integration has been that traditional political science has retained a narrow, old-fashioned perception of the relationship. Today, it is necessary to break out of the old conceptual confines which assumed that federalism 'always' led to federation.

This chapter suggests that both federal and confederal ideas, influences and strategies lie at the heart of the debate about the theory and practice of European integration. They have been especially prominent during the last decade because of the recent shift towards the building of 'political' Europe. Indeed, the public debate about the future of Europe has been controversial precisely because it is a 'constitutional' debate – a debate about constitutionalizing the European construction. Federal and confederal notions have been catapulted to the forefront of the debate because we have finally engaged the critical issue of institutional reform and the 'new' architecture. Most theorists of European integration do not acknowledge this, although many of them do recognise that there has been a significant change in the nature of European integration since the SEA. Most theories of European integration, as Schmitter has observed, focus on process not outcome but federalism alone confronts both of these. Our theoretical analysis suggests that the EC/EU is neither a federation nor a confederation in the classic sense. But it does claim that European political and economic elites have shaped and moulded the EC/EU into a new form of international organization, namely, a species of 'new' confederation. Finally, this chapter reminds us that it is important to distinguish between federalism and federation as an approach to the study of the EC/EU and confederation and federation as analytical descriptions of the EC/EU itself.

It is time now to turn away from the theoretical discourse of federalism and federation, and its implications for the study of the EC/EU, and look instead at the historical context within which federal and confederal ideas first emerged in the post-war years. We will investigate the historical period between 1950, when the commitment to a federal Europe was first enunciated by Robert Schuman, and 1972, when the goal of a 'European Union' was first proclaimed by nine member states of the EC. In order to underline the continuity of the theoretical discourse in this book, we will begin our post-war historical review and revision with an examination of the dominant mainstream inter-governmental school of thought which suggests that both the origins and subsequent development of European integration were due entirely to the role of national governments and to the changing perceptions of national interests entertained by national political and bureaucratic elites. It is time to reinstate the relevance of federalism to the historical evolution of European integration.

## NOTES

1   K.C. Wheare, *Federal government*, 4th edn, London: Oxford University Press, 1963.
2   E.A. Freeman, *History of federal government in Greece and Italy*, 2nd edn, Freeport, N.Y.: Books for Libraries Press, 1972.
3   W.S. Livingston, 'A note on the nature of federalism', *Political Science Quarterly*, 67, pp. 81–95, 1952.
4   C.J. Friedrich, *Trends of federalism in theory and practice*, New York: Praeger, 1968.
5   P. King, *Federalism and federation*, London: Croom Helm, 1982.
6   M. Burgess (ed.), *Federalism and federation in Western Europe*, London: Croom Helm, 1986; and M. Burgess and A.G. Gagnon (eds), *Comparative federalism and federation: competing traditions and future directions*, London: Harvester Wheatsheaf, 1993.
7   Launched by C.L. Brown-John with the support of D. Elazar in 1982 at the twelfth IPSA World Congress in Rio de Janeiro, Brazil, the Research Committee has grown rapidly and adopted its current title in 1985 at the thirteenth IPSA World Congress in Paris, France. The author is at present Vice-chairman of the Research Committee.
8   P. King, *Federalism and federation*, p. 20.
9   P. King, *Federalism and federation*, p. 77.
10  P. King, *Federalism and federation*, pp. 91 and 140.
11  R. Dikshit, *The Political geography of federalism: an inquiry into origins and stability*, Delhi: Macmillan, 1975, p. 4.
12  D.J. Elazar, *Exploring federalism*, Tuscaloosa, AL: University of Alabama Press, 1987, p. 12.
13  P. King, *Federalism and federation*, p. 90.
14  P. King, 'Against federalism', in R. Benewick, R.N. Berki and B. Parekh (eds), *Knowledge and belief in politics*, pp. 151–76, London: Allen & Unwin, 1973.
15  P. King, *Federalism and federation*, p. 76.
16  See M. Burgess, *Federalism and European Union: political ideas, influences and strategies in the European Community*, London: Routledge, 1989.
17  See L. Moreno, 'Ethnoterritorial concurrence and imperfect federalism in Spain', in B. De Villiers (ed.), *Evaluating federal systems*, pp. 162–93, London: Martinus Nijhoff Publishers, 1994, and L. Moreno, *La federalizacion de España: poder politico y territorio*, Madrid: Siglo Veintiuno de España Editores, S.A., 1997.
18  See M. Burgess, *Federalism and European Union*, pp. 43–63.
19  J. Pinder, 'European Community and nation-state: a case for a neo-federalism?', *International Affairs*, 62, pp. 41–54, January 1986.
20  J. Monnet, *Memoirs*, New York: Doubleday, 1978, p. 519.
21  F. Duchene, 'Jean Monnet's methods', in D. Brinkley and C. Hackett (eds), *Jean Monnet: the path to European unity*, pp. 184–209, London: Macmillan, 1991.
22  J. Monnet, *Memoirs*, p. 523.
23  R. Mayne, 'The role of Jean Monnet', *Government and Opposition*, 2, pp. 351–52, 1966–67.
24  They were first published in French in 1976. In an anonymous review of his *Memoirs* by 'Z', Monnet's own recollections were especially welcome because there was 'no very easily accessible record of his utterances and opinions'. See 'Z', 'What Jean Monnet wrought', *Foreign Affairs*, 55, pp. 630–35, 1977.
25  J. Monnet, *Memoirs*, pp. 221, 356 and 511.
26  J. Monnet, *Memoirs*, pp. 37, 76, 87, and 511.
27  J. Monnet, *Memoirs*, p. 291.
28  J. Monnet, *Memoirs*, pp. 304 and 384.

29  J. Monnet, *Memoirs*, pp. 46, 109, 140 and 417.

30  J. Monnet, *Memoirs*, pp. 93, 286, 295, 367, 383 and 392–93. This would create 'a "silent" revolution in men's minds' which would lead one day to 'a European federation'. See J. Monnet, 'A ferment of change', *Journal of Common Market Studies*, 1, pp. 203–11, 1962.

31  J. Monnet, *Memoirs*, pp. 394–95.

32  Interview with Spinelli, 15 September 1983 and 14 February 1985, European Parliament, Strasbourg, France.

33  A. Spinelli, 'Reflections on the institutional crisis in the European Community', *West European Politics*, 1(1), pp. 79–80, February 1978.

34  C. Pentland, *International theory and European integration*, London: Faber & Faber Ltd, 1973, p. 21.

35  W. Diebold, 'The relevance of federalism to Western European economic integration', in A.W. Macmahon (ed.), *Federalism: mature and emergent*, p. 455, New York: Russell and Russell, 1962.

36  W. Diebold, 'The relevance of federalism', p. 441.

37  F. Duchene, *Jean Monnet: The first statesman of interdependence*, London: W.W. Norton and Co., 1994, p. 405.

38  F. Duchene, *Jean Monnet*, p. 407.

39  F. Kinsky, 'Personalism and federalism', *Publius*, 9(4), pp. 151–52, 1979. See also his 'The impact of Proudhon and the personalist movement on federalism', in A. Bosco (ed.), *The Federal Idea: The history of federalism from enlightenment to 1945*, 1, pp. 91–98, London: Lothian Foundation Press, 1991, and R.W. Rauch, Jr., *Politics and belief in contemporary France: Emmanuel Mounier and Christian democracy, 1932–1950*, The Hague: Martin Nijhoff, 1972.

40  F. Kinsky, 'Personalism and federalism', p. 152.

41  F. Kinsky, 'Personalism and federalism', p. 156. For another brief survey of this subject, see G.L. Ulmen, 'What is integral federalism?', *Telos*, 91(2), pp. 135–49, 1992.

42  F. Kinsky, 'Personalism and federalism', p. 155.

43  See, for example, S. Garcia (ed.), *European identity and the search for legitimacy*, London: Pinter Publishers, 1993, and M. Wintle (ed.), *Culture and identity in Europe: perceptions of divergence and unity in past and present*, Aldershot: Avebury, 1996. For a recent summary of some key sources on integral federalism and regional identities in Europe, see J. Loughlin, 'Europe of the regions and the federalization of Europe', in M. Burgess (ed.), *Federalism and European Union, Publius*, Special Issue, 26(4), 141–62, Fall 1996.

44  M. Forsyth, *Unions of states: the theory and practice of confederation*, Leicester: Leicester University Press, 1981, pp. 2–3 and 6.

45  M. Forsyth, *Unions of states*, p. 183.

46  M. Forsyth, 'The political theory of federalism: the relevance of classical approaches', in J.J. Hesse and V. Wright (eds), *Federalizing Europe? the costs, benefits, and preconditions of federal political systems*, pp. 43–44, Oxford: Oxford University Press, 1996.

47  D.J. Elazar, 'From statism to federalism: a paradigm shift', *Publius*, 25(2), p. 12, Spring 1995.

48  I have concentrated on the main intellectual debate between the 'neorealists' and the 'neoliberal institutionalists'. See R. Keohane, 'Neoliberal institutionalism: a perspective on world politics.' in R. Keohane (ed.), *International institutions and state power*, pp. 1–20, Boulder, CO: Westview Press, 1989, and J.M. Grieco, 'Anarchy and the limits of cooperation: a realist critique of the newest liberal institutionalism', *International Organization*, 42(3), pp. 485–507, Summer 1988.

49  R. Keohane, 'Neoliberal institutionalism', pp. 2–3.

50  R. Keohane, 'Neoliberal institutionalism', p. 6.

51  R. Keohane and S. Hoffman, 'Conclusion: Community politics and institutional change', in W. Wallace (ed.), *The dynamics of European integration*, p. 276, London: Pinter Publishers, 1990.

52  R. Keohane and S. Hoffman, 'Conclusions: Community politics and institutional change', p. 293.

53  R. Keohane and S. Hoffman, 'Institutional change in Europe in the 1980s', in R. Keohane and S. Hoffman (eds), *The new European Community: decision-making and institutional change*, p. 25, Oxford: Westview Press, 1991. Keohane and Hoffman acknowledged that an earlier version of this chapter was published in W. Wallace (ed.), *The dynamics of European integration*, London: Pinter Publishers, 1990. See fn. 51. above.

54  The most detailed advocacy of 'liberal intergovernmentalism' is in the work of A. Moravcsik. See his 'Negotiating the Single European Act: national interests and conventional statecraft in the European Community', *International Organization*, 45, pp. 19–56, Winter 1991, and 'Preferences and power in the European Community: a liberal intergovernmentalist approach', *Journal of Common Market Studies*, 31(4), pp. 473–524, December 1993.

55  J. Pinder, 'European Community and nation-state: a case for a neo-federalism?', p. 54.

56  J. Pinder, 'European Community and nation-state: a case for a neo-federalism?', pp. 53–4. See also his *European Community: the building of a union*, Oxford: Oxford University Press, 1991, pp. 203–222.

57  J. Pinder, 'The new European federalism: the idea and the achievements', in M. Burgess and A.-G. Gagnon (eds), *Comparative federalism and federation: competing traditions and future directions*, p. 46, London: Harvester Wheatsheaf, 1993.

58  J. Pinder, 'The new European federalism', p. 64.

59  The debate between S. Hix, 'The study of the European Community: the challenge of comparative politics', *West European Politics*, 17(1), pp. 1–30, January 1994, and A. Hurrell and A. Menon, 'Politics like any other? comparative politics, international relations and the study of the EU', *West European Politics*, 19(2), pp. 386–402, April 1996, while interesting as an intellectual jousting match, seems to be largely a phoney war.

60  The group of scholars most closely associated with these sorts of approaches to European integration include *inter alia*: Alan Milward, Stanley Hoffman, Simon Bulmer, Andrew Moravcsik, William Wallace and Robert Keohane. They are identified in M. O'Neill (ed.), *The politics of European integration: a reader*, London: Routledge, 1996.

61  It is already possible to detect the beginnings of an intellectual backlash against the dominant 'liberal intergovernmentalist' school of thought. See, for example, D. Wincott, 'Institutional interaction and European integration: towards an everyday critique of liberal intergovernmentalism', *Journal of Common Market Studies*, 33(4), pp. 597–610, December 1995, and A. Moravcsik, 'Liberal intergovernmentalism and integration: a rejoinder', *Journal of Common Market Studies*, 33(4), pp. 611–28, December 1995.

62  Apart from A. Moravcsik, 'Negotiating the Single European Act', pp. 19–56, see W. Sandholtz and J. Zysman, '1992: recasting the European bargain', *World Politics*, 42(1), pp. 95–128, October 1989, and D.R. Cameron, 'The 1992 initiative: causes and consequences', in A.M. Sbragia (ed.), *Euro-Politics: institutions and policymaking in the New European Community*, pp. 23–74, Washington, D.C.: The Brookings Institution, 1992. On EMU, see D. Andrews, 'The global origins of the Maastricht Treaty on EMU: closing the window of opportunity', in

A. Cafruny and G. Rosenthal (eds), *The state of the European Community: the Maastricht debates and beyond*, pp. 107–23, Boulder, CO: Lynne Rienner, 1993; W. Sandholtz, 'Monetary bargains: the treaty on EMU', in A. Cafruny and G. Rosenthal (eds), *The state of the European Community*, pp. 125–41; W. Sandholtz, 'Choosing union: monetary politics and Maastricht', *International Organisation*, 47(1), pp. 1–39, 1993; and J. Grieco, 'The Maastricht treaty, economic and monetary union and the neo-realist research programme', *Review of International Studies*, 21(1), pp. 21–40, January 1995.

63 A.M. Sbragia, 'Thinking about the European future: the uses of comparison', in A.M. Sbragia (ed.), *Euro-Politics*, pp. 257–91.

64 A.M. Sbragia, 'Thinking about the European future', in A.M. Sbragia (ed.), *Euro-Politics*, pp. 262–63.

65 W. Wallace, 'Theory and practice in European integration', in S. Bulmer and A. Scott (eds), *Economic and political integration in Europe: internal dynamics and global context*, pp. 272–77, Oxford: Basil Blackwell, 1994. The title of William Wallace's earlier confrontation with these conceptual issues is 'Less than a federation, more than a regime: the community as a political system', in H. Wallace and W. Wallace (eds), *Policy-Making in the European Community*, pp. 403–36, 2nd edn, Chichester: John Wiley & Sons, 1983.

66 W. Wallace, 'Theory and practice in European integration', p. 275.

67 P. Schmitter, 'Some alternative futures for the European polity and their implications for European public policy', in Y. Meny, P. Muller and J.-L. Quermonne (eds), *Adjusting to Europe: the impact of the European Union on national institutions and policies*, pp. 25–40, London: Routledge, 1996.

68 P. Schmitter, 'Some alternative futures', pp. 32 and 37.

69 P. Schmitter, 'Some alternative futures', p. 25.

70 A.M. Sbragia, 'Thinking about the European future', in A.M. Sbragia (ed.), *Euro-Politics*, p. 262.

# 3   Federalism and the building of Europe, 1950–72

History is about explaining and understanding the past. However, interpreting the past is always difficult because it is at the mercy of the present and what we want to do with the future. The past is condemned to be assessed in terms of the events and circumstances which follow it. Our experience of the present impels us to rethink and reassess the past. History is, therefore, constantly reappraised and reinterpreted precisely because the past, present and future are inescapably intertwined. But scholarly historical analysis of this complex relationship must be distinguished from the political uses of history. As Francis H. Hinsley remarked, 'People often study history less for what they might learn than for what they want to prove'.[1] It is in this sense that recent historical revisionism concerning the origins and nature of post-war European integration must be judged. Corrective zeal has its merits but in justifiably seeking to disprove and debunk much of the early history, often written by enthusiasts, the great danger is that revisionism can go too far. History itself then becomes the casualty.

Hinsley's statement serves as a useful reminder of this danger. The motives of the revisionist historian and the particular approach which he or she employs are of crucial significance. In this chapter, I intend to investigate the nature of recent historical revisionism in the light of the European Community's (EC) federal heritage.[2] I want to look closely at some of the recent scholarly contributions to the debate about the origins and early development of European integration in order to clarify and assess the implications of this revisionism. I shall also attempt to 'reappraise the reappraisals' by restoring the significance of federalism to the building of Europe in the years between 1950 and 1972. My general hypothesis is that some of the historical revisionism has distorted our understanding of the driving forces and political influences behind European integration in its determination to challenge the myths and folklore in post-war European history. In this quest, which involves both historical reappraisal and theoretical reassessment, my underlying purpose is to reinstate federal political ideas, influences and strategies in the overall evolution of the EC during this period. My interpretation of the building of Europe in these years is, therefore, intended to challenge those aspects of the recent historical revisionism which deny the importance of political ideas and visions entertained by particular statesmen, groups and movements in their search to change the nature of inter-state relations in post-war Europe. Let us begin our quest by looking first at the new orthodoxy recently established by both historians and political scientists.

## History and theory: reappraisals reappraised

In an influential study first published in 1984, Alan Milward quickly became the standard-bearer of the new historical revisionism when he successfully challenged many of the hallowed conventional wisdoms related to the early post-war economic and political reconstruction of Europe.[3] For our purposes here, it is necessary to focus only upon those aspects of the revisions which are relevant to federalism, federal theory and the federalists. We will start with a summary of Milward's arguments which relate, however broadly, to these issues.

Milward's basic purpose was to provide a comprehensive explanation of both the economic and political nature of the rebuilding process which occurred in Europe during 1945–51. His general conclusion, put simply, was that the success of Western Europe's post-war reconstruction derived from the creation of 'its own pattern of institutionalized international economic interdependence'.[4] Based upon a detailed study of the available statistical information and archival research into official government records, the main arguments of the book were unavoidably confined to 'the macro-economic level' which sought to explain 'the way in which governments shaped the pattern of economic interdependence to suit their own national objectives'. The overall thrust of Milward's impressive study which emphasized the pivotal role of national governments and their political and bureaucratic elites was clear: the very limited degree of integration that was achieved came about through the pursuit of the narrow self-interest of what were still powerful national states.[5] There was no room at all for what he variously called the human idealism, idealism(s) and higher ideals of men like Adenauer, Schuman, Sforza, Spaak and Monnet. According to Milward, previous writers had always failed to show through what political mechanisms the idealisms which supported west European integration 'actually influenced governmental policy-making in the nation-states'. On the contrary, the evidence clearly indicated that the limited economic integration which had emerged had been created not by the espousal of high ideals but by national bureaucracies 'out of the internal expression of national political interest' rather than by 'the major statesmen who implemented policy'.[6]

Another argument central to Milward's iconoclastic purpose was his assertion that the origins and early evolution of the EC were relative and contingent rather than expressive of fundamental principles which might be universal and timeless. Accordingly, the EC came into existence not as part of any grand design but merely 'to cope with certain historically-specific and well-defined economic and political problems'. The European Coal and Steel Community (ECSC), the Common Agricultural Policy (CAP) and the EC itself were indispensable pillars of Europe's continued economic prosperity but 'each was and is designed to resolve a particular and limited, not a generalized and universal, problem'. There was, in short, 'no necessary implication in any of these carefully controlled acts of economic integration that the supersession of the nation state was an inevitable continuing process.' Moreover, the process of integration was 'neither a thread woven into the fabric of Europe's political destiny nor one woven into the destiny of all highly developed capitalist nation states'.[7]

In uncompromising language which foreshadowed the emergence of the so-called 'liberal intergovernmentalist' school of thought in the 1990s, Milward acknowledged that further steps in the direction of economic integration would have to be 'equally specific to the resolution of economic and politicial problems not otherwise resolvable'. He conceded, however, that there might well be such problems in the future; the theoretical possibility therefore certainly existed that the pattern of integrative activity peculiar to the reconstruction period under review could be repeated. Evidently what was necessary for this to happen was a conjunction of circumstances which would produce a durable consensus among west European governments sufficient to support new forms of international and/or supra-national organizations which would, like the ECSC, be created 'as an arm of the nation states to do things which could not otherwise be achieved' by themselves acting independently.[8]

This cursory survey of Milward's vintage 1984 broadside against the prevailing historiography of the age explains why he was firmly placed in the realist category of scholars who emphasized the role of the national state in controlling the integration process. He was somewhat reticent about the precise nature of the relationship between 'interdependence' and 'integration' at this time, but his historical analysis of the latter, as it evolved between 1947 and 1951, conceded that it was 'significantly different in form and final implication from anything previously seen', even if it was not then possible to arrive at any firm conclusions about its nature and meaning.[9] There remained more questions than answers. Nevertheless Milward's reappraisal of post-war European integration chimed perfectly with the established intellectual position of the American realist, Stanley Hoffman, whose observations in 1982 had already reaffirmed the fundamental role of the EC in serving 'not only to preserve the nation-states, but paradoxically to regenerate them and to adapt them to the world of today.'[10] The EC was not involved in a zero-sum game with its constituent member states; rather, it corresponded to an 'international regime' of the sort originally identified in 1977 by Robert Keohane and Joseph Nye

which required 'long-term reciprocation' to survive in the world of international relations.[11]

In 1992, Milward's entrenched position in the realist camp of scholars
was reinforced when his subsequent historical study of the relationship
between the EC and the national state in the 1950s was published. The
central argument of this study was twofold: first, that the evolution of the
EC since 1945 had been an integral part of the reassertion of the national
state; and, second, that the very process of European integration had been
a necessary part of the post-war rescue of the national state. Indeed 'the
EC only evolved as an aspect of that national reassertion and without it the
reassertion might well have proved impossible'.[12] The major reason for the
origins, early evolution and the continued existence of the EC was quite
straightforward: it was simply one more stage in the long evolution of the
European state. And the economic historian in Milward could not resist
the temptation to state categorically that 'the true origins of the European
Community are economic and social'.[13]

In order for him to pursue his twofold argument, Milward began by
denouncing what he took to be a false assumption which had been
absorbed into popular discussion, namely, the assumed antithesis between
the EC and the national state. His view was that no such antithesis existed.
The EC and its constituent member states could coexist alongside each
other quite easily. Indeed, since it was the national states that had created
the EC, its subsequent evolution had been state-directed. Member state
governments were in control of both the pace and the direction of European integration. Nevertheless, he acknowledged that this false assumption had endured and remained at the core of virtually every attempt at
comprehensive theoretical explanations of the origins and evolution of
the EC. According to Milward, it was historians who were to blame, by
default of silence, for allowing this false assumption to continue to serve as
the historical foundation for much theory-building. Moreover, much of
the theory which had emerged was due to a predominantly ahistorical
stance on the part of many of the enthusiasts of integration who were able
to 'argue as though there were no history whose influence could not be
set aside with no more cost than an effort of will'.[14]

In a nutshell, then, Milward set himself an ambitious twofold task: first,
to use historical evidence to triumph over the prevailing but inadequate
theories of European integration; and, second, to attempt to replace them
with a new theoretical explanation which was rooted in 'a new set of
assumptions in conformity with the facts which historical research has
brought to light'.[15] This, he believed, would enable him to reconcile two
dominant aspects of European history in the last half-century: the reassertion of the national state as the fundamental organizational unit of political, economic and social existence with the undeniable surrender of
limited areas of national sovereignty to the EC. Milward's conclusions confirmed his original hypothesis that the EC was the European rescue of the

national state. The cumulative surrenders of national sovereignty during the 1950s were just one aspect, albeit the most important one, of the successful reassertion of the national state as the basic organizational unit of Europe. The new theory which he claimed to have constructed rested upon the historical evidence assembled from the official archives located in eight different countries as well as those of the EC itself. It boiled down to what he called 'an open-ended theory' based upon the nature of national domestic policy choices which did not forecast any particular outcome but allowed for several possibilities. The theory suggested that the broad choices available to EC member state governments between either a framework of interdependence or an integrationist framework depended entirely upon a series of strategic decisions leading to a convergence of national policy choices. The theory's greatest merit was that it fitted 'the historical facts'.[16]

This important scholarly contribution to the history and theory of European integration was bolstered and enriched in 1993 when Milward and his colleagues, working at the European University Institute in Florence (EUI), Italy, extended their historical analysis from the 1950s into the early 1990s. This project was an intellectually bold but risky attempt to persist with the pursuit of the goal toward which Milward was already moving, namely, the construction of a theory of integration derived from empirical research into Europe's own history. The problem with investigating the historical evidence of recent events, however, was recognised at the outset: it was 'not yet susceptible to a full analysis'.[17] But Milward et al. were undaunted by this obstacle and concluded their brief survey of the early 1990s convinced that these developments in European integration did not seem in any way to modify their original hypotheses about either the process of integration or the EC itself; rather, they served to confirm them.[18] But what was vitally necessary nonetheless remained seemingly unattainable, namely, a theory which could actually predict the future nature of national policy choices. Accordingly, the only predictive value of a theory derived from historically-based research would be 'that once national policies were specified, their international consequences for the nation-state could be specified'.[19]

The crucial theoretical significance of this was that European integration contained no inherent logic or momentum which was driving the national state inexorably forward toward a supra-national or federal denouement. The national state had surrendered its sovereignty to the EC only gradually and in piecemeal fashion, with certain limited and specific purposes in mind. And this itself suggested that the frontier of national sovereignty, which was approached within varying distances by national policy choices, remained essentially where it had been fixed in 1952 and 1957.[20] All that could be realistically postulated, based upon the existing empirical evidence, was actually a recommendation to both politicians and Euro-enthusiasts: to descend to the detail of the relationship of each specific policy proposal to the available international frameworks for advancing it.[21] In other words, public support for European integration could best be promoted and sustained by relating each national policy choice to the appropriate international framework deemed necessary to implement it. Mass publics could then relate the achievement of national policy goals directly to the existence of the EC.

What are we to make of this impressive historical revisionism? How does it impinge upon the relationship between federalism and European integration and what impact does it have upon the historical role of the federalists themselves in their drive toward a federal Europe? Clearly there is much in Milward's sceptical reappraisal of both the history and the mainstream theories of European integration that helps us to understand better the driving-forces and centripetal pressures propelling the national state toward the building of Europe. He has explained and clarified what was previously unclear. But while he is quite right to expose and criticize the blatant over-simplifications and value judgements embodied in some of the earlier accounts of European integration, his approach to the subject is not without its own problems and pitfalls.

The first problem with this searching reappraisal is the methodology and sources used to arrive at conclusions of such far-reaching historical and theoretical significance. Milward's heavy reliance upon official records and statistical information as the dominant basis for his arguments and interpretations meant that his conclusions were to some extent self-fulfilling prophecies. If the historian who is already self-consciously revisionist is compelled to rely heavily upon official documentary evidence it is hardly surprising if he/she reaches conclusions which reflect what is 'available official evidence' and fails to appreciate the significance of the wider political context within which policy is decided. In short, the political environment is equally significant. One consistent thread which characterizes each of these revisionist contributions is the obsession with 'historical facts'. Like the stiff, inflexible and dictatorial schoolmaster, Thomas Gradgrind, in Charles Dickens's *Hard Times*, there is a relentless pursuit of the 'facts' – facts, facts and more facts – as if they existed in objective isolation from their political and historical contexts. Milward, to be fair, does acknowledge this problem as the most obvious limitation of historical research as a conscious test of political theory. The standard 30-year rule for the release of historical records is clearly the most difficult obstacle to overcome. This is perfectly understandable. However, the attempt to utilize an historically-based hypothesis which was originally rooted in the early post-war years to explain events in the early 1990s suggests more than a little optimism about the capacity of historical method to bear the weight of such scholarly expectations. In short, Milward's ambitious goal of seeking to construct an historically-based theory of integration which would have predictive value is bedevilled by the acknowledged need to support it with 'a further theory which could predict the choice of national domestic policies' because 'the process of integration is not sepa-rable from the evolution of domestic politics'.[22]

The implications for federalism and the federalists of this approach to the history and theory of European integration are palpably obvious. His acknowledgement that he deliberately 'set aside the great body of popular, semi-popular and synthetic literature' about the evolution of the EC and that 'politicians leave few traces' in west European government records effectively blinds Milward to other important rival influences and pressures for political change.[23] Indeed, it makes the federalists and others that wanted a more binding and integrated EC almost invisible. It con-signs them to oblivion as if their existence was simply irrelevant. This is the dangerous result of a kind of barefoot historical empiricism which recog-nises only the 'facts' derived from official sources. Aside from the pre-sumption that we know precisely what an historical 'fact' is and that it is incontestable, it enables the historian virtually to dismiss as mere 'ideal-ism' the combined influence and impact of such giants of the integration process as Robert Schuman, Jean Monnet, Alcide De Gasperi, Paul-Henri Spaak, Walter Hallstein, Konrad Adenauer and Johan Willem Beyen.

In a ferocious attack in 1992 on the historical significance of the so-called 'European saints', Milward railed against the hagiographers, fabu-lists and theologians who had dominated the historiography of European integration. As an antidote to this kind of propagandist history, he juxta-posed the weighty empirical evidence of a history culled from the access-ible memoranda of national bureaucrats against the impressionistic and fragmentary perceptions of the founding fathers of the EC. The impera-tive was to arrive at an accurate understanding of their role, unobscured by the received and heavily contaminated accounts of their disciples and apologists. This corrective zeal was, once again, perfectly justifiable. Indeed, it was essential to put the record straight. But it is also important to be clear about what it was that Milward wanted so desperately to chal-lenge and correct. A close analysis of his critique of 'the lives and teach-ings of the European saints' suggests that his main purpose was twofold: first, to expose the colossal over-simplifications and value judgements which purported to be accurate, objective historical accounts of the build-ing of Europe by a small band of leading statesmen imbued with a shared, if grandiose, vision; and, second, to demolish the widely-held presumption that these men fervently believed in the ultimate dissolution of the national state as a direct consequence of European integration. He largely succeeded in achieving both of these goals. But his assertion that so few of these men 'achieved anything of political significance' remains a quite untenable position when we look at the concrete progress of post-war European integration.[24] On the contrary, the collective achievements of men like Monnet, Schuman, Beyen and Spaak in this cause have been of lasting significance.

It is certainly true that some European federalists envisaged the eventual disappearance of the national state. It appeared, for example, in some of the intellectual thought of the Resistance movements but this was born out of their wartime experiences and the devastating consequences of war, and it was relevant largely to the immediate post-war years when almost anything must have seemed possible. Their hopes, like the aspirations of the so-called European saints, were doubtless construed in eminently practical terms; their political ideas were valid only for the time and place in which they formulated them.[25] However, it is important to clarify the distinction which Milward makes between the advocacy of political ideas and proposals which purport to have a philosophical universality and those which are merely specific to both time and place. It is perfectly possible, as Milward himself has admitted, to advocate a set of integrative policy proposals which are specific to time and place but which 'once chosen may be retained even if the dissimilarities between national policy bundles become wide'. Leading European statesmen knew perfectly well that what they were constructing in 1952 and 1957 might serve as a 'framework for the future' because once created the EC 'profoundly changed power relations within Western Europe'.[26] In other words, European political elites were able to construe principles specific to the ECSC and the EEC in terms of implications much wider than just these particular experiments. 'Integration', as Milward and his associates have reminded us, had far greater implications for Europe and the national state than did mere 'interdependence'. Decisions about integration were, and still are, a calculated risk involving strategic political judgements, rooted in time and place, about practical policy choices which had enormous implications for the future. And integration implied a future in which national states would conceivably have much less independent control. Their national autonomy could, therefore, be reasserted only as part of a larger union of states with congruent interests.

Let us summarize our reappraisal of Milward's research with regard to federalism and the federalists. There seems to be an implicit, and sometimes explicit, assumption in his work that federalism implies either the destruction of the national state or at the very least a determination in some way to by-pass it. This is a mistake. As we have indicated above, there was some evidence for this in the federalist literature of the early post-war years and it still figures in the assumptions of the contemporary Utopian federalists who seek to uncover a European federal society. However, it is certainly not the primary purpose of federalism when related to European integration. Milward and his colleagues do not explain precisely what they understand by federalism, nor do they always identify which federalists they are referring to. The vast majority of federalists, like both Monnet and Spinelli, accepted the national state at face value and had predicated their respective political strategies upon its continued existence. To do otherwise would have been to risk certain political impotence as Spinelli gradually came to realise in the 1960s. In reality, what most federalists shared – and continue to believe – was a view of the national state as a potentially dangerous force for violent conflict in international relations but a force which ironically possessed a much reduced capacity to determine itself in world affairs.

It is also unclear from Milward's detailed historical analyses just what it is that the national state must be rescued from. The import of his research suggests only that it is determined to survive in a much more uncertain global and competitive post-war environment. The spectacle of an intermittently beleaguered national state struggling to survive in a rapidly changing world of states by constantly adjusting and readjusting its internal and external relations is hardly a novel hypothesis. Nonetheless, his basic thesis about the origins and evolution of the EC as merely an aspect of the post-war rescue of the national state is certainly attractive to realists because it furnishes the comforting impression that the national state is always in control of its own destiny. Contrary to alternative beliefs, it has retained the capacity for independent self-determination. In retrospect, the reality was very different. In consenting to novel forms of economic and political integration, which conceded institutional space and autonomy at the supra-national level, national governments had *ipso facto* furnished a federal context for European decision-making.

Milward might, then, be judged to have persistently overstated his case in claiming that the European national states had been so weakened by their experiences during 1929–45 that they 'more or less had to re-create themselves as functioning units in the immediate post-war period'. Indeed, one historian who also worked at the EUI in Florence, Richard Griffiths, has argued that 'Europe's post-War productive capacity was not as damaged as has often been claimed' and its industrial capacity was in some respects 'better adapted to the needs of the post-War era'. Already, by 1947, most west European countries had surpassed their pre-war levels of industrial output.[27] Clearly, the national state did not need to be 'rescued' with respect to its post-war industrial recovery. And it is also clear that the European mass publics, much to the dismay of the federalists, returned to their national state governments in droves in the immediate post-war years. The federalists' so-called heyday during 1945–50 did not stretch to the occupancy of national government. Their significance could be found in what Milward's dour Gradgrind approach ignored, namely, the political context of the post-war debate about European integration.

Milward's thesis about the rescue of the national state in the early post-war years and its relationship to progress in European integration merits further investigation. The links between the survival of the national state and the timing of the moves toward European integration do not seem to have been fully explored. It may be objected that the national state had already reasserted itself successfully and did not need 'rescuing' by the time the ECSC was launched in 1952. But this partly depends upon what particular significance is attached to the ECSC. These are important questions for historians. For political scientists, the focus turns away from the nuts and bolts of historical archives, official memoranda and autobiographical reflections and toward concept formation and reformation, theory-building and the search for persistent patterns of development. To their credit, Milward and his colleagues have confronted some of these things. Indeed, they have claimed that 'history offers clearer, although not always decisive, answers to these questions than other subjects, such as economics and political science, which are usually used to answer them'.[28]

These disputes go to the very heart of the intellectual debate about European integration, and we will return to them at the end of the chapter. Mindful of Milward's critique of federalism and the federalists, our purpose now is to examine in some detail the building of Europe in the years between 1950 and 1972 in order principally to present an alternative perspective to the narrow national state-centred interpretation which is fashionable among the historians, comparative political scientists and international relations theorists of today. As we shall see, it is possible to accept much of this contemporary analysis and simultaneously reinstate the relevance of federalism to the evolution of European integration.

## The origins and growth of European integration, 1950–57

In his *Memoirs,* Jean Monnet, claimed that he and his small band of friends and advisors – Pierre Uri, Etienne Hirsch and Paul Reuter – were responsible for the original idea, the political initiative and the subsequent blueprint of the ECSC.[29] Whatever contemporary economic historians might suggest about it, the ECSC was, at least in Monnet's mind, another example of that lateral thinking required to transform the nature of a seemingly intractable problem by transforming the facts. Monnet construed the ECSC essentially as a means of overcoming two major post-war problems, namely, the French fear of future West German industrial hegemony and the German desire for equality of treatment. The genius of the ECSC lay in its ability to link these two problems to a single solution which would also have far-reaching implications for Western Europe as a whole. In other words, the Franco-German problem had to be approached as a European problem and the ECSC would become 'the germ of European unity'.[30]

In a famous public speech on 9 May 1950, the French Foreign Minister, Robert Schuman, declared the goal of a united Europe:

> Europe will not be made all at once, or according to a single plan. It will be built through concrete achievements which first creat a *de facto* solidarity. The coming together of the nations of Europe requires the elimination of the age-old opposition of France and Germany. Any action taken must in the first place concern these two countries.... The pooling of coal and steel production should immediately provide

for the setting up of common foundations for economic development as a first step in the federation of Europe … this proposal will lead to the realization of the first concrete foundation of a European federation indispensable to the preservation of peace.[31]

And in a recently published biography of Monnet, François Duchene confirmed that 'one theme was consistent': Monnet saw European integration as 'an effort to order peace'. 'Though often tactically convenient, this was always more than a slogan'.[32]

With typical iconoclastic fervour, Milward's trenchant claim that the ECSC was merely a 'proto-plasmic organization able to take any shape it wished according to the pressures on it from the nation states' was designed to destroy any illusions about its purported teleological destiny. Whether or not it would be the forerunner of a 'federation of Europe' could be judged only by its subsequent history, and that remained to be written.[33] But while Milward's detailed historical analysis of the ECSC – replete with its archival focus upon Western Europe's steel industries, the role of the American and British governments, the Paris–Bonn axis, the complexity of the interests of other countries and a clutch of external factors like the Saarland and events in Korea – downgrades the significance of its novel 'supra-national' institutions and its 'fine language about European unity', it nonetheless recognised, albeit reluctantly, that it 'ended eighty years of bitter and deadly dispute and made the reconstruction of Western Europe possible'.[34] And its originality could not be gainsaid. Even Milward, for all his determination to emphasize that the ECSC was based on 'the real interests of the nation states which signed it', conceded that it created 'a formalized network of institutional economic interdependence' which provided an alternative to the conventional national state-centred diplomacy of the past.[35]

It is also perfectly possible to accept that Monnet may have exaggerated his role and those of his advisors in first creating and then launching a new policy in a dramatic and highly original way on unsuspecting west European governments. Monnet's *Memoirs*, after all, are somewhat self-serving. But this does not in any way dilute either the significance or the originality of the political ideas and strategy which lay behind them. And Milward's claim that the ultimate credit for the Schuman plan should go not to Monnet at all but to Schuman himself seems to go too far in the other direction.[36] The political origins of the ECSC might indeed be much more mundane than we have been led to believe, but it is simply too dismissive to suggest that Schuman and Monnet merely 'associated a diplomative initiative with a cause'.[37] As John Pinder has recently remarked, if the Quai d'Orsay had really been responsible for the Schuman Plan 'it is hardly to be expected that they would have designed the Community with an independent executive and a basis for federal parliamentary and judicial institutions'.[38] The 9 May 1950 was indeed a radically new departure in post-war west European history and in the larger world of international relations itself. Contrary to what Milward has stated, the ECSC not only solved a past and seemingly intractable problem but it also heralded colossal possibilities for the future, a future which would be built upon many of the novel political ideas and assumptions inherent in the ECSC.

What, then, are we to make of Milward's historical revisionism in respect of the ECSC? Apart from a few small details, has his analysis succeeded in destroying that 'certain saintliness' which had been conferred 'on all those who had touched the Schuman proposals from Monnet and Schuman down to the professor of law who drafted a version of them'?[39] Certainly it was necessary to ransack official government archives as well as those of interested non-governmental parties in order to discover the motives and vested interests of the many actors involved. But once again this laudable quest must not be allowed to impose a new orthodoxy which conveniently ignores the radical originality inherent in the ECSC. Leaving aside the gallery of European saints, there remains a strong body of old and recent literature which continues to support the view that the ECSC did harbour unique features and qualities which had massive implications for both the future of European integration and the national state. It is not necessary to accept 'saintliness' in order to acknowledge the remarkable characteristics inherent in the ECSC. Nor does it matter if the ECSC did not entirely succeed in its specific economic goals in the 1950s. One recent commentator on Monnet's role in the creation and operation of the ECSC, John Gillingham, has already acknowledged that the ECSC was 'in many respects a disappointment'. The High Authority was 'never able either to govern supranationally or create genuinely common markets'.[40] But the practical political experience of bringing six separate sovereign national states together to work in an unprecedented supra-national decision-making context was itself a remarkable achievement. Indeed, in what Milward acknowledged to be the best general account of the early history of the ECSC, William Diebold remarked that if a federal Europe was established sometime in the future the ECSC would 'appear as one of the first stages by which it was achieved'. But his most interesting and perceptive observation was his belief that in these circumstances it would be 'institution-building' rather than just 'economic foundation-laying' that would 'seem most important'. Indeed, it was the federal elements in the ECSC which confirmed that 'sovereign nations' could work well together in novel ways.[41]

What is characteristic of the early accounts of the ECSC is the sense of novelty and the widespread recognition that the era of national sovereignty was already over.[42] It was not that national states needed to be 'rescued' from anything so much as the fact that they could no longer pursue their separate national interests independently from other countries. Their future integrity depended not upon some formal fictitious concept of 'sovereignty' but upon a more relative realistic notion of 'autonomy'.[43] And the practical post-war experience of conventional international organizations, like the Organization for European Economic Cooperation (OEEC) and the Council of Europe, strongly suggested that something much more binding and regulated than these bodies was necessary if the national state was to guarantee its future self-determination in however attenuated a form. Whether or not the resurgence of the national state would have been so effective with conventional international cooperation instead of European integration is a question which is now redundant. However, the word 'rescue' does seem rather theatrical in the absence of a clear explanation of the particular threat and of a measured consideration of the alternative forms of economic and political adaptation which might then have been possible. In the light of this interpretation, then, we might be better advised to construe Milward's research more in terms of the post-war 'resurgence' of the national state rather than its 'rescue'. The former term is less dramatic than the latter and it seems to convey more accurately the realist purpose of the Florence school of historical thought.

Historical controversy also continues to surround the sudden and dramatic appearance during 1952–54 of two remarkable projects which had enormous implications for post-war Western European integration. A complex combination of international and domestic events and circumstances in the aftermath of the Schuman Declaration in May 1950, and the period leading up to the launching of the ECSC in July 1952, catapulted the far-reaching proposals for a European Defence Community (EDC) and a European Political Community (EPC) into the forefront of west European politics. Much has already been written about these notable events and I do not intend to rehearse them here. My purpose instead is to reinstate the significance of federal ideas and influences in the unfolding of these projects.

The outbreak of the Korean War in June 1950 set in motion a chain of events which culminated in the EDC Treaty signed in Paris in May 1952. Indeed the years between 1950 and 1954 were dominated by military issues: the activities of the North Atlantic Treaty Organization (NATO); the American pressure for European rearmament; Franco-German military negotiations; the military intentions of Stalin; and the Korean and Indochina wars. And national domestic policy preferences, of course, were pivotal in the ultimate outcome of these issues. Nonetheless, the role of Monnet and of the European federalists must not be underestimated. On 11 August 1950, the Consultative Assembly of the Council of Europe, led by Winston Churchill, called for 'the immediate creation of a unified European army, under the authority of a European minister of defence, subject to European democratic control'.[44] On 23 August, Monnet wrote to his old associate, Rene Pleven, the French Prime Minister, urging the following proposal which was communicated to him on 3 September 1950:

> What ... we need ... is a political concept, that is, a spiritual and
> ethical one.... I propose you bring to the partnership a strong, con-
> structive concept as well as a determination to build up a stout exter-
> nal defence ... the establishment of a structured Atlantic free world,
> accommodating the diversity of its three constituent parts, the United
> States, the British Empire and continental Western Europe federated
> around an expanded Schuman Plan.... The hope ... lies in the fact
> that the team leader is the United States. Of all the countries of the
> West, it is the readiest to accept change and listen to strong straight
> talk, so long as one throws a constructive idea into the ring.... Alone,
> they will not develop the political vision of which the world stands in
> need. I think that is our task.[45]

In his *Memoirs*, Monnet confirmed his belief that the building of Europe
would not be achieved via defence. It might certainly be 'one task for the
future federation' but it did not offer 'the most powerful or compelling
motive for unity'.[46] What altered this rock-solid view of European integration was Monnet's famous conception of 'the course of events'. 'Change',
he reflected, 'had already affected events before it had affected our thinking'.[47] The ECSC could no longer operate in isolation from these new circumstances:

> We were forced to take short cuts. Now, the federation of Europe
> would have to become an immediate objective. The army, its weapons,
> and basic production would all have to be placed simultaneously
> under joint sovereignty. We could no longer wait, as we had once
> planned, for political Europe to be the culminating point of a gradual
> process, since its joint defence was inconceivable without a joint polit-
> ical authority from the start.[48]

Events were clearly in command and Monnet sought to utilize them in a
way which would resolve two major but seemingly discrete issues: to preserve the preponderance of French military power in the face of the
inevitable rearmament of West Germany, and to promote the wider cause
of European integration. The Pleven Plan was the result of Monnet's political strategy. And if it is true that 'the notion was very much in the air in
1950', it is also true that 'Monnet himself established the link between the
Schuman and Pleven Plans', the latter furnishing the solution to the
problem of German rearmament 'in the same spirit and by the same
methods as for coal and steel'.[49] Duchene noted that Monnet had not
claimed to have 'invented' the Pleven Plan for a European army; what
Monnet did was 'to take it up, put it into shape for the more or less willing
group at the heart of government in Paris, and push it through'.[50]

The Pleven Plan, which was really an ingenious way of rearming
Germans without rearming Germany, was welcomed by the NATO

Council in October 1950 and, in addition to the Paris–Bonn axis, was supported by Italy, Belgium, Luxembourg and eventually the Netherlands, after a short delay while the Dutch waited in vain for a positive response from the British. An EDC treaty-making diplomatic conference was convened in Paris in February 1951, chaired by the French diplomat, Herve Alphand. Details of these events have already been chronicled in the mainstream scholarly literature on the EDC and EPC and there is no need to repeat them here. It is important, however, to emphasize the crucial role of the European federalists in the feverish activities of this period. Apart from Monnet and his close circle of federalist friends and associates, we must include Altiero Spinelli, Paul-Henri Spaak, Fernand Dehousse, Henri Frenay, Andre Philip, Ivan Matteo Lombardo, Ludovico Benvenuti, Piero Calamandrei and Alcide De Gasperi, the Italian Prime Minister.[51] Together with the support of those statesmen and former statesmen who, like Schuman, Adenauer, Pleven, Reynaud and von Brentano, were not avowed federalists but who were nevertheless quite willing to embrace the Community idea, the European federalists were able to exert a political influence out of all proportion to their size. External events had altered the political environment sufficiently to open up a window of opportunity for Monnet, Spinelli and the federalist movement to exploit. They did so with great vigour and tenacity.

Concrete evidence of the federalists' impact upon both west European politics and the process of European integration can best be gauged by the critical role that they played in the struggle to achieve a European Political Community (EPC) to democratize the EDC. Led by De Gasperi, the Italian government took the lead in advocating a federal model with a fully-fledged European Assembly directly elected by European citizens and having powers of taxation in a joint decision-making structure. Other governments however were less enthusiastic and the EDC Conference could not decide whether the structure of the future permanent organization should be federal or confederal. In consequence, the Italian delegation secured the insertion of a special Article 38 in the EDC treaty which ensured that these discussions, although temporarily delayed, would not be abandoned. The upshot of these discussions was to entrust the tasks of Article 38 to the ECSC Assembly which adopted the title of 'Ad Hoc Assembly' for these purposes and assigned a 26-member constitutional committee to draw up a preliminary draft treaty for its consideration.[52] Preoccupied with shoring up the ECSC, Monnet played no part in the EPC episode but Pinder's detailed research has shown that the federalists occupied key positions in the committee and were able to shape the proposals, in the form of a draft treaty, for an EPC constitution which was presented to the Ad Hoc Assembly in March 1953.[53]

These EPC proposals have been well-documented and the best academic monument to this remarkable episode in the struggle to build Europe in the early 1950s remains *Studies in Federalism*, edited by Robert R. Bowie and Carl J. Friedrich, which was published in 1954. In his Introduction to the volume of essays, Friedrich stressed that the Study Committee did not concern itself with formal questions, such as whether the European Community (EC) was to be a federation or confederation, noting that the EDC Treaty had also 'left this question open'. What mattered were 'the concrete issues' but the Draft Treaty did refer to the EC as 'supranational' and it was founded upon 'a union of peoples and states' which would be 'indissoluble'.[54] In brief, the EC was to assume the functions of both the ECSC and the EDC with additional powers relating to foreign affairs and economic policy. Its institutional structure was to be based upon the separation of powers and a bicameral representative system, as specified in Article 38 of the EDC Treaty, and although the EC was endowed with the institutions of a federal government, its powers were sharply circumscribed. Friedrich claimed that when Spaak presented the Treaty to the Council of Foreign Ministers in Strasbourg on 10 March 1953, he identified the proposed constitution as 'partly federal and partly confederal'.[55] Spinelli, who had been 'one of the Committee's most active members', acknowledged that the EC was not a federation but that it had federal structures which could evolve into something more substantive in the future.[56]

Because the EDC, and with it the EPC, was rejected by the French National Assembly in August 1954, it is common even for informed historians and political scientists to dismiss the whole affair as confirmation that national governments would never sacrifice their sovereignty in such circumstances. Defence in particular was a matter of 'high politics' which, along with foreign policy, constituted the very essence of what it meant to be an independent sovereign state. But a very different gloss can be put on these events if we recall that the EDC treaty actually came within a whisker of being ratified. West Germany and the Benelux countries ratified it while Italy waited for French endorsement. It should be noted, therefore, not simply that it failed but that it almost succeeded. Its greatest legacy was that, in coming so close to success, the EDC–EPC episode confirmed that federal ideas and influences could have a major impact upon practical policy-making in Europe. In hindsight, the episode put down an important marker for future federalist attempts to build Europe. The historian of the EDC, Edward Fursdon, claimed that it was 'one of the most important episodes in post-war European history', but one of the least known. Yet the outcome of the EDC experience, he noted, laid the foundations of today's defence and security of Western Europe and 'in this, following the unique series of paradoxes characteristic of the EDC, its failure was its success'.[57] And, in the extent to which contemporary Europe has moved closer to a Common Foreign and Security Policy (CFSP), both the Treaty on European Union (TEU), ratified in 1993, and the Treaty of Amsterdam (TA), signed in 1997, have their origins in the EDC–EPC precedent.

Perhaps because European integration reached a temporary impasse in 1954, Alan Milward had virtually no comment to make about the

EDC–EPC affair except to dismiss it as 'foredoomed to failure'.[58] After all, to the barefoot empiricist, it had ended in abject failure. But the revisionist's instincts were certainly reactivated when Milward turned his attention to matters of more direct concern to the economic historian. If we look now at the origins and development of the shift from narrow sectoral politics to the broad embrace of a common market in the mid-1950s, we encounter once again the unrelenting, almost visceral, logic of the iconoclast. The main focus of Milward's attack on the federalists and other enthusiasts of European integration is his rejection of the conventional assumption that the idea of a united Europe was 'relaunched' by 'the two great federalists Monnet and Spaak in the twin projects for Euratom and the common market' which led directly to the Treaties of Rome as the 'culminating triumph of this relaunch'. In uncompromising but now-familiar language, Milward claimed that 'most of this is myth, nurtured by federalists and other advocates of political unification as an end in itself'.[59]

As with the ECSC and EDC–EPC, Milward has little time for the purported influences of the federalists on policy-making and none at all for those federalist influences upon policies which were never implemented. Let us look a little closer at what is unquestionably the subject of a serious searching historical reappraisal. One consequence of recent historical research suggests that it was the growing recognition of West Germany's post-war position as the economic and commercial pivot of Western Europe's growth, combined with the separate national economic interests of the negotiating parties, that was responsible for the Treaties of Rome signed in 1957. In short, 'the real origins of the common market' were located in the strength of West Germany's economic prosperity which was 'so essential to the growth of incomes elsewhere in Western Europe'.[60] And since the project for a customs union was 'of much earlier gestation than the notion of a relaunch implies', the 'widespread notion of the failure and relaunch of the project for European integration over the years 1954–6 is mainly fanciful political propaganda'.[61]

In dealing with the origins of the European Economic Community (EEC), Milward is clearly on comfortable ground. And there is no doubt that his detailed analysis of the factors which combined to bring the idea of a customs union into the realm of practical politics during 1955–57 is impressive. There are plenty of foreign trade statistics which enable him to marshal the facts and propel him relentlessly forward toward his realist destination. Distilled into simple logic, his general conclusion is unequivocal: West Germany had to be firmly anchored in place not because of its likely future military prowess but rather because of its economic strength and vitality which was 'indispensable to the rescue of the European nation-state'.[62]

This thesis, in concentrating mainly upon economic and social criteria, is neat and tidy but not entirely convincing. In his single-minded determination to analyse and explore the motives for the creation of the EEC,

Milward has been selective by omission. Once again the political context has been sacrificed in pursuit of 'the facts'. Where, then, were the federal influences in this explanation and what role did the federalists play in the events and circumstances which led up to the Rome Treaties? We know that Monnet, having resigned as President of the ECSC's High Authority in November 1954 in order to channel his political activities into the Action Committee for the United States of Europe, played no visible part in the emergence of the EEC. Monnet's primary purpose was to add more sectors, especially atomic energy and transport, to the ECSC. But we should recall that the idea of shifting from sectoral to common market integration was itself not a novel one during 1955–57. A European customs union had already been proposed by the Dutch Foreign Minister, Johan Willem Beyen, in 1953, as part of the economic supporting structure for the EPC. And, as Milward has argued, the earliest proposals for this project 'emanated from Paris before the Marshall Plan'.[63] We now know that the key to progress in the customs union was to entice the French government to the negotiating table by the prospect of research on the use of nuclear technology. For either of the projects to be successful, therefore, it was necessary for Monnet's Euratom plan to be incorporated into the discussions. In this way, 'the link between the common market and Euratom was born'.[64]

Federal influences derive from institutional context. Several points are worth noting about these influences which are easily overlooked. It is broadly accepted that all the important provisions in the Treaty of Rome were foreshadowed in the Spaak Report of April 1956. Indeed, on most points, 'the provisions in the Treaty of Rome simply developed further or refined principles and procedures discussed in the Report'. And since it lay 'somewhere between an objective blue-print and a negotiated plan', it is reasonable to assume that the small committee of three which drafted the Report played an influential role in the outcome.[65] Historical analysis should not, therefore, ignore the important 'fact' that two of the three men who together drafted the Report – Pierre Uri and Hans von der Groeben – were self-confessed federalists. Uri was the principal economist of the ECSC's High Authority and a close associate of Monnet, while von der Groeben had been head of the Coal and Steel Community Section in the German Ministry of Economic Affairs. It was certainly no accident that the ECSC served as an institutional model for the EEC. Uri's conception was of a common market whose institutions could be appropriately woven into the existing ECSC framework. The institutional balance between the national and supra-national elements may have been altered in favour of the former, but the inclusion of Article 201 which furnished the basis for an independent source of EC revenue together with Article 138 which provided for direct elections to the European Assembly in the future, had enormous federal implications. Moreover the introduction of qualified majority voting (QMV) in the Council of Ministers was an innovation which, it was hoped, would be extended in the future. The federalist imprint of Uri was unmistakable, and Spaak wrote much later that the Report had been 'largely the fruit of his efforts'. Indeed, he was 'one of the principal architects of the Treaty of Rome'.[66]

Within the general framework of the Treaty, then, there was much that was effectively open-ended. It was possible, in short, for it to be very much an outline treaty. Naturally, each national delegation construed the treaty negotiations in the context of its own perceived national interests, but some were more positive than others in the extent to which they were able to make national and European interests converge. The Italians, for example, were particularly keen to make a success of the venture. The federalist, Benvenuti, led the Italian delegation and since its members were 'trained in the De Gasperi era of Europeanism, and frankly admitted their continuing belief in those ideals', it was easy to see in this work the perpetuation of 'De Gasperi's continuing contribution to the cause that had dominated his last years of life'. In the end, the Italian delegation was able to negotiate a treaty that satisfied 'the moral exigencies of Europeanism' and the need for 'direct international help in the solution of long-standing national problems'.[67]

Institutional context was also important in another respect. Von der Groeben, himself a member of the European Commission during 1958–70, has underlined the significance of elite activists in the Community institutions.[68] Progress in European integration would be heavily dependent upon the opinions and objectives advocated by politicians and officials active in them. The early role of the Commission was crucial for the federalists. The appointment of Walter Hallstein, an avowed federalist, as its first President in 1958 was clearly a political decision and enabled these influences to percolate throughout the institution during the pioneering period of integration.[69] Apart from Hallstein, both Sicco Mansholt and Jean Rey were 'openly pursuing federalist objectives'.[70] And with several senior European ministers in West Germany, Italy and Benelux – like Adenauer, Spaak and Beyen – sympathetic to the Community idea in these formative years, it is not at all surprising to learn that federal ideas and influences helped to promote a dynamic interpretation of the wording and context of the Rome Treaties. Even the renowned Euro-sceptic, Robert Marjolin, who was no friend of the federalists, acknowledged that with certain pragmatic reservations he 'was not then, nor am I now, in profound disagreement with the "federalists"'. However, he really believed in what he called 'a middle way' whereby the result would be 'a Europe which, if perhaps not wholly unified economically, would nevertheless present a degree of unity unachieved hitherto'.[71] Coming from Marjolin, this was a major concession even if his own conception of a federal Europe remained somewhat inflexible and unimaginative.

If we now summarize the years between 1950 and 1957, it can be seen that federalism and the federalists played a significant part in the origins and evolution of European integration. And, contrary to the arguments advanced by Milward, both Monnet and Spaak promoted federal influences which helped to transform the idea of European unity into the practical politics of European integration. They helped to shape and mould the three emergent Communities – ECSC, Euratom and the EEC – into initially self-contained polities founded upon the interaction of federal, supra-national and intergovernmental institutions unprecedented in international politics. Because the concept of 'political influence' is admittedly difficult to operationalize, Milward has overlooked Monnet's intricate, wide-ranging network of personal contacts which enabled him, like Spinelli after him, to pick up the telephone and speak directly with the President of France. As von der Groeben noted, Monnet exercised a profound influence upon 'the responsible statesmen and elites in the political parties, industrial associations, trade unions and bureaucracy' in promoting integration. He was also successful in winning over many sceptical and understandably hesitant politicians like those in the West German Social Democratic Party (SPD).[72]

It would also be a serious historical mistake to overlook Spaak's pivotal role in the negotiations of the eponymous committee which led more or less directly to the Rome Treaty. The Belgian Foreign Minister's energetic and persuasive political leadership in the public debates and negotiations surrounding the emergence of the EEC during 1956–57 was vital in ensuring that the disparate interests and motives of the national delegations coincided sufficiently to secure a new European bargain. Although not a federalist, Spaak was one of those European statesmen who, like Adenauer and Schuman, preferred to act as one rather than to use the word itself. As Pinder has commented, Spaak's conviction that national sovereignty was redundant brought him 'to act as a federalist between 1952 and 1956'. Indeed, it would not be an exaggeration to claim that Spaak, Adenauer, Schuman and Beyen were among the leading lights of European integration in this period who, rather like many European leaders today, 'appeared to prefer a federal reality to the federal word'.[73]

How, then, should we assess the emergence of the Rome Treaties in 1957? Is Milward correct to claim that they had nothing to do with the popular idea of a relaunching of the project for European integration during 1955–57? One German political scientist, Hanns Kusters, found himself in agreement with Milward but for different reasons. He claimed that the EEC and Euratom did not constitute a 'reactivation' of the European idea simply because, after the failure of the EDC in 1954, 'the efforts towards integration never came to a halt'. Accordingly, it was rather more a matter of the Rome Treaties occurring under 'uniquely favourable historical circumstances that were neither foreseeable nor consciously contrived'.[74] This view construed the successful conclusion in 1955 of security and defence arrangements in the Western European Union (WEU) – an extension of the Brussels Treaty Organization of 1948 – as removing a crucial obstacle in the path of further political progress towards closer economic integration. In satisfying the American demand for German rearmament and British and European concerns about it, the creation of the WEU along with West German membership of NATO facilitated further discussions about economic and commercial matters.

In short, this interpretation stresses historical continuity rather than the dramatic rupture implicit in the *relance europeenne*. Federalists, too, would concur with this view. Historians and political scientists all too often overlook the fundamental continuities which lie beneath the apparent but sensational discontinuities of dramatic events. Federal ideas, influences and strategies are just such a case in point. As we shall see, they continued quietly and unobtrusively to prompt, promote and pressurize for an alternative conception of Europe throughout the years which witnessed the arrival and demise of the figure Pinder has felicitously called 'God's gift to the realist school of international relations', namely, General de Gaulle.[75]

Before we leave the contentious intellectual debate about the origins and growth of European integration during this period, it is appropriate to reflect upon Milward's own concluding remarks about the Rome Treaties. Given his previous assertion, quoted above, about the primarily social and economic origins of the EC, it is important for us to be crystal clear about what Milward's claims are.

Let us begin with what is perhaps a surprising statement by Milward. In his hugely detailed survey of the 1950s, he is at pains to clarify his basic thesis, lest it be misunderstood. He acknowledges that, in bringing so much evidence relating to the economic and social foundations of the Rome Treaties, 'there is no intention to deny the political motivations which are conventionally and correctly ascribed to the Treaties'. These are that the EC 'was a further guarantee of the peace settlement in Western Europe; that it made central to this peace settlement a still closer Franco-German association; that in doing so it reasserted French political leadership in Western Europe; and that it represented a yearning that Europe should have a greater voice in world affairs'. However, in accepting the validity of these political motivations, Milward is keen to emphasize that 'the economic foundation of the treaties was more fundamental, because without it they could not have achieved their additional political objectives'. In any case, he argues, these were 'not truly separable from the economic ones'.[76]

On the face of it, these are curious statements to make in the light of his earlier arguments and observations. He appears to be riding postillion. He would also appear to have confused the meaning of origins and motivations. The implication of his thesis is that the origins of the EC were primarily economic and social but that they were politically motivated. This intellectual position is unconvincing, especially when we are constantly reminded in the mainstream literature that both the origins and the goals of European integration were 'political' and that it was the means to achieve them that were 'economic'. Monnet's approach to European integration confirms this, but this assumption is also the bedrock of virtually every post-war theory of political integration. In other words, it is in Milward's 'political motivations' that we will find the 'true origins' of the Rome Treaties in particular, and of European integration in general. One explanation for this apparent conundrum is simple: Milward is an economic historian rather than a political scientist. His academic discipline, like any other, pushes him in a particular direction and impels him to construe European integration in mainly economic and social terms rather than in terms of political ideas, strategies and goals. We will return to this question at the end of the chapter. For the moment, let us return to historical matters.

### From Rome to Paris, 1958–72

The Treaties of Rome, establishing the EEC and Euratom, were signed on 27 March 1957 and entered into force on 1 January 1958. During the years between the declared commitment to 'an ever closer union among European peoples' and the agreement in October 1972 at the Paris Summit to 'transform before the end of the present decade, and with the fullest respect for the Treaties already signed, the whole complex of the relations of the Member States into a European Union', European integration was firmly consolidated.[77] But this period of consolidation is often regarded as evidence of the end of the EC's federal heritage – the so-called federalist dream – an archaeological monument to an age which effectively ended in 1954 with the demise of the EDC and EPC. For those who continue to oppose the building of a federal Europe, federalism is conveniently consigned to history. It has, they claim, no enduring relevance to European integration.

At first glance, it does seem that the economic and political evolution of the EC in this period overshadows the federalist pressures for further integration. Federal ideas appear to be invisible. And it is, of course, perfectly understandable for historians to look chiefly for a history which is largely intergovernmental, one which emphasizes the role of national governments. It is once again a history which overlooks and dismisses the role of political ideas as part of the explanation of political events. The marked shift from sectoral policies to the common market project is construed as a reaffirmation of the realist and/or neorealist paradigm: it is evidence of pragmatic intergovernmental politics which emphasizes national interests and policy preferences over and above the ideas that surround these events.

The conventional interpretation of EC history, however, is once again selective by omission. Unlike the Council of Europe of 1949, the EEC of

1957 was not its own greatest achievement. Inherent in it was the capacity to go beyond what existed. The experience of operating the institutional system of the ECSC had sensitized European political elites to both the possibilities and the limitations of supra-national politics. And, as Pinder has reminded us, once the impulse for a federalizing step has been given, the existing institutional framework makes it easier for that step to be taken.[78] We must also recall that in establishing a much more sophisticated institutional framework than previous intergovernmental organizations, the member states had also deliberately left many questions unresolved. These were to be worked out later once the EEC was in full operation. In these circumstances, then, it was hardly surprising to learn that federalists were highly optimistic about the EEC. It contained within it the germ of a Europe which had great federal possibilities. As Griffiths has already remarked, 'for some, at least, it carried the hopes of a future federal European state'.[79]

Another preconception of many commentators on the post-war history of European integration is that the great political rupture of 1966, when General de Gaulle successfully challenged the political authority of the European Commission, constitutes an important historical turning-point which sounded the death-knell of a supra-national Europe. According to this historical interpretation of events, de Gaulle's unerring victory over the Commission signified the inauguration of an intergovernmental Europe often referred to as a *Europe des patries*. It reflected, in short, the triumph of the national state over its putative European successor. The significance of this event, however, has to be reassessed in the light of the subsequent political evolution of the EEC. Because history refuses to stand still, it is subject to constant reinterpretation. De Gaulle's actions during 1965–66 were certainly a blow to the supra-national pretensions of the Commission, but their significance should not be exaggerated. They did not represent the end of a supra-national Europe nor did they usher in an undisputed era of intergovernmentalism. This is an over-simplification which fails to convey the institutional and policy complexities of the EEC. Moreover, federal ideas, influences and strategies did not disappear with the advent of de Gaulle as the new French President in June 1958; they merely bolstered what we might call the 'creative tensions' inherent in the Community.

Because de Gaulle dominated Community affairs in the 1960s, it is reasonable to expect him to loom large in the mainstream literature on the EEC which addresses that decade. But we must not allow him and his singular activities to completely overshadow the progress made in European integration. Despite his heroics in championing French national sovereignty, the EEC began its life in favourable conditions. Griffiths has claimed that 'the early years of the EEC were startlingly successful', and there appears to be a significant consensus which supports this view.[80] In *Wirtschaftspolitik für Europa*, von der Groeben identified the following favourable preconditions for success: 'the general willingness to liberalize and to limit protectionism after the Second World War; the USA's support of all integration initiatives; the post-war boom, with high growth rates and a prevailing mood of optimism; and entrepreneurs' expectation of being able to improve the production process and thereby the productivity of their businesses by a better division of labour in a large European market, without creating difficult problems of adjustment in the fact of the rapid growth of national economies'. But he also noted another factor which he called 'the psychological effect created by the EEC, the dynamism of its institutions and the first successes'. Success breeds success, and the balance sheet of the Community's early years was summed up as one in which 'faith in the Common Market contributed a lot to its success and accelerated the process of fusion and integration'.[81]

The sense of getting off to a good start was also echoed by Monnet who, although believing that the Rome Treaties had 'disappointed the hopes of the federalists', nonetheless felt that the Community's consolidation and future enlargement would 'bring closer the time when a political Europe could be built'.[82] The buoyant optimism of the time appears to have been justified. Griffiths has gone so far as to suggest that the EEC 'soon found itself basking in a golden age' with a young and inexperienced supranational Commission that quickly became 'a formidable force in European politics'.[83] But in 1960, the focus of EEC politics was suddenly and dramatically riveted upon a subject which typified the Gaullist conception of European unity, namely, political union.

De Gaulle had viewed the supra-national elements in the Rome Treaties with a conspicuous scepticism. But he recognized the support for the Treaties in French industrial and especially agrarian circles, and they chimed appropriately with his main objective of liberalizing the French economy. His own conception of European unity was a limited one in which the national states, under the political leadership of France, could cooperate in matters of mutual economic interest, preserve their independence from the Atlantic Alliance dominated by the United States, and move closer together in matters of foreign policy and defence where the EEC was weak. He had no intention of allowing the EEC's Commission to expand its powers and functions in the area of foreign external relations where it had already begun to flex its muscles in connection with the GATT trade rounds. Politically, he thought only in terms of consultation and cooperation by heads of government and small ministerial committees. His initiative in the summer of 1960, therefore, was regarded by the advocates of a more integrationist conception of Europe, both federalists and non-federalists alike, with considerable caution and not a little suspicion.

The background context to de Gaulle's political initiative in 1960 is already well-documented and I do not intend to rehearse the details here.[84] It is sufficient for our purposes to emphasize the connecting links between this initiative and the void left by the collapse of the EDC and EPC in 1954. Pierre Gerbet has noted that de Gaulle had put his finger on the striking contrast between an EEC well along the road toward economic integration and the absence of any diplomatic and military Community.[85] It was this lacuna in the EEC's institutional and policy-making capacity which de Gaulle sought to address. But it was also a golden opportunity for him to assert the role of France in Europe's political evolution. Von der Groeben put it succinctly: de Gaulle probably chose this relatively early date for his initiative because 'European development was taking place within an institutional framework that did not accord with his ideas, and he feared that it might consolidate itself and that the integration process might spill over into the political field'.[86] The new French President did not initially intend to subvert the EEC, but he feared the political implications of its early economic successes which might propel it in a supra-national direction against French national interests. Here was a set of circumstances which he could turn to his own best advantage and close the gap between France's post-war economic recovery and its international failure. Europe could exorcize the French demons of Indochina, Suez and Algeria.[87]

The key to de Gaulle's strategy, as we have come to expect in most of post-war Europe's forward moments, was the Paris–Bonn axis. Relations with the West German Chancellor, Konrad Adenauer, were crucial to its success, and de Gaulle was able to successfully present a new Franco-German *rapprochement* as the firm basis for a strengthening of the Federal Republic's international position, as well as anchoring it even more securely in the European domain. Adenauer's principal concern was to balance West Germany's interests in European integration with those in the Atlantic Alliance, defence being of paramount importance in the presence of the Soviet military threat. The bold statement by de Gaulle at a press conference in May 1960, announcing his intention of 'building Western Europe into a political, economic, cultural and human grouping organised for action and self-defence … through organised cooperation between states, with the expectation of perhaps one day growing into an imposing confederation'[88] was both a challenge and a threat to the rival concept of a 'European Europe' founded upon economic and political integration. And the dangers inherent in it were perceived as such by the EEC Commission which could hardly fail to appreciate that these assumptions and goals were hostile to its own evolution. The main danger of course was that de Gaulle intended to construct a new and separate political edifice alongside the EEC instead of using the existing Community system, and especially the Council of Ministers, for this purpose. Moreover, it was obvious that de Gaulle's real intention was for this new organization, dealing initially with foreign policy and defence matters, ultimately to absorb the whole Community system.

During the years between 1960 and 1962, when the proposals for political union, enshrined in the Fouchet Plan, dominated Community politics, it is evident that the federalists were fighting a rearguard action. De Gaulle's political activities amounted to a scathing attack upon federalism and the federalists. But his plans to neutralize the supra-national basis of the infant European enterprise met stiff resistance from federalists such as Hallstein in the Commission and federalist sympathizers like Spaak. Restored as Belgian Foreign Minister, he described de Gaulle's ideas as 'vague' and the whole project as 'marked by a certain confusion'.[89] Monnet's response to de Gaulle's political initiative was interesting. Far from opposing it, he welcomed the opportunity of progress in an area where none had been achieved since the conclusion of the Rome Treaties. Fully aware of de Gaulle's resilient, if antiquated, conception of European unity, Monnet determined to exploit the new situation and to see the positive side of the General's 'Europe of the States', a scheme which to his mind 'remained obscure'.[90]

Since 1955, Monnet's energies had been channelled into the Action Committee for the United States of Europe, a political lobby and pressure group of influential political and economic leaders for keeping up the momentum in favour of European integration, but his own network of political influence was no less effective for that. Indeed, his personal contacts with and private access to the French Foreign Minister, Maurice Couve de Murville and Chancellor Adenauer were put to good use. When the Fouchet–Cattani negotiations eventually failed, Monnet's conviction that Europe could not be built by intergovernmental compromises alone seemed once again to have been confirmed. But it is important to note that he was not implacably opposed to political cooperation as a mechanism for bringing national political leaders together to arrive at international agreements. His only proviso was that it should strengthen the union of Europe. In a letter to Adenauer on 21 November 1960, Monnet sketched the outlines of what this union might involve:

> I believe that it is a useful suggestion that the Heads of Government should meet as frequently and regularly as possible to discuss our six countries' common policy, and that there should be meetings of Foreign Ministers and also of Ministers of Education and Defence. For the time being, ... I think that cooperation is a necessary stage. It will be a step forward, above all if the whole European system – the integrated Community and the organizations for cooperation, different as they are – be included in a single whole, a European confederation.[91]

In hindsight this correspondence was remarkably prescient. It not only underlined Monnet's willingness to be flexible about the building of Europe, but in resembling so closely the Europe of the 1990s his vision also indicated the institutional shape of things to come.

The failure of the Fouchet Plan, according to Monnet, was implicit from the very outset in the way that the negotiations were conducted. 'If any grand design existed', he wrote, 'it certainly had no time to take shape'. Instead, the Community of the Six 'plunged right away into a defensive quest for reciprocal concessions'. It was important, therefore, to be clear about the nature of this failure: 'it was the failure of an intergovernmental conference not of the Community method'.[92] De Gaulle's memorable definition of Community Europe, forever immortalized in his infamous and petulant riposte about European integration, embodied all of the dogmatic assumptions of the national mindset and foreshadowed the later convulsions about Europe of the British Prime Minister, Margaret Thatcher. The French President's visceral remarks are worth summarizing:

> Only the States, in this respect, are valid, legitimate, and capable of achieving it. I repeat that at present there is and can be no Europe other than a Europe of the States – except of course for myths, fictions and pageants.... A so-called 'integrated Europe', which would have no policy, would come to depend on someone outside; and that someone would have a policy of his own. There would perhaps be a federator, but it would not be European. And that, perhaps, is what sometimes and in some degree inspires some of the remarks of one or another of the champions of 'European integration'.[93]

De Gaulle's use of the word 'federator' clearly referred to the United States and incensed Monnet for the way that it caricatured 'the great venture that for twelve years had been uniting the peoples of Europe'. The Action Committee's caustic rejoinder is also worth more than a moment's reflection:

> The prospects open to Europe today are the outcome of the decision of European countries not to treat their economic problems as national ones but as common to them all. To solve these problems, they have adopted a new method of collective action.... This is a completely new approach. It does not create a central Government. But it does result in Community decisions being taken within the Council of Ministers notably because the proposal of solutions to common difficulties by the independent European body makes it possible, without risk, to give up the unanimity rule. The Parliament and the Court of Justice underline the Community character of the whole. This new method is the real 'federator' of Europe.[94]

In the end, the plan for political union was reduced to the Franco-German Treaty of 23 January 1963, a sort of 'bilateral' Fouchet Plan. Spaak was disappointed with this new, solemn accord because, although it was loudly trumpeted as something which could be extended later to the other member states, he believed it to be against both the letter and the spirit of the Rome Treaties. Private Franco-German consultations held prior to Community discussions 'introduced a new and unforeseen element in the EEC' which he did not think would prove to be 'helpful'. The depth of his dismay even prompted him to suggest that the treaty had been agreed partly as 'a revenge for certain attitudes which emerged during the debate on the so-called Fouchet Plan'.[95] Spaak was alluding to the pivotal role played at this time by the small EEC member states like Belgium and the Netherlands which had effectively torpedoed de Gaulle's scheme for a 'Union of States'. But it is also important to remember that the failure of de Gaulle's plan for political union in 1962 was also the failure of the Gaullist conception of European unity. And his unilateral termination of negotiations for British membership of the EEC shortly before the signing of the Franco-German Treaty on 14 January 1963 could not compensate for this abject failure. There would be no Gaullist Europe.

The failure of the project for political union meant that there was no formal political cooperation in the EEC for the rest of the 1960s. The periodic meetings of the foreign ministers begun in 1960 were not continued after January 1963. De Gaulle's high-handedness had alienated the Benelux countries and from the outset the wide divergence of views among the member states about the structure, pace and direction of political union could not be overcome. For federalists, there was relief that the Community had emerged from a very difficult episode with its political integrity intact and undoubtedly a certain confirmation that intergovernmental cooperation alone was simply inadequate as a basis for a new European order. An interesting legacy of this memorable series of events is of particular interest in the context of this book. This was the gradual emergence of the phrase 'European Union' in the context of the debates about the Fouchet Plan. Gerbet has noted that it appeared without either fanfare or success early in 1962 and was to reappear ten years later 'when the old files were dusted and re-read' by the leaders of the enlarged Community.[96]

The Community did not escape the wrath of de Gaulle for very long after 1963. Several attempts were made by the governments of West Germany, Belgium and Italy to restart the negotiations on political union during 1964–65 but they came to nothing. The series of events which created the first major constitutional and political crisis in the infant Community, however, had nothing to do with political union. Instead they had a lot to do with the early evolution of the EEC's peculiar institutional system and the institutional relationships that it implied. Informed opinion on this question remains divided. Von der Groeben has claimed that the deterioration of the climate of integration which followed the failure of the Fouchet Plan and the collapse of the accession negotiations led to an increased concern with national interests on the part of all the member governments which 'found practical expression in large-scale involvement of their own officials in the decision-making process and limited the Commission's potential, frequently even forcing it to accept compromises which were at variance with its proposals'. There was, then, a discernible weakening of the Commission's influence and a corresponding tendency for the Council to 'lose sight of its responsibility as a Community institution and upholder of the Community interest'.[97] Indeed, it resorted increasingly to hard-fought compromises.

The gist of this interpretation was that the crisis was endemic. It was always in the making, given the institutional imbalance resulting from the peculiar distribution of powers and functions allocated to the Commission and the European Parliament (EP). It was the Commission's bold interpretation of its own legitimate function as the driving-force behind the process of integration that led it in 1965, with Hallstein at the helm, to make spirited proposals to finance the Common Agricultural Policy (CAP) and strengthen the EP's budgetary powers. In doing so, it felt that it was acting according to the letter and the spirit of the Treaty. The crisis which this initiative provoked in the decisive Council meeting of 29–30 June 1965 was, according to von der Groeben, 'one of the strangest episodes in the Community's fluctuating history' and clearly 'bore the stamp of confrontation'.[98] But if the crisis was always waiting to happen, responsibility for it must also be shared by the French government. It might conceivably be argued that de Gaulle had been waiting impatiently for an excuse to confront the Commission in order to clip its wings. Hallstein's view, not unnaturally, confirmed this. He believed that French diplomacy chose June 1965 as the 'particular moment' to launch an attack on two basic principles which governed the EEC, namely, the majority voting system in the Council and the institutional position of the Commission.[99] As a federalist, Hallstein probably regarded his tactical approach as a calculated risk worth taking, but it underlined once again the potential for conflict inherent in the unique but uneasy combination of intergovernmental and supra-national institutions that was the hallmark of the Community.

It is, of course, perfectly possible to take a completely different view of the June 1965 crisis. Robert Marjolin, still a Commission Vice-President at this time, described the episode in rather more dramatic terms as 'the failure … of "federalist" Europe with supra-national institutions'. In branding Hallstein as the culprit who wanted the Commission to become, at least in budget matters, 'a kind of government of the Community', he openly confessed that his position separated him from most of his colleagues in the Commission.[100] Marjolin's opposition to what he called Hallstein's 'strange legal construct' seems not to have been a principled objection; it was rather a dispute about tactics. He believed that, given the sentiments which prevailed in Paris but also in government and civil service circles elsewhere, there was not the slightest chance of the project being accepted. If pursued, it would be a retrograde step that might even damage the construction of Europe. Moreover, Hallstein's insistence upon launching his proposals in the EP in Strasbourg before the Council knew about them was itself a departure from custom, quite apart from the fact that it had not expected them to be so far-reaching. According to Marjolin, the whole affair was the result of a Commission blunder and ensured that 'the idea of a federal Europe made its last appearance'.[101] Besides:

> The truth is that between Europe, as we know it, and a European federation with legislative power and an executive power, both set in place by the will of the people, it is difficult to imagine an intermediate position. What one regarded twenty or thirty years ago as steady progress towards a political reality of this kind – a High Authority invested with sovereign power or a Commission that would try to behave like a government, or again a Council of Ministers in which the major decisions would be taken by majority vote – has all proved illusory. The Common Market is not a federation and is not on the way to becoming one.[102]

The historical verdict about what happened and how it happened in 1965 remains disputed. Its legacy – the infamous 'Luxembourg Compromise' of January 1966 – was also the subject of continuing disagreement and debate in the following two decades.[103] Clearly its appellation was a misnomer since there was only an agreement to disagree, and significant majority voting was effectively abandoned for the following twenty years. Marjolin's interpretation of events from inside the Commission contrasts sharply with that of von der Groeben, another inside observer. Nonetheless, we can see from this brief summary of events and circumstances that the so-called Luxembourg Compromise was a major setback for the federalists. It is understandable, therefore, that most historians and political scientists have regarded the crisis of 1965–66 as another watershed in the Community's political evolution, one which signified its movement away from supra-nationalism and federalism. But in their eagerness to dismiss these ideas and influences, it is also important for them to acknowledge that 1965–66 did not, as even Marjolin admitted, signify the triumph of a Gaullist Europe. It consecrated the victory of Gaullist conceptions in the matter of the Community institutions, but it did not confirm support for Gaullist ideas about 'political Europe'.[104] And it is appropriate at this juncture to remember the sober, almost philosophical views of Spinelli in this imbroglio: new ideas needed to experience some initial defeats because that was the only way to test whether or not they were capable of survival. If they survived, there was a good chance that they were serious and relevant; if they disappeared then their intentions were either irrelevant or at best premature.[105]

In retrospect, both Hallstein's objectives and his actions in 1965, given the political environment of the time, were probably premature, ill-advised and therefore highly risky. Even Monnet and the Action

Committee were guarded in their support, regarding the challenge to the French government as unwise largely because the tension between it and Hallstein had become personal. In the years which followed what Monnet referred to as the 'ambiguous accommodation', Community politics must have seemed much less turbulent but also much less exciting.[106] During 1966–68 little effort seems to have been made to repair the damage inflicted on Community relations, with de Gaulle insistent on rebuffing a second British application for membership in 1967 and no resumption of negotiations on political union. But solid if unspectacular progress was made in other policy arenas. A brief summary of the economic achievements of the EEC in the decade between 1958 and 1968 included the following areas of progress: the customs union and the CAP were in place by 1 July 1968 (a year and a half ahead of the time limit set by the Rome Treaty); intra-European trade grew rapidly; trade with the rest of the world increased appreciably; productivity and output grew at unprecedented rates; the GATT multilateral trade negotiations known as the Kennedy Round were brought to a successful conclusion with some significant tariff reductions in June 1967; Association Agreements were agreed with Greece in 1962 and Turkey in 1964; the Yaounde Convention, which regulated trade relations between the EEC and African countries, entered into force in June 1964; some small progress was made in the coordination of the member states' monetary policies with the establishment of a Standing Committee of Governors of Central Banks in 1964; and freedom of movement for all categories of workers was implemented on schedule in May 1964. This is by no means an exhaustive list of EEC achievements but in itself it does explain why, despite the political upheavals wrought by the divisive political union debates and the seismic rift over constitutional questions, member state governments continued to support the Community. For all of the disruptions and frustrations that had arisen, it was still considered to be an indispensable framework within which their economic activities could prosper.

In his *Memoirs*, Marjolin claimed that the decade of the 1960s confronted the EEC with 'a complex skein of interests, ambitions and national calculations that was often difficult to unravel'. The problems were 'infinitely complicated' but the Community that emerged in 1967–68 was 'not that different from the one we know today, nor from the one which the negotiators of the Rome Treaty had conceived in 1956–7'.[107] Broadly speaking, this judgement was correct. It did seem to have reached a new crossroads in its economic and political development. One legacy of the infamous 'ambiguous accommodation' of 1966 in Luxembourg was atmospheric: there had been a dramatic change in the climate of opinion within Community circles. The former optimistic sense of purpose and steady progress was swiftly replaced by a morose caution and inertia. 'Everyone had lost a few more illusions', Miriam Camps observed in 1966, 'the experience of the crisis will breed caution on all sides.... Further progress will doubtless be slow'.[108] The aura of pessimism was corroborated by Annette Morgan:

> The second half of the 1960s was marked by a decline in the decision-making capabilities of the Community, and no fresh initiative was taken in the fields of economic or political union, both the Council and Commission appeared to mark time and to have lost their sense of purpose.[109]

The tenth anniversary of the signing of the Treaty of Rome, belatedly celebrated in May 1967 in Rome, was a dull affair. Indeed, as we have already noted, 1967 was remembered chiefly for the second French veto of British attempts to join the Community. But the Community did not stand completely still. The treaty obligations guaranteed some momentum. The Merger Treaty, signed in Brussels on 8 April 1965, entered into force on 1 July 1967, following ratification by the national parliaments and introduced an institutional rationalization which streamlined the three Communities (ECSC, EEC and Euratom) creating a single Commission, Council, Court and EP for what subsequently became known collectively as the 'European Community' (EC).

It was really only the political balance-sheet that registered on the debit side. Europe's concrete economic achievements were undeniable, yet they nonetheless seemed incapable of generating a corresponding political momentum. Hallstein found reasons to be cheerful, remarking subtly that it would be wrong to portray European unification as falling back: 'Our problem was not to reverse a backward trend but to speed up a rate of progress which had been slowed down'.[110] What, then, spurred the Community of the Six to make a breakthrough to fresh ground' with the Hague Summit in 1969? And what comfort could the federalist perspective take from what happened in 1969, given that it was once again an elite intergovernmental initiative?

Spinelli's observation that 'at the end of 1969 the wind began to change and from then until ... mid-1972 the European theme was revitalized' merely begged the key question.[111] Why should the governments, institutions and assorted public opinions of the EC experience 'an increasing realisation that decisive steps forward in European affairs must be taken?'[112] The answer, at a general level, lies in three intimately interrelated contexts which furnish several competing perspectives: the changing international arena; domestic policy priorities; and intra-Community relationships. In the mainstream literature on the breakthrough achieved in 1969, it would appear that the disappearance of de Gaulle, the shifting nature of French domestic and foreign priorities, the competitive European dispositions of the new French President, Georges Pompidou and the new West German Chancellor, Willy Brandt, and the contextual debate over the impending enlargement of the EC combined to alter the prospects for significant progress in Community relationships on a number of levels and in different dimensions. And if we add to this the various timetables and achievements foreshadowed in the Treaty of Rome, it becomes clear why the Hague Summit represented an appropriate stock-taking enterprise: looking both backward at past accomplishments and forward to new ambitions. In this sense, the Hague Summit was merely the necessary and logical outcome of a particular stage in the EC's economic, social and political development.

Unfortunately for federalists, the triptych of completion, deepening and enlargement evocatively inscribed in the French formula for Community progress conveniently circumvented the sort of institutional issues which they would have preferred to address. Nonetheless, there were compensations. Hallstein invoked that comfortable sense of piecemeal inevitability to which some federalists adhered when he gauged that 'integration was fast approaching the stage where economic and monetary policies … had to be fused'. His sense that these questions came 'close to tackling the core of the Community's concept and its practical implications' raised the time-honoured question of federalist strategy.[113] Which approach to federal union in Europe was likely to be successful? Hallstein felt that his view coincided with the inexorable moving forces of history. Economic and monetary union (EMU) followed logically from the idea of a customs union. Spinelli, too, came to the same conclusion: the Community must 'set itself the goal of the progressive implementation of a monetary and economic union'. He viewed 1971 as yet another 'moment of creative tension' which would probably extend into the early 1970s.[114] But monetary instability at this time of course was not new. It had permeated the economic atmosphere at least as far back as 1968–69 and had undoubtedly strengthened the argument for EMU even as a viable approach to inter-governmental unity and cooperation. The key question was how far national governments were prepared in the prevailing circumstances to increase Community competence in these areas.

French and West German currency movements during late 1969 also appear to have been instrumental in Brandt's own initiative on EMU at the Hague. But both the source and the purpose of this stand on new monetary policies were deep-seated and complex. Monnet claimed that Brandt's proposals 'came from a long way back: several of the ideas we had worked out together in the Action Committee were given their chance to succeed'.[115] In his personal recollections, Brandt acknowledged Monnet's 'encouragement' but it is important here to underline the complicated overarching nature of Brandt's own political strategy for West Germany which has been noticeably neglected in the mainstream literature.[116] Brandt was a federalist whose federal ideas can be traced back at least to his exile years as a socialist pariah from Hitler's Germany. These ideas became central to the complex links which he forged in his later post-war policies of *Ostpolitik*, *Westpolitik* and *Deutschlandpolitik* that gave rise to the notion of a 'European Peace Order'. In short-hand, this linkage came to mean the 'Europeanization of Germany' and the 'Europeanization of Europe'.[117]

The role of Pompidou was also crucial as the chief instigator of what came to be known as 'summit politics'. His period of office as French President during 1969–74 marked a transitional post-de Gaulle adjustment of French policy and attitudes toward the EC. Brandt's penchant for 'incorporating wide vistas' in his approach to contemporary problems was sharply counterbalanced by Pompidou's more day-to-day businesslike realism. Nonetheless, Pompidou's belief in the future of the Community, tempered by caution and continuity, did help to strengthen the European dimensions to French foreign policy and assisted toward the changed atmosphere in Community relations at the end of the 1960s.

The coincidence of interests which occurred in 1969 between Paris and Bonn, then, must not be allowed to disguise the differing motives existing between Pompidou and Brandt. These motives have been the subject of a detailed reassessment and they confirm the extent to which Brandt linked the closer coordination of economic and monetary policies to closer coordination in foreign policy.[118] Brandt wanted to 'invest the European Community with a new quality' at the Hague while Pompidou strove to limit and confine progress in these areas to strictly intergovernmental gains.[119] Presidential opposition to institutional reforms which might serve to buttress the supra-national features of the EC was consistently exerted. And given Pompidou's unshakable resistance to strengthening the central institutions, Brandt's initial enthusiasm for direct elections to the EP was eventually quelled. But even if his ardent support for European integration at the Hague represented 'only a partial exception' to his overriding concern for *Ostpolitik*, it would nonetheless be a mistake to completely ignore the complex motives, both short- and long-term, which impelled him to readjust his political tactics at different times, shifting the emphasis between its several component parts.[120]

Monnet may have been correct to claim that Brandt 'persuaded the Hague Summit to adopt the plan for economic and monetary union, with a European Reserve Fund, as the Action Committee had proposed', but this is to overlook the deep-rooted driving forces outlined above which propelled him into the forceful, self-confident posture he displayed and which so ebulliently overshadowed Pompidou as a progressive European. Brandt could hardly be depicted as a fervent agitator for a federal Europe in 1969, but the success of the Hague Summit was crucial to his larger political strategy: it was 'widely judged as a prerequisite for Brandt's Eastern policy'.[121]

The Hague Summit signified the *relance* (relaunching) of the European idea. Hence the Summit and its aftermath replaced the stagnation and inertia that seemed to characterize the period after the Luxembourg Compromise. But it can be seen that the forces which were at work for a general revitalization of the EC also gave a fresh impetus to federalist hopes. Federalists, we must remember, had to rely upon whatever concessions could be wrung from a predominantly intergovernmental organization in practice. Spinelli certainly had no illusions both about the value and the limitations of summits. Like Monnet, he recognized that they could be useful for launching new initiatives, as with the Hague, but their necessity was itself symptomatic of the EC's most debilitating handicap, namely, its general institutional deficiencies. As long as its central institutions remained weak and unable to 'develop subsequently their own fields of common action and correspondingly to carry out reforms within themselves' the Community's progress would be pedestrian.[122] Whatever collection of favourable events and circumstances propelled the governments to move ahead in particular directions at certain times, the major results of summitry would remain disappointing. Governments would prevaricate and compromise to the point where most of the genuine Community characteristics of new common policies would deteriorate in the hands of national officials.

In some instances, as with the CAP, concrete achievements could be made. But Spinelli's interpretation of what happened at the Hague in 1969 left no doubts about his opinion of the yawning chasm between rhetoric and reality:

> when nothing further than a declaration of principle was made, in the belief that practical progress could be made through the existing channels, then nothing of moment was achieved: the ambitious vision of economic and monetary union was implemented with fragile promises which were completely inadequate and which were rapidly overturned by the monetary crisis.[123]

From the standpoint of the end of the century this judgement now seems harsh, if not actually erroneous. Summits, as we shall see, were formally institutionalized in 1975 and several significant advances, including the European Monetary System (EMS) and direct elections to the EP, were to spring from them. But Spinelli's fundamental argument about the need for strong, autonomous central institutions remained a compelling one at this time. Spinelli had just been appointed to the Commission in 1970, and his purpose was to try to make an impact in the very institution that he had been criticizing in the previous decade. It was his presence, largely behind the scenes, in the 1970s that brought the public debate between the federalists and the intergovernmentalists into much sharper focus. Nonetheless, the Hague Summit demonstrated that any major breakthrough to fresh ground in the EC's economic and political development still required a considerable push from national governments.

Not unnaturally, the final declaration of the Summit boldly claimed that the Community had 'arrived at a turning-point in its history'. But while the determination of governments to make substantial headway in the fields of EMU and foreign policy coordination (POCO) seemed assured in the establishment respectively of the Werner and Davignon Committees, and in the new French attitude toward enlargement, the hopes raised for the EC's future had to be qualified from a federalist point of view. Hallstein provided a realistic summary of what he felt were the 'significant omissions' in the Hague Conference communique:

> We search in vain for measures actually to restore majority voting in the Council of Ministers, or to introduce direct elections to the European Parliament. There is no provision for strengthening the position of the Commission, for example, by having it invested with its powers and functions by the European Parliament, or by defining its role in negotiations with countries seeking membership. Finally, most of the dates fixed for the completion of the talks ... smack of diplomatic compromise ... they lie too far in the future.[124]

To federalists like Hallstein the progress achieved at the Hague Summit was unsatisfactory. The commitments entered into by the national governments had to be seen in this light. There was no attempt at all to address the question of institutional reform that federalists wanted so earnestly to achieve. But even if the results were disappointing, something had obviously happened to the EC at the end of the 1960s. Why, after all, should governments commit themselves to such potentially far-reaching goals? What did the notions of entrenching the Community's constitutional authority over its own financial resources, and of strengthening the EP's budgetary powers, mean if they were not intended to enhance EC competences in a manner which would gradually, and in piecemeal fashion, supersede nation state parameters though not the nation state itself?

Pompidou's well-known reservations about the institutional implications of the projected political secretariat arising out of the POCO discussions, and his lukewarm attitude toward the ambitious ideas envisaged in the Werner Report on EMU, did not augur well for major institutional reform. His much-heralded press conference speech of January 1971, in which he called for a 'European confederation' with a European government rendered 'the dispute over supranationality ... irrelevant'.[125] What, then, did the Paris Summit of October 1972 achieve and how did 'European Union' emerge from these discussions? Its achievements once again were determined largely by French and West German predispositions, although British inclinations were also accommodated this time. According to Spinelli, Pompidou was at last 'quietly but continuously moving away from the European conception' of de Gaulle, but 'intergovernmentalism remained his touchstone'.[126]

In hindsight it was obvious that progress at the Paris Summit, because it could only ever be an elite intergovernmental bargaining affair, would be

modest. Paul Taylor, the historian of intergovernmentalism, observed that
the member state governments were 'caught up in the dynamic process
which had begun at the Hague'.[127] 'This view very much reflected the
rhetoric of Pompidou at his 1971 press conference. Monnet acknowledged that it 'had been full of good intentions and the objectives it had
set for Europe had been both ambitious and precise'.[128] Others, however,
took a less than sanguine view. Brandt lamented that 'the effects of the
programme agreed there remained disappointing, perhaps because we
reached too far into the future'.[129] Another commentator remarked:

> The Paris Summit contained the elements of a deal, but it was an
> unbalanced one.... In practice, it did little more than salute, in some-
> what vague and pompous terms, the desirability of creating a more
> agreeable and better coordinated Community, thus avoiding any
> precise commitment.[130]

Three broad sets of issues faced the enlarged Community: EMU; POCO;
and the strengthening of the EC institutions. Those who favoured a
federal Europe could, at least in principle, be comfortable with all three
objectives. The lengthy communique amalgamated the various governmental priorities in a 16-point programme which amounted to an
omnibus statement: EMU, to be realised by 1980, would be accompanied
by an effective regional policy and support for a vigorous social policy;
agreement on a single industrial base included common scientific, technological and environmental policies; further steps toward the progressive
liberalization of trade; and moves toward a common commercial policy
*vis à vis* Eastern Europe. Finally, there was an agreement to strengthen
POCO consultations and an 'invitation' to the Community institutions to
study ways of improving their decision-making procedures, submitting
individual reports on 'European Union' by the end of 1975.

'Probably the oddest feature of the summit was the concept of a "European Union" raised by Pompidou'.[131] As we noted at the beginning of this
section, it was announced in appropriately innocuous phraseology. One
writer, Christian Franck, has commented: 'How exactly this last decision
came to be taken is a story which remains to be told'.[132] Monnet remarked
that 'the final form of that union was not further defined' and like
Brandt's own European Peace Order, the phrase remained nebulous –
'the evocation of a grand and popular but undefined ambition'.[133] But the
phrase 'European Union' was not new. It had been part of the vocabulary
of European culture and philosophy for centuries. And in the immediate
post-war years, it had been used often by advocates of an integrated
Europe to indicate a generic goal. Its strength lay less in specific details
than in the general idea which it conveyed, and we have already seen that
it had been resuscitated in 1962 for a particular purpose during the
contentious negotiations surrounding the Fouchet Plan. In so far as its

deployment ten years later meant anything, it suggested a much more all-encompassing idea denoting an organic but as yet abstract over-arching framework which would be filled in and pieced together only gradually as changing events and circumstances dictated. In this way, it committed EC member state governments to nothing. Intergovernmentalists could feel as comfortable with it as federalists. *Le Monde* summarized its utility most accurately: ' "European Union" diverted attention away from differences in other areas, notably institutions, by opening up vast but vague vistas for the future'. For Pompidou, it represented 'a vague formula that was readily so in order to avoid useless and paralysing doctrinal disputes'.[134] And it clearly suited both the spiritual and electoral priorities of Brandt and Edward Heath, the British Prime Minister. Its advocacy reinforced their domestic and international images as progressive Europeans. To this extent, our need specifically to identify the architect of the phrase 'European Union' is not important. It clearly emerged, as Spinelli would have put it, as yet another intergovernmental compromise. In 1972 it was simply an expedient. The task of converting the expedient into something much more substantive and significant lay in the future. With this thought in mind, it is time to conclude our theoretical and historical survey of this exciting, if often tempestuous, era in the building of Europe.

## Conclusion: the imprint of federalism

This chapter has underlined the significance of federal ideas, influences and strategies in the attempt to build Europe during 1950–72. It has chronicled the sequence of events which serve to demonstrate the resilience and continuing relevance of these ideas to the debate about post-war European integration. In doing so, however, it has not suggested that federalism was the only driving-force behind the multifarious efforts to bind both states and peoples closer together in some form of problem-solving framework. Rather, the main purpose has been to reinstate federal ideas in the overall evolution of European integration. Its goal has been, in short, to restore their significance to the theoretical and historical debate about the building of post-war Europe.

Mindful of Hinsley's candid warning that people often study history less for what they might learn than for what they want to prove, it has been necessary to venture into the intellectual world of the new orthodoxy recently established by both historians and political scientists. The new orthodoxy is the result of recent historical revisionism which has sought to replace the old, often impressionistic, conventional wisdoms about post-war European integration with contemporary arguments and interpretations based upon rigorous, empirically-verifiable evidence. History and theory have been judiciously combined in this new school of thought which has effectively adopted the neorealist paradigm based almost exclusively upon state-centric assumptions that give little or no credence to actors, institutions and procedures existing beyond the gravitational pull of the national state. The most important and influential representative of this school of thought is the economic historian, Alan Milward, together with his associates in the EUI in Florence. Together, their seminal research on post-war European integration has been the source of much fresh insight and not a little scholarly controversy. But the establishment of the new orthodoxy has made it the legitimate target of continuing investigations. Consequently, it has been appropriate to interrogate certain important aspects of this historical revisionism as part of the quest to restore the significance of federal ideas to post-war European integration.

The chapter has demonstrated that, if we harness conceptual lenses different from those used by Milward to the historical analysis of this period, the empirical evidence exhumed is correspondingly different. In consequence, a very different gloss is put on the historical interpretation of post-war European integration. The historical emphasis shifts away from simple, straightforward economic facts and statistics and toward the more sophisticated political context of ideas, actors, institutions and procedures where federalism and the federalists re-emerge from the shadows. Familiar figures which disappeared completely from view suddenly reappear in the company of new actors and influences. The so-called 'saints' of the integration process – rendered virtually invisible by recent revisionist rigour – are now rescued from an unrelenting obscurity, their political significance restored.

It is important to note that, in reappraising the reappraisals, there is no intention to turn the clock back. Much of Milward's historical revisionism is to be welcomed. And, indeed, it is perfectly possible to reinstate the relevance of federal ideas to the integration process, while simultaneously accepting many of the arguments and interpretations of the new school of thought. As Griffiths has emphasized, the juxtaposing of the new version of history against the earlier federalist accounts does not mean that the two are necessarily irreconcilable. We have to avoid replacing one over-simplified historical orthodoxy with yet another equally flawed school of thought. Part of the problem undoubtedly lies in the two very different approaches to the subject, one being that of the political scientist and the other that of the economic historian. Each is looking for very different things. This is why Milward seems to have had some difficulty in deciding whether or not the origins of the EC were social and economic or political. Obviously, it is impossible in the real world to entirely separate social science criteria and treat them as individual categories. When we do so, it is only for scholarly convenience. In practice, it is usual to stress the unity of the social sciences and to investigate their complex interactions. But the conundrum with which we are confronted here can be explained simply by each scholar's understanding of the term 'origins'. It is a matter of historical interpretation and terminological definition.

It would seem, therefore, that the search for a coherent alternative explanation to federalist accounts will continue. But it has to be recognised that the earlier, often subjective and propagandist, federalist accounts against which Milward railed so vehemently have themselves been superseded by new, more empirically-based, explanations. This primary purpose, for example, is precisely what lies behind the recent research of John Pinder in his own determination to put the historical record of the federalists straight.

The past, then, has many meanings. But history is often the unfortunate victim of competing and conflicting motives and half-truths. Accordingly, it has not been my purpose to distort history by seeking to overstate the case for federalism and the federalists. Instead, I have merely tried to reintroduce them to the emerging historical analysis of contemporary scholarship which had omitted them completely from explanation. My principal aim, then, was to situate them in the complex totality of the available evidence; evidence which is not narrowly confined to the methodological ghetto of official archives and statistics. A close re-examination of the role of Monnet and the activities of leading federalists and federal sympathizers like Schuman, Spaak, Hallstein and De Gasperi in the ECSC, EEC and Euratom experiments, together with another look at the peculiar supranational context of the Community's institutional relationships, and the intermittently favourable predispositions of key figures like Beyen and Brandt in the intergovernmental arena explain how and why there was an indelible imprint of federal ideas and strategies in these years. There was no inherent logic in the integration process which drove it inexorably toward a federal goal; the idea had to be fought for mainly in the terrestrial world of national politics, although the supra-national arena clearly lent an additional impetus to it.

It is also true that nothing could prevent the sort of damage which a de Gaulle could inflict upon the process of European integration. The early neofunctionalists grappled heroically to conceptualize the Gaullist phenomenon in order to integrate it into integration theory. It was not an unqualified success. But they were, in fairness, the first empirical theorists to test their concepts and assumptions using the emergent Community as their laboratory. And if de Gaulle could effectively hold the federalist forces back, it was only a temporary abeyance. They did not disappear nor was their rival conception of Europe displaced. Quite the reverse. They believed that history was on their side. Two world wars in the twentieth century, the Cold War, the rise of two nuclear hegemons, decolonization and huge changes in the global economy combined to convince them that the national state in Western Europe had to resort to new forms of institutional innovation if it was to meet these enormous post-war challenges. National leaders required political imagination if the nation state was to survive in this much more hostile and competitive post-war world.

The economic and political evolution of the Community in this period, then, signified a dramatic recognition of this fact, involving an unprecedented shift in both inter- and intra-state relations. But this shift was not symptomatic of the 'rescue' of the national state between 1950 and 1972. The EC furnished the basis for a 'resurgence' of the nation state, but it was a resurgence which, in itself, changed the nature of the national state for ever. The readjustment of its internal domestic relations and its external capacity for action meant that it would survive and prosper, perhaps even with increased influence, but not with the same political independence. This is why these years can be accurately portrayed as the struggle to adapt the rules of future rather than existing political behaviour. This, in a nutshell, was the primary goal – a goal which, as Griffiths has emphasized, persisted even if it required a surrender of consistency or elegance in the short-term.

It is now time to shift the focus of our study away from the early period when Europeans first explored the embryonic ideas of political union and European Union and toward the years when these ideas gradually matured into practical political and economic achievements. We will resume our journey by reflecting upon the relationship between federalism and European Union.

## NOTES

1  F.H. Hinsley, *Power and the pursuit of peace*, Cambridge: Cambridge University Press, 1980, p. 13.
2  In this period, I am dealing with the European Community (EC) rather than with the European Union (EU) into which it later developed when the Treaty on European Union (TEU) was ratified in 1993.
3  A.S. Milward, *The reconstruction of Western Europe, 1945–51*, London: Methuen & Co. Ltd, 1984.
4  A.S. Milward, *The reconstruction of Western Europe*, Preface, p. xvi.
5  A.S. Milward, *The reconstruction of Western Europe*, Preface, pp. xvi and 492.
6  A.S. Milward, *The reconstruction of Western Europe*, p. 492.
7  A.S. Milward, *The reconstruction of Western Europe*, p. 493.
8  A.S. Milward, *The reconstruction of Western Europe*, pp. 493–94.
9  A.S. Milward, *The reconstruction of Western Europe*, p. 494.
10  S. Hoffmann, 'Reflections on the nation-state in Western Europe today', in S. Hoffmann (ed.), *The European sisyphus: essays on Europe, 1964–1994*, p. 223, Oxford: Westview Press, 1995, reprinted from the *Journal of Common Market Studies*, 21(1–2), pp. 21–37, September/December 1982.
11  R.O. Keohane and J.S. Nye, *Power and interdependence: world politics in transition*, Boston: Little Brown, 1977.
12  A.S. Milward, *The European rescue of the nation-state*, London: Routledge, 1992, pp. 2–4.
13  A.S. Milward, *The European rescue of the nation-state*, Preface, p. xi.
14  A.S. Milward, *The European rescue of the nation-state*, Preface, p. x.
15  A.S. Milward, *The European rescue of the nation-state*, p. 18.
16  A.S. Milward, *The European rescue of the nation-state*, pp. 438–40.
17  A.S. Milward and V. Sorensen, 'Interdependence or integration? A national

choice', in A.S. Milward et al., *The frontier of national sovereignty: history and theory, 1945–1992*, p. 22, London: Routledge, 1994.

18  A.S. Milward and V. Sorensen, '*Interdependence or integration?*', p. 31.
19  A.S. Milward and V. Sorensen, '*Interdependence or integration?*', p. 12.
20  A.S. Milward and V. Sorensen, '*Interdependence or integration?*', p. 31.
21  A.S. Milward and V. Sorensen, '*Interdependence or integration?*', pp. 31–2.
22  A.S. Milward, 'Conclusions: the value of history', in *The frontier of national sovereignty*, pp. 187 and 196.
23  A.S. Milward, '*Conclusions: the value of history*', p. 183.
24  A.S. Milward, *The European rescue of the nation-state*, p. 340.
25  A.S. Milward and V. Sorensen, '*Interdependence or integration?*', pp. 15–17.
26  A.S. Milward and V. Sorensen, '*Interdependence or integration?*', p. 5.
27  R.T. Griffiths, 'The European integration experience, 1945–58', in K. Middlemas, *Orchestrating Europe: the informal politics of European union, 1973–1995*, p. 4, London: Fontana Press, 1995.
28  A.S. Milward et al., *The frontier of national sovereignty*, Preface, p. viii.
29  J. Monnet, *Memoirs*, New York: Doubleday & Co. Inc., 1978, p. 292–317.
30  J. Monnet, *Memoirs*, p. 293.
31  'The Schuman Declaration' in B.F. Nelsen and A. C.-G. Stubb (eds), *The European Union: readings on the theory and practice of European integration*, pp. 11–12, Boulder, CO.: Lynne Rienner Publishers, 1994.
32  F. Duchene, *Jean Monnet: the first statesman of interdependence*, London: W.W. Norton & Co., 1994, p. 198.
33  A.S. Milward, *The reconstruction of Western Europe, 1945–51*, p. 420.
34  A.S. Milward, *The reconstruction of Western Europe*, p. 418.
35  A.S. Milward, *The reconstruction of Western Europe*, pp. 418 and 420.
36  For a contrary view, see F. Duchene, *Jean Monnet: the first statesman of interdependence*, pp. 223–25.
37  A.S. Milward, *The reconstruction of Western Europe*, p. 398.
38  J. Pinder, 'The influence of European federalists in the 1950s', in T.B. Olesen (ed.), *Interdependence versus integration: Denmark, Scandinavia and Western Europe, 1945–1960*, pp. 220–21, Odense: Odense University Press, 1997.
39  A.S. Milward, *The reconstruction of Western Europe*, p. 396.
40  J. Gillingham, 'Jean Monnet and the European coal and steel community: a preliminary appraisal', in D. Brinkley and C. Hackett (eds), *Jean Monnet: The Path to European Unity*, p. 157, London: Macmillan, 1991.
41  W. Diebold Jr., *The Schuman Plan: a study in economic cooperation, 1950–1959*, New York: F.A. Praeger, 1959, p. 664.
42  See, for example, W. Diebold Jr., 'The relevance of federalism to Western European economic integration', in A.W. Macmahon (ed.), *Federalism: mature and emergent*, pp. 433–57, New York: Russell & Russell Inc., 1962; T.C. Clark, 'Inaugurating the coal and steel community' in the same volume of essays, pp. 471–90; and H.A. Schmitt, *The path to European Union: from the Marshall Plan to the Common Market*, Baton Rouge, La: Louisiana State University Press, 1962.
43  For the conceptual distinction and its implications, see W. Wallace, 'Rescue or retreat? the nation state in Western Europe, 1945–93', in J. Dunn (ed.), *Contemporary crisis of the nation state?*, *Political Studies*, Special Issue, 42, pp. 52–76, 1994.
44  See R. Mayne and J. Pinder with J. Roberts, *Federal Union: The Pioneers*, London: Macmillan, 1990, p. 106.
45  F. Duchene, *Jean Monnet: first statesman of interdependence*, p. 228.
46  J. Monnet, *Memoirs*, p. 338.

47  J. Monnet, *Memoirs*, p. 340.

48  J. Monnet, *Memoirs*, p. 343.

49  See I.M. Wall, 'Jean Monnet, the United States and the French Economic Plan', in D. Brinkley and C. Hackett (eds), *Jean Monnet: the path to European unity*, p. 108; and J. Monnet, *Memoirs*, 346.

50  F. Duchene, *Jean Monnet: first statesman of interdependence*, p. 229.

51  A detailed analysis of the whole EPC episode is provided in R. Cardozo, 'The project for a political community, 1952–54', in R. Pryce (ed), *The dynamics of European union*, pp. 49–77, London: Croom Helm, 1987; while J. Pinder, 'The influence of European federalists in the 1950s' identifies the federalists and assesses their significance.

52  R. Cardozo, 'The project for a political community', pp. 52–53.

53  J. Pinder, 'The influence of European federalists in the 1950s', pp. 227–28.

54  C.J. Friedrich, 'Introduction', in R.R. Bowie and C.J. Friedrich (eds.), *Studies in federalism*, p. xxix, Boston: Little, Brown & Co., 1954. The Draft Treaty is in Appendix II, pp. 828–53.

55  C.J. Friedrich, 'Introduction', in *Studies in federalism*, p. xxxiii.

56  C.J. Friedrich, 'Introduction', in *Studies in federalism*, p. xxix and J. Pinder, 'The influence of European federalists in the 1950s', p. 228

57  E. Fursdon, *The European defence community: a history*, London: Macmillan, 1980, p. 341–43.

58  A.S. Milward, *The European rescue of the nation-state*, p. 119.

59  A.S. Milward, *The European rescue of the nation-state*, p. 119.

60  A.S. Milward, *The European rescue of the nation-state*, p. 134.

61  A.S. Milward, *The European rescue of the nation-state*, p. 120.

62  A.S. Milward, *The European rescue of the nation-state*, p. 167.

63  A.S. Milward, *The European rescue of the nation-state*, pp. 121–22.

64  H.J. Kusters, 'The Treaties of Rome (1955–57)', in R. Pryce (ed.), *The dynamics of European union*, p. 83.

65  M. Camps, *Britain and the European community, 1955–1963*, London: OUP, 1964, pp. 57 and 60.

66  P.-H. Spaak, *The continuing battle: memoirs of a European, 1936–1966*, London: Weidenfeld & Nicholson, 1971, p. 231.

67  F.R. Willis, *Italy chooses Europe*, New York: OUP, 1971, pp. 59 and 64.

68  H. von der Groeben, *The European community: the formative years (1958–66)*, Luxembourg: Office for Official Publications of the EC, 1987.

69  For a detailed survey of Hallstein's federal ideas, see W. Hallstein, *Europe in the making*, New York: W.W. Norton & Co. Inc., 1972.

70  H. von der Groeben, *The European community*, p. 31.

71  R. Marjolin, *Memoirs, 1911–1986: architect of European unity*, London: Weidenfeld & Nicholson, 1986, pp. 266–67.

72  H. von der Groeben, *The European community*, p. 251.

73  J. Pinder, 'The influence of European federalists in the 1950s', pp. 226 and 231.

74  H.J. Kusters, 'The Treaties of Rome (1955–57)', in R. Pryce (ed.), *The dynamics of European union*, pp. 96–97.

75  J. Pinder, 'The influence of European federalists in the 1950s', p. 233.

76  A.S. Milward, *The European rescue of the nation-state*, p. 208.

77  *Bulletin of the European communities*, 10, part 1, Ch. 1, 1972.

78  J. Pinder, 'The influence of European federalists in the 1950s', p. 239.

79  R.T. Griffiths, 'The European integration experience', p. 36.

80  R.T. Griffiths, 'The European integration experience', p. 46.

81  Quoted in H. von der Groeben, *The European community: the formative years*, pp. 86–7.

82  J. Monnet, *Memoirs*, p. 430.
83  R.T. Griffiths, 'The European integration experience', p. 46.
84  See, for example, S.J. Bodenheimer, *Political union: a microcosm of European politics, 1960–1966*, Leiden: A.W. Sijthoff, 1967.
85  P. Gerbet, 'In search of political union: the Fouchet plan negotiations', in R. Pryce, (ed.), *The dynamics of European union*, p. 106.
86  H. von der Groeben, *The European community: the formative years*, p. 91.
87  S.J. Bodenheimer, *Political union: a microcosm of European politics*, p. 48.
88  Quoted in R.T. Griffiths, 'The European integration experience', p. 43.
89  P.-H. Spaak, *The continuing battle*, p. 436.
90  J. Monnet, *Memoirs*, p. 440.
91  J. Monnet, *Memoirs*, p. 436.
92  J. Monnet, *Memoirs*, pp. 438 and 443.
93  De Gaulle quoted in J. Monnet, *Memoirs*, p. 441.
94  J. Monnet, *Memoirs*, pp. 441–42.
95  P.-H. Spaak, *The continuing battle*, p. 454.
96  P. Gerbet, 'In search of political union', p. 122.
97  H. von der Groeben, *The European community: the formative years*, p. 166.
98  H. von der Groeben, *The European community: the formative years*, p. 182.
99  W. Hallstein, *Europe in the making*, p. 51.
100 R. Marjolin, *Memoirs*, pp. 327 and 350.
101 R. Marjolin, *Memoirs*, p. 350.
102 R. Marjolin, *Memoirs*, pp. 356–57.
103 See A.L. Teasedale, 'The Life and death of the Luxembourg compromise', *Journal of Common Market Studies* 31(4), pp. 567–79, 1993.
104 R. Marjolin, *Memoirs*, p. 347.
105 Interview with Spinelli, 14 February 1985, EP, Strasbourg.
106 J. Monnet, *Memoirs*, p. 484.
107 R. Marjolin, *Memoirs*, p. 327.
108 M. Camps, *European unification in the sixties: from the veto to the crisis*, London: McGraw-Hill, 1966, p. 124.
109 A. Morgan, *From summit to council: evolution in the EEC*, London: PEP, Chatham House, 1976, p. 11.
110 W. Hallstein, *Europe in the making*, p. 97.
111 A. Spinelli, *The European adventure*, London: Charles Knight & Co. Ltd, 1972, p. 20.
112 A. Spinelli, *The European adventure*, p. 20.
113 W. Hallstein, *Europe in the making*, p. 94.
114 A. Spinelli, *The European adventure*, p. 20–21.
115 J. Monnet, *Memoirs*, p. 494.
116 W. Brandt, *People and politics: the years 1960–1975*, London: Collins, 1970, p. 247.
117 See W. Brandt, *In exile: essays, reflections and letters, 1933–1947*, London: Oswald Wolff, 1971 and H. Simonian, *The privileged partnership: Franco-German relations in the European Community*, Oxford: Clarendon Press, 1985.
118 See H. Simonian, *The privileged partnership*, pp. 78–100.
119 W. Brandt, *People and Politics*, p. 254.
120 S. Bulmer and W. Paterson, *The Federal Republic of Germany and the European Community*, London: Allen & Unwin, 1987, p. 138.
121 H. Simonian, *The privileged partnership*, p. 82.
122 A. Spinelli, *The European adventure*, p. 23.
123 A. Spinelli, *The European adventure*, p. 25.
124 W. Hallstein, *Europe in the making*, p. 101.

125 Press conference by the President of the French Republic, 21 January 1971, Extracts from the *French Documentation on political and social problems*, Supplement, 61, February 1971.
126 H. Simonian, *The privileged partnership*, p. 143.
127 P. Taylor, *The Limits of European Integration*, London: Croom Helm, 1983, p. 64.
128 J. Monnet, *Memoirs*, p. 501.
129 W. Brandt, *People and politics*, p. 264.
130 A. Morgan, *From summit to council*, pp. 16–17.
131 H. Simonian, *The privileged partnership*, p. 147.
132 C. Franck, 'New ambitions: from the Hague to Paris summits (1969–72)', in R. Pryce (ed.), *The dynamics of European union*, p. 144.
133 H. Simonian, *The privileged partnership*, p. 147.
134 H. Simonian, *The privileged partnership*, p. 148.

# 4 Federalism and the struggle for European Union, 1973–84

The Paris Summit of October 1972 had committed the European Community (EC) to achieve the goal of 'European Union' by the end of the decade. The commitment, however, remained unclear. As we have already seen, the emergence of the phrase 'European Union' was as curious as its meaning was vague. Christian Franck noted that it expressed 'a teleology which was intended to mobilise political will and energies'. Clearly, 'a new objective had been set – but what it meant and how it was to be achieved were problems deliberately set aside for later consideration'. He believed that it merely 'reflected a driving force which the period 1969–72 appeared to have fired with new life', but it also 'symbolised the way ahead'.[1] If this view is correct, what was the way ahead from the standpoint of 1973? What practical progress could be made toward an objective which remained so nebulous?

Ambiguity has its advantages and 'European Union' met a whole range of different approaches to the future of the EC, including both federal and confederal scenarios. Above all, federal strategies for Europe's unknown destination remained valid. The public commitment to European Union furnished both a reason and an opportunity to ensure that the Community's future political development would be guided in a federal direction. This might have seemed overly optimistic in January 1973 when the EC's first enlargement to include the United Kingdom (UK), Ireland and Denmark was completed. Neither the UK nor Denmark were widely perceived as countries which were predisposed to integrationist rather than conventional intergovernmentalist solutions to European problems. Their collective conception of Europe was one which subordinated supra-national considerations to the more narrowly pragmatic, if less visionary, concerns of national self-interest. This perception construed the EC as no more than the mere aggregate of its component member state parts. Accordingly, the institutional implications of this view of Europe were extremely limited, stopping well short of the aims of many federalists and a moonshot away from the diagnosis of Altiero Spinelli who watched events with some despair from his strategic position in the Commission. His remedy at a time of great economic and political ferment was characteristically far-sighted:

> It is finally no longer possible to conceal the fact that the present insti-
> tutions of the Community, whatever their past merits, are no longer
> suitable for the dimensions and new tasks of the present Community
> and should be modified, probably in a very profound manner ... The
> long and as yet uncertain meditation on the state of the Community is
> drawing to one central and obvious conclusion: if the countries of the
> enlarged Community are not capable of taking common international
> action – be it monetary, commercial or political – then everything may
> collapse.[2]

This gloomy, almost apocalyptic, warning placed Europe's leading federalist in the vanguard of the political elite in Brussels, which regarded the
institutional reform of the EC as imperative. For the time being, however,
the political circumstances were not conducive to such a major step
forward. Indeed, they were to unfold in a manner which made not only
major advances in political integration unlikely but also further steps in
economic integration extremely difficult.

The year 1973 is often regarded as another turning-point in the political
and economic evolution of the EC. The first Community enlargement
coincided with a series of events and circumstances which combined to
cast a dark shadow over the optimistic goals outlined in Paris the previous
year. The upheaval in monetary relations which dated back at least to the
late 1960s returned with a vengeance in January 1973 and promptly catapulted the Italian lira out of the currency agreement, known as the Snake,
designed in 1972 to introduce stability into exchange rates. The currency
crisis forced the EC to abandon attempts to move toward the first stage of
monetary union and correspondingly dampened the overall prospects for
economic and monetary union (EMU). Other less visible but no less damaging circumstances suggested further problems for the European project.
Richard Griffiths remarked that the 'treasured assumptions that had
marked the 1950s and 1960s were destined to be discarded: economic
growth, full employment, efficacious Keynesian economic management
[and] technological leadership'.[3] International events also dashed the
hopes for progress in European integration when, on 6 October 1973, the
Yom Kippur War broke out in the Middle East. The subsequent oil
embargo which precipitated a recession also ushered in a new era of
lasting economic stagnation: thirty years of post-war world boom was suddenly and dramatically brought to an end. Indeed, it gave the years
between 1973 and 1984 a sense of dismal, lugubrious continuity: a gloomy
period which was characterized by a 'pattern of self-interested national bargaining vying with rare bursts of collective altruism'.[4] Stanley Hoffmann
referred to the period as the Community's 'dark years' when national policies had only limited success and the result was 'a sense of failure'.[5]

The purpose of this chapter is to pursue the federalist odyssey in
European integration during 1973–84 in order once again to demonstrate

the fundamental continuity of federal ideas, influences and strategies in the EC. This approach to understanding the Community is all the more important when we consider that most historical interpretations of these years refer to intergovernmentalism as the preponderant model of inter-state relations. In other words, relations between the EC member states were fundamentally much the same as those between states elsewhere. There was, in short, nothing particularly unique about the EC's institutional framework in terms of the dynamics between states. The policy outcomes conformed to the realist school of international relations. But this did not mean that it was acceptable to impose a blanket interpretation of intergovernmentalism upon this period. There was, as Paul Taylor has remarked, no 'single plateau of intergovernmentalism through the 1970s'. In reality, the character of intergovernmentalism in the EC in the late 1970s and early 1980s was 'significantly different from that in the early seventies' and there were 'various shades of intergovernmentalism'.[6] Nonetheless, intergovernmentalism, of whatever shade, became the hallmark of these years.[7]

I do not wish to challenge the primarily intergovernmental nature of the policy outcomes suggested above. I do, however, want to suggest that there is more than one reality when we seek more fully to understand the EC, even in an era of intergovernmentalism. One of the problems with looking at the EC through exclusively intergovernmentalist lenses is that it often conveniently ignores its supra-national reality as well as the existence of federal ideas and influences. It is selective by omission and is in this respect an over-simplification. From a federalist perspective, the decade of the 1970s is usually viewed as an era of myopic intergovernmentalism whose lasting legacy was national solutions to European problems. It was a failure of political will. There was certainly no concerted European response to the economic recession of 1973–74. Moreover, the Copenhagen Summit during 14–15 December 1973 was widely acknowledged as an abject failure, even by conventional intergovernmentalist standards. The EC's disarray was never more blatantly obvious to the outside world than in the protracted conflict between the British Prime Minister, Edward Heath, and the West German Chancellor, Willy Brandt, over the vexed questions of energy policy, on which Brandt wanted progress, and the establishment of a regional fund, which Heath was determined to secure for the UK. And relations between Pompidou and Brandt also left much to be desired as the French President looked with suspicion at the diplomatic pace with which the *Ostpolitik* was being pursued by Bonn. Pompidou's 'Copenhagen initiative' was founded upon a mixture of motives but the critical factor lay in his wish to 'recapture and perpetuate' an upsurge of public enthusiasm for Europe which, in his view, only regular institutionalized summit meetings could guarantee. His hopes and expectations, however, were quickly torpedoed. The summit was 'inconclusive on every single issue' and is remembered chiefly for the subsequent emergence in March 1975 of the European Council as a permanent feature of the Community's institutional landscape.[8]

The Paris Summit of December 1974 was, in contrast, of great significance to federalists and intergovernmentalists alike. Before we consider the innovations agreed by the member state governments, it is important to underline the elite personnel changes which had by then occurred. Brandt, Heath and Pompidou had gone and in their place Helmut Schmidt, Harold Wilson and Valéry Giscard d'Estaing respectively heralded a new era in Community relations. And, as before, their motives at the summit varied widely. From the federalist perspective, Paris was a distinct improvement upon Copenhagen. One writer has gone as far as endowing this summit with an importance comparable to the Hague Summit of 1969. Another Franco-German convergence of interest enabled the EC to break new ground; both Giscard and Schmidt 'firmly felt that some powerful demonstration of the Community's cohesion and its future prospects was especially desirable'.[9]

Giscard's arrival in particular facilitated a far more flexible and pragmatic approach to Community affairs. Progress in economic policy coordination proved easier than expected, as did agreement on the establishment of a regional fund and on the UK's budgetary contributions. Federalists, however, could take particular comfort from the very promising commitments made in the area of institutional reform. Several fresh initiatives were launched and included the following:

> The Heads of Government would meet, accompanied by the Ministers of Foreign Affairs, three times a year and, when necessary, in the Council of the Communities and in the context of political cooperation. They would reaffirm their determination gradually to adopt common positions and coordinate their diplomatic action in all areas of international affairs which affected the European Community. The European Parliament was to be more closely associated with the work of the Presidency in political cooperation (POCO) and it was to submit proposals to the Council on the issue of direct elections which could take place at any time in or after 1978. A working party would be set up to study the possibility of creating a Passport Union, leading eventually to a uniform passport, and another group would examine the conditions and timing under which Community citizens could acquire special rights. Agreement was reached to renounce the practice of requiring unanimity among member states in the Council of Ministers which had governed decision-making since the Luxembourg Agreement of January 1966 and Permanent Representatives would be given greater latitude so that only the most important political problems need be discussed in the Council. They consider that the time has come to agree as soon as possible on an overall concept of European Union. Leo Tindemans, the Belgian Prime Minister, was invited

to submit a comprehensive report to the Heads of Government, based upon reports from the Community institutions, consultations with Governments and public opinion throughout the Community, before the end of 1975.[10]

These public commitments paved the way for the Tindemans Report of 1975–76, and for the introduction of direct elections to the European Parliament (EP) in 1979. A bird's eye view of these institutional reform proposals revealed what seemed to be a clear logic: the institutionalization of the summits by the creation of the European Council buttressed the executive fulcrum of the Community by strengthening its capacity to resolve conflicts and launch fresh initiatives; the introduction of direct elections to the EP would reinforce the democratic nature of the EC by acknowledging a European electorate and giving the Community a new relevance and popular electoral legitimacy in a parliamentary Europe; and the Tindemans exercise would surround and integrate these proposals, via a comprehensive report, in a new – as yet unknown – overarching institutional framework.

It should be emphasized that there was no mention of augmenting the role of the Commission and that, even where the EP's powers would be increased in the budgetary and legislative spheres, these concessions, though important to the new Members of the EP (MEPs), were modest. Taylor claimed that these reforms, including the teleological ambiguity of European Union, were 'merely expedient: there was not much chance that they would be realised, or have any effect, and they could therefore be safely offered'.[11] Certainly Giscard's Community policy did not represent a complete break with the past. The shadows of de Gaulle and Pompidou still darkened French perceptions of Europe's future.

The overall significance attached to the Paris Summit of 1974 depends upon whether an integrationist or an intergovernmentalist approach is adopted. It is obvious that the new driving-force for building Europe at this time came to be summit politics, formalized later by the European Council. The first enlargement of the EC coupled with a revival of the Paris–Bonn axis seemed merely to endorse this view. Yet even in this enhanced intergovernmental arena, there could be cause for hope. Taylor, for all his scepticism about European Union, acknowledged that, at the Paris Summit, there were several proposals which 'seemed to confirm the commitment of members to integration of a rather advanced kind'.[12] And Haig Simonian has claimed that 'only the Paris Summit of December 1974 can be said to have rivalled the Hague Conference in terms of importance for the Community's future'.[13] Research on the evolution of the European Council confirms this and underlines the important concessions granted to 'the sceptics who saw summitry as a threat to the EC's supra-national aspirations'.[14] Bulmer and Wessels emphasized that the commitment to direct elections, the efforts to abandon the unanimity principle in the Council and the Tindemans Report were 'the first institutional improvements to have been agreed at a summit conference' (leaving aside POCO arrangements initiated at the Hague) and that these were 'components in favour of a more supranational or federal form of integration'.[15]

The role of the smaller states in Benelux and Italy during these years seems conspicuous by their absence. In reality, of course, they were anything but inactive. And it was no accident that they were the four countries most warmly disposed to institutional reform which would strengthen the Commission and the EP against the Council. Brandt acknowledged that 'the Dutch and the Italians were foremost among those in favour' of direct elections at the Paris Summit of 1972, and we should also remember that it was the Belgian Prime Minister, Gaston Eyskens, who took the initiative in the same year in proposing 'European Union'.[16] Indeed, the Commission in the past had been able to rely upon the periodic mobilization of this support in the Council. It had been of mutual benefit, giving these states a guaranteed voice and influence against the highly exclusive Paris–Bonn dialogue from which they were excluded and preserving the original supra-national basis of the Community. During 1973–74, however, their collective impact upon the greater intergovernmentalism of these years – with its attendant emphasis upon Paris, Bonn and later London – was severely restricted. But their potential influence remained a future mobilizing force for institutional reform, and it was to be reasserted during the 1980s.

In the mid-1970s, then, federal ideas, influences and strategies in the Community were not absent from the revitalization of the European idea, but they struggled in a difficult intergovernmental environment. Nonetheless, Europe was moving again and it was in some important respects movement in the right direction. Some of the commitments, if accomplished, would at least accentuate the federal nature of the Community, even if this was not the intention of the leading member states. Meanwhile, attention was focused upon the Tindemans Report and its implications, and it is to this that we shall now turn our attention in the next section.

## The Tindemans Report, 1975–76: means to ends

Prepared for and on behalf of the European Council, the Tindemans Report was formally submitted to it by letter on 29 December 1975, and officially published on 7 January 1976. It was originally to have been based upon the reports propounded by the Commission, the EP and the Court of Justice, but on its own initiative the Economic and Social Committee of the EC and the Dutch government also prepared similar reports, the latter known as the Spierenberg Report, published in May 1975.[17] Tindemans' brief also included consultations with the member state governments and with a wide spectrum of public opinion throughout the Community.[18]

The Spierenberg Committee determined to make its report available to Tindemans as 'a fruitful and constructive contribution to the formation of ideas' which would eventually form part of the discussions between heads of government at the next meeting of the European Council in Luxembourg during April 1976.[19] There is no conclusive evidence as to how far this report influenced Tindemans' final proposals, but in part one of its general references to questions of the 'desirable and the attainable' it placed the federal goal in sober perspective:

> The committee does not believe that the restructuring of this system of states into a European federation is within the bounds of possibility in the period under consideration.... The gap between the present situation and a European federation is so wide that there is still plenty of room for intermediate structures which would leave open a variety of other possibilities for evolution.... The question of whether a future European government will develop first from the European Commission or from the Council of Ministers or from any combination of the two ... can be left to the course of events.[20]

Federalist strategies, however, did not always mean an automatic quantum jump into federation. Most federalists in the mid-1970s would probably have been pleased to change the economic and political atmosphere within the Community in order to render it more conducive to piecemeal federal institutional reform, such as direct elections to the EP. Step-by-step federal instalments, both in matters of Community policy and institutional change, doubtless seemed the most profitable strategy. The most significant exception to this general strategic rule, however, proved to be the Commission. For reasons which will become clear in our survey of the Tindemans episode, the Commission's report proved far more ambitious, both in ends and means, than the final report.

For our purposes it is the Commission and the EP reports which are the most instructive. Both of these central institutions had a vested interest in promoting policy and institutional reforms which would lever them into the forefront of Community decision-making. Only by reasserting the supra-national driving-force of integration and democratizing the decision-making arena could the Community be revitalized and the European idea regenerated. Let us look at the way this perspective was channelled into practical proposals by the Commission.

At this juncture, it is imperative that we take account of the role played by Spinelli in the Commission's initiative. Spinelli, it will be recalled, became the Commissioner responsible for Industry, Research and Technology in 1970, and regarded his position as an opportunity to explore the possibilities of further progress in the European construction. His personal strategy was 'to learn what it meant to be a Commissioner, to have a certain influence in the Commission and to pay attention to how we could have the institutional developments' necessary to go beyond merely the coordination of national policies.[21] His influence and inspiration lay behind the Commission's Report, published on 26 June 1975, which urged Tindemans to adopt an ambitious approach to European Union. What, then, did the Commission propose and where were the federalist influences most explicit?

We shall emphasize here those aspects of the report which particularly reflected federalist priorities. Clearly it was important to take note of two significant clauses in the famous statement made at the Paris Summit of October 1972. These were what was meant by 'the fullest respect for the Treaties already signed' and what meaning should be attached to the expression 'whole complex of relations'.[22] The Commission Report did not assume 'that European Union must necessarily encompass every type of relation between the member states ... European Union is not to give birth to a centralizing super-state'.[23] It recognised, therefore, two vital concerns and anxieties present in contemporary west European societies: the fear of and growing resistance to attempts to centralize power, and the need to build on what had already been achieved – the Community patrimony. An ambitious approach to European Union did not rule out time-honoured pragmatism. These were not and are still not mutually exclusive.

Bearing these two important qualifications in mind, the report carefully outlined both the fields of competence of the union and the new institutional Europe. It listed those competences already enshrined in the Rome Treaties in which significant progress had been made – commercial policy, competition, social, agricultural, regional, nuclear research and development aid policies – and those requiring further improvement – the convergence of national economic priorities, industrial, energy, environmental and research policies. But it concluded that the main Community objective should be EMU. Competence, powers and means of action were identified in five main areas: monetary policy; budgetary expenditure; budgetary revenue; improving economic structures in order to reduce imbalances; and social affairs. In general, the report emphasized the many possibilities already implicit in the Treaties to achieve these policy changes including, ultimately, treaty amendment under Article 236. But it also argued that 'the creation of European Union should also make it possible to go beyond the present limits by explicitly vesting new powers and new fields of competence in the European institutions'.[24] These included foreign policy, defence and human rights. Political cooperation (POCO) being drawn into the formal union framework logically necessitated the incorporation of defence in order for the union to be organized coherently, while human rights reflected the gradual extension of the Community's competence in the daily life of the European citizen.

What were the institutional implications of these common policies? We should remember that, for Spinelli, the institutional reform of the

Community and the attempt to achieve European Union were 'one and the same thing'.[25] His paramount concern was to give these central institutions the capacity to go beyond what existed – to furnish them with an autonomous vitality to maintain the inexorable momentum toward an ever closer union. The key point was that federalists regarded the Community as more than a loose association of national states:

> It is also a political entity with its own personality, superior in certain aspects to the states, possessing its own organization, producing decisions which must be accepted by the member states and respected by their citizens. Thus that for which the states is a treaty, is for the Community its own constitution; that which for the states is a revision of the treaty is for the Community a revision of its constitution.[26]

The contrasting and conflicting versions of federalists and intergovernmentalists in the building of Europe could hardly have been better summarized. Thinking federally required a mental predisposition to interpret the Community as something much more than just a loose association of states. It required the political imagination to see in the Community a union of states and peoples which, built upon federal and confederal principles, was gravitating slowly toward a federal and/or confederal destination. Whether or not it would ever become a union of states representing a single people was something which would be decided in the future. It was certainly not inevitable. The Commission's Report confined itself to one simple goal, namely, the constitutionalization of new and old practices.

Briefly, the Commission opted firmly for a single institutional structure covering all the fields of competence vested in the union, rather than separate bodies dealing with different policy areas. Basing its interpretation of the Paris communique (1972) upon the need both to build upon what already existed and to reinforce and make more effective the existing institutional structure, the report expressed a preference for a qualitative leap forward rather than an incremental step-by-step evolution. Its authors seem to have been influenced by the method chosen when the Treaties were adopted during 1955–57. Seeking 'a certain stability', the report emphasized:

> The aim would be to set up the political organs required to enable the Union over a period which will, of necessity, be rather long, gradually to assume effective responsibility in its various fields of competence. This period of time will allow real political relations ... to develop between the various organs ... European Union means nothing if it does not involve the development of a European governmental executive. The Commission sees the European Government as an executive body with political authority ... comparable with those normally

possessed by a Government – a body which would carry out its activities under the supervision of a Parliament to which it would be responsible.[27]

The influence of Spinelli was clear. Europe had to have a real political centre with effective powers. The report identified three institutional models. It rejected the first in which executive authority would be vested in a body comprising national ministers, independent of a bicameral parliament. Its own stated preference was for the second model in which the governmental organ would be a collegiate body, absorbing the existing Commission and Council of Ministers, independent of the national governments. This model also posited a bicameral parliament having the legislative power and in some way able to hold the executive authority responsible to it. The third model, whereby a Committee of Ministers representing national governments would operate alongside the new collegiate governmental organ and bicameral parliament, was deemed a more satisfactory solution to the problem of organizing cooperation but involved a more ponderous institutional structure. It was viewed as appropriate only for a limited transitional period.[28]

In its emphasis upon gradual piecemeal evolution designed to foster genuine organic constitutional and political relations, the report, notwithstanding its belief in the qualitative leap forward, recognised the immediate need to reactivate the building of Europe. In order to give European Union a new impetus, a precondition for the major step lay in direct elections to the EP and fresh initiatives in existing common policies. These would be neither a transitional phase nor a first step toward European Union, but a precondition for the major step.

What did the EP propose? In the form of two resolutions adopted on 17 October 1984 and 10 July 1975 respectively, it declared that European Union could be achieved only by strengthening and extending Community powers to include foreign policy and security as well as economic, monetary, social and cultural policy. Its conception of European Union was a 'pluralist and democratic Community'. To this end it specified 'a single decision-making centre' which would be 'in the nature of a real European government, independent of the national parliaments and responsible to the Parliament of the Union', a European Court of Justice, a consultative Economic and Social Committee and a European Court of Auditors. The EP would have both budgetary and control powers, and would participate 'on at least an equal footing' in the legislative process. Like the Commission, it urged immediate action by calling for direct elections, but it also called upon the Commission to submit an overall programme of priority action in furtherance of the Union and recommended the substantial reinforcement of the Parliament's power by 1980.[29]

Given the various inputs into the Tindemans exercise, what conclusions did the Belgian Prime Minister arrive at? However the report is assessed, it is perfectly clear that he did attempt to spell out precisely what European Union meant. In two short pages of the report, he identified six 'different components of European Union' which were 'closely connected'. Without delving into these facets in great detail, it is nonetheless worth underlining one of Tindemans' most telling remarks: 'the development of the Union's external relations cannot occur without a parallel development of common policies internally'. In practice, this meant that European Union was conceptualized as a totality – foreign policy, defence, economic relations and development aid were inextricably intertwined with common monetary, industrial, agricultural, regional and social policies. But it was the new European Council's responsibility to decide 'in which general prospect the joint endeavour' would be pursued 'in the Union phase'. Both the scope and the consequences of specific actions in these different but cognate fields would have to be judged according to 'their importance and the chances of success'.[30]

Before we examine the institutional aspects of the report, it is important to pause and look more closely at what Tindemans meant by his references to 'the Union phase'. He described it as 'a new phase in the history of the unification of Europe', which was 'a continuous process'.[31] In one account of the Tindemans Report, Jacques Vandamme reaffirmed this, adding that the measures taken by the European Council were to have constituted 'qualitative progress capable of leading, at a later stage, to a new treaty confirming this progress in legally binding texts'. And 'a new element appeared ... namely the quality of progress' which implied 'a complete package of measures' designed to achieve a 'qualitative transformation of the whole'.[32] Tindemans' own contribution was to set the December 1974 Paris Summit commitments in a wider overarching context which would facilitate and nourish the evolving qualitative progress toward a new – as yet undefined – totality.

What kind of institutional reforms did Tindemans recommend in order to get Europe on the move toward this new totality? Like Spinelli, Tindemans regarded institutional reform as crucial to the achievement of European Union. Wisely, he did not suggest an institutional upheaval. Rather he concluded that:

> To achieve European Union we must henceforth be able to find in the different European institutions the authority needed to define a policy, the efficiency needed for common action and the legitimacy needed for democratic control. It also implies that the institutions should have that coherence of vision and of action which alone will allow them to define and then pursue a policy.[33]

In consequence, the four criteria of authority, efficiency, legitimacy and coherence determined Tindemans' conception of institutional reform designed to bring about qualitative change.

Designed both to strengthen the institutional machinery and improve its overall performance, Tindemans' recommendations began with the EP. Direct elections were deemed the first necessity. This would give it a new political authority and reinforce the democratic legitimacy of the whole Community apparatus. In addition, it should be empowered to consider all questions within the competence of the Union, whether or not they lay outside the scope of the Treaties, and should gradually, as the Union evolved, be given the legal right of initiative. Concerning the European Council, Tindemans proposed that, in order to strengthen the Union's decision-making capacity, the Heads of Government should provide coherent general policy guidelines based upon a comprehensive panoramic vision of the major problems. They were to search constantly for that political agreement without which dynamic progress would be impossible. The Council of Ministers should prepare the meetings of the European Council and should itself become more coherent, speedy and continuous. This meant *inter alia* more majority voting as normal practice, the abolition of the distinction between ministerial meetings devoted to political cooperation (POCO) and conventional Community business, and extending the term of the Council Presidency to a full year.

Tindemans acknowledged that the Commission possessed its own inherent brand of dynamism in helping to construct Europe via common policies, and he sought to reassert its freedom of action within the framework of agreed Community policies. More specifically, he proposed amendments to the Treaties so that the President of the Commission would be appointed by the European Council, subject to confirmation by the EP, and he in turn would appoint the other Commissioners. Finally the existing powers of the Court of Justice were reaffirmed in the new sectors of the Union and Community citizens would have the right of appeal directly to it if their basic rights were infringed.[34]

What are we to make of this particular episode in the struggle to achieve European Union? Given that 'all those involved in the Tindemans exercise came up with solutions ... essentially federal in character', how should we assess the Report's significance?[35] Scholarly opinion, though divided, was predominantly critical. Philip Taylor claimed that it was 'generally believed to be the most pragmatic of all the documents on European Union', but he acknowledged that Tindemans' 'modest approach' had been criticized as at once both too modest and too ambitious.[36] Stanley Henig believed that the whole event had been 'a futile exercise' simply because his task from the very beginning was 'impossible'.[37] A more detailed and charitable view was taken by James Mitchell who, although highly critical of some of the legal–constitutional relationships encountered in the Report, nonetheless welcomed it for underlining the Community's structural defects which impeded closer union and for effectively re-opening the debate 'in real terms'.[38]

The most thorough apologia of the Tindemans Report, however, was that of Vandamme. Here a series of detailed explanations were listed for Tindemans' failure to deliver the goods. But the Report, according to Vandamme, had two redeeming features: first, it restated and reaffirmed the long-term aims which had been formulated at the Paris Summit in 1972 and, consequently, gave a much more precise content both to the concept of European Union and to the mechanism required to achieve it; and, second, it fully exposed the wide differences of opinion which existed among the member states regarding the goals and substance of European Union.[39]

Tindemans' mission was clearly very difficult. It originated, we must not forget, in an intergovernmental arena. What else, we may ask, could realistically have been achieved? Tindemans was fully aware of an inherent intergovernmental scepticism and confessed that he 'deliberately refused to draw up a report claiming to be, at least in part, the Constitution for the future European Union'.[40] This would indeed have been futile. But were the steps which he advocated be taken to advance toward European Union the appropriate ones? It is here that federalist strategy in this exercise becomes pertinent. Let us look at the Tindemans episode through Spinelli's eyes.

Spinelli did not agree that the various reports of the Community institutions should have been entrusted to 'a political wise man' in the first place. He urged the Commission, as the supra-national authority, to forge an alliance with the EP and the Court in order to present a united front to the Heads of Government. In his view, such a mobilization of opinion would have been much more politically effective than diluting the institutional proposals at the compromising behest of nine separate national constituencies. At least the Community institutions would have nailed their colours to the mast and stood firm on what they believed in. Tindemans' realism, in contrast, produced only words. The Heads of Government could quietly and conveniently put the Tindemans Report into cold storage.

Spinelli's view of the Tindemans episode was quite categorical. He regarded Tindemans as he regarded all European Christian Democrats: they were good Europeans in an ideological sense but bad operators of the European construction. Full of good intentions, they capitulated at the first sign of resistance and did not guarantee the means to achieve their undoubtedly genuine ends. Tindemans, according to Spinelli, succeeded in defining European Union in the mid-1970s, but he failed to specify and insist upon what was needed to achieve it. It was a classic case of ends without means. In his inimitable words, the Tindemans Report 'had the consequence that it remained without consequence'.[41]

The great weakness of the Tindemans Report was that it did not provide the mechanism to enable the central institutions to develop a sufficiently autonomous capacity to go beyond what existed. Tindemans' diplomatic faith ensured that the main thrust of European integration would remain firmly in the hands of the Heads of Government. This was why Spinelli dismissed it and why he determined to retire in 1976. In the event he did not retire but, his own personal liaison with the Commission having failed, he moved instead to the EP to begin again.

The intergovernmental response to the Report was, as Spinelli had predicted, disappointing. According to Haig Simonian, Bonn was 'enthusiastic about the proposals for increasing the powers of the Commission and boosting the role of its President'. They were also 'pleased about the suggestion for the European Parliament being given the right to initiate and not just rubber-stamp policy', but these 'federalist options' were unacceptable to the French who took a 'minimalist view'. Giscard was stoutly opposed to the institutional recommendations concerning the Commission and the EP: they were seen as 'highly undesirable, smacking much too strongly of supranationalism'.[42] The two European Council meetings which discussed the Tindemans Report during April 1976 in Luxembourg and November 1976 in the Hague yielded one meagre outcome – the Commission and Council of Ministers were invited to produce an annual report on the progress toward European Union without even defining what it meant.

And what, finally, of Tindemans? What was his view, given that he was a self-confessed federalist as regards Europe? In an official speech entitled 'The Future of Europe', given at the Foreign Affairs Club in London during December 1976, the Belgian Prime Minister lamented the practical results. The following extract from that speech is worth quoting:

> I have done all that I could in my report to sidestep doctrinal controversies which have already caused Europe so much harm. Not once did I write the word 'supranational' and ... this was not from a lack of conviction on my part. But so strong are susceptibilities in this respect that it is impossible not to give offence when you want to say something pertinent. ... it is difficult to give a detailed description of the final form of Europe's unification. This form will depend ... on the psychological evolution [which] ... is still incomplete, partial, unfinished.... Today, if we want an overall picture, we must limit ourselves to indications on the various directions of our action, refraining from an exact description of the final result. That is what I wanted in my report ... to attempt.... While writing my report, I tried to keep as close as possible to political reality, to suggest only measures that seemed feasible, to refrain from dreaming, to stick to what was practical and concrete ... [but] the ... conclusions were more than disappointing. Several proposals were discarded because there was no agreement, others were described as premature ... many have been so hedged about with provisos and qualifications that they have lost much of their value. The idea of innovation, a new start, a qualitative leap forward ... had almost disappeared from the documents

submitted to the European Council.... I think that this is only a matter of political will, but that our capability to act has been impaired.[43]

The last sentence from this extract of Tindemans' speech is particularly revealing. He was to return to its implications during the early 1980s. Meanwhile, having accepted the chairmanship of the European People's Party (EPP) in the EP, Tindemans, like Spinelli, had moved into a completely different institutional forum to continue his own efforts to bring about European Union. Before we leave this episode in the history of European Union, it is important to look again at the overall significance of the Tindemans Report. In hindsight, neither Tindemans nor his Report have been given the credit which they deserve.

From the 'first step' of Schuman in 1950, and the cumulative steps of Monnet which followed, Europe has been built according to a gradual process leading up to European Union in the 1990s. If we consider for a moment the piecemeal, incremental approach to European Union achieved as a result of the Single European Act (SEA), 1987, the Maastricht Treaty on European Union (TEU), 1993, and the Treaty of Amsterdam (TA) 1998, it is abundantly clear that both the policy content and the institutional reforms established by these treaties were foreshadowed much earlier in the Tindemans Report. Small steps were often taken because they made it 'easier to take the large steps' which would have to be taken at a later date. But the policy of 'small steps' could not always apply; sometimes it was necessary to take a 'large step'.[44] Tindemans has not been given the credit which he deserves for a vision of European Union, much of which has either already come to pass or is still in the process of implementation. A bird's eye view of what his European Union looked like included the following: direct elections to the EP; a single institutional system; a common foreign policy; EMU; a common external policy on multilateral trade and the Third World; a common analysis of defence problems leading ultimately to a common defence policy; a common industrial policy for the manufacture of armaments; a common energy policy; a common research policy; the expansion of regional policy in line with progress toward EMU; the establishment of citizens' rights and fundamental freedoms; a common policy on nuclear energy and power stations; the disappearance of frontier controls; and the introduction of equivalence in educational qualifications. In retrospect, then, Tindemans and his Report established what has become an enduring legacy.

Looking back from the standpoint of the end of the century, the continuity of policy content and recommendations for institutional reform is quite remarkable. And Tindemans even anticipated the notion of a 'double speed' Europe by at least a decade when he observed that it would have been impossible to fashion a credible programme of action if it was 'deemed absolutely necessary that in every case all stages should be reached by all the states at the same time'. Instead, those states which were able to progress had 'a duty to forge ahead', while those states which were unable to move ahead immediately simply delayed their progress to a later date. But this did not mean 'Europe à la carte' since every state would be bound by the agreement of all regarding the final objective to be achieved in common; it was only the timescales for achievement which would vary.[45] And Tindemans was quite categorical about the implications of these political choices: they could not occur without 'a transfer of competences to common institutions'. The internal reforms dovetailed neatly with the external changes to produce a grand teleology. In this vast scheme, he claimed that everything touched everything else: it was the 'sum of the progress achieved in parallel' which constituted 'the qualitative change' that was European Union.[46]

In summary, then, it is time to reassess and reappraise both Tindemans and his Report. The Tindemans episode should not be dismissed as an exercise in futility; it was much more of a stock-taking exercise which recognised the short-term need to make concrete progress in several areas while simultaneously looking ahead in the long-term to a federal Europe. What was self-evident to Tindemans, however, was not shared by every member state government and it is clear that the whole episode under-lined the frustrations, difficulties and disappointments attendant upon attempts at general institutional reform during the mid-1970s. Nonethe-less, there is a sense in which his exertions did contribute to practical progress in one specific area, namely, direct elections to the EP. We will turn now to look more closely at the institutional arena which was to become the focus of so much feverish activity in the cause of European Union in the 1980s.

## The European Parliament, direct elections and federalism

The issue of direct elections to the EP was a single institutional reform which necessitated no treaty amendment. It was, therefore, a reform which it was possible, at least temporarily, to isolate as incremental change not necessarily presaging wholesale institutional upheaval. Both in theory and in practice, of course, the question of direct elections did suggest far-reaching consequences for the future relations between member state gov-ernments and Community institutions. Moreover, it had important implications for inter-institutional Community relations. We shall examine the relevance of these issues as they relate to federalism and the EC, but first we will investigate the context within which the question of direct elections emerged during the early 1970s.

The goal of direct elections was firmly entrenched, via Article 138, in the Treaty of Rome in 1957. Its inclusion in the treaty, however, had inter-esting contextual origins. Spinelli observed that the role of the EP – known as the Common Assembly up until 1962 – was 'an almost purely formal concession made by the treaty negotiators to the democratic-federalist approach'.[47] Given his view of Monnet's approach to European integration, Spinelli considered that 'the Common Assembly was not in the logic of the functionalist plan in which the institutional mechanism consisted essentially in the dialogue between Eurocrats who proposed and governments which disposed'. Consequently it was 'circumscribed by limitations ... for the same reason that preceding assemblies had been'.[48] There was room in Monnet's conception of Europe for an elected assembly. We can trace it back at least to the Schuman Plan Conference of June 1950 which set up the ECSC.[49] But Spinelli's federalist approach to the European construction – the direct route via constitutionalism – naturally predisposed him to give the institution of parliament a central, indeed pivotal, place in treaty negotiations. Monnet's idea of exploiting the possibilities of functionalism to achieve constitutionalism in contrast placed the role of the EP in constant jeopardy. It risked being permanently marginalised in the process of unification. In this light the future of the EP was something of a gamble. The role of the EP in the evolving Community hence was determined at the outset by the rival European interpretations of Monnet and Spinelli which we have already designated in Chapter 2 as the two faces of federalism.

The success of Monnet's European conception, then, meant that the EP's future role in the Community was inherently ambiguous. This legacy more than anything else explains the difficulties and frustrations which have characterized the EP's incessant struggle to assert itself in the Community's political and constitutional progress since 1957. And it is not enough to equate this struggle with historical comparisons of the evolution of national parliaments. Understandable though these might be, the building of Europe is not synonymous with the conventional processes of state-building and national integration which political scientists have identified with the creation of the national state. We have already underlined this mistaken assumption and its implications in our earlier analysis of Monnet's European conception. The institutional reality of the Community lacks a political authority sufficiently autonomous to express a genuine European perspective. In the absence of an authoritative European Government, the EP has had to grow and develop in an institutional space with only tenuous connections to a fragmented executive authority.

Monnet's approach to federation provided a place for the EP, but it was secondary to his overriding concern for concrete functional achievements which would enable political institutions to grow, as it were, organically out of the daily practice of European experience. Given the major flaws which Spinelli identified in Monnet's conception of Europe, however, the anticipated shift to 'political Europe' was inherently difficult. Member state governments would block significant progress in this direction. Monnet's strategy hence determined that a parliamentary Europe would not necessarily be the logical outcome of European integration. It was a possibility which would have to be fought for.

It is against this contextual background that we should assess the significance of direct elections to the EP. Monnet's legacy has imposed a heavy burden upon a fundamental political principle which informs the very core of Western liberal democracy. The principle of direct elections, engaging the European citizenry beyond their states, was attached to a weakly-conceived institution with an inherently ambiguous role. Small wonder, then, that the President of the Commission, Walter Hallstein, believed the Treaty of Rome to be designed 'to encourage the removal of the inadequacies in the Community's parliamentary system at the earliest possible moment'.[50] The EP's role since 1957 has been preoccupied with attempts to break free from the institutional prison in which Monnet's Europe confined it. Beginning as early as 1960, considerable pressure was brought to bear by the EP upon the Council of Ministers to implement direct universal suffrage in accordance with a uniform procedure in all member states. Article 138, paragraph three, of the Treaty of Rome, however, was ignored until May 1969 when it surfaced again, at the EP's insistence, on the agenda of the Committee of Permanent Representatives (COREPER) and of the Council. Brief mention was made of it later at the Hague Summit in 1969 but it was the strengthening of the EP's budgetary powers in 1970 and 1975 which eventually compelled the Council to agree to the implementation of direct elections in September 1976.[51] It could be argued that the delay in holding the elections of twenty-two years between 1957 and 1979 vindicated Monnet's 'functionalist–federalist' strategy. Political Europe would be built only slowly upon concrete practical achievements. Federalists, however, would argue that the Community's very practice and progress has, on the contrary, exposed the inherent weaknesses and flaws of Monnet's Europe. The Community is still dominated by its member states, unable to move ahead via significant institutional reform in order to solve European problems. Direct elections arrived late, in grudging fashion, and were themselves symptomatic of a Europe which urgently required further constitutionalism if it was to acquire and express that autonomous political life which was so palpably absent in Monnet's Europe. Direct elections were only a step, albeit an important step, in this direction. For federalists the question of direct elections transcended the obvious need to lend some democratic legitimacy to the European enterprise and went beyond mere concession to western liberal democratic ideology. They were part of a much larger overall strategy of institutional reform intended to organize power at the European level – a means by which the European political will could be nurtured and canalized.

Spinelli himself had long ago recognised that, once the Community institutions had begun to operate, 'practice would in one way or the other alter the role and relative positions of each of them'.[52] He had consistently urged the Commission to support the EP in its persistent quest to come in from the cold. In his view, these two supra-national bodies 'should and ought to have made common cause before the Council'. Such an alliance, neither prescribed nor prohibited by the Treaty of Rome, could have enabled both institutions to wring the maximum of advantage from their respective decision-making powers and rights of initiative, and would have made the EP 'one of the real decision centres and ... increased its sense of importance'. Had this liaison been sensibly developed, Spinelli believed that the Community's institutional history could have been different, and that of the EP especially so:

> Capable parliamentarians would have been induced to participate in it and a fruitful tension between Parliament and Council would have taken shape. The subject of European elections and the reform of Parliament's powers and of the political community in general would have developed in a very different way.[53]

But the Commission eschewed this possibility until the limits of its supra-national initiatives were firmly underlined by de Gaulle during 1965–66. Until then it regarded the EP merely as 'one of several sounding boards to publicise its own actions', and Spinelli correctly observed the comical aspect of the Commission defending governmental prerogatives against that status without the concomitant growth of the EP's role. Indeed the Commission's 'substantial indifference' toward the EP actually guaranteed its own impotence in the face of enhanced intergovernmental cooperation. It defended not its strengths but its weaknesses.[54]

We can now understand more fully the change in the attitude of the Commission toward direct elections during the early 1970s. It had slowly come to recognise the potential value of its parliamentary ally and Spinelli, as a new Commissioner, was determined to forge a closer alliance both with the EP and the Court of Justice. His overriding aim in joining the Commission in 1970 was 'to try to see what was possible ... and to pay attention to how we could have further institutional developments'. This meant learning 'what it means to be a Commissioner and to have a certain influence in the Commission'. Spinelli was convinced that the antidote to the Commission's weakness in the overall institutional framework lay in 'proposing some stronger legislative powers for the EP'. This, he claimed, was how and why the Vedel Report emerged in March 1972.[55]

This report, which was completed in six months, arose from a Commission initiative taken in July 1971 to set up an ad hoc working party under the chairmanship of the French constitutional lawyer, Professor Georges Vedel, to 'examine the whole corpus of problems connected with the enlargement of the powers of the European Parliament'.[56] We shall not examine the details of the report here but content ourselves with emphasizing the importance once again of federalist ideas and influences. It is

clear, as Avi Shlaim has acknowledged, that both moderation and gradual-
ism were the hallmarks of the working party's approach, conditioned by
the prevailing political climate, in their efforts to make a significant
impact upon the outcome of the Paris Summit of October 1972. Since the
subject of institutions was on the agenda of the summit conference, 'it was
hoped that the group's recommendations would not only help to shape
the Commission's own proposals to the heads of state but would also influence government and non-governmental elites and make an important
contribution to the public debate on the institutional reforms called for by
the enlargement of the Communities'. With this intention in mind, 'it saw
little point in making proposals which, whatever their general merit, had
no chance of being accepted'.[57]

But if there was no mention made of a European government responsible to a directly-elected EP, it is nonetheless true that federal ideas did cir-
culate in the group's early discussions.[58] And if we remember that one
driving-force behind the Vedel Report, Spinelli, viewed the episode as part
of a federalist strategy to reinstate the Commission at the centre of
Community affairs, the ubiquity of the federal idea is once again evident.
As the only federalist in the Mansholt Commission in the early 1970s,
Spinelli was forced to operate in isolated militancy and he was unable to
persuade his colleagues to adopt the Vedel proposals and persevere with
them after 1972. The Commission supported ideas of codecision for the
EP, and it actually went further than the Vedel proposals in recommend-
ing a date for the introduction of direct elections. But it would not be
pressurised into supporting Spinelli's bold plan for radical reform, including direct elections together with full legislative and budgetary powers for
the EP, which he touted in 1973.[59]

The two separate issues of direct elections and increased legislative and
budgetary powers for the EP have come to be associated with federalism in
both a direct and an indirect fashion. They are directly linked to federalism in the sense that they were, after all, part of an overall federalist
strategy. This can hardly be refuted if we examine Spinelli's role and
thinking in the evolving life of the Community. But there is another, more
indirect, sense in which they have gradually been equated with a federal
Europe. The basis and underlying assumptions for reasoning along these
lines was cogently analysed before the introduction of direct elections in
1978 by Val Herman and Juliet Lodge, and rests upon a number of fundamental misconceptions and misunderstandings about federalism, supra-
nationalism, intergovernmentalism and national sovereignty. We shall not
re-examine the detailed assumptions which underpin much of the thinking about direct elections and the road to a federal Europe. Rather than
trace the various steps which have led to this equation, it is more important here to underline the extent to which such thinking fostered an assortment of myths, fears, suspicions and anxieties about federalism and
European Union. This is important because it has encouraged distorted

images of the Community and because it has nurtured deep misgivings among member state governments about the Community's future constitutional and political development.

It should be emphasized at the very outset that just as direct elections did not automatically endow Community decision-making with a sudden democratic legitimacy, neither did they necessarily imply a federal Europe.[60] A parliamentary federal Europe would certainly be predicated upon direct elections, but the reverse logic did not automatically follow. Herman and Lodge put it this way:

> National parliaments and governments fear that they [direct elections] are but the first step in a process likely to culminate in the creation of a federal union in which the member governments and national parliaments will be relegated to roles akin to those of regional parliaments in federations.... However, ... power ultimately lies with the member governments. In other words, the implications of direct elections being detrimental to the autonomy and authority of the member states and national parliaments have been exaggerated.[61]

The source of such a perception was familiar and arose from repeated mistaken analogies with national state evolution. Transplanted to the European level, the conventional processes of state-building and national integration would lead, so the logic follows, to the erosion of national sovereignty and the eventual withering away of the national state itself. The distorted image of the Community's future was further misrepresented, as Herman and Lodge remarked, by 'an inadequate appreciation of both the position of regional parliaments in federations and of the political nature of federalism itself'.[62]

A general misunderstanding of the EP's intentions had fuelled a paranoia among some national parliamentarians and member state governments that sovereignty was once again under threat. MEPs had been perceived as ambitious competitors with national parliaments for a growing range of legislative powers. In reality, of course, all that MEPs wanted was to fill an expanding gap in democratic parliamentary scrutiny and accountability which national parliaments were simply unable to bridge. As Spinelli emphasized, the EP's efforts to assert itself were not inspired by theoretical federalists' assumptions, but by the very practical experience of the Community itself: it was particularly sensitive to 'the undemocratic aspect and the intrinsic weakness of a situation in which large segments of legislative power and control of public monies were passing into the hands of the Community administrators.[63] Only the EP could effectively respond to changes in the EC which were beyond the capacity of national parliaments to deal with. There was never any suggestion, as Lodge remarked, that the EP should acquire powers at the expense of national parliaments: 'on the contrary, the two sets of parliamentarians were expected to have complementary, not competing, functions'.[64]

The discussions about the prospect of direct elections during the 1970s certainly helped to focus public attention upon some fundamental questions about both the nature and purpose of the Community. In particular, they rekindled the debate about institutional powers and relationships. They forced some old issues and questions to resurface in changed circumstances. What powers should the Community's central institutions possess and what should their relationships be to each other? What sort of relationship should exist between these institutions and the member state governments? These and other questions often generated more heat than light. Anxieties and misconceptions abounded. But it was at least important to have such a debate and to return to fundamentals. In this way, the Community and the European idea which it represented were thrust into the limelight and given a prominence continually sought but often denied to them. Certainly the issue of direct elections enabled Spinelli to prepare the platform from which he was later to launch a fresh federalist initiative, and it facilitated his seemingly ubiquitous activities behind both the Vedel and the Tindemans Reports.

At the end of the twentieth century, it probably makes little sense to speculate about the implicit assumptions of the architects of the Treaties of Rome as they relate to a directly-elected EP. Whatever their intentions, the EP has slowly but persistently accumulated new formal powers and procedures which it has coupled with an extensive network of influence to increase its visibility, stature and vitality. Direct elections have not yet distilled the aggregate of national biases and perceptions into the common political will of EC citizens as federalists would have liked, but history suggests that such processes should be counted in generations rather than years. Spinelli certainly did not expect it to happen overnight. But it was important for the EP during this period to act and behave as if it was already pivotal in the decision-making procedures of the EC. If it had behaved like a sheep it would have been eaten by the wolves. The EP's powers did not grow as fast as its influence but its overall institutional strength – its capacity to take initiatives, to invade new public policy spheres previously unoccupied and to interpret its own role ambitiously – was undeniable.

The silent disregard for the limitations placed upon it by the Rome Treaties partly explains its somewhat lacklustre appearance in the past. Many reasons have been advanced for its presumed failure to establish and sustain a reputation worthy of the name 'Parliament', but in retrospect the policy of stealth, of the gradual accretion of power, authority and influence, eventually yielded some invaluable gains. The tendency to link direct elections with federalism probably harmed the EP in some member states, notably the UK and Denmark, but this did not prevent it from evolving into something considerably more significant than a mere debating chamber. And its federal potential remained and continues to furnish the prospect, much closer today than in the 1970s, of a parliamentary federal Europe encased in a European Union. In providing a direct channel linking the central institutions to the European citizenry the member state governments created the basis for new perceptions and attitudes among the EC's mass publics. Small wonder that the EP has been viewed suspiciously by particular member state governments for many years.

Our discussion of the relationship between direct elections to the EP and federalism is critical to both the theoretical and empirical aspects of building Europe. It raised and continues to prompt serious questions about the nature and meaning of the European project. But we must also acknowledge the existence of other, perhaps less significant, developments which occurred at the end of the 1970s and which played a constructive role in the diagnosis of the Community's institutional shortcomings. These developments, however, involved only minor adjustments to what existed and were essentially engaged in tinkering with the Community system.

## Tinkering with the system: Spierenberg and the committee of three

According to Emile Noel, the Secretary-General of the Commission between 1958 and 1987, the year 1979 was 'a year of movement and of innovation'.[65] Leaving aside direct elections to the EP, several other developments prompted him to observe that, after a long period of stagnation, Europe had 'taken off again, with new methods and a different impetus'.[66] Clearly a new combination of events lay at the root of his optimism. What were these fresh developments and was his optimism justified? We shall briefly survey the background to a series of events during 1979 which account for the Community's condition of institutional health at the end of the decade when European Union, originally promulgated at the Paris Summit of October 1972, was officially to be consummated.

Noel apportioned credit for the achievements of 1979 to the established Community institutions of the Commission and Council of Ministers, and to the much younger European Council, in roughly equal measure. The latter had been largely responsible for implementing direct elections to the EP as well as providing the impetus for the common position on energy policy (aimed at regulating oil imports) and the creation of the European Monetary System (EMS), while the former had been pivotal in the enlargement negotiations involving Greece, and the multilateral trade discussions of the Tokyo Round Table and the delicate renewal of the Lome Convention on overseas aid and development. Together, these concrete gains reflected the value of a combined communitarian and intergovernmental approach to Community progress.

Arising out of this conjunction of achievements, federalists were particularly active and interested in the the emergence of the EMS. Monetary integration, as we have already noted, was considered by many federalists to be the most fruitful approach to European Union. Re-launched in 1977 by Roy Jenkins, the newly-appointed Commission President, the goal of monetary union was a bold but not original step. Jenkins claimed that although the Paris–Bonn axis was working well internally, it was 'doing no good for Europe'. He was casting around for ideas and fastened upon advice from Monnet:

> The lesson he taught me was always to advance along the line of least resistance provided that it led in approximately the right direction. It was against this background that I came firmly to the view that the best axis of advance for the Community in the circumstances of 1977 lay in re-proclaiming the goal of monetary union.... I decided that there was a better chance of advance by qualitative leap than by cautious shuffle. And such a leap was desirable both to get the blood of the Community coursing again after the relative stagnation of the mid-1970s and on its own merits – because it could move Europe to a more favourable bank of the stream.[67]

This was reminiscent of Tindemans' belief that occasionally it was necessary to take a large step. Jenkins did not expect that member state governments would launch themselves on the 'qualitative leap' in 1978 but the important thing from the Commission's standpoint was that the sustained advocacy of monetary union gave his presidency both 'a theme and a focus which had been lacking'.[68]

When the EMS was launched in December 1978, it was primarily directed toward exchange rate stability but gradual progress toward the full convertibility of European currencies subsequently yielded the European Currency Unit (ECU) as the new system's benchmark. Full convertibility remained the ultimate goal of monetary federalists who believed that not until there was a real common monetary organization would the customs union and the Common Agricultural Policy (CAP) be properly managed. The role of the ECU and of the revamped European Monetary Cooperation Fund represented slow, albeit significant, progress in this direction but the contradictions which existed between a single market for agricultural produce and industrial products, and the existence of separate financial markets had been clearly exposed.[69]

No new institutions appeared in 1979 as part of the fresh monetary impetus, although Jenkins noted that once the EMS had been launched it very much became the creature of European Councils which, if nothing else, justified 'this early institutional innovation of President Giscard's'.[70] There were, however, two acts of institutional self-appraisal which occurred in this year and which together represented the culminating progress toward European Union at the end of the intergovernmental decade when 'governments were less likely to choose integrative solutions' to contemporary problems.[71] Noel believed that the process of institutional self-appraisal was a sign of their maturity and confidence, and it seemed to confirm the continuing vitality of the European Union idea itself. Let us look briefly at the Spierenberg Report and the Report of the Committee of Three (known as the 'Three Wise Men') and comment upon their respective relevance to federalism and European Union.

The origins of the independent review body chaired by the Dutchman, Dirk Spierenberg, to submit proposals for the reform of the Commission date back to the decision taken in 1978 by the Jenkins Commission to reassess its overall efficiency and coherence. In consequence, the Spierenberg Committee had a narrow institutional focus. Moreover, its cautious pragmatic approach to reform, concentrating in the main upon improving the Commission's general performance, was reflected in proposals requiring only procedural agreement rather than protracted treaty amendments. As Henig correctly observed, there was indeed a clear acceptance of existing reality as a starting point.[72] No constitutional blueprint was intended nor was there any attempt to contemplate long-term aims for the EC. The atmosphere which surrounded the whole exercise was one of level-headed caution.

Since the proposals contained in the Spierenberg Report are well-known to most seasoned observers of Community institutional affairs, we will not provide another detailed survey of them here. Rather, what we shall emphasize are those aspects of the Report which were perceived to have particular significance from the federalist standpoint. What parts of the Report were relevant to federalism and European Union? One central concern of the Report was especially germane to federalists thought and strategy, namely, the widely-perceived decline of the Commission. The centrality of the Commission's position in the overall Community institutional framework has always been of paramount importance to federalist thinking, and Spierenberg's underlying purpose to counteract some of the forces responsible for its decline earned federalist support. Decline had to be halted and reversed. The Commission required revitalization from within since its reassertion from without seemed highly improbable.

Reform from within at least equipped the Commission to put its own house in order without requiring other institutions to be involved. For example, recommendations affecting the role of and relationships between directors general and cabinets and those concerning the recruitment and career prospects of the Commission staff were practical proposals designed to improve overall efficiency. Their suggestions for the strengthening of the Commission President's role and for reducing the number of Commissioners and portfolios, however, were controversial and did require member states' approval. Briefly, they identified the appointment process as the source of Commission weakness. Mindful of the impending membership of Greece, and aware of Spanish and

Portuguese intentions, the Report sought to place a curb on old practices. It recommended that member states should have just one Commissioner each, and that portfolios be similarly rationalised. The President should also be able to play a greater role in the appointment of Commissioners and receive support in the work of coordination and control by one designated Vice-President instead of the several nominal ones which customarily existed.

There was very little in all of this for federalists to find inspiring. They saw the sense in seeking to streamline the Commission's internal administration and in proposing other reforms intended to improve performance, but they did not view these as effective in reversing the Commission's decline. This would have needed a genuine change of heart by member state governments and a closer working relationship with the directly-elected EP – presaging wider institutional reform – before it could recover its former political leadership role in Community affairs. Nonetheless, the Spierenberg Report was indicative of movement, of a fresh initiative to breathe new life into an old institution. It was an attempt to tinker with the system in a manner designed to avoid controversy.

The Committee of Three – Berend Biesheuvel, Edmund Dell and Robert Marjolin – was established in December 1978 by the European Council to consider adjustments to the machinery and procedures of the Community institutions. Its mandate applied formally to all the institutions but in the knowledge that Spierenberg was examining the Commission at the same time, its focus came to rest mainly upon the Council of Ministers and other parts of the EC framework. As the Three Wise Men underlined in their prefatory remarks to their Report, they were influenced in their practical conception of their task by two imperatives: that their proposals should not entail treaty amendments and that their proposals should be 'specific' in order to be 'implemented swiftly'.[73] These two imperatives placed clear limitations upon the scope and effectiveness of their recommendations.

Before we look a little closer at these proposals, it is worth our while to examine the origins of this report, especially in view of the European Council's weak response to the Tindemans Report which it had also been instrumental in launching four years previously. It is significant that the initiative to set up a fresh institutional study came from the French President, Giscard d'Estaing, who, like his predecessor, Pompidou, was invariably willing to invoke French conceptions of European Union. Indeed, it is particularly interesting to note the emphasis placed in the Report upon 'progress toward European Union', a guarantee of safety in ambiguity.[74] However, the Commission's role in prompting Giscard's initiative appears to have been crucial. One writer has gone as far as arguing that the Committee of Three had been appointed in order to counter the Commission's annual report of 1978 on the state of progress toward European Union which had made several incisive remarks about the enlargement of the Community and the need for certain treaty amendments.[75] In this light, it was an intergovernmental determination not to be upstaged by the Commission which accounted for the decision.

Given these somewhat obscure origins to the Report, coupled with the clear limitations imposed by their mandate, the Committee of Three worked with admirable speed and efficiency to complete their task in October 1979, one month after the release of the Spierenberg Report. Visiting all of the member states either individually or together, they had confidential discussions with heads of governments, senior ministers and officials, and met separately with the presidents of all the Community institutions as well as COREPER and the Council Secretariat. Without wishing to enter into a detailed analysis of the Report, it is nonetheless significant to recognise their assumptions about the need for institutional reform. They were naturally very guarded about the scope for and value of institutional reform. In their view, it was not the key that would unlock the door to further progress. Instead they blamed existing failures upon 'political circumstances and attitudes that sometimes produced no clear conception at all'.[76] A conspicuous lack of political consensus rather than institutional deficiencies was deemed the main culprit. And, as the Three Wise Men acknowledged, they could do nothing about that. It went beyond the boundaries of their mandate.

The bulk of the Report concentrated upon the respective roles and workloads of the European Council and the Council of Ministers. Indeed, 33 pages of the 73-page Report were devoted exclusively to these two institutions. There was much here to interest federalists but nothing to excite them. The EP was to be able to debate the Council's objectives for the next six months as outlined by the Council President. The use of majority voting in the Council was to be encouraged, albeit in the spirit of the 1974 Paris Summit which had committed governments to using the veto less. The main focus of interest in the Report clearly lay in issues of inter-institutional efficiency and coordination, especially involving the European Council, the Council of Ministers, COREPER and the general responsibilities of the Presidency. The recommendations of the Report served to confirm the future role of the European Council in evaluating overall Community priorities and the essentially political purpose of the Council of Ministers *vis-à-vis* preparation and execution, without which the former could not effectively function.

With the intergovernmentalist perspective firmly entrenched, federalists doubtless expected little of significance from those short sections of the Report which looked at the Commission and EP. Here, perceived caution and pragmatism were especially evident. Nothing of much import was suggested for the Commission. The Report identified some prosaic reasons for its decline and broadly agreed with the proposals advocated by the Spierenberg Committee, although there was more than a hint about the Commission's ability to reassert its political role by acting in a more

independent manner during technical consultations with national officials. A close analysis of this section of the Report reveals a distinct sympathy for the Commission's pivotal position conveying 'something more
than an approximation of the separate interests of member states'. It
should demonstrate what kind of actions would best reflect 'the larger
interests of Europe as a whole'.[77]

Two specific developments influenced the Committee's proposals
regarding the EP: first, the growth of its budgetary powers via the treaty
amendments of 1970 and 1975; and, secondly, the implications of direct
elections. Their recommendations, however, deliberately eschewed the
anticipated closer relationship between the EP and the Commission which
Spinelli had so earnestly advocated, although they did favour the EP
having some involvement in the appointment of the Commission President. But their real focus was upon what they labelled a 'triangular
pattern' of Commission, Council and EP. This would create 'a more complete and stable institutional balance'.[78] Direct contact between the EP
and the European Council was also envisaged in order to promote communication and cooperation in the launching of major initiatives. A
regular six-monthly report by the President of the European Council to
the EP in person was deemed appropriate. In the Committee's opinion
the EP was to develop its full potential as 'a sounding-board for the large
policy issues of the day'.[79]

Since the Report of the Three Wise Men was predisposed to comment
upon progress toward European Union, it is appropriate for us to look at
this final aspect of their work before bringing this section to a close. Their
remarks about European Union were characteristically vague and cautious
given the various mandatory constraints imposed upon them. Indeed, in
the concluding paragraph to the Report they acknowledged that their 'few
thoughts' on European Union may have seemed to some to be 'insuffi-
ciently ambitious'. Anticipating such criticism they reminded their potential detractors of the imperative for their proposals to be implemented
swiftly. The late 1970s, they observed, was 'ill-suited to futuristic visions'
which predisposed a profound and rapid change of attitudes within the
Community.[80]

What, then, did they say about European Union? The following brief
extract from this section of the Report is revealing:

> European Union ... is a term the meaning of which has been hotly
> contested during the last few years. ... our own practical and imme-
> diate approach ... has been that everything which strengthens the
> Community's internal unity, and its unity and that of the Nine in deal-
> ings with the rest of the world, constitutes progress towards European
> Union. When we speak of European Union ... we are speaking not so
> much of a definite goal as of a direction of movement.... The concept
> needs to be defined and measured in relation to the obstacles which

will have to be overcome.... It is through the efforts of the Community and its states to tackle the dangers ... that European Union however one defines it, will be built.[81]

There was no Tindemans-type teleology here. European Union, whatever it meant, would evolve in time-honoured piecemeal fashion as a result of successive responses, both communitarian and intergovernmental, to the prevailing problems of the age. In particular, monetary and budgetary policies to combat inflation, Community solidarity over energy shortages in oil and gas, and the adjustments required to accommodate Greece, Spain and Portugal in the next enlargement, were identified as the areas where opportunities to promote European Union loomed largest. Political cooperation was also mentioned, as were industrial, regional and social policies in which concrete and limited actions were deemed possible. The atmosphere conveyed by this section of the Report was clearly congruent with the perceived crisis surrounding Community affairs and Europe in general. 'Over-large or ill-defined projects in whatever area of policy' were considered inopportune.[82]

In his *Memoirs*, Robert Marjolin confessed that European Union had become 'a catchword in speeches and sometimes in official texts' but that the Three Wise Men had 'found it very difficult' to conceal their 'scepticism'. Indeed, they would probably never have used the expression if it could have been avoided.[83] And his summary of the 1970s – the decade of intergovernmentalism – was generally pessimistic. The new objectives, 'notably those spelled out in the summit declarations of 1972 and 1974, had not been achieved; the new initiatives had not cohered into one or more full-scale "common policies"'. Member states' governments, owing to the acute economic problems of the 1970s, had taken 'more nationalistic stances' and refused to accept the advice of the Commission which alone could distil the Community interest. He believed that the Committee of Three were 'almost completely at a loss to do anything about a trend of this kind'.[84]

In complete contrast to Marjolin's sombre disappointment, Emile Noel had watched events with a lively anticipation. He believed that Community developments which had occurred in or about 1979 suggested optimism about the progress made, especially regarding direct elections to the EP and the launching of the EMS. Neither the content nor the consequences of the two reports sketched out above, however, could really be construed as successful. Some of the institutional proposals of the Three Wise Men were significant from the standpoint of the federalists, particularly those advocating closer contact between the EP and the Council, but tinkering with the system was really all that was implied. Indeed, judging by the outcome of the proposals contained in both the Spierenburg and the Committee of Three Reports, it seems fair to conclude that very little was intended from the outset.

Henig observed that in the immediate aftermath of the presentation of the Spierenberg Report the member states rejected the proposal to reduce the number of Commissioners – 'a very rapid justification of the cautious approach which was adopted'.[85] The Report of the Three Wise Men fared no better. The prospects of closer institutional relationships and of a greater political consensus among member state governments about European Union seemed just as remote. The European Council prevented the EP from having access to the Report before they had considered it themselves for fear that MEPs might 'pre-empt their discussion of its contents'.[86] And after referral to the Council of Ministers, the European Council returned to the Report at its December 1980 meeting in Luxembourg 'where, in effect, it was shelved'. Once again, as Bulmer and Wessels remarked, the European Council was found 'unable to transform vague commitments to European Union into a practical programme, even though the Report stressed concrete and practical steps forward'.[87]

In retrospect, neither the Spierenberg nor the Committee of Three Reports appear to have had much impact upon subsequent Community developments and this is probably why very little attention has been paid to them. From the federalist perspective they seemed to represent relatively unimportant milestones along the road toward European Union. Marjolin later expressed sadness that 'in the years that followed the submission of this report so little was done to implement the proposals'. Nonetheless he also referred in his *Memoirs* to Jacques Delors, the Commission President, who in the mid-1980s remarked in positive vein that the report was 'still topical' and that 'the solutions offered were still valid'.[88] In one particular sense both reports were significant: they served to confirm the views of Spinelli and other federalists that the way forward lay not in intergovernmentalist-inspired initiatives. Other routes were likely to be more promising.

## European Union relaunched, 1980–84

The years 1980–81 represented something of a coincidence in the history of federalism and European Union. They marked both the beginning of a new federalist initiative by Altiero Spinelli in June 1980 and the culmination of a series of reports and debates about institutional reform emanating from the EP during 1974–81.[89] This is why the role of the EP appeared suddenly to assume such a large prominence in discussions about European Union after 1979. Direct elections were certainly a key factor in prompting the EP to adopt a more assertive position regarding European Union in the early 1980s but it was not the only explanation for the renewed impetus. The revitalization of parliamentary activity must be set against the background of consistent efforts at inter-institutional reform stretching back several years, at least to the initial Kirk Report of 1974.

According to Michael Palmer, the Kirk-Reay Report retained its significance as a landmark in the history of the EP's development mainly because it 'represented the clearest and most complete survey of the whole range of inter-institutional problems confronting the European Parliament' since 1963, and because of the way in which it pointed to 'the inadequacy of Parliament's relationship with the Council and to the lack of political accountability from Council to Parliament', a deficiency which remains to be corrected today.[90] Testimony to the importance of much of the institutional thinking behind the Kirk-Reay Report was quickly demonstrated in October 1979 when the EP's Political Affairs Committee (PAC) established a new subcommittee to deal with institutional problems. Given the specific task of investigating relations between the EP and other Community institutions, the eight reports which followed retraced several of the steps of inter-institutional relations already trodden by Sir Peter Kirk. Taken together, the Rey, Van Miert, Hansch, Diligent, Elles, Baduel Glorioso, Antoniozzi and Blumenfeld Reports amounted to a comprehensive review of the EP's relations with other Community institutions with a view to strengthening its overall influence in the decision-making process.[91] These resolutions, it should be noted, conformed to the goal of institutional reform 'within the existing treaties'. The Rey Report was the first to be debated and adopted in April 1980 while the Van Miert, Hansch, Diligent, Elles and Baduel Glorioso reports were discussed and approved in a major institutional debate in July 1981. The Antoniozzi and Blumenfeld reports were debated in December 1981 and February 1982 respectively.

Several proposals made in the eight reports identified above were accepted by the Council of Ministers within a very short space of time.[92] And many of the suggestions outlined in the Blumenfeld, Hansch and Antoniozzi reports were later incorporated in the Genscher-Colombo Act which we shall briefly survey in the next section of the chapter. This background information confirms that the first directly-elected EP of the Community had already renewed its quest for institutional reform within the existing treaties before Spinelli launched his own personal initiative in 1980. But many of these proposals were not original; they had been aired much earlier without success. Palmer summarised the circumstances succinctly:

> By and large, the ideas which were developed concerning relations with the Council, relations with the Commission and a greater role for the Parliament in European political cooperation and in the handling of the Community's external relations, represent a completion of ideas originally put forward in the years preceding direct elections by Sir Peter Kirk and Lord Reay. A number of ideas which seemed unattainable and unrealistic at the time when they were originally proposed … were taken over – in appropriately modified forms – by a number of *rapporteurs* of the institutional subcommittee, were adopted

by Parliament ... and, in certain cases, have been accepted by the Council, the European Council and the foreign ministers meeting in political cooperation.[93]

This background perspective is important for an accurate understanding of the events of 1980–81. It demonstrates an extant parliamentary strategy of piecemeal 'small steps' institutional reform alongside the more illustrious episodes of Tindemans and direct elections which effectively overshadowed it. But, in retrospect, the strategy of 'small steps' had been particularly submerged beneath the welter of attention thrust upon Spinelli's far more radical federalist strategy for wholesale treaty revision which began in earnest in July 1981 when the EP agreed to the creation of a new committee to deal with institutional issues involving treaty amendments leading ultimately to European Union.[94] This was a fresh departure of approach for the EP but, as two inside observers remarked:

> A considerable body of opinion had come to believe that more radical proposals for amending the treaties were [also] necessary.... They simply did not think it [the 'small steps' strategy] would be sufficient. The fact that the decision to set up a new committee to consider treaty revision was taken the same day as the adoption of resolutions advocating incremental changes in institutional relations showed that the EP saw no contradiction in following both approaches.[95]

Initiatives, however, came from more than one direction and a peculiar conjunction of circumstances occurred about 1980–81 which also acted as a spur to renewed activity. Let us look briefly at these events and circumstances in order to obtain an overall picture of the evolving process of historical change.

That these years witnessed a widespread recognition of the need for significant change within the EC across an extensive range of issues and policies was clearly demonstrated by the European Council decision of 30 May 1980. This gave the Commission a mandate to examine existing policies, their financing and the budgetary problems they posed to certain member states. The acrimonious controversy over the UK's financial contribution to the Community budget may have been the main explanation for the European Council's decision, but it is more instructive to view this development from a longer perspective. The changing economic climate had a debilitating effect upon Community policies and served to expose and underline the deficiencies of the whole European enterprise. The development and subsequent deepening of the world recession from the early 1970s showed the Community to be wholly incapable of solving the major problems of the era such as chronic unemployment and monetary instability. This increasing awareness of its own impotence and the public image of incessant intergovernmental bickering sparked a bout of self-examination. The EC was on the defensive and had to be seen to be fighting back.

Indissolubly-linked to the Community's impotence caused by the world recession was its manifest inability to arrive at speedy and concordant decisions. Economic depression had served to emphasize the differences of interest among member states. Budgetary problems and the CAP in particular presented the Community decision-making process as a veritable war of attrition in which each state, or group of states, stood its ground with the sole intention of extracting concessions by wearing down its adversaries. The early 1980s seemed symptomatic of a deep and underlying lack of political commitment to act together to solve common problems. Criticisms inevitably gravitated towards the decision-making machinery itself. The sense of being continually locked in mortal combat over issues repeatedly conceived as zero-sum conflicts began to take its toll upon morale. In this sense the special problem of the UK's budgetary position merely sharpened the growing Community introspection and led to the gradual reappraisal of the totality of the European apparatus.

Consequently, the Commission did not interpret the 30 May Mandate as 'a mere accounting exercise'. Instead it chose to 'map out the major pathways towards a common relaunching of the European ideal'.[96] Gaston Thorn, the President of the Commission, diagnosed the Community's ills as lacking respect for the rules of democracy and, in particular, 'respect for the rule of majority'.[97] When the Commission's report was submitted to the European Council on 24 June 1981, it identified the following main areas as requiring immediate attention: tighter coordination of national monetary and economic policies; the expansion of the EMS; accelerating the shift toward a single market; a better coordination of national efforts and Community participation in solving energy problems; the promotion of investment in research and technology; and an active competition policy to bring about economic convergence. But Thorn urged that the Commission report should be seen as 'a comprehensive view both of the Community and of the way the institutions work'. The problem posed by the 30 May Mandate was 'much more than simply a difficult economic situation which could be solved purely by a change of machinery'. Indeed, it was 'the very existence of the Community that could ultimately be put at risk'.[98]

Commission thinking, therefore, extended beyond structural policy changes to include the institutional machinery of the Community. In this way, it assumed a positive participatory role in the intensified parliamentary debate about institutional reform in the summer of 1981. Its involvement in this great debate, and its subsequent declaration of support for improving inter-institutional relations, added weight to the conjunction of events and circumstances which promoted the relaunching of European Union.[99] But this advocacy of institutional reform – confined mainly to urging more majority voting in the Council of Ministers, improving the

Commission–EP dialogue and exploiting the EP's existing powers and procedural reforms to the full – did not extend to major treaty revision. Here,
the Commission trod warily. Thorn's position was cautious, advocating
new working methods for the institutions and reverting to the procedures
already laid down in the Treaties. If we stand back and take stock of the
events of these years, we can now understand precisely why there was a
renewed impetus for European Union. The EP, Commission and European Council had each, deliberately or unwittingly, assisted in that conjunction of developments which served to rekindle interest in the goal of
European Union. A series of separate initiatives and circumstances provided a fresh opportunity to make further progress. The coincidence
existed in the meeting-point of two separate developments during
1980–81: the culmination of a long parliamentary drive for institutional
reform and the decisive initiative of Altiero Spinelli. It was Spinelli whose
federalist strategy pushed the EP toward wholesale treaty amendments
beyond anything that the Commission dared to contemplate. We will
return to Spinelli's federalist initiative later in the chapter. For the
moment, let us turn our attention to another development in the quest
for European Union which it has been convenient to investigate separately. This is the Genscher–Colombo initiative which spanned the years
1981–83, and resulted in the 'Solemn Declaration on European Union'
agreed at the Stuttgart European Council of 19 June 1983.

## The Genscher–Colombo initiative, 1981–83

The public launching of the Genscher–Colombo plan to revitalize European Union occurred on 6 January 1981 at the Free Democrat Party's
(FDP) party congress in Stuttgart. It culminated in what eventually came
to be known as the 'Solemn Declaration on European Union' formally
agreed at the Stuttgart European Council of 19 June 1983. During this
short period of two-and-a-half years, it is important to remember that this
initiative which emanated from outside the established Community institutional framework ran parallel to the separate federalist enterprise of
Spinelli in the EP. Mindful of the purpose of this book, we do not intend
to present yet another detailed analysis of the origins, nature and purpose
of these fresh proposals other than to discuss their relationship to federalism and European Union. The details of these proposals and their evolution have already been researched.[100] It is useful, however, to set these
developments against the background of the events already discussed in
order to establish their place in the overall context of European Union in
this period.

There remains some element of mystery about Genscher's real motives
in activating this enterprise. As the West German Foreign Minister in the
SPD–FDP coalition led by Helmut Schmidt, Genscher may have been
driven by purely domestic party political concerns rather than by

high-minded European ideals.[101] Nonetheless, the proposals were presented officially as those of the Federal German government in coordination with the Italian government whose own Foreign Minister, Emilio Colombo, lent his name to the initiative.[102] A certain irony existed at the outset in their diagnosis of the EC's problems in the extent to which, as Joseph Weiler remarked, they themselves as prominent representatives of the intergovernmental Community apparatus were also part of these problems.[103] This institutional paradox was soon exposed as the source of the many difficulties and obstacles which they faced during their quest for European Union. And, as we shall see, it was scathingly underlined by many members of the EP, including Spinelli himself.

Since the so-called Draft European Act was first propelled into the Community framework in November 1981 – via a letter to all member states and the Commission, and by a formal presentation to the EP – it is convenient to use the ensuing parliamentary debate as an entrance to our discussions. Genscher's opening remarks were instructive. Echoing the deficiencies of Monnet's concept of Europe, Genscher called attention to the 'widespread hope that economic constraints would automatically bring about political unification' and dismissed it as 'illusory'. Clearly, political unification could be achieved only via a new political initiative, a strategic assertion which federalists like Spinelli had consistently made. The Community's major economic problems could not be solved without 'a definite political dimension'.[104] Genscher's analysis certainly did not indicate that he had become a convert to federalist strategy, but it served to emphasize yet again the fundamental dilemma of intergovernmentalists seeking to move from economic to political Europe.

Addressing himself to the concept of European Union, Genscher observed that it would become 'a special kind of entity not covered by the traditional concepts of the federal state or the confederation of states'. In the disarming language reminiscent of Tindemans, he referred to the intended European Act as formulating the aim of European Union to encompass the 'many-faceted process of the unification of European activities'.[105] Distilled as practical proposals, this meant a wholesale consolidation of existing Community practices and procedures which would provide an impetus for the further development of economic and political integration. The specific targets were an extension of political cooperation (POCO) and the consolidation of its procedures, together with the central decision-making structures of the Community under the aegis of the European Council; improved cooperation and dialogue between the major Community institutions, with particular emphasis upon the EP's participation and watchdog functions; the reassertion of majority voting in the Council of Ministers; and the inclusion of security policy in the Community's evolving POCO process. Additional institutional details spelled out new specialized ministerial councils, including culture and security, the strengthening of the presidency and the creation of a small, independent secretariat further to facilitate the POCO procedure. Arising mainly out of Italian priorities, there was also a draft declaration on questions of economic integration which emphasized *inter alia* the internal market, economic convergence, the further development of the EMS and the completion of the southerly enlargement of the Community.[106]

We will not examine in detail the content of each of these broad policy objectives here. It is worth directing the reader's attention to the significant emphasis placed upon both political cooperation and security issues, since this study does not attempt to grapple with these subjects. Evident progress in POCO had already been made by means of the London Report in 1981, which facilitated discussions about some political and economic aspects of security and inaugurated regular reports from the European Council Presidency to the EP.[107] It is also worth noting the congruence between the position of the Italian government and that of the Commission as revealed above in the 30 May Mandate. Italian and West German priorities were clearly never identical during this episode.[108]

The history and politics of this initiative served to confirm the worst fears and predictions of those, like Spinelli, who advocated a different strategy to achieve European Union. The Genscher–Colombo initiative suffered at the outset from a deliberate and purposive determination to downgrade and devalue its importance within the Community. Successive rebuttals by the European Council, the relative silence of the Commission and an aggressive posture by the EP, seeking stronger proposals combined to reduce its status from an 'Act' to a 'Solemn Declaration' by June 1983. A comparison of the original Draft European Act of 1981 with the Solemn Declaration of 1983 reveals precisely how far evisceration had occurred. The original contents of the proposal were effectively emptied both of substance and significance.[109] This disappointing conclusion to yet another genuine attempt to break out of the institutional paralysis which had come increasingly to characterize Community affairs in the early 1980s was particularly ironic when it is recalled that Genscher had already uttered a warning, in November 1981, against ambitious intentions:

> We have deliberately confined our draft European Act to proposals which we believe are capable of producing a consensus among the member states in the present circumstances. Rather than saying what we would like to happen, we have tried to formulate what we believe to be feasible. We have learned from past failed initiatives that unification can only be achieved as a result of a continuous step-by-step approach, and that any premature attempt to make a great leap forward is more likely to put us back to a point behind our original starting point.[110]

He had first wanted a solid treaty, legally and politically binding, consolidating existing Community achievements, but had abandoned the idea as 'little short of unrealistic'. And it was also intended that, five years after the signing of the proposed European Act, the member states would subject it to a review 'in the light of the aim of a treaty on European Union'. Colombo, too, had viewed the intended Act as 'a new phase of dynamism in the building of Europe', which would lead eventually to its revision and the participation of the EP in preparing a 'draft treaty on European Union'.[111] These hopes and beliefs, which collapsed in the intergovernmental bear-pit of the European Council in 1982–83, were soon to be resurrected in a different arena in 1984.

Let us look not at the Draft European Act or at its pale legacy in the shape of the Solemn Declaration, but at Spinelli's federalist critique of the whole enterprise. There is no doubt that the fate of the initiative was precisely what Spinelli had expected. In the EP in 1981, he had already warned Genscher about intergovernmental sabotage. Very little progress would come from national elites whose limited vision was yet more intergovernmental cooperation, lacking both substance and durability. His attack upon this approach to European Union was trenchant:

> In your 'Act' you call for the setting up of an army of councils, committees and subcommittees as part of a preposterous secretariat whose structure and location will not be fixed. In other words you want to create a leviathan of a bureaucracy but manned only by intergovernmental agents. And when this monster of committees and boards has chewed everything over and disgorged it, you believe that each member state is going to tot up the political experience acquired.[112]

This was vintage Spinelli. He was adamant that only the EP could have risen above this aggregative arithmetical experience as the only genuine constituent body capable of a vision going beyond what existed. Europe could not be built using the same old tools.

Both Genscher and Colombo were fully aware of the EP's own separate intiative for European Union and of the many searching criticisms of their proposals. Parliamentary support was evident but qualified. Not unnaturally, the main concern of the EP was to ensure that no discussions by the Council, in the wake of the Genscher–Colombo proposals, would be taken about its own future role without the EP itself being involved. Otherwise there seemed to be little cause for concern about the duality of the two initiatives. They were deemed not to be in direct competition with each other. Indeed, Genscher reaffirmed his own belief, first stated publicly in December 1981, that the Draft Act he advanced with Colombo would be an initial step in the direction toward the revision of the Treaties already being pursued by the EP.[113] This interpretation undoubtedly gained credence during 1982 as the original Draft Act lost its impetus and was gradually watered down to innocuous proportions. By October 1982, the Commission claimed that to accept the diluted version of the Act would have been insufficient. Its task was also to 'trigger off a series of decisions' which would 'bring the European idea a step forward in practical terms', such as in agriculture and budgetary policies, and to provide the starting point for more far-reaching institutional reforms. Policy and institutional reform were in this way indissolubly linked.[114]

Looking back from the vantage point of the end of the century, we can see that the Genscher–Colombo episode was in some respects a variation on the theme of de Gaulle's earlier 'Political Union' but without the French bravado: foreign policy and security were its main concerns. But it is difficult to view the Genscher–Colombo initiative as anything more than yet another piecemeal intergovernmental milestone on the road toward a more pronounced intergovernmental Europe. The best that can be said for it is that it helped to intensify the debate about Europe's future, and raised some of the fundamental issues surrounding the process of European integration. It also furnished some useful minor improvements in Community procedures, such as the onus on the European Council to submit an annual report to the EP on progress toward European Union.[115] And perhaps its enduring legacy lay in the extent to which some of its concerns, like POCO, were later to be fully incorporated in the SEA in 1987.

It is also clear in retrospect that Genscher and Colombo were doomed to fail from the very beginning. Their initiative was well-intentioned but it never secured the necessary support from the Heads of Government whose different priorities and motivations were gradually revealed as the concrete implications of closer political integration became clear. Indeed, as we have already noted, it was not certain that Italian and West German interests were identical. The Genscher–Colombo initiative seemed to underline, once again, the narrow limits of an intergovernmental strategy. And this, of course, was what lay at the heart of the federalist critique. Mauro Ferri, the first chairman of the EP's new Committee of Institutional Affairs, summarised this inherent strategic weakness in unequivocal terms:

> On the course we have taken no form of consultation with the Council of Ministers and the Commission is possible.... The work itself ... will be carried out in complete autonomy. The institutional committee expressed no judgement on the Genscher–Colombo Act. This was not its job. Moreover, the Act is situated on a different plane and it is part of a different philosophy: that of 'small steps' to be taken by the governments through common declarations of intention in the context of the Treaties, ... without exploring the possibilities of modifying the Treaties themselves.... The fact is ... that beyond the good intentions ... the approach ... is not feasible; it cannot produce the desired results.[116]

Spinelli's conclusion was equally damning. The Genscher–Colombo proposals were futile. Their realistic, pragmatic approach merely repeated the same mistakes made a decade earlier when European Union was first enunciated. They were now confronted with the unpleasant realities of their strategy. Spinelli's federalist analysis pinpointed this error: they were in a dilemma not because of their aims but because of the means they proposed to achieve them.[117] With these remarks, we can conveniently bring our discussion of the Genscher–Colombo episode to a close. Spinelli had unmasked what he considered to be the strategic self-deception of well-intentioned but myopic Europeans. In order for real progress to be made toward achieving European Union, the old methods would have to be set aside. At best they furnished hope and some minor improvements; at worst they were demoralising and sterile. Having looked at the congested contextual background of the early 1980s, it is time to devote some attention to the activities of Spinelli and the EP in their joint quest to define and distil the meaning of European Union in 1984. We will begin with a short introduction about Spinelli's federal strategy. This amounts to a reprise of our earlier analysis and discussion about Monnet and Spinelli in Chapter 2.

## Spinelli, federalism and the European Union Treaty, 1984

Spinelli's contemporary political actions in the early 1980s must be set in historical context. The intellectual origins of his federal ideas stretched back at least to the inter-war years and were a testimony to a long progeniture. We will not investigate these origins here because they have already been analysed and explained elsewhere.[118] It is important, nonetheless, to recognise their significance because they underline the existence of a strong, unbroken continuity of federal ideas, influences and strategies for building Europe, of which the EP's European Union Treaty (EUT) was simply the latest manifestation. To trace the life and career of Altiero Spinelli is to uncover the links between the inter-war years and the post-war era in terms of European integration. The continuity of political ideas is quite remarkable and they furnish the basis for demonstrating that the Europe that would be built would become, in an incremental but unerring step-by-step process, a federal Europe.

We have already seen that the early 1980s were construed by most informed observers of Community affairs as a period of great anxiety and despair. Spinelli, too, viewed them as a 'state of profound crisis' for the Community, but they afforded an opportunity to be exploited.[119] In a letter dated 25 June 1980, which was circulated to all MEPs, Spinelli launched his initiative for European Union with the idea of the EP assuming a constituent role as the legitimate voice of the people of Europe. He warned his colleagues that each intergovernmental solution to the Community's major structural and resource problems had only 'a temporary character', and that its existing institutions, procedures and competences condemned it to 'pass through more and more frequent paralysing crises'. In these circumstances, the EP had to act and seek compromise in a 'European perspective and not one that would be only the sum of the national ones'. Reform of the Community's institutions was too serious to be left in the hands of statesmen and diplomats'.[120] The letter outlined a lucid federalist strategy for proposing a new draft treaty for European Union which both modified and integrated the existing treaties and would be ratified by the national parliaments of the member states. The initial response must have been disappointing to Spinelli since only eight members from various political groups and nationalities responded, but it marked the practical origins of a huge mobilization of parliamentary support for European Union which culminated in 1984 in the EUT. Meeting in the Crocodile restaurant in Strasbourg on 9 July 1980, the nine MEPs agreed upon both the goal and the strategy required to achieve it. Subsequently, it was decided to form a club in order to exert pressure in the respective transnational political groups of the EP, and in this way the new Crocodile Club was founded, taking its name from the Strasbourg restaurant.

In their research on 'The Crocodile Initiative', Rita Cardozo and Richard Corbett have already provided us with a detailed analysis of how the EP set up the new Committee on Institutional Affairs which began its work on the draft treaty in January 1982.[121] We shall not duplicate their work. It is sufficient for our purpose here to remind ourselves of the peculiar conjunction of circumstances and events which combined to exert pressure for both new and old attempts to flesh out the meaning of European Union so ambiguously enunciated in 1972.

It is clear that, from 1982, the evolution of European Union was predominantly a trial of strength between federalism and intergovernmentalism. From a strategic standpoint, Spinelli had finally reached the position for which he had been struggling for most of his life. He had arrived at the destination of his long journey in the Community experience which dated back almost to its beginning in the early attempts to establish the European Defence Community (EDC) and the European Political Community (EPC) in 1953. Given the many compromises which he had made, the EUT was certainly not his own ideal model for Europe, nor was it intended to be the final goal of European unification. But it was probably the best achievement which he could have secured in the circumstances of the early 1980s. We shall not enter into a detailed discussion of every clause of the new draft treaty. This subject has already been well-researched.[122] Instead, we will concentrate our attentions upon the federalist ideas and influences which permeated both the letter and the spirit of the EP's text. First, however, it is appropriate to return to the role of Spinelli in mobilizing a large parliamentary support for what was tantamount to yet another of those federalist initiatives in post-war European political development.

It is important to distinguish between the EUT itself and the political environment out of which it emerged. The political weight which was accorded the new treaty can be attributed to Spinelli. It was his single-minded determination and clarity of purpose which laid down the formula which should be the basis for future action. Earlier efforts by the EP and the Commission had encapsulated the goal of European Union, but had never spelled out both a clear purposive strategy or an end to be attained. Spinelli had the purpose, the energy, the strategy and the breadth of vision necessary to push the EP towards a new treaty via the various resolutions required to achieve it during 1981–83. His own personal charisma, influence and reputation both within and without the EP enabled him to gather widespread support for the project which initially did not look promising in the circumstances of the time. This particular role he played was vital and cannot be exaggerated. And, in this sense, his contribution to the movement for European Union was more important than the actual imprint he stamped upon the content of the EUT itself.

It was much easier to persuade the EP to agree to the general principle of European Union than it was to obtain a majority in support of a specific treaty. This was Spinelli's great achievement, and it enabled the EP to travel a long way in a short time. From a minority position and stigmatised by some as having the Communist label, Spinelli had to convince parliamentary opinion to overcome its reluctance to commit itself to a formal treaty. This was a formidable task. It was not like seeking to obtain support for human rights in Afghanistan or Nicaragua but, instead, of mobilizing a majority in favour of a particular concept of European integration which was simultaneously competing with the EP's own, more familiar strategy of 'small steps' toward European Union. The agenda for institutional reform was already crowded. Parliamentary opinion concerning a new treaty was, at best, lukewarm. Spinelli had to put enormous physical and intellectual weight into uniting MEPs behind the treaty. Once this decisive momentum had been achieved, and the project kept in the public limelight, of course, parliamentarians gradually began to accept responsibility for it and incorporate it in public debate over a period of time. The longer it was debated, the more it acquired a dynamic of its own and, correspondingly, the less the enterprise needed Spinelli.

Without wishing to labour the point, it is worth underlining the parliamentary context in which Spinelli struggled to mobilize support. His federalist reputation certainly generated stiff competition in the federalist-minded EPP, and it has to be emphasized categorically that he encountered a rivalry rooted in jealousy from several quarters – jealousy of his impeccable federalist credentials, of his capacity to successfully convince and persuade people to support his cause, and of his renowned personal contacts. Few MEPs, after all, possessed the esteem which he had, for example, to obtain a personal reply of substance from the French President, François Mitterrand. Only Monnet, as we have seen, could rival him in this respect. It would probably be an exaggeration to suggest that such rivalries stretched to actual sabotage, but their very existence scarcely smoothed his own path towards European Union.

A good example of the unremitting presence of alternative ideas and strategies was the model constitution proposed by the EPP which envisaged the Community of Ten transformed into a federal state. Dated 13 September 1983, this draft constitution was timed to coincide with the EP's vote on the substance of the preliminary draft treaty emanating from the Committee on Institutional Affairs.[123] Tabled by two West German Christian Democrats, Rudolf Luster and Gero Pfennig, the authors of the new constitution for Europe denied that theirs was a counter-proposal to the work of the Committee on Institutional Affairs. They presented it as a useful model which indicated the form that the final objective of European Union might take. It was to be viewed ostensibly as a contribution by the EPP which would provide criteria establishing at each stage whether the EUT was along the right lines. This meant that the yardstick by which the EUT should have been judged was a federation.

It remains difficult in hindsight to regard this EPP initiative so late in the day as anything other than mischief. The bulk of the work on the draft treaty had already been completed. Pending the necessary parliamentary majority, all that was required was a final text to be drawn up in legal form by the four lawyers appointed by the EP. A generous interpretation of the EPP's motives would emphasize their own dissatisfaction with the EUT and their legitimate concern to ensure that certain key matters were not omitted from the final text. There was some basis for this argument. When the draft treaty was formally adopted by the EP on 14 February 1984 (237 votes in favour, 31 against and 43 abstentions), several criticisms of its content were made by EPP members. And it is significant that in the Lusters/Pfennig proposal cited above, there had been a whole section devoted to listing basic human rights and freedoms – something absent from the EUT.[124] Leaving this aside, it nonetheless has to be said that the EPP did to some extent hamper the work of the Committee of Institutional Affairs. Ortensio Zecchino, the EPP rapporteur responsible for institutional aspects of the EUT in the Committee on Institutional Affairs, was particularly troublesome in his eccentric insistence upon floating new proposals and using overtly federalist rhetoric which was far too ambitious and divisive. The Italian lawyer and university professor even managed to exasperate Spinelli, who regarded his temporary absence from the committee during the final voting on institutions as 'divine intervention' in their favour.[125] Zecchino's ideas and the Luster/Pfennig model constitution both serve once again to illustrate the continuity and resilience of federalism in the drive for European Union, but they also underline the distinction between what was desirable and what was feasible. Federalists were sometimes too detailed when it paid to be general and too vague when clarity was necessary. It was to Spinelli's credit that he understood perfectly the delicate relationship between these two conflicting imperatives.

What, then, should we say about the EUT itself? In what sense did it incorporate federalist ideas and influences? The EUT which the EP adopted in February 1984 was carefully constructed upon the existing Community apparatus. It was built upon the *acquis communautaire*, thus respecting the legal and political continuity between the existing Treaties and the new union. Nowhere did controversial terms like 'federation' or 'European government' appear in the text. Not only was the Community patrimony accepted as the starting point for the union – beginning, as Spinelli had always said, with what had already been implemented – but the same institutions were the basis of the EUT. Institutional continuity was, therefore, also deliberately preserved.

The EUT took the form of an international treaty which required ratification by the appropriate constitutional authorities within the member states. Spinelli devised an ingenious means by which to prevent national elites from grasping the treaty first and watering it down to insignificant proportions. Avoiding the conventional use of Article 236 of the Rome Treaty, which would have placed the EUT's destiny in the hands of the customary guardians of national sovereignty, Spinelli prolonged the possibilities of the new treaty's survival with the intention that it would be carried along by the momentum of a majority of member states unhindered by minority opposition. In short, his strategy centred upon the ability to give clear expression to the will of the majority. Here the unanimity required by Article 236, effectively giving any single member state the power to veto the project and bring the whole enterprise to a halt, was circumvented and replaced by a majoritarian formula enabling the EUT journey to proceed by overcoming the usual obstacles inherent in narrow national perspectives. This federalist strategy, consistent throughout Spinelli's long career, raised more than a few legal eyebrows and provided fertile ground for a number of labyrinthine legal arguments and interpretations.[126] The preamble and the 87 articles of the EUT, for the first time, were to encapsulate that hitherto elusive common European political will which had been only intermittently present during the previous forty years of the European construction.

In order for future progress to be guaranteed, the EUT altered the institutional balance of the Community by revising the competences, in particular, of the Commission, EP, European Council and Council of Ministers. Crucial to these changes, however, was the inclusion of the key principle of subsidiarity which had been part and parcel of Catholic social theory for centuries and had permeated the post-war ranks of the Christian Democratic parties throughout Europe. Despite its origins and Spinelli's own personal indifference to the use of the term itself, 'subsidiarity' was incorporated in the EUT in Article 12(2). The principle emphasized that the Union would act only in those areas that could be dealt with in common more effectively than by the member states acting separately. Briefly stated, Union law could lay down only 'the fundamental principles governing common action' and would 'entrust the responsible authorities in the Union or the Member States with setting out in detail the procedures for their implementation'.[127] Mindful of the dilemma confronting federalists in their pursuit of federation, namely, of advocating movement in a unitary direction without seeking a unitary state, this principle was crucial.[128] It was a definitive answer to those critics who repeatedly pointed the finger of excessive centralization at federalist intentions. Articles 12 and 34 were designed to ensure that the Union did not become a centralized leviathan encroaching upon national sensitivities.

As a direct extension of the existing Community, the Union was intended to complement the member states not to substitute for them. Consequently, an important distinction was made between those areas where the Union had exclusive competence to act (as at present, for example, competition policy and customs duties) and those areas in which the Union and member states had concurrent competences. Should the Union wish to initiate or extend common action in a new field, it could do so only via qualified majority approval by each branch of the legislature – designated in the EUT as the EP and the Council. Furthermore Article 11(2) was important to prevent what Juliet Lodge called 'creeping intergovernmentalism' characteristic of the EC: 'in the fields subject to common action, common action may not be replaced by cooperation'.[129] The ever-present temptation to fall back upon intergovernmental solutions was thus effectively thwarted. In general, the EUT established a single institutional system which would incorporate all of those fields formerly subject to Community competence and those subject to cooperation, or intergovernmentalism, among member states while maintaining both the methods of cooperation and common action.

In this short sketch of common action, cooperation and the subsidiarity principle, we can already detect the underlying distinctions and relationships that typify conventional federations. A more detailed analysis of the EUT would reveal further federal elements, and those who wish to pursue this search can be profitably directed to the main texts already identified at the beginning of this chapter. Meanwhile, let us look briefly at the institutional relationships laid down in the EUT. Given what we already know about Spinelli's own intellectual background, it came as no surprise to learn that standard Western liberal democratic notions of parliamentary representation, constitutional and judicial guarantees and legislative–executive relations were the hallmark of the institutional provisions. No radical restructuring of the institutional framework was intended but a major modification of the legislative power was proposed. It was shared jointly by the Council of the Union and the EP, thus providing two arms of the legislative authority akin to traditional federal practice whereby democratic accountability was assured to citizens as members both of the European Union and of their member state. The imposition of majority voting procedures and deadlines was deemed of vital importance in order, once again, to ensure that, at the end of the day, a firm decision guaranteeing positive action would be taken instead of the all-too-familiar inertia so characteristic of contemporary Community practice. The EP's elevation to the legislative arena was, of course, entirely in keeping with its recently-acquired democratic legitimacy derived from having been directly elected. Its elevation, therefore, remedied, at least in part, the so-called 'democratic deficit' in Community affairs and, apart from the additional advantage of combating the notorious deficiencies in decision-making mentioned above, it also created a new accountability of both the Council and the Commission to the elected body of the European Union. Finally the new Council–EP relationship also included the ratification of international treaties and agreements, thereby, in part, foreshadowing an important aspect of the subsequent SEA.

If we reflect broadly upon the Council–EP linkage in the EUT – one that had been consistently sought by the EP, at least as far back as the Kirk–Reay Report of 1974 – it would appear that the EP had been the main beneficiary of a significant shift in institutional relationships. But, if we turn our attention to the reform of the Commission's role, we obtain a somewhat different picture. Spinelli always remarked that something very important had been obscured in the public discussions about the EUT. If we recall his original intentions and beliefs analysed in Chapter 2, we will also remember that it was, in reality, the Commission, not the EP, which was central to his conception of European Union. His own explanation was tantalisingly simple:

> If a parliament does not have a Government it is a source of chaos; the really important problem – the first one – is the King.... The King is the political element ... in our case we must have the real nucleus of a European Government because the most important thing is the authority we have given to the Commission in the formation of the Community. If we have this, then this is the political centre; in order to have it democratic Parliament is necessary.[130]

Here was a paradox which Spinelli was convinced the majority of parliamentarians had failed fully to grasp: normally, parliaments attempt to check the power of the executive whereas the EP sought consciously to increase it. By strengthening the Commission, the EP would also be strengthened. Hence by altering the Community's institutional balance in favour of the Commission and the EP, the two main pivots of supranationalism, the 'common elaboration' would be released to develop and determine itself.

How, then, did the EUT reform the Commission? First it established a clear link between its term of office and the term of the EP. The Commission's tenure was extended from four to five years, appointed after each European parliamentary election which would consequently raise the political profile of both institutions as well as the elections themselves. But the method of the Commission's appointment, deemed by one friendly critic to be 'a somewhat awkward procedure', involved the designation of its President by the European Council and the subsequent selection of other Commission members by the new President.[131] Finally, the whole Commission was to be invested by the EP on the strength of its programme. The EUT did not alter the Commission's power to initiate legislation, nor its executive power to implement it, and it was guaranteed a voice in the new legislative process. The EP's underlying assumption in this novel triangular institutional relationship was that 'the President of the Commission, whose authority originated from the European Council, would seek an understanding with Parliament on the choice of his colleagues' and it seems clear in retrospect that the architects of the EUT wanted 'to turn the Commission into an executive vested with real authority', authority derived from its manner of appointment via governments and citizens.[132]

The European Council emerged relatively unchanged in appearance but not entirely unscathed. It retained its authority for intergovernmental cooperation and its supremacy in international affairs, and it acquired the decisive power to determine the transfer of areas of cooperation to common action. Its formal incorporation in the EUT, however, seems to have been something of a puzzle. Roland Bieber claimed that it was included 'somewhat reluctantly', while Lodge suggested that its accommodation actually entailed a distinct diminution in its power to initiate legislative proposals.[133] Whatever conclusions are drawn from these observations, part of the answer to this apparent conundrum lay in one simple fact: the European Council was not really a European *institution qua institution* at all but a cumbersome device for patching together intergovernmental compromises. The EUT merely exposed its expedient quality.

We shall now make a few general observations about the EUT, before commenting upon its relationship to federal ideas and influences. Our survey has been far from exhaustive, but it does enable us to obtain a general picture of the EP's interpretation of European Union in the mid-1980s. One outstanding question of controversy resided in Article 23(3) which confirmed member states' right of veto in the Council of the Union – a right designed to extend over a transitional period of ten years. It requires little imagination to appreciate how far this decision was the product of heated compromise. It satisfied few participants. Even Thorn found it difficult to swallow, perpetuating as it did the very principle the Commission had fought against for nearly two decades. Other aspects of the EUT which generated fierce criticism for being either too ambitious or too anaemic were Article 38, dealing with complicated voting procedures for draft laws, Article 82 concerning the legal and political imbroglio of the treaty's entry into force, and the conspicuous silence of the treaty concerning security matters. These complaints, however, had to be set against the overall content of the EUT which stood in perspective as having 'an appealing internal balance and a surprising modesty in its reformism'.[134]

Given the Community patrimony, the retention of familiar institutional identities within a single institutional system, the maintenance of intergovernmentalism and the principle of subsidiarity, the EUT could hardly be described as a blueprint for a European federation. Paulo Barbi, the EPP President in 1983, summed up his interpretation of the new treaty in lucid terms:

> This proposal does not do away with the sovereignty of our states, it does not set up a federation, ... it does not create the United States of Europe; but it does lay the institutional basis for that European Union which our political leaders said they wanted to bring about ten years ago.[135]

This view of the EP's project was endorsed by Zecchino in a perhaps unusually modest statement:

> It will not be a federation for the fundamental reason that the member states will retain their sovereignty, but it will have important federal characteristics, 'such as the complexity and subdivision of the institutional system (with a directly elected parliamentary body) and the possibility of taking legal action which, in given cases, may be of immediate concern to the citizens of the member states.[136]

But it was obviously wrong to underestimate the degree of change inherent in the EUT. The key Article 38 set out a new legislative procedure involving a bicameral system of codecision by the EP and the Council, together with a series of deadlines, albeit flexible ones, for each stage of the legislative process, and specific majorities for voting in both institutions. The EUT could accurately be described as a federal document only in the extent to which it enhanced the decision-making capacity of the Union. Lodge claimed that 'the institutional set-up envisaged for European Union accords with a vision of a federal system of open government and representative democracy in which an elected chamber plays a pivotal role scrutinising and controlling the executive and legislating for the people on the basis of the majority views of the "common good", instead of according to a blocking minority of national interests'.[137]

Rival interpretations may have been just as valid. The EUT, after all, claimed no competence in the fields traditionally associated with a federal authority: defence, foreign policy, currency and the money supply, and internal security. Institutionally much remained unchanged. The Commission retained its powers of initiation and implementation, the Council remained the dominant authority despite having to share its legislative role with the EP and acknowledge formally in specific areas the supremacy of the European Council, and the three existing Community treaties remained valid in so far as they had not been either modified or superseded by the EUT. How, then, should we assess the EUT in the light of federalist ideas and influences? Was the spectre of a federal Europe in this treaty a myth or a reality?

At the levels of political ideas and political strategy, the federalist impetus was unmistakable. Here the search for a distinctive federal imprint in the EUT should not be confined solely to the examination of political institutions and legislative competences. This would overlook, and thereby underestimate, the federalist influences and aspirations which lay at the root of the treaty. The absence of federation should not blind us to the presence of federalism. The EUT could conceivably be assessed as a case of federalism without federation. But our conclusion must not be allowed to end so abruptly. There is another important observation which must be made before we investigate the intergovernmental response to this remarkable episode in the EP's recent history.

The basic ingredient of the EUT was not just that it was a political document which reflected a broad consensus of European parliamentary opinion, but that it contained within it the cornerstone of Spinelli's federalist strategy: an essential dynamic which would enable the Community to break out of Monnet's Europe. In short, it provided the means by which the Community could go beyond what existed. This is also why Spinelli's role in the whole enterprise would have declined in direct proportion to the success of what, at the beginning, was his project. The EUT was indeed wisely moderate, gradualist and pragmatic. Derek Prag remarked that it contained nothing federalist and that such hopes had been deeply disappointed precisely because of its practical and realistic content.[138] But the key to understanding the full implications of the EUT was to realise that it presupposed a decisive quality leap. The EUT represented the embryo of an overall political system with its own political legitimacy. In a general sense, it proposed a structure, seemingly harmless, with little actual power, but with considerable potential power, having a full legitimacy of its own. Here was a profound difference in conceptual approach from what already existed. The Rome and Paris Treaties had been suffocated and stifled by pragmatic intergovernmental cooperation. The EUT provided the mechanism for the nurturing of that autonomous European political life which Spinelli had persistently sought to cultivate for over 40 years.

The construction of the EUT was significant from a number of different standpoints.[139] Even so-called 'pragmatism' – reputed to be open-minded and amenable to experimentation – could not justifiably exclude the EP's attempt to make the existing Community institutions more effective. Using pragmatic terms of reference, it was simply nonsense for member state governments and other national elites to continually complain that the EC did not work properly while, at the same time, opposing genuine efforts to make it operate more effectively. The EUT was not a take-it-or-leave-it proposition, but a basis for agreement between the member state governments. It remained to be seen how they would respond.

Spinelli, of course, knew that the EP's treaty, having survived for so long by being kept out of the hands of national elites, would ultimately be compelled to confront both the governments and parliaments of the member states in order to seek their approval. This was as it should have been. And this, as he often remarked, was when the real battle for the Union would begin in earnest. The EUT had been launched into the intergovernmental arena where its future was uncertain. It was now set on a different course from that originally envisaged. We will shortly turn our attention to the intergovernmental response to the EUT, but first let us summarize the period which Richard Griffiths has dubbed 'The stagnant decade'.[140]

## Conclusion: The dawn of a new era

The years between 1973 and 1984 were predominantly an era of Euro-pessimism. National strategies for economic growth had failed to rescue member states and Europe was in the grip of what many politicians and economists had traditionally thought of as a contradiction in terms, namely, 'stagflation'. The old Keynesian model of national economic development, with its associated political bargains, no longer provided Europe with a formula guaranteed to bring about economic prosperity. National responses to the long-term structural changes in the global economy after the oil shock of 1973 were simply bankrupt. The comfortable post-war political strategy of assuming governmental responsibility for full employment and the provision of the welfare state in most of Western Europe had run its course. Everywhere there seemed to be anguish and despair at the apparent impotence of the national state to provide an effective response to the changed western political economy. It was, in hindsight, the end of an era.

Perception in politics is more important than reality, and it is usually difficult to detect with precision when the old era has crumbled. The signs are often confusing; they sometimes point to short-term revivals. In retro-spect, it is clear that these years signalled the failure of the national state in Europe to cope effectively with these new circumstances, but it also underlined the absence of a concerted European response. Member state governments were not yet ready to pool their energies and resources into a genuine European strategy, while the Community did not have the institutions, powers and competences necessary to respond with a coherent and robust solution. In the EC, intergovernmentalism reigned supreme over integration.

What relevance did federalism have in these difficult circumstances and why did the EUT emerge in the early 1980s? What, in short, did it signify?

We should remember that the European Council did act in 1980 to provoke a supra-national response from the Commission with the 30 May Mandate. And it should also be remembered that many of the recommendations of the Commission, such as the tighter coordination of national economic and monetary policies and the sharper focus upon the single market, contained remedies which were to be implemented by the Community and by the member states acting together in intergovernmental fashion only later, in the era of Jaques Delors. In other words, the political strategies and economic responses to the new political economy were evident in the early 1980s, but the political will of the member states and the capacity of the Community to be able to act effectively were absent.

The federalists believed that only by Europe having the capacity to go beyond what existed would it have any hope of reaching a concerted integrationist solution to contemporary economic problems. The EUT must be seen in this light as being the first stage in the empowerment of the Community to respond effectively to these problems. Apart from the enormous influence of Spinelli, the Commission and the EP, the emergence of the EUT should also be construed as a direct response to Spinelli's 'state of profound crisis'. The EUT signified once again the impotence of intergovernmentalism, the failure of the national state to solve the problems of the age, and the dawn of a new era. Looking back upon the history of this episode, we can now appreciate fully the real significance of the EUT. But like so many of these events in the evolution of the EC, the alarming lack of vision and the failure of member state governments to understand that these problems were common problems which required common solutions were the consequences of the narrow national mindset.

From the Tindemans Report, direct elections to the EP, the reports of Spierenberg and the Three Wise Men and the Genscher–Colombo Solemn Declaration to the EP's draft treaty and the EUT, we can identify clearly the significance of federalism and the federalists. As with the Tindemans Report, the EUT embodied an enduring legacy for the European construction. Both were visionary with far-sighted proposals and long-term goals many of which were later to be implemented by member state governments as if they were novel intergovernmental solutions. In reality, the road to Damascus had been signposted by the federalists much earlier.

Today, both the Tindemans Report and the EUT have been largely forgotten. It is nonetheless uncanny how far so many of their ideas and proposals have been implemented to take their place as part and parcel of the evolving European Union. The principle of subsidiarity, for example, was to be incorporated first rather modestly in the SEA and later, much more robustly, in the TEU, while it was consolidated in the TA only in 1997. Meanwhile the federalization of the appointment procedures for the Commission President and of codecision for the EP finally saw the light of day in the TEU and TA in the 1990s. In the public fuss and fanfare of notorious intergovernmental bargains, however, these considerations are usually overlooked. What was yesterday's unthinkable eccentricity is often today's practical convention. In these circumstances, the past clearly has a future.

It is time to shift our focus of attention away from the era of Euro-pessimism and toward the age of Euro-dynamism. It was no accident that this new age coincided with a new sense of purpose and direction in the EC nor that its chief inspiration and prime motivator, Jacques Delors, was a confirmed federalist.

## NOTES

1  C. Franck, 'New ambitions: from the Hague to Paris summits', in R. Pryce (ed.), *The dynamics of European union*, pp. 145–46, London: Croom Helm, 1987.

2  A. Spinelli, *The European adventure*, London: Charles Knight & Co. Ltd, 1972, p. 21.

3  R.T. Griffiths, '1958–1973', in K. Middlemas, *Orchestrating Europe: the informal politics of European union, 1973–1995*, p. 70, London: Fontana Press, 1995.

4  R.T. Griffiths, 'The stagnant decade, 1973–83', in *Orchestrating Europe*, p. 72.

5  S. Hoffmann, 'The European Community and 1992', in S. Hoffmann (ed.), *The European sisyphus: essays on Europe. 1964–1994*, p. 231, Boulder, CO: West-view Press, 1995.

6  P. Taylor, *The limits of European integration*, London: Croom Helm, 1983, p. 60.

7  This is now the conventional interpretation of the decade of the 1970s. Apart from the sources identified above, see P.M.R. Stirk, *A history of European integration since 1914*, London: Pinter, 1996, pp. 187–94.

8  A. Morgan, *From summit to council: evolution in the EEC*, London: PEP, Chatham House, 1976, pp. 18–19.

9  H. Simonian, *The privileged partnership: Franco-German relations in the European Community, 1969–1984*, Oxford: Clarendon Press, 1985, p. 259.

10  Extracts from the communique issued after the Paris meeting of heads of state and government, 10 December 1974, *Bulletin of the European Communities (EC)*, 12, pp. 7–12, 1974.

11  P. Taylor, *The limits of European integration*, p. 75.

12  P. Taylor, *The limits of European integration*, p. 70.

13  H. Simonian, *The privileged partnership*, p. 349.

14  S. Bulmer and W. Wessels, *The European Council: decision-making in European politics*, London: Macmillan, 1987, p. 46.

15  S. Bulmer and W. Wessels, *The European Council*, pp. 45–6.

16  See W. Brandt, *People and politics: the years 1960–1975*, London: Collins, 1970, p. 267 and C. Franck, 'New ambitions', in R. Pryce (ed.), *The dynamics of European union*, p. 145.

17  These EC reports have been gathered together and republished in *Selection of texts concerning institutional matters of the Community from 1950–1982*, Luxembourg: European Parliament, 1982, pp. 304–65. I have obtained an unofficial translation of the Spierenburg Report from the Dutch Embassy in London. More conveniently, each of these reports has been discussed separately in P. Taylor, *When Europe speaks with one voice: the external relations of the European Community*, London: Aldwych Press, 1979, pp. 27–41.

18  He consulted over a thousand people and about 200 organizations. The personalities and organizations met are identified in the *Annex to the Tindemans report, memo from Belgium: views and surveys,* No. 171. Brussels: Ministry of Foreign Affairs, 1976.

19  *The Spierenburg Report,* London: Dutch Embassy, 1975, p. 3.

20  *The Spierenburg Report,* pp. 6–7.

21  Interview with Spinelli, 14 February 1985, European Parliament, Strasbourg.

22  Point 16 of the final communique, sixth General Report, *Bulletin of the EC,* 10, part one, chap. one, 1972.

23  The report has been republished in *Selection of texts,* pp. 308–41.

24  *Selection of texts,* p. 315.

25  A. Spinelli, *The European adventure,* p. 176.

26  A. Spinelli, *The European adventure,* p. 26.

27  *Selection of texts,* p. 329.

28  For details of these models, see *Selection of texts,* pp. 330–2.

29  *Selection of texts,* pp. 340–2.

30  *The Tindemans report, memo from Belgium,* pp. 12–14.

31  *The Tindemans report, Text of letter to the European Council,* p. 4, 29 December 1975.

32  J. Vandamme, 'The Tindemans report, (1975–1976)', R. Pryce (ed.), in *The dynamics of European Union,* pp. 149–60.

33  *The Tindemans report, memo from Belgium,* p. 45.

34  For the complete institutional recommendations, see *The Tindemans report, memo from Belgium,* pp. 45–54.

35  Such was the opinion of the study group set up by the University Association of Contemporary European Studies (UACES) to analyse the Tindemans Report. See the *Report of UACES study group on European union,* London: King's College, 1976, p. 13.

36  P. Taylor, *When Europe speaks with one voice,* pp. 27–8.

37  S. Henig, *Power and decision in Europe: the political institutions of the European Community,* London: Euro-potentials Press, 1980, pp. 109–10.

38  J.D.B. Mitchell, 'The Tindemans report: retrospect and prospect', *The Common Market Law Review,* 13, pp. 455–84, 1976.

39  J. Vandamme, *The Tindemans report,* pp. 166–7.

40  *The Tindemans report, text of letter to the European Council,* p. 4.

41  Interview with Spinelli, 14 February 1985.

42  H. Simonian, *The privileged partnership,* p. 262. On Brandt's continued support for European union, see J. Vandamme, 'The Tindemans report', pp. 163–4.

43  L. Tindemans, 'The future of Europe', address to the foreign affairs club, London, press report, 7 December 1976.

44  *The Tindemans report, memo from Belgium,* p. 31.

45  *The Tindemans report, memo from Belgium,* p. 27.

46  *The Tindemans report, memo from Belgium,* p. 14.

47  A. Spinelli, *The eurocrats: conflict and crisis in the European Community,* Baltimore: Johns Hopkins Press, 1966, pp. 151–2.

48  A. Spinelli, *The eurocrats,* p. 151.

49  J. Monnet, *Memoirs,* New York: Doubleday & Company, 1978, pp. 321–4.

50  W. Hallstein, *Europe in the making,* New York: W.W. Norton & Company, 1972, p. 75.

51  The various efforts to implement Art. 138(3) of the Treaty of Rome are summarised in V. Herman and J. Lodge, *The European Parliament and the European Community,* London: Macmillan, 1978, p. 3.

52  A. Spinelli, *The eurocrats,* p. 165.

53  A. Spinelli, *The eurocrats*, pp. 165–6.
54  A. Spinelli, *The eurocrats*, pp. 166–7.
55  Interview with Spinelli, 14 February 1985.
56  See the Report of the working party examining the problem of enlargement of the powers of the European Parliament, *Bulletin of the EC*, supplement 4/72. A detailed analysis of the origins and content of the report is given in A. Shlaim, 'The Vedel report and the reform of the European Parliament', *Parliamentary Affairs*, 27(2), pp. 159–70, 1974.
57  A. Shlaim, 'The Vedel report', p. 161.
58  See M.T.W. Robinson, 'The political implications of the Vedel report', *Government and Opposition*, 7(4), p. 427, Autumn 1972.
59  A. Shlaim, 'The Vedel report', p. 169.
60  See J. Lodge, 'Nation-states versus supranationalism: the political future of the European Community', *Journal of European Integration*, 2(2), pp. 161–81, 1979.
61  V. Herman and J. Lodge, *European Parliament and European Community*, p. 7.
62  V. Herman and J. Lodge, *European Parliament and European Community*, p. 160.
63  A. Spinelli, *The eurocrats*, p. 162.
64  J. Lodge, 'Nation-states versus supranationalism', p. 178.
65  E. Noel, 'Reflections on the state of the European Community at the end of the seventies', *Government and Opposition*, 15(2), p. 134, 1980.
66  E. Noel, 'Reflections', p. 133.
67  R. Jenkins, *European diary, 1977–1981*, London: Collins, 1989, p. 23.
68  R. Jenkins, *European diary*, p. 24.
69  For a short account of 'monetary federalism', see A. Jozzo, 'Towards a federal European economy: pre-federal monetary union', *The Federalist*, XXXVII(3), pp. 195–201, 1985.
70  R. Jenkins, *European diary*, p. 198.
71  P. Taylor, *The limits to European integration*, p. 77.
72  For a short discussion of the Spierenburg Report, see S. Henig, *Power and decision in Europe*, pp. 110–15.
73  *Report on European institutions*, presented by the Committee of three to the European Council, text of mandate, Brussels: EC, 1979, p. 81.
74  *Report on European institutions*, p. 7.
75  A.N. Duff, 'The Report of the three wise men', *Journal of Common Market Studies*, XIX(3), pp. 239–40, 1981.
76  *Report on European institutions*, p. 7.
77  *Report on European institutions*, p. 53.
78  *Report on European institutions*, p. 61.
79  *Report on European institutions*, p. 62.
80  *Report on European institutions*, p. 80.
81  *Report on European institutions*, pp. 73–8.
82  *Report on European institutions*, p. 79.
83  R. Marjolin, *Memoirs, 1911–1986*, London: Weidenfeld and Nicholson, 1989, p. 370.
84  R. Marjolin, *Memoirs*, p. 369.
85  S. Henig, *Power and decision in Europe*, p. 115.
86  S. Bulmer and W. Wessels, *The European Council*, p. 115.
87  S. Bulmer and W. Wessels, *The European Council*, p. 89.
88  R. Marjolin, *Memoirs*, p. 365.
89  For a detailed discussion of these reports and debates concerning the EP's own views of its institutional role, see M. Palmer, 'The development of the European Parliament's institutional role within the European Community, 1974–1983', *Journal of European Integration*, VI(2/3), pp. 183–202, 1983.

90  M. Palmer, 'The development of the European Parliament's institutional role', pp. 187–8.

91  M. Palmer, 'The development of the European Parliament's institutional role', pp. 188–9.

92  For a detailed survey of these successful proposals, see M. Palmer, 'The development of the European Parliament's institutional role', pp. 192–3.

93  M. Palmer, 'The development of the European Parliament's institutional role', pp. 193–4.

94  *Official journal of the EC*, C234/48, September 1981.

95  R. Cardozo and R. Corbett, 'The crocodile initiative', in J. Lodge (ed.), *European Union: the European Community in search of a future*, pp. 20–21.

96  'The 30 May Mandate and the relaunching of the European Community', *European File*, 16/81, Brussels: Commission of the EC, October 1981.

97  Thorn's speech to the EP, *Debates in the EP*, (DEP), 1–273, p. 32, 7 July 1981.

98  Thorn's speech to the EP, *DEP*, 1–273, p. 31.

99  'Relations between the institutions of the Community', Brussels: Commission of the EC, 1981, Com. (81), 581 final.

100 See J.H. Weiler, 'The Genscher–Colombo draft European act: the politics of indecision', *Journal of European Integration*, VI(2/3), pp. 129–53, 1983; and G. Bonvicini, 'The Genscher–Colombo plan and the "solemn declaration on European Union", 1981–1983', in R. Pryce (ed.), *The dynamics of European Union*, pp. 174–87.

101 See G. Bonvicini, 'The Genscher–Colombo Plan', pp. 176–7; and S. Bulmer and W. Wessels, *The federal republic of Germany and the European Community*, London: Allen & Unwin Ltd, 1987; pp. 134–5.

102 See Genscher's speech to the EP, 19 November 1981, *DEP*, *OJ*, Annex No. 1–277, pp. 216–19.

103 J. Weiler, 'The Genscher–Colombo draft European act', p. 130.

104 Genscher's speech, 19 November 1981, *DEP*, pp. 216–17.

105 Genscher's speech, 19 November 1981, *DEP*, p. 217.

106 For a complete summary of the initial details, see *Bulletin of the EC*, 14(11/18), pp. 87–91.

107 See the Report on European political cooperation, 13 October 1981, *Bulletin of the EC*, supplement, 3/19/81.

108 On their differences and the tensions between them, see G. Bonvicini, 'The Genscher–Colombo plan', pp. 177–8.

109 See G. Bonvicini, 'The Genscher–Colombo plan', pp. 182–4.

110 Genscher's speech, 19 November 1981, *DEP*, pp. 218–19.

111 Colombo's speech, 19 November 1981, *DEP*, p. 220.

112 Spinelli's remarks, 19 November 1981, *DEP*, p. 228.

113 Genscher's speech, 14 October 1982, *DEP*, *OJ*, Annex No. 1–289, p. 246.

114 Andriessen representing the Commission, 14 October 1982, *DEP*, *OJ*, Annex No. 1–289, p. 248.

115 For the details, see the solemn declaration on European Union, *Bulletin of the EC*, 6, 1983, pp. 25–6.

116 Ferri's analysis, 14 October 1982, *DEP*, p. 263.

117 Spinelli's remarks, 14 October 1982, *DEP*, p. 263.

118 See M. Burgess, *Federalism and European Union: political ideas, interests and strategies in the European Community, 1972–1987*, London: Routledge, 1989.

119 A. Spinelli, 'Towards European Union', Sixth Jean Monnet Conference, 13 June 1983, *Europe Documents*, Agence Internationale, Brussels, pp. 1–9.

120 Copy of Spinelli's letter, addressed in Rome, obtained courtesy of Derek Prag,

British Conservative MEP, who kindly placed his own private archive at my disposal.

121 See R. Cardozo and R. Corbett, 'The Crocodile initiative', in *European Union: Europe in search of a future*, pp. 15–46.

122 See, for example, J. Lodge, 'European Union and the first elected European Parliament: the Spinelli initiative', *Journal of Common Market Studies*, XXII (4), pp. 377–402, 1984; R. Bieber et al., (eds), *An ever closer union: a critical analysis of the draft treaty establishing the European Union*, Brussels–Luxembourg: European Perspectives Series, 1985; J. Lodge (ed.), *European Union: Europe in search of a future*; and O. Schmuck, 'The European Parliament's draft treaty establishing the European Union', in R. Pryce (ed.), *The dynamics of European Union*, pp. 188–216.

123 See EP working document, 1-659/83.

124 See article 49(3) of the draft treaty establishing the European Union, Luxembourg: European Parliament, 1984, 12. This task was to be entrusted to the Union itself which would adopt its own declaration on fundamental human rights within five years. The treaty has been published in J. Lodge (ed.), *European Union*, pp. 188–227.

125 Private observations of Derek Prag, MEP, rapporteur on international relations.

126 This legal debate is lucidly discussed by R. Corbett and J. Lodge, in J. Lodge (ed.), 'Progress and prospects', *European Union*, Chap. 8.

127 Article 34(1), draft treaty, p. 23.

128 See Chap. 2 of this volume.

129 J. Lodge (ed.), *European Union*, p. 60; and Article 11(2), draft treaty, p. 16.

130 Interview with Spinelli, 15 September 1983, European Parliament, Strasbourg.

131 R. Bieber, 'The institutions and the decision-making procedure in the draft treaty establishing the European Union', in R. Bieber et al., (eds), *An ever closer union*, p. 38.

132 R. Bieber et al., (eds), *An ever closer union*, p. 36; and J.-P. Jacque, 'The draft treaty: an overview', in R. Bieber et al., (eds), *An ever closer union*, p. 25.

133 R. Bieber et al., (eds), *An ever closer union*, p. 36; and J. Lodge, 'European Union and the first elected European Parliament', p. 391.

134 R. Bieber, 'Introduction', in R. Bieber et al., (eds), *An ever closer union*, p. 9.

135 Barbi's speech to the EP, 13 September 1983, *DEP*, *OJ*, 1–303, p. 46.

136 Zecchino's remarks, 15 July 1983, EP working documents, Doc. 1–575/83/C, p. 142.

137 J. Lodge (ed.), *European Union*, p. 291.

138 Derek Prag's remarks, European Union file.

139 See the useful summary by O. Schmuck, 'The European Parliament's draft treaty: an overview', pp. 210–11.

140 R. Griffiths, 'The stagnant decade, 1973–83', in K. Middlemas (ed.), *Orchestrating Europe*, Chap. 3.

# 5  Federalism, European Union and the Single European Act, 1985–88

The years between 1985 and 1988 constitute another crossroads in the political and economic development of the European Community (EC). During this period, the EC experienced a number of important changes which most commentators have since regarded as a remarkable reversal of fortune. In moving from 'its stagnant to its dynamic phase', it underwent 'an extraordinary transformation' which was tantamount to the rebirth of the European idea.[1] Consequently, the years 1985–88 can be conveniently construed as a time when the European construction entered perhaps its most vigorous and fruitful period since 1955–57.

What factors were responsible for this turn of the tide? Why did the EC suddenly find itself able to make considerable progress in both economic and political integration in a way which had seemed so unlikely only a few years earlier? The answers to these questions lie in a combination of national, intra-European and international circumstances which produced yet another of those invaluable opportunities to push forward with new ideas and fresh initiatives. It was reminiscent of the conception of 'crisis exploitation' to which both Jean Monnet and Altiero Spinelli had so frequently referred in their political strategies. The quest to build Europe, we are reminded, would occasionally experience certain 'moments' when national governments were prepared to take crucial integrationist steps forward to solve contemporary problems which they were unable to resolve separately. But these occasions would have to be perceived and seized upon quickly if genuine progress in European integration was to be successfully pursued. To delay was to miss the chance and to allow national responses to European problems.

Recent research on the origins of the Single European Act (SEA) has acknowledged that one of the chief driving-forces behind the revival of the European idea in the mid-1980s was a new consensus among member state governments about the decline in Europe's ability to compete, in both domestic and world markets, with the United States and Japan. Changes in the international political economy, which could be traced back to the early 1970s, indicated that national economic strategies could no longer be relied upon to keep European states' economies competitive with those of their main rivals. Stanley Hoffmann's explanation of the SEA indicated precisely where the main threat to European competitiveness lay:

> While the United States remains a major trading partner of the Community, the new effort is aimed much less at establishing a 'partner' of equal weight to cooperate with, and to resist domination by, the United States than at resisting the challenge from Japan, whose aggressive external economic expansion and fierce protection of its own market the Europeans resent.[2]

His diagnosis of the failure of national solutions in a world in which the number of industrial and commercial players had multiplied prompted a new outlook on Europe. Regional integration would be the appropriate response to global market competition. Indeed, 'if national solutions did not work, there remained one way out: an escape by a forward leap – into Europe'.[3] Evidently the perceived threat to member states' economies in the EC was less that of the United States and more those of Japan and the newly-industrializing economies of Asia.

Against this background of changes in international economic structures, especially in trade and technology, there were other factors which were propitious for a forward leap. The resolution of the protracted British budgetary problem and the agreement to take long overdue steps to reform the Common Agricultural Policy (CAP) at the Fontainebleau meeting of the European Council in June 1984 cleared a congested agenda and helped to change the political environment in the Community. The economic climate in the EC had also changed. When the French attempt during 1981–83 to pursue a Keynesian policy of spending its way out of the recession failed, it signified a new acceptance of monetary stability and the retrenchment of public expenditure. The so-called 'market model' propounded by the British Conservative Prime Minister, Margaret Thatcher, heralded the dawn of the new era of privatization, deregulation, the enterprise culture, the downsizing of the state and freer trade in Western Europe. Added to these circumstances was a significant change in the political leaderhip of the EC. The new Commission President, Jacques Delors, assumed office in January 1985 and arrived with a glowing reputation as President Mitterrand's former finance minister and a strong self-determination to put his own ideas into practice.

The West German Chancellor, Helmut Kohl, and the French President, François Mitterrand, began to inject new life into the Paris–Bonn axis in the mid-1980s. Together with Delors, they forged a dynamic partnership which also worked well with those in the European Parliament (EP) who wanted to give the EC the capacity to go beyond what existed. The federalists played a crucial role in making the most of these favourable circumstances. They provided both the initiative and the political leadership in the EP, and Spinelli's dogged determination to promote institutional reform via the European Union Treaty (EUT) furnished the basis for what later became the SEA.

## From the EUT to the SEA

The context out of which the EUT emerged during 1980–84 was very different from that into which it was catapulted during the succeeding years. The world of intergovernmental relations, built upon fragile, shifting coalitions, was uncertain. It lacked the sort of institutional continuity which both the EP and the Commission possessed for the successful achievement of European Union. Furthermore, the EUT had, in a sense, been shielded from the full blast of intergovernmental bickering and turbulence over the British budgetary problem which had so dominated this arena during the early 1980s. Hence, the political atmosphere in which the EUT surfaced during the first half of 1984 was exceptionally uninviting. It did not suggest that there would be a healthy environment for the serious discussion of major treaty revision. The EUT was prey to the vicissitudes of intergovernmental politics and personalities, but it also needed elevated status for the impending EP elections due in June 1984. All in all, the interim period of four months between 14 February and 14–17 June seemed a palpably insufficient interval within which to mobilize national governments, political parties, interest groups, parliaments and mass publics in support of the new treaty. Spinelli's original strategy appeared to have been mistimed.

What changed this somewhat bleak scenario was the unexpected public intervention of François Mitterrand in the EUT equation. During the important parliamentary debate of 14 February, which resulted in the adoption of the EUT, Spinelli had already challenged the French government – as occupants of the Presidency of the Council – to 'ponder the crisis in Europe' and to deal with it 'with greater intensity and more imagination than in past years'.[4] His appeal could hardly have been more candid:

> Our Parliament must ... say to all the people of France, but above all to the President of the Republic, who recently appealed for a return to the spirit of the Congress of the Hague and spoke of the need to achieve political unity, that we look to the French Presidency of the Council to do more than come and speak to us in ritual fashion. ... we look to the French government – I really do mean the French government, not the European Council – to adopt the draft treaty.... In that case these six months of the French Presidency would go down in history.[5]

Within the space of three-and-a-half months, Mitterrand addressed the EP on 24 May 1984 and provided the important fillip which the EUT required. Mitterrand's speech was significant if only for the way in which it changed the political climate surrounding the debate about Europe. But in his public remarks, he did not believe that a new treaty had to be 'a substitute' for the existing treaties, but only an extension of them to fields they did not already cover.[6] Close analysis of this speech, then, did not confirm the French President's own support for the EUT itself; it was only qualified approval of the EP's predilections.

Nonetheless, Mitterrand's intervention gave a lift to the EUT's prospects. At the memorable European Council meeting at Fontainebleau on 25–26 June 1984, agreement was reached to establish two committees to advance the concept of European Union. The first, the Adonnino Committee, was instructed to make proposals to promote the image of a 'people's' Europe, such as a Community flag and anthem designed to give EC citizens a sense of common identity, but the second committee was given a much more searching task.[7] It was described as 'an ad hoc committee consisting of personal representatives of the Heads of State or Government on the lines of the "Spaak Committee"' whose function was 'to make suggestions for the improvement of the operation of European cooperation in both the Community field and that of political, or any other, cooperation'.[8] The President of the European Council would take the necessary steps to implement the Fontainebleau decision. Since Ireland occupied the Council presidency during July–December 1984, the new Ad Hoc Committee for Institutional Affairs was commonly referred to as the Dooge Committee after the majority leader of the Irish Senate, James Dooge. For the next twelve months, the ten personal representatives of the Heads of State or Government, along with the Commission, served as the main forum for the evolving intergovernmental debate about European Union.

Why did Mitterrand take this initiative? What was he seeking to achieve? Whenever we focus upon the intentions of member state governments and of heads of state, it is usual to ascribe their actions to domestic strategies and tactics. Their real motives are determined less by the Community arena itself than by what they perceive as necessary for their success at home. This means that factors such as the complexities of coalition government, impending national elections and economic difficulties over currency, inflation or unemployment usually explain their actions in the Community arena. Domestic priorities are elevated to the Community level. Here, Mitterrand was no exception. The French socialist government, having taken a nosedive in public popularity, was about to enter a critical period with elections due in 1986. And the British budgetary imbroglio cannot be ignored. Fontainebleau brought to an end the very painful and damaging episode of *juste retour*. Mitterrand's initiative, which was never supported by the *Quai d'Orsay*, could be portrayed as tactical. In contrast to the British, who appeared niggardly and intransigent, the French seemed suddenly to don the mantle of good Europeans. Was this all that lay behind Mitterrand's personal initiative?

Spinelli's view of Mitterrand was pertinent because it provides us with an interesting explanation for the French position in 1984. Taking into account the broad international context construed in terms of the military and economic policies of the Reagan Presidency in the United States, Mitterrand viewed a new European initiative as appropriate to French national interests. But Spinelli also believed in Mitterrand's own past as a man of Europe. Unlike any other French President of the Fifth Republic, Mitterrand could legitimately claim to have a pedigree as a European. He was a man of the Fourth Republic, not of the Gaullist era. Indeed, he was the first President of the Fifth Republic who was not a man of the Fifth Republic. De Gaulle invented it, Pompidou and Giscard d'Estaing were products of it, but Mitterrand was a political animal from an earlier era. Spinelli did not ignore Mitterrand's 'Florentine' reputation, but his Machiavellian instincts were not allowed to obscure his European past:

> He was a man who had been there at the beginning and supported the first steps.... At the Hague Congress (1948) he could say I was there and I believed in it. When Schuman began (1950) he could say I was there and believed in it. And this has lain dormant in his spirit but it existed. When it awakened in his mind he discovered again that he believed in it.[9]

In other words, Mitterrand was a genuine European socialized in the European spirit of the Hague and well acquainted with the heyday of Schuman and Monnet in the 1950s. But he continued to preside over a divided France on the question of Europe's future and of the place of France within it. In consequence, he was driven to balance national interests and those of his party against his own deeply-rooted commitment to European integration. In pursuit of this strategy, it was necessary for him to sacrifice clarity to ambiguity. Recent research has confirmed that Mitterrand was a convinced federalist but one who was also pragmatic about it:

> Mitterrand has on several occasions claimed to be a federalist ... (who) believed in a political authority, in the idea of a European Political Community – a theme to which he returned with increasing emphasis following his election in 1981 – yet he is a pragmatist who will accept a second-best option if the primary goal is unattainable.... Mitterrand affirmed that a federal Europe was desirable as a long-term objective, and ... repeated references over more than 30 years to the desirability of a European federation.[10]

In hindsight, this description of Mitterrand's personal commitment to European integration based upon federal principles could equally have been written to describe another pioneering Frenchman, Jean Monnet.

Mitterrand's own role in the intergovernmental response to the EUT was, therefore, of critical importance. He also required the support of the West German Chancellor, Helmut Kohl, in the customary Paris–Bonn axis approach to Community affairs. As we shall shortly discover, a series of unexpected events and circumstances emerged during the first six months of 1985, which soured the atmosphere and damaged the prospects of an early agreement on European Union. But, immediately after Fontainebleau, both Mitterrand and Kohl gave the impression that Europe needed a big leap forward. In particular, their public rhetoric and demeanour provided a useful impetus to the first phase: the work of the Dooge Committee.

What was the relationship between the Dooge Report of March 1985 and the EP's EUT? In order to clarify the precise nature of this relationship, it is vitally important to look first at the composition of this so-called 'Spaak II Committee'. The EUT, though never actually on the table for discussion, was very much in the background of the debate because it was very much in the minds of some of the members of the Dooge Committee. The Italian representative, Mauro Ferri, for example, was a former MEP and an ex-chairman of the EP's Committee on Institutional Affairs which had laboured over the EUT. Fernand Herman, the Belgian representative, had also been a very active and committed MEP who had sat on the Committee on Institutional Affairs and worked in the avowedly federalist cause of the EPP. It is also worth mentioning Frans Andriessen, who represented the Commission and whose enthusiastic alliance with Gaston Thorn, the Commission President, had been an important source of support for the EP's project. Andriessen remained until the end of 1984 when he was replaced by the much less committed Ripa de Meana in the new Commission of Jacques Delors.

The Commission's role was interesting. It had achieved the immediate objective of 'being there', and it followed the same favourable line which Thorn had originally adopted on the EP's EUT. But it had to walk a very difficult tightrope in order to avoid being divisive. The Dooge Committee had an independent life of its own, and the Commission's purpose was to play an active part in these proceedings. Keeping a low profile in view of its delicate position, it sought overall unity. This meant allying with the majority of the seven – France, West Germany, Italy, Ireland and Benelux – but seeking simultaneously to bring the remaining minority of three – the UK, Greece and Denmark – closer to the majority position.[11] This tactical dilemma had two broad implications for the Commission. First, it was essential not to be isolated or marooned. It could not afford to be alone against all of the member states, or even of alignments of member states. And, secondly, its search for compromise between the majority group and the minority group meant that it had to be more ambitious with the former and less ambitious with the latter. But the intellectual lead within the Dooge Committee at the beginning lay elsewhere. Here we must return to the French position.

The French representative was Maurice Faure, a well-known European of long-standing, who had been a signatory to the Treaty of Rome in 1957, a former foreign minister and an ex-MEP. Faure, however, did not participate on behalf of the French government. He was, therefore, independent from the clutches of the *Quai d'Orsay*. Unlike Jurgen Ruhfus of West Germany and Malcolm Rifkind of the UK, Faure had been appointed as the personal representative of a Head of State rather than as a government spokesman. Mitterrand thus ensured that Faure's independence was protected. And it was Faure who produced the first draft outline which served as the basis for discussion within the committee. His text, though much less ambitious than the EUT, was nonetheless along the same lines as the EP's project. Conceptually at least, there was no fundamental contradiction. Thus, although the final Dooge Report and the EUT were not identical, the Report did follow the spirit and, in some cases, even the letter of the EUT. The French position, therefore, remained constant during this first phase. Faure and Mitterrand maintained an autonomous position distinct from both the *Quai d'Orsay* and the French government.

Before we look in more detail at the Dooge Report, it is important to underline a fundamental conceptual distinction between the Report and the EUT. The Dooge Report in its concluding sentences advocated:

> a conference of the representatives of the governments of the member states should be convened in the near future to negotiate a Draft European Union Treaty based upon the *'acqui communautaire'*, the present document and the Stuttgart Solemn Declaration on European Union and guided by the spirit and method of the draft treaty voted by the European Parliament.... The very decision of the Heads of State or Government to convene such a conference would have great symbolic value and would represent the initial act of European Union.[12]

What did this mean? If we compare this statement of intent with the actual content of the Dooge Report, it is difficult not to view it both as demagogic and rhetorical. A careful analysis of the Dooge Report reveals the main difference between it and the EUT. The latter was written deliberately by people within the EC system who wanted consciously to replace the existing treaties with something completely different. The former, however, was written by people of goodwill who remained within the system, while changing and modifying it even substantially, but who nonetheless preserved the existing balance of the Rome Treaty, namely, intergovernmental cooperation. Of course, it was important for the EP to downgrade the differences between the two texts, but they remained significant nonetheless.[13]

In the Dooge Report, there was no real merger between the Community and political cooperation (POCO) as there was in the EUT. Energy policy, included in the EUT, was conspicuous by its absence in the Report, and it was also less elaborate about the EMS than the EUT. Leaving aside the role of the European Council, which was to remain outside the institutional scope, the approach of the Dooge Committee was very similar to that of the EUT. But their verdict on the future role of the Commission was not identical. In the EUT, the role of the Commission was substantially altered, while in the Dooge Report it was merely strengthened. There was a significant difference. As we have already observed, the EUT outlined an overall political system with its own legitimacy; this was not the case with the Dooge Report. From an analytical standpoint, the main differences between the two texts were much more significant than the EP, Commission and Dooge Committee were prepared to admit. For obvious reasons they did not want to split the European camp.

In retrospect, there were some areas where the Dooge Report went beyond the EUT and many fields in which it lagged behind. The Report was more advanced on security issues, for example, though a close scrutiny suggested that its institutional implications were extremely thin. In effect, both texts seemed to acknowledge that the Community had not yet reached the stage where defence in Europe could be approached from an institutional standpoint. Taking a broad perspective, we can conclude that the Dooge Report did not really alter the basic institutional position whereby legitimacy was derived directly from the member states. It was a political document not a legal text. It defined the political objectives, policies and institutional reforms deemed necessary to 'restore to Europe the vigour and ambition of its inception', but this did not commit it to 'draft a new treaty in legal form'.[14] There did seem to be some ambiguity in the language of the Dooge Report on this question. The Report was obviously less precise than the EUT; it was clearly not of the same order or character of its counterpart, and this led to much initial confusion. Did it advocate a new treaty or merely a supplementary treaty? Did it suggest a new treaty going beyond the existing treaties as regards additional policy areas, or did it simply mean a modification of the existing treaties in order to accommodate new institutional procedures? These questions were left open in the minds of many informed observers. What was really at issue, however, was a supplementary treaty which would add to the existing Community patrimony rather than sweep it all away and return to first principles.

The Dooge Committee presented an interim report to the Dublin European Council on 3–4 December 1984 which merely noted its submission and decided to defer it to the Brussels European Council due to meet on 29–30 March 1985. There, the final report could be thoroughly discussed. However, as Patrick Keatinge and Anna Murphy have emphasized in their detailed analysis of the whole episode, the Dooge Committee was not engaged in negotiations: 'its members were not the plenipotentiaries of governments but rather were involved in a preliminary exploration of the national leaders' positions in order to clarify the extent of agreement which might be possible'.[15] What happened between the Dublin meeting and the decisive Milan European Council at the end of June 1985 remains, to some extent, a matter for conjecture. It was a period open to many different interpretations.[16] One conclusion, however, is unequivocal: the intergovernmental arena, always prey to sudden unexpected shifts in member states' positions, produced a new climate much less favourable to the progress of European Union. The Milan decision to hold an inter-governmental conference in the teeth of British opposition reflected an unusual permutation of member state influences with Italy and the Benelux countries playing a decisive role in keeping up the pressure for progress toward European Union. The Italians, in particular, were able to crown their European Council Presidency with an important legacy which was eventually brought to fruition in December 1985 by the subsequent Luxembourg Presidency paving the way for the SEA.

## Federalism and the Single European Act, 1985–87

If we look back from the standpoint of the end of the century, the period between June and December 1985 – when the Intergovernmental Conference (IGC) met to fashion a series of compromises on reforming the treaties which would be the central focus of the Luxembourg European Council – suggested something very important. This was that, at last, the status quo was not an option. The political momentum generated by the EP's EUT and the subsequent Dooge Report, culminating in the Milan decision to have an IGC, meant that institutional reform of some sort was kept on the agenda. Thatcher had been forced to go along with this momentum and the three most sceptical member states – the UK, Denmark and Greece – were compelled at the very least to attend the IGC for fear of being marginalized by the decisions likely to be taken by the majority of seven. The British Prime Minister's room for manoeuvre had been narrowly circumscribed but national sovereignty was not at risk because within the IGC, unlike in Milan where a qualified majority vote was sufficient, unanimity was required for the approval of treaty amend-ments. From the federalist perspective, at this crucial stage, it was vital simply to keep up the pressure on the governments.

The IGC was formally convened on 22 July 1985, and the first ministerial meeting took place on 9 September 1985, agreeing to 'take account in its work of the Draft Treaty adopted by the European Parliament' as well as 'any further proposal which the European Parliament may wish to submit'.[17] We shall not attempt a detailed analysis of what occurred inside the IGC during the important months of September to November 1985, because this has already been researched by Richard Corbett.[18] But it is important to underline the point which he has stressed concerning the IGC:

In convening the IGC on this basis, Council broke with precedent. Previous revisions of the Treaty were negotiated within the Council, often in close association with the other institutions, and the IGC had merely provided formal assent. This time the real negotiations were to take place in the IGC, the outcome of which was unknown when the other institutions gave their favourable opinions.[19]

We can see that in these circumstances the EP had to use its best skill and diplomacy in order to keep its foot in the door of institutional reform. The approach of the IGC was not institutional reform at all. Instead, it chose to examine and discuss what it perceived as necessary from a policy perspective and only then to consider the institutional implications.

It was obvious by this stage of the proceedings that, despite the rhetoric of the IGC, it had no intention of considering a new treaty in the sense of the EUT. It was engaged in a very different enterprise. Jacques Santer, the Luxembourg Prime Minister, identified five main themes which had come to dominate the attention of the European Council: improved decision-making in the Council of Ministers; an enhanced role for the EP; the Commission's executive responsibilities; the extension of EC activities into new areas; and the strengthening of POCO.[20] Here we can already detect the skeletal outline of what later became the SEA. There was no real difference of opinion between member state governments about the problems to be solved; the differences emerged over the methods to be used. Santer's five main themes prompted different responses from the Heads of State or Government. The familiar question reappeared: should the reforms considered necessary be achieved by making better use of the existing structures without treaty revision, or should a new departure be made requiring treaty amendment? The Luxembourg Presidency resolved to adhere strictly to Article 236 of the Rome Treaty in order to reach a unanimous agreement among the Twelve. This was deemed inescapable. But Santer expressed the view that complementarity of proposals would suffice to make an historic step forward, built upon unanimity, which would 'represent a major step towards the final objective of a European Union'.[21] Any contributions towards the achievement of this goal, whether or not they entailed 'modifying the treaties', were in his view ultimately 'complementary'.[22]

Treaty modification was, therefore, not excluded. The main aim of the Commission, and of some of the small member states like Belgium and Luxembourg, was to avoid a conclusion which yielded two separate texts – one on political cooperation and the other on modifications to the Rome Treaty. Delors spelled this out very clearly to the EP.[23] The first reason for this was purely tactical. The Commission wanted to prevent the IGC from dishing reforms to the Rome Treaty in order to be able to claim modest successes in political cooperation. In this event, member state governments could plausibly jettison changes to the Rome Treaty but still argue that the IGC had been successful. POCO would therefore constitute the sole area of progress. With one single text, however, it would have been very difficult for member state governments to claim success in one area while confessing to failure in the other. The second reason was substantive. To allow two separate texts would effectively impede the gradual approximation of POCO to the main Community arena.

The Commission's position, then, was once again tactical – the predicament of a supra-national institution reacting to an intergovernmental strategy. It had, after all, not chosen the approach. Its main concern was to ensure that headway was made in the areas of new competences and in decison-making procedures. The latter meant increased use of majority voting in the Council of Ministers and new powers of co-decision for the EP. Delors had put the internal market and technological cooperation at the forefront of the Commission's proposals but, in following what he perceived to be a wise response to the IGC, there were two obvious dangers. First, the Commission's acquiescence risked losing sight of the importance of the overall institutional question. The grand design might be forfeited. Second, the IGC might conceivably degenerate into a fragmentary discussion in which only a number of very specific points were developed into a working programme rather than constitutional change. Hence, if the Commission wanted to retain the advantage of the Luxembourg Presidency approach while avoiding its pitfalls, it was compelled to discuss competences in a global sense. This was in order to determine what would be necessary to facilitate Community progress during the next generation while simultaneously keeping attention focused upon decision-making procedures.

From the Commission's perspective, the IGC could not be allowed to fail. Its conclusions would probably determine the scope of the treaties for the next 20 years and, therefore, the pace and evolution of Europe. But the Commission also feared a cosmetic result. Even if successful, a cosmetic conference would have been seen as just that. Still worse would have been intergovernmental disagreement even on cosmetics. In this event, the Community would have been divided about nothing and Europe would not have even been able to explain to public opinion that its disarray was about real issues. This would have been the worst possible outcome. And it should be noted that this was precisely why Delors had deliberately set the IGC at such an audaciously high level of ambition. Having called the IGC into existence, he reasoned that its conclusions could not afford to be cosmetic. This was where the federalist strategy of keeping up the pressure on member state governments was demonstrably effective. They were to some extent imprisoned by their own decision to go ahead with the IGC in Milan. In short, they had to confront the consequences of their own actions.

The Luxembourg Presidency was confronted by two pressing demands. First, there was the requirement of unanimity and, second, there was the imperative of national ratification by twelve separate parliaments. Given these constraints, it came as little surprise to learn that the SEA fell far short of European Union as conceptualized by the EP and by several member states, notably Italy and Belgium. Certainly, if it was compared with the EUT, though there were some limited resemblances, it was only a pale reflection of what the EP's project had intended. We will not provide a detailed examination of the SEA here, since it has already been analysed elsewhere.[24] Instead, we will approach it from the federalist standpoint in order to suggest how far the SEA could conceivably have moved the Community closer towards federalism and European Union.

Before we look more closely at the SEA, it is useful to bear in mind two important preliminary considerations. First, it was possible to adopt either a minimalist or a maximalist postion. Certain member state governments, notably the British, Danish and Greek, interpreted the new treaty revision for different reasons from the standpoint of restricting both its policy and its institutional implications to very modest proportions. Others, including Italy and the Benelux countries, perceived it in much more ambitious terms. And federalists, of course, believed that, as it was the first major overhaul of the Treaties – leaving aside the 1970 and 1975 budgetary revisions – the maximum of advantage could be wrung from the policy extensions and institutional reforms enshrined within it. Even seemingly modest adaptations could be very significant. If persistent pressure could be applied discreetly, these changes could be made to work in a federalist direction, thus altering the institutional imbalance in ways unforeseen by intergovernmental elites. Second, we should remember the federalist conception of policies and institutions from a political strategy viewpoint. Some federalists believed that concrete progress could be made by extending Community competences, like POCO and the EMS, within the existing institutional framework, while others focused almost exclusively upon institutional reform as the most productive route to European Union. The SEA contained reforms in both of these dimensions. Let us look first at the extensions of formal competences to new areas.

Community competence in research and technological development, the environment, regional policy and social policy was formally extended. In particular, neither environment policy nor regional policy were treaty-based. Hitherto, environment policy had been implemented only as part of a series of environment programmes dating from 1973. In the SEA, it was at last an official EC policy, albeit subject to unanimity in the Council of Ministers on questions of principle. Similarly with regional policy, the Regional Development Fund was formally integrated into the EC, and the SEA made some provision for majority voting in the Council of Ministers concerning the implementation of decisions. In both of these cases, there was clearly some scope for further extensions of policy evolution.

Turning to look at POCO and the EMS, federalists' hopes were disappointed. There was no merger of political cooperation and the

Community arena as had originally been proposed in the EUT. Certainly it had been formally incorporated in the SEA, but although linked, it remained a distinctly separate structure from the EC with no mechanism provided for its gradual transfer from the intergovernmental arena to the more integrated Community framework. A secretariat based in Brussels was established which at least provided an institutional basis for the future, but it remained to be seen how far it would be allowed to develop as a centripetal force for POCO. In summary, 'none of these novelties' changed 'the character of the cooperation'. They remained 'a statement of intent', especially as the competence of the Court of Justice was not enlarged to include POCO.[25] Similarly with the EMS, it was mentioned in the preamble to the SEA (implementing monetary cooperation) and both the EMS and the ECU were acknowledged in the treaty revision (Article 102A). It was notable, however, that any institutional changes deemed necessary by the further development of economic and monetary policy were subject to Article 236 of the EEC Treaty which required unanimity of agreement by the member states. In short, although both the EMS and the ECU were treaty-based, the procedures for their future development within the framework of existing competences appeared to have become more cumbersome rather than less so.

The modest outcome of the SEA in the monetary field brought the question of the internal market and majority voting in the Council of Ministers into sharp focus. Among the outstanding unfulfilled commitments in the Treaty of Rome, the idea of a seamless common market, to be achieved by 1992, had been given great prominence in the SEA and subsequently in the economic liberalism espoused by many in the media world of Western Europe. Clearly, qualified majority voting (QMV), which applied with few exceptions to the completion of the single market by 1992, represented a significant milestone in the gradual legal surrender by member states of their national sovereignty in the areas delineated. In hindsight, we can see that this concession did not necessarily mean that all of the single market proposals subject to QMV would be implemented. The distinction between policy-making and policy-implementation was quickly brought into sharp relief, but QMV nonetheless had a powerful symbolic importance which flagged up the direction that member states had agreed European integration should take.

If we look finally at the institutional provisions laid down in the SEA concerning the Commission, Court of Justice, Council of Ministers and the EP, we can see that much remained unclear. The Commission's role was theoretically strengthened in that it was given 'powers for the implementation of the rules which the Council lays down' but the latter was able to 'reserve the right, in specific cases, to exercise directly implementing powers itself' and to specify the 'principles and rules to be laid down' which governed Commission action.[26] The treaty revision also extended to the Court of Justice in that a subsidiary Court of First Instance was created principally to relieve the workload of the main court, but it was granted no specific powers. It was in the area of the EP's altered institutional role that federalists drew most hope. Here a new cooperation procedure was introduced, albeit limited to ten articles, which provided for a second reading in the EP's participation in the decision-making procedure of the EC. Used wisely, it had the potential in certain circumstances to translate cooperation effectively into co-decision for the EP. MEPs were not slow to realise that this new procedure gave them a toe in the door of co-decision and their astute exploitation of this opportunity in subsequent years paved the way for the huge gains that the EP was to make in the Maastricht Treaty on European Union (TEU).

Viewed, as it were, in the round, it was sensible for member state governments to have resisted the temptation to equate the SEA with European Union. Even this short survey of it amply testifies to the fact that it fell far short of that goal. Indeed the phrase 'European Union' was alluded to just twice and only in the preamble to the SEA. This brief analysis of the SEA, then, demonstrates that there was both security for the intergovernmentalists and hope for the federalists. It was a typical Community compromise which could be conveniently reduced to minimalism versus maximalism. Some competences were carefully safeguarded for the member states and, on some issues such as culture, education, energy and consumer protection the SEA's silence was deafening. Here the intergovernmental interpretation was confirmed. But if the door to institutional reform appeared to have been firmly closed to federalists in 1986, there were several windows open to them for the future. The significance of the cooperation procedure could not be underestimated if the emphasis which both Monnet and Spinelli had placed upon institutions and procedures affecting people's perceptions of problems was recalled. Old views, habits and roles, we are reminded, could be radically altered by working within new procedures.

The SEA was not ratified until July 1987 and its political significance was easily underestimated even by federalists. If the provisions about competences and institutions seemed rather insipid at the time, the constitutional and political implications of the internal market were colossal. Above all, the main breakthrough in treaty revision had at last been made and the SEA became another of those key steps which enabled further progress toward European Union to be taken in the foreseeable future. And that future would be guided and inspired largely by a revitalized Commission led by the man whose towering political presence and intellectual ability came to dominate the EC arena for virtually the next decade.

## Jacques Delors, federalism and European Union

When Jacques Delors was first appointed President of the European Commission in July 1984, few informed observers could have foreseen the enormous impact he would have upon the institution of the Commission, the EC as a political system and European economic and political integration. It was not as if he had risen without trace, but the complicated political circumstances of his appointment at the helm of the Commission did not suggest that his succession to Gaston Thorn would herald any major strategic policy departures, let alone a grand project for the building of Europe. Had it done so, it is reasonable to assume that Margaret Thatcher, who along with Helmut Kohl had rejected the previous nomination of Claude Cheysson as Commission President, would have withheld her approval of Delors as an acceptable alternative. In hindsight, it is ironic that the renaissance of European integration 'thus began partly from serendipity'.[27]

Much has been written about the life and political career of Jacques Delors and it is not my purpose to duplicate it here. Instead, I intend to furnish a short intellectual and political profile of the man of Europe – a self-styled leader of Europe's would-be polity – whose social, economic and political preconceptions of European integration placed him at the forefront of the movement for a federal Europe in the late twentieth century. Together with Monnet and Spinelli, Delors represented yet another architect and builder of the European construction whose single-minded pursuit of the federal goal brought him into repeated conflict with the narrow national mindset in his approach to contemporary problems. We will return to the ideological and strategic characteristics which Delors shared with Monnet and Spinelli later in the section. For the moment, let us concentrate upon the intellectual origins of Delors' personal commitment to federalism and a federal Europe.

For a book like this whose principal purpose is to reinstate the federal idea in the building of Europe since 1950, it is crucial that we recognise the significance of the political ideas and strategies of perhaps the Community's first genuine European statesman. What, then, were the intellectual origins of Delors' federal ideas, and how did they shape his political strategy to build Europe in the years between 1985 and 1995? Charles Grant has claimed that when he began to research a biography of Delors, Pascal Lamy, his *chef de cabinet* for most of the time that he was Commission President, told him that if he wanted to understand Delors he should read Emmanuel Mounier.[28] The political ideas of Mounier, the twentieth-century French Roman Catholic philosopher, stretch back to the inter-war years when he was one of the intellectual fathers of personalism. We have already addressed this issue in Chapter 2, but it is appropriate to recall some of its basic philosophical assumptions and beliefs here since they help to explain the motives which drove Delors to champion a particular conception of Europe. The personalist view of the world is one which is concerned to rescue man from the anonymity associated with the dominant materialist values of capitalist states and societies. It is, in essence, a sharp critique of capitalism and the capitalist state. Personalists want to restore man's identity – his sense of himself – as a whole human person in order to reconnect him with his own social life, his family and, ultimately, himself. It is a perception of the world which is societal rather than state-based and one which makes for a peculiar brand of federalism and a particular kind of federalist.

The views of the personalists, sometimes known as 'integral' or Proudhonian federalists, predispose them to a certain view of Europe in which man escapes from the narrow-minded atomism of liberal individualism on the one hand and the tyrannical bureaucratic centralization of collectivism on the other. From this point of view, Delors was able to construe the building of Europe not as a huge state-like leviathan centred in Brussels; this was the very opposite of his intentions. His personalist assumptions required him to see the European construction in all of its human dimensions. This meant that the Europe of the single market was not to be reduced merely to an economic Europe of single-minded profit-seeking entrepreneurs; it also had an important social dimension which was integral to the fostering of a federal European society. And the political dimension, which we have already discussed, required federal values and institutions capable of establishing local autonomy and decentralization to facilitate participation down to the grassroots of society.

This unique combination of social, economic and political ideas is admittedly complex, but its basic driving-force is simple to appreciate. And we can also understand how far its fundamental structure of thought and practice have both emerged from and served to enrich Roman Catholic social theory. It was no accident that both federalism and subsidiarity were suffused within Christian Democracy throughout Europe, nor that the European People's Party (EPP) in the EP championed these ideas in their own manifesto for a federal Europe.[29] Ultimately, the source of this body of thought is the human person: a complex being with spiritual, temporal and material needs. Personalism requires that human beings, as whole persons, can determine themselves via participation in political organizations which are also human organizations operating close to their daily lives. This is why the principle of subsidiarity was so firmly embedded in personalism and federalism. It acted as a guarantor of local participation, autonomy and self-determination to facilitate human agency. As political animals with self-conscious ideas and energies, people must have the capacity to shape their own lives through active participation in political, economic and social institutions close to their needs. Put simply, Delors entertained an ethical conception of Europe.

We can already see from this brief sketch outline of the contours of Delors' political faith that his conception of the European construction was both authentic and deep-rooted. In short, he was driven by a coherent set of values, beliefs and assumptions about man, the state and society which rendered his view of Europe overtly ideological. His political ideology was that of a personalist federalist. He was driven by what was a fundamentally messianic cause; his mission was to help build a Europe with which ordinary men and women could identify. It would be a Europe which was relevant to their daily lives. The social, economic, political, intellectual, spiritual and philosophical dimensions fitted together neatly to produce a new totality of, above all, 'human' experience. This remarkable unity of thought determined a unity of practice. It explained Delors' particular approach to problem-solving. It also explained his political strategy as a federalist, and why he behaved in many ways as though Europe was already a fully-fledged, self-contained polity in its own right. The reality of European Union was in the making of it.

In this light, it is much easier to understand the politics which Delors practised in Brussels. The principles of federalism, subsidiarity and social solidarity, the social dialogue, his anathema to the unbridled neoliberal market capitalism of Thatcher, his Roman Catholicism, his sympathy for the communitarian values and principles of equity and fraternity enshrined in socialism and his unswerving belief in a 'European model of society' each combined to create what Grant has called 'the foundations of Delorism'.[30] How, then, were these ideological principles and beliefs translated into practice in the EC? After all, Delors' historical significance, as Grant has reminded us, rests on 'the practice rather than the theory of Delorism'.[31]

In his recent monograph on Delors, George Ross has demonstrated the clear logic behind the Commission President's federal political strategy. Beginning with what had already been implemented, Delors and his team in the Commission sought to 'build out from the EC's economic mandate towards broader, federalizing, state-building goals'. If the post-1985 EC's renaissance was construed as a market-based revival, the Commission and its other Community and member state allies 'attempted to graft an ambitious state-building strategy onto it in order to make important changes in the very definition of the European game'.[32] The gradual shift from market-building to state-building involved a protracted journey from the internal market via the SEA to social policy, regional economic redistribution, EMU and a single currency, a common foreign and security policy (CFSP) and, ultimately, political union (which meant federal political institutions). There was more than a hint of Monnet's method in this. Delors, like Monnet before him, sought to change the context of the problems which confronted Europe. We will recall Monnet's basic premise that, by changing the context, the problems themselves are changed. And this was to be conducted in the authentic, sure-footed Monnet-style method of small steps to build concrete practical achievements.

Delors' central goal was to create a new integrationist momentum out of the results of the '1992' Single Market launching pad. With a convergence of national, intra-EC and international factors working in favour of further European integration, Delors determined fully to exploit the results of the '1992' project to 'create new opportunities for wide-ranging programmatic initiatives'. Ross distilled the essence of the federal political strategy:

The hope was that successful new European activism would shift the location of member state problem-solving more to Community level and create an irresistible logic of Europeanization. There was therefore a great deal of the 'Monnet method' in the Delors strategy. A premium was placed on locating new programs which promised linkages to more far-reaching areas, pulling 'on the thread which would untangle some knots and, step by step, the rest would fall into place'. Member states would be carried forward in their commitments to European integration by the unintended consequences of decisions made to resolve specific problems.[33]

This strategy, both in conception and operation, revealed once again a fundamental continuity of federalist thought and practice. The similarities with the so-called 'Monnet method' were undeniable. Let us look, therefore, at this basic continuity of federalist thought and practice through the prismatic relationship between Monnet, Spinelli and Delors: the triad of federalists.

It is remarkable, though entirely predictable, that contemporary theorists of European integration should conveniently overlook the thought and practice of the triad of federalists in their determination to ignore the significance of federalism in their explanation of the Community's evolution. Despite the glaring empirical evidence that stares them squarely in the face, such theorists cannot bring themselves to acknowledge the often pivotal role which federal ideas and strategies have played in the EC's economic and political evolution. We will return to this extraordinary predicament a little later in the chapter. For the moment, let us focus sharply upon the links between our three federalists.

There were many similarities and some significant differences between Monnet, Spinelli and Delors. The intellectual origins of their federal ideas are interesting but, since we have already analysed those of Monnet and Spinelli in Chapter 2, only a cursory comparative focus will be utilized here. Like Spinelli but unlike Monnet, Delors came from the Catholic Left and derived his federalism from this source and his personalism from Mounier. Grant noted that Delors' close friendship with Helmut Kohl had prompted the West German Chancellor to remark that if the Commission President 'had been born in Germany he would have become a Christian democrat'.[34] And Ross observed that Delors 'occupied a situation on the overlapping boundaries between social democracy and Christian democracy'.[35] Spinelli, too, came from the Left in Italy but he had rejected Catholicism. Nonetheless his federal ideas, like those of Delors, possessed a strong ideological basis completely absent in Monnet. Delors and Monnet, however, share similarities in respect of their step-by-step federalist strategies which hinged on the perception of opportunities, the force of events and the belief that nothing could happen without ideas. And the combination of political ideas and institutions, of course, was something that bound all three federalists together just as their unswerving sense of mission drove them to devote their lives to the European federal cause. Ross referred to Delors' 'inner-directed moral convictions' and described him colourfully as being 'inhabited by deep spiritual motivations' which furnished a '*grande mission*'.[36] Delors also 'instinctively agreed with the logic of the "Monnet method"' locating policy changes which 'would later "spillover" into other areas'.[37] Linkage was the fulcrum of European integration.

This short profile of Jacques Delors the federalist amply testifies to the practical impact of federal ideas and strategies on the EC in particular, and on European integration in general. The singular focus upon Delors inevitably stretches beyond the historical period with which this chapter is principally concerned, but it points up once again the striking continuity of federalist thought and practice in the evolution of the Community, and serves to expose and underline the abject failure of most contemporary theorists of European integration to accommodate federalism in their explanations of the building of Europe. It also demonstrates, yet again, the importance of networks of influence promoting the federalist cause. A study of Delors' cabinets reveals distinctly similar federalist networks to those which we have already surveyed in the Hallstein Commission a quarter of a century earlier. There was a veritable web of behind-the-scenes federalists who were able to weave their influence in putting the ideas and strategies of Delors into practice. The activities of his long-serving *chef de cabinet*, Pascal Lamy, his deputy *chef de cabinet*, Francois Lamoureux, and later Riccardo Perissich who became the director-general for the single market, Jerome Vignon, head of the Commission think-tank, and the secretary general, David Williamson, all worked in the federal cause. The network should also be stretched to include those Commissioners, like Carlo Ripa di Meana, who were either self-confessed federalists or federalist sympathizers. The Commission, we are reminded, was always sympathetic, albeit diplomatically, to forward movement in a federal direction. Its institutional context predisposed it toward the federal goal. But the caution with which it had traditionally allowed itself to be associated with federalism suddenly seemed to evaporate in the late 1980s. Even the term 'federalism' itself ceased to be taboo in Community circles.

The years between 1985 and 1988 therefore were heady years for Delors and the Commission. It was a period of buoyant optimism for both federalists and intergovernmentalists alike. Each could take comfort from contemporary achievements. The goal of the Single Market by 1992 was inextricably linked to support for the SEA. Thatcher had endorsed the SEA principally to secure the benefits of the internal market for the UK. She viewed it as an end in itself and was determined to reduce the implications of other parts of the Act to very modest proportions. It was a calculated gamble. Delors, as we have seen, viewed it in a completely different light. It was only a part, although an integral part, of his much larger federal strategy, designed to achieve a much larger federal goal. In any event, December 1988 brought Delors to the end of his first term as Commission President – a term which could boast the achievement *inter alia* of what he had called the 'triptych'. This referred to the Single Market, the SEA and the so-called 'Delors package' of budgetary measures which were also a crucial element in his overall federal strategy. The saviour of his package, and probably his greatest ally among the political leaders of the member state governments, was Chancellor Kohl. By the end of 1988, Delors had not only salvaged his budgetary package but he had also reactivated EMU as the chairman of the eponymous Delors Committee, and had taken the first steps to promote his notion of the 'European Model of Society' which presaged the European 'Social Charter' in the summer of 1989.

Grant claimed that at the end of Delors' first presidency, the Community had moved much closer to a federal system of government in two important respects: first, member states had transferred powers to EC institutions via constitutional changes and new laws; and, second, they had transferred money from their own budgets to that of the Community.[38] It had been impossible to introduce the sort of fiscal federalism that is the hallmark of every established federation, but he had at least managed to introduce the principle of regional economic redistribution into Community affairs. As we bring this section to a close, it is worth reflecting upon the nature of Delors' political leadership during his first term as Commission President.[39] He had achieved a great deal in a short space of time, especially if we consider the doom and gloom of the early 1980s. And, unlike Monnet and Spinelli, he had been in a prominent position at the helm of the Commission to place his public office at the service of the federalist cause. This he did with great energy and gusto. And when he discovered that he had no formal power to implement his federal ideas, he resorted to Monnet's tactics: persuade others to promote them. Helmut Kohl's EMU initiative in 1988 was a classic example of his ability to do this.

Delors knew, however, that support from the intergovernmental arena was always transient and unreliable. It was liable to be undermined at any moment by shifting domestic policy priorities and electoral calculations. During these years, he moved swiftly to implement the largely economic foundations of his grand project which were critical to the creation of his socio-political community. As we have seen, 1992 was integral to his master plan. Since everything was linked, it would be the crucial connecting link to what was to follow. Let us look, then, at two principal features of the Single Market which continue to arouse considerable scholarly controversy, namely, the putative political consequences of 1992 and its theoretical implications.

## Federalism, integration theory and the single market

There seems to be a general scholarly consensus that the plans to complete the Single Market by 1992 were responsible for a dramatic revival of academic interest in the EC. Helen Wallace and Alasdair Young observed in 1996 that 'new theoretical approaches to the study of European integration' had 'taken the single market as their main point of reference'. Indeed the Single Market project had been elevated so much that for many it constituted the 'critical turning point between stagnation and dynamism, between the "old" politics of European integration and the "new" politics of European regulation'.[40] What are these new theoretical approaches to the study of European integration and how far has their focus upon the Single Market succeeded in advancing our understanding of the complex processes involved in shaping the EC's political destiny? In particular where, if at all, do federal ideas, influences and strategies fit into these new theoretical approaches?

It is not our purpose to provide a detailed investigative account of these new theoretical approaches here. The constraints of space prevent this. Instead I intend to refer to several of the more well-known theoretical contributions, which together have constituted the academic revival of interest in the EC from about the late 1980s, with a particular purpose in mind. I want to examine the relationship between federalism and these recent theoretical revisions in order to reinstate it as part of the explanation of the SEA. First, let us review the origins and nature of the Single Market project which formed the centrepiece of the SEA.

In ratifying the SEA in July 1987, the Community of the Twelve committed themselves to the progressive establishment, by the end of 1992, of an internal market defined as 'an area without internal frontiers in which the free movement of goods, persons, services and capital is ensured'.[41] This commitment included certain procedural changes deemed necessary to the effective implementation of the internal market plan, which was based upon 279 proposals contained in the 1985 Commission White Paper spearheaded by the British Commissioner for the Internal Market, Lord Cockfield. It is evident that the origins of the Single Market project can be traced back at least to the 1970s and the early 1980s. Structural changes in the global political economy, the failure of national economic strategies, new trends in international competition, and the arrival of new national political elites combined to prompt a west European reappraisal of the economic goals of the EC. But as Wayne Sandholtz and John Zysman have emphasized, structural change was 'a necessary, though not a sufficient, condition for the renewal of the European project. It was a trigger. Other factors were equally necessary and, in combination, sufficient'. In short, 'the international changes did not produce 1992: they provoked a rethinking'.[42]

Sandholtz and Zysman's analysis of the 1992 project suggested that the initiative to recast, if not unify, the European market was 'a disjunction, a dramatic new start, rather than the fulfilment of the original effort to construct Europe'.[43] Theirs is the first of the new theoretical approaches to the study of European integration which we shall briefly survey and we will return to their important claim about 1992 as a new start later in the section. In a nutshell, they proposed a composite theoretical explanation which incorporated three basic elements: the Commission's pivotal role as policy entrepreneur; the support of a transnational industry coalition; and a favourable collective (domestic) setting whereby a coalition of intergovernmental elites were receptive to market unification based upon the domestic political contexts of each member state. For a number of reasons, they did not think that conventional integration theories were well suited for analysing the events of 1992.[44] Moreover, the domestic political context alone could not carry the full analytical burden of explanation: 'the project did not bubble up spontaneously from the various national political contexts'. Political leadership for 1992 actually came 'from outside the national settings; it came from the Commission'.[45]

This analysis contained several contradictions and seemed somewhat confused about precisely which actors and institutions were responsible for the Single Market project. Its main strength lay in its rejection of a single theory to explain 1992 and in its acknowledgement of the need for a much more sophisticated multicausal explanation. Despite elements of confusion, however, they did edge slowly toward a theoretical explanation that recognised the interplay of international and domestic factors which furnished the Community institutions – and the Commission in particular – with a golden opportunity to exercise adroit political leadership. We can see from the focus of their analysis that there was also an acknowledgement of some old, largely discredited, neofunctionalist assumptions.

David Cameron, in his theoretical contribution which appeared in 1992, incorporated many of the assumptions and assertions of Sandholtz and Zysman, but his thesis was much less muddled. He concluded in what was a neorealist vein: 'however inexorable the integrationist impulses in the Community, in the final analysis it will be the states, acting through the European Council, rather than the supra-national organizations of the Community, that will by and large define, shape and control policy, at least in the realm of economic, monetary and political union'. His concession to the influence of the Commission and other non-state actors did not amount to much: 'however powerful the economic and institutional forces favoring integration may appear, and however consequential the spillover effects of the 1992 initiative, the Community has been, is now, and will remain a community of states'.[46] Cameron's detailed analysis did not leave much room here for the active leadership role of the supranational institutions, the transnational business organizations or the ubiquitous influence of the federalists.

It was to be expected that the new dynamism of the post-1985 EC, especially with its emphasis upon the Single Market, would attract conventional reappraisals of neofunctionalism. Two appeared in fairly quick succession. David Mutimer looked at the relationship between economic integration and political unification with a view to assessing the political implications of market completion. He claimed that the successful internal market would have political spillover effects particularly in the areas of national economic policies: 1992 was a useful test case of the validity of neofunctionalism precisely because 'the blatantly political implications of so many of the economic measures being taken' made them 'perfect candidates for spillover'.[47] The Single Market, if successful, would have a strong centripetal impact upon the Community towards centralizing decision-making in Brussels, intensifying the pressures for monetary union and strengthening both the political legitimacy of and political identification with Brussels. Indeed, since both the Commission and the EP were actively engaged in promoting 'enhanced political integration', there was already a framework in place 'into which political authority' could 'spill, and to which political identification' could shift. But he seemed nonetheless disappointed with his own conclusions, confessing that neofunctionalism was 'not sufficient for understanding the progress of political integration'.[48]

The second theoretical contribution to the purported revival of neofunctionalism, by Jeppe Tranholm-Mikkelsen, was optimistic about its explanatory value. This author claimed that, since 1985, the Commission had made a conscious effort to pursue a neofunctionalist strategy much more openly, skilfully and with more successful results than previously. In other words, strong neofunctionalist pressures – functional, political and cultivated – were in evidence, and they had 'played an important part in speeding up integration'. There had also been 'a re-emergence of the neo-functionalist logic'.[49] And the resilience of the logic of spillover implied that neofunctionalism was 'by no means obsolete'. Indeed, it was 'indispensable to the understanding of European integration'.[50] Neofunctionalism did not however 'constitute an all-encompassing framework for the understanding of the integration process'. Alternative frameworks, like intergovernmentalism and interdependence theories, also contained important insights into the integration process. Neofunctionalism remained only 'a partial theory' of European integration, even in its post-1985 dynamic phase.[51]

Both of these neofunctionalist revisions suggested elements of an accommodation with realism. The analyses of Sandholtz and Zysman and Cameron also suggested some attempt at a theoretical convergence between those who stressed the importance of supra-national organizations and other non-state actors, and those whose main focus was the member states. Put simply, these contemporary analytical surveys pointed to some kind of theoretical *rapprochement* between neofunctionalism, realism and neorealism the combination of which was much closer to reality than each would be separately. Cameron, although he arrived at a largely neorealist destination, nonetheless stated his position bluntly: 'neither neofunctionalism nor neorealism seems to fully explain the process by which 1992 came into being. And, taken alone, neither serves as a reliable guide to the Community of the future'.[52] No such concession was offered by the more hardline realists like Stanley Hoffmann and Andrew Moravcsik, although the self-styled 'neoliberal institutionalist', Robert Keohane, did appear more sympathetic to the incorporation of non-state actors in his explanation of 1992. It is, therefore, to these theorists that we must finally turn in our brief survey of 1992 and integration theory.

Since we have already paid some attention, albeit brief, to the theoretical contributions of Keohane and Hoffmann in Chapter 2, we will concentrate upon the recent realist analysis of Moravcsik. Here we return to the standard intergovernmentalist explanation of 1992, essentially an application of the realist image of international relations (IR) to the EC. Moravcsik's explanation was empirically-based, testing the historical evidence of the SEA against what he called a particular variant of neofunctionalism, namely, 'supra-national institutionalism'. His detailed research claimed that none of the three supra-national variables – European institutional momentum, transnational business interest group activity, and international political leadership – could account for the timing, content and process of negotiating the SEA. Instead, it was 'intergovernmental institutionalism' – rooted in hard zero-sum bargaining between member state governments, relative power relations and domestic policy preferences – that explained the creation of the SEA. Moravcsik concluded that supra-national institutions, like the Commission, had an important role to play in 'cementing existing interstate bargains', but he insisted that the primary source of integration lay 'in the interests of the states themselves and the relative power' that each brought to Brussels.[53]

What are we to make of this impressive intergovernmentalist thesis about the SEA? Moravcsik was later to extend his explanation into a much more fully-developed analysis, based upon the origins of domestic policy preferences, which came to be known as 'liberal intergovernmentalism'.[54] For the moment, however, we will focus upon his theoretical contribution concerning the SEA. There is no doubt that plenty of empirical evidence existed to confirm that both the European Council and the Thorn Commission were behind the internal market initiative. It had already been taking shape at least four years before Delors and the Commission that took office in January 1985 entered the EC arena as propulsive forces in favour of renewed integration. But since Moravcsik's critique of the neofunctionalist variant focused largely upon the timing, content and process of negotiating the SEA, federalists would challenge much of his historical interpretation of the events that led up to its approval by the European Council in February 1986. They would argue that his self-styled 'intergovernmental institutionalism' was far too narrow and exclusive to be convincing. In its failure to accommodate the subtleties and complexities of key elements of the peculiar political environment of 1984–85 – which included the strong federalist propensities of both Mitterrand and Kohl, the individual contributions of Delors and Cockfield to the Commission's White Paper on the internal market, the influence of the Italians, especially Craxi, at the Milan summit, and the ubiquity of federalist elites operating across the spectrum of the Community institutions and in the Dooge Committee – his thesis simultaneously ignored the federalist sympathies of key state elites and was too dismissive of non-state actors. It denied even a relative institutional autonomy for the Commission and EP from the member states, and it ignored the decisive role that the supranational Court of Justice played in the *Cassis de Dijon* case (1979) which paved the way for the internal market programme. Federalists from Monnet to Delors, we will recall, believed that institutions and ideas mattered in the world of politics. Consequently, Moravcsik's assertion that the Commission could do little more than merely 'cement interstate bargains' seemed empirically invalid: the Commission, Court of Justice and EP together had exerted autonomous Community preferences and pressures upon the member states as well as being influenced by them. It was a two-way traffic of ideas and influences.

In summary, then, Moravcsik's thesis can be taken to task for several deficiencies of historical analysis and interpretation which have resulted in selective omissions and some sweeping over-simplifications. He signally failed to bridge the gap between domestic policy formulation and national preferences and the autonomy of the EC's evolution with its growing impact upon an increasingly global environment. For federalists, the Community was more than just a bargain among governments. Mrs Thatcher had famously asserted that there was no such thing as 'a separate Community interest'; it was merely the aggregate of the constituent state units that composed it.[55] Federalists, however, construed it as an emergent European polity in the making, with all that this implied.

Returning to neofunctionalism, there was certainly some evidence of a theoretical convergence with federal ideas and interpretations. Both Mutimer and Tranholm-Mikkelsen acknowledged the resilience of linkage (the logic of spillover survived), the trend towards more centralized decision-making in Brussels and the political implications of stronger central institutions. These observations chimed conveniently with the federalists' political strategy of step-by-step progress and institutional reform. There was also a consensus between them about 'automaticity'. The SEA confirmed that if integration was to occur in the future it would not be according to any inherent logic propelling it forward, as it were, by its own volition. It would require a firm push. And the pushing would be successful only if the circumstances were propitious. Political elites would first have to perceive the opportunity and then act decisively. This was the predicament that both Monnet and Spinelli had described as 'crisis exploitation' and George Ross has recently dubbed 'political opportunity structure'.[56]

Before we conclude this section on integration theory and the SEA, it is necessary to return to the important claim that Sandholtz and Zysman made about 1992 as 'a dramatic new start' which bore no direct linkage to the Treaty of Rome. This assertion seems to be driven by realist and/or neorealist assumptions which reject the idea of any kind of inherent institutional or policy determinism. Hoffmann, too, argued that the 'new enterprise' built on the institutions and achievements of the 'earlier one' but that it was not 'a mere continuation'.[57] And both Moravcsik and Milward insisted that European integration had never proceeded steadily and incrementally in linear fashion. On the contrary, it had moved forward in fits and starts. Like Moravcsik, Milward claimed that the SEA was the result of a rational choice by member state governments 'for the advancement of new national policy objectives'. The SEA underlined the fact that there was 'nothing automatic' about the realignment of common policies; it merely signified the extent to which member states were prepared to alter the balance between using integration and interdependence to further their national policy objectives.[58] In short, the SEA episode was, not surprisingly, construed by realists to confirm the basic assumptions of realism.

The realists clearly believed that they were on safe ground when they rejected the notion of an inherent logic or a self-sustaining momentum in the integration process. The empirical evidence simply failed to support it. Member state governments in the European Council remained firmly in control of the EC's destiny. It could go nowhere without their consent. But this fundamental axiom of realism needed to be carefully weighed against the contemporary realities of international change. The realists needed to be realistic. If Sandholtz and Zysman were correct to argue that structural changes in the global economy had not caused 1992, there is certainly a case for claiming that they shaped and circumscribed the possible outcomes. The reality was that the policy choices were limited and the EC clearly proved to be the most compelling of those available. It was precisely at this juncture that Moravcsik's 'supra-national variables' came into play. The role of both the Thorn and the Delors Commissions cannot simply be brushed aside on the basis of timing, content and negotiations. As Ross has argued, extensive supra-national action played 'a central role in the entire EC story after 1985'.[59] Consequently both realism and neorealism need to be more flexible and adjust their somewhat narrow emphasis upon inter-state bargains and constraints on further reform in order to incorporate pressures coming from elsewhere. The member state governments took important decisions about their perceived national interests in a specific EC context: what IR theorists would call a high degree of institutionalization.

### Conclusion: history, theory and practice

It was not possible at the historical juncture of 1985–88 to know if the SEA and 1992 would lead logically to further movement toward European integration, or if they were simply a set of specific historical events with no necessary implications for the future. But it was already clear in 1988 that there were several state and non-state actors which were determined that they would have far-reaching consequences. Mitterrand, Kohl, Delors, the Commission, the EP and a veritable ant hill of federalist elites across the Community framework acted with purpose to ensure that the Single Market would be implemented, that EMU would be relentlessly pursued, that a CFSP would be gradually brought into focus and that the foundations for a 'social Europe' would be firmly put in place. These incisive goals, if successfully implemented, would present realism with further intellectual challenges. The theory would be outstripped by an unfolding and apparently inexplicable reality. After all, if spillover and linkage were as redundant as the realists suggested, why and how could these developments be explained? And if the federalist step-by-step teleology was as irrelevant as they had always argued, how could events unfold in the manner predicted by federalists?

The years between 1989 and 1993 would demonstrate that the federalist conception of European integration was anything but irrelevant. The longer the Community's evolution moved in a federal direction, the more it was possible to converse convincingly about long-term federal trends. It all depended upon which perspective was adopted. If the realists and neo-realists were correct in their insistence upon the 'discontinuity' of European integration, they could not equally deny that there was an unbroken line of descent from the European Coal and Steel Community (ECSC) via the European Community (EC) to the SEA. As François Duchene put it: 'there was a direct line of descent from the Schuman Plan to the Common Market, as indeed there is to the Single Market'.[60] Of course, lineage is not causation, and this is not to claim that each of these building blocks led logically to the next one in the style of an automatic chain-reaction. But it could not be denied that each forward movement had built largely upon the existing *acquis communautaire* which had, in turn, helped to shape and direct national policy priorities. As Milward acknowledged, the *acquis* offered guarantees based upon political judgements about the long-term national interest: it was 'less easily reversed, more exclusive and more law-abiding'.[61] The theoretical implication of this observation was that, while more research was needed on domestic policy, it should also take account of the established and increasingly supra-national EC policy base.

Having looked at the history, theory and practice of federalism, European Union and the SEA, it is clear why Wallace and Young were reluctant to endorse any interpretation of events in 1985 that sought to offer 'monocausal explanation'. The striking picture, they claimed, was of 'a clustering of factors'.[62] Our survey of these years suggests that, once again, reality was much more complex and untidy than the conventional theories of neofunctionalism, realism, neorealism, and the 'supra-national institutionalism' and 'intergovernmental institutionalism' of Moravcsik suggested.

Indeed the SEA and 1992 confirm a sense of theoretical disarray. No single theory of European integration is able to explain the SEA and 1992. What seems to have emerged is an attempt to bring together different elements of these theories to provide a composite explanation. Keohane and Hoffmann, for example, have conceded that if the concept of spillover retained any theoretical significance, it required 'prior programmatic agreement among governments, expressed in an intergovernmental bargain'.[63] But even if we agree to build upon statist notions of political leadership in the European Council, it is not sufficient for the neorealists simply to leave it at that. It is also important for them to recognise that the key state actors, especially in the Paris–Bonn axis, were federalists whose evaluation of their respective national interests coincided with and, in some cases, was driven by a particular conception of Europe.

Our purpose in this chapter was not to suggest an alternative theory of European integration. This would have been far too presumptuous. Instead, we have tried once again to underline the influence of federalism and the federalists, and to demonstrate that without Delors, Spinelli, the EP and the EUT, the SEA would probably never have been achieved. 1992 might have come about in some fashion, but the SEA would probably not have emerged at all or, at least, not in the form that it did. In reality, of course, the two were inextricably linked. But without the remarkable momentum achieved by the federalists – including Mitterrand, Kohl and Craxi – the Community would not have been able to take another crucial step in the direction of European Union. Delors knew that once the EC had taken 1992 on board, the pressure for constitutional reform would grow. It was not by accident that he revered the SEA: 'I knew that if this treaty was accepted, it was an important moment and that historians would one day recognise the value of this mouse'.[64] History demonstrates that Delors and the federalists were right; the subsequent years were to witness further federalist momentum in the shape of the Treaty on European Union (TEU) which shifted more power from national governments to Community institutions. With these thoughts in mind, it is time to shift the focus of our attention to the most convulsive period in post-war European history: a period in which the relationship between federalism and European Union became much more dynamic and transparent. We will begin with some reflections upon the significance of 1989 for federalism and European Union and then examine in some detail the political implications of 1992 before looking closely at the TEU.

## NOTES

1   D. Dinan, *Ever closer union? An introduction to the European Community*, London: Macmillan, 1994, p. 129; and J. Pinder, *European Community: the building of a union*, Oxford: OUP, 1991, p. 68.

2  S. Hoffmann, 'The European Community and 1992', in S. Hoffmann (ed.), *The European sisyphus: essays on Europe, 1964–1994*, p. 234, Boulder, CO: West-view Press, 1995.

3  S. Hoffmann, 'The European Community and 1992', p. 231.

4  Spinelli's speech, 14 February 1984, *OJ, DEP*, 1–309, p. 28.

5  Spinelli's speech, 14 February 1984, *OJ, DEP*, 1–309, p. 28.

6  Mitterrand's speech, 24 May 1984, *OJ, DEP*, 1–314, pp. 262–63.

7  See the Report from the ad hoc committee on a people's Europe, *Bulletin of the EC*, 3–1985, pp. 3–10.

8  For the conclusions of the Fontainebleau European Council, see *Agence Europe*, 28 June 1984.

9  Interview with Spinelli, 14 February 1985, European Parliament, Strasbourg.

10  E. Haywood, 'The European policy of François Mitterrand', *Journal of Common Market Studies*, 31, pp. 275–77, June 1993.

11  It is important to note that this equation was not a fixed majority–minority relationship. There were shifting alignments on different policy issues, eg. Eire and security.

12  Ad hoc committee for institutional affairs, *Report to the European Council*, 29–30 March 1985, Brussels, p. 33.

13  The EP published an official comparison of the Dooge Report and the EUT in order to demonstrate how 'strikingly similar' they were. See *D.G. for Committees and Interparliamentary Delegations*, 16 April 1985, P.E. 97. p. 407.

14  *Report to the European Council*, p. 2.

15  P. Keatinge and A. Murphy, 'The European Council's ad hoc committee on institutional affairs, 1984–1985', in R. Pryce (ed.), *The dynamics of European Union*, p. 223.

16  See M. Burgess, *Federalism and European Union: political ideas, influences and strategies in the European Community, 1972–1987*, London: Routledge, 1989, pp. 190–91.

17  *EP Bulletin*, No. 39, (special edition) 26 September 1985, p. 6.

18  See R. Corbett, 'The 1985 intergovernmental conference and the Single Euro-pean Act', in R. Pryce (ed.), *The dynamics of European Union*, pp. 238–72.

19  R. Corbett, 'The 1985 intergovernmental conference', p. 239.

20  See Santer's speech to the EP on the results and implications of the Milan European Council and the Luxembourg Presidency's intentions regarding the IGC, *OJ, DEP*, No. 2–328, 9 July 1985, pp. 36–41 and pp. 68–69.

21  Santer's speech to the EP, No. 2–328/41.

22  Santer's speech to the EP, No. 2–328/41.

23  See Delors' speech to the EP on the Commission's position, *OJ, DEP*, No. 2–328, 9 July 1985, pp. 41–46.

24  See J. Lodge, 'The Single European Act: towards a new euro-dynamism?', *Journal of Common Market Studies*, 24, pp. 203–23, March 1986; and R. Corbett, 'The 1985 intergovernmental conference', pp. 238–72.

25  R. Corbett, 'The 1985 intergovernmental conference', p. 261.

26  Single European Act, (SEA), *EC Bulletin*, supplement 2/86, p. 10.

27  G. Ross, *Jacques Delors and European integration*, Cambridge: Polity Press, 1995, p. 28.

28  C. Grant, 'The theory and practice of Delorism', in M. Bond, et al., (eds), *Eminent Europeans: Personalities who shaped contemporary Europe*, pp. 285–307, London: The Greycoat Press, 1996.

29  For a detailed analysis of the ideological background to federalism and Chris-tian Democracy, see M. Burgess, 'The European tradition of federalism: christian democracy and federalism', in M. Burgess and A.-G. Gagnon (eds),

*Comparative federalism and federation: competing traditions and future directions*, pp. 138–53, Hemel Hempstead: Harvester Wheatsheaf, 1993.

30  C. Grant, 'The theory and practice of Delorism', p. 286.
31  C. Grant, 'The theory and practice of Delorism', p. 293.
32  G. Ross, *Jacques Delors and European integration*, pp. 4 and 12.
33  G. Ross, *Jacques Delors and European integration*, p. 230.
34  C. Grant, *Delors: inside the house that Jacques built*, London: Nicholas Brealey Publishers, 1994, p. 141.
35  G. Ross, *Jacques Delors and European integration*, p. 244.
36  G. Ross, *Jacques Delors and European integration*, p. 70.
37  G. Ross, *Jacques Delors and European integration*, p. 29.
38  C. Grant, *Delors: inside the house that Jacques built*, p. 76.
39  On this aspect of Delors' presidencies, see H. Drake, 'Political leadership and European integration: The case of Jacques Delors', *West European Politics*, 18(1), pp. 140–60, January 1995.
40  H. Wallace and A.R. Young, 'The single market: a new approach to policy', in H. Wallace and W. Wallace (eds), *Policy-making in the European Union*, p. 126, Oxford: OUP, 1996.
41  Article 8A, Section II(1), Single European Act (SEA), *Bulletin of the EC*, supplement 2/86, Commission of the EC, Luxembourg, 1986, p. 11.
42  W. Sandholtz and J. Zysman, '1992: recasting the European bargain', *World Politics*, 42(1), p. 106, October 1989.
43  W. Sandholtz and J. Zysman, '1992', p. 95.
44  These are explained in W. Sandholtz and J. Zysman, '1992', p. 99.
45  W. Sandholtz and J. Zysman, '1992', p. 100.
46  D.R. Cameron, 'The 1992 initiative: causes and consequences', in A.M. Sbragia (ed.), *Euro-Politics: institutions and policy-making*, p. 74, Washington DC: The Brookings Institution, 1992.
47  D. Mutimer, '1992 and the political integration of Europe: neofunctionalism reconsidered', *Journal of European Integration*, 13, p. 100, 1989.
48  D. Mutimer, '1992 and the political integration of Europe', pp. 100–101.
49  J. Transholm-Mikkelsen, 'Neofunctionalism: obstinate or obsolete? A reappraisal in the light of the new dynamism of the EC', *Millennium: Journal of International Studies*, 20(1), p. 16, 1991.
50  J. Transholm-Mikkelsen, 'Neofunctionalism: obstinate or obsolete?', p. 19.
51  J. Transholm-Mikkelsen, 'Neofunctionalism: obstinate or obsolete?', p. 18.
52  D.R. Cameron, 'The 1992 initiative: causes and consequences', p. 30.
53  A. Moravcsik, 'Negotiating the Single European Act', in R.O. Keohane and S. Hoffmann (eds), *The new European Community: decision-making and institutional change*, p. 75, Oxford: Westview Press, 1991.
54  A. Moravcsik, 'Preferences and power in the European Community: a liberal intergovernmentalist approach', *Journal of Common Market Studies*, 31, pp. 473–524, December 1993.
55  *The Times*, 3 February 1981.
56  G. Ross, *Jacques Delors and European integration*, pp. 5–6.
57  S. Hoffmann, 'The European Community and 1992', in *The European sisyphus*, p. 233.
58  A.S. Milward and V. Sorensen, 'Interdependence or integration? a national choice', in A.S. Milward et al. (eds), *The frontier of national sovereignty: history and theory, 1945–1992*, pp. 20–21, London: Routledge, 1994.
59  G. Ross, *Jacques Delors and European integration*, p. 10.
60  F. Duchene, *Jean Monnet: the first statesman of interdependence*, London: W.W. Norton & Co., 1994, p. 399.

61  A.S. Milward and V. Sorensen, 'Interdependence or integration?', p. 19.
62  H. Wallace and A.R. Young, 'The single market: a new approach to policy', p. 137.
63  R.O. Keohane and S. Hoffmann, 'Institutional change in Europe in the 1980s', in R.O. Keohane and S. Hoffmann (eds), *The new European Community: decision-making and institutional change*, p. 17.
64  C. Grant, *Delors: inside the house that Jacques built*, p. 75.

# 6 Maastricht: the last treaty of the Cold War, 1989–93

The collapse of the Berlin Wall in November 1989 signified the end of the Cold War. Indeed, its significance has been construed by some scholars as having effectively brought the history of the twentieth century to an abrupt and premature close. This is largely because the years between the Russian Revolution in October 1917 and the events of November 1989 are considered to have been dominated by the titanic contest between capitalism and communism (or socialism). 1989 has apparently resolved that conflict once and for all. In what Eric Hobsbawm has dubbed the 'Short Twentieth Century', there is no doubt that 'in the late 1980s and early 1990s an era in world history ended and a new one began'.[1] Let us look briefly at some of the long- and short-term implications of 1989 for federalism, European Union and European integration.

The significance of 1989 is multifaceted. It spreads out in many directions, is often only dimly perceived and continues today to perplex us. We remain uncertain about its long-term impact. The euphoria which accompanied the much vaunted material and moral victory of liberal capitalist values and market economics over the centralized state-controlled command economies rooted in Marxist–Leninist ideology was understandable, but it was also short-lived and short-sighted. The triumphalist tone set by both the British Prime Minister, Mrs Thatcher, and the American President, Ronald Reagan, came later to be regarded by many percipient observers as a hollow triumphalism. The most immediate consequence of the crumbling of the Berlin Wall was German unification: the absorption in 1990 of 18 million east Germans into a new German colossus situated in the heart of Europe. Berlin replaced Bonn: Germany moved physically eastwards, as did the centre of Europe. And Europe began to return to itself, although not in the same way. The process of regeneration earlier in the 1980s in Poland, and the re-emergence of Hungary, Romania, Czechoslovakia and Bulgaria together with Latvia, Lithuania, Estonia and new states like Croatia, Slovenia and Slovakia (from the peaceful break-up of Czechoslovakia in 1992) in the early 1990s engendered a massive reappraisal of what the new Europe meant.

A particular focus of this public debate has been the revival of the concept of 'central' Europe. Since the Cold War realities of the East–West divide had effectively obliterated what was considered to have been central Europe in the inter-war years, the post-1989 era has reopened the old question of where the limits, divisions and boundaries of Europe are. Like Europe itself, there has never been a general consensus about where central Europe begins or ends. For forty years it had disappeared; it had become, in Timothy Garton Ash's words, 'an assertion about the past', an aspiration, an idea, a 'kingdom of the spirit'. Today it has been rediscovered; it is 'an assertion of the present'.[2] This partly intellectual and partly public debate continues to have enormous implications for the European Union (EU) in particular and European integration in general. But in the years immediately after 1989 the primary concern of countries like Hungary and Czechoslovakia was to put in place the mechanisms which would establish the market economy on which, it was generally assumed, liberal democracy was predicated. Economic strength and stability was the foundation for political stability.

The tumultuous events of 1989 were really about central and eastern Europe rather than the Soviet Union. Yet it is nonetheless true that the demise of communism there and the unravelling of the Soviet empire in the early 1990s to yield a reformulated Russian federation has left the enduring impression that this historic transition was merely a postscript to 1989. In reality, the Soviet path toward a basic restructuring of the economy and a fundamental modernization of the state, though not its destruction, had been foreshadowed at least as far back as 1985 when Mikhail Gorbachev ascended to the leadership of party and state. But the release of the central and east European states from Soviet tutelage and the reshaping of the Russian state itself left a region of dangerous economic, political, military and cultural instability. Around the periphery of the Russian federation, ethnic rivalries and hostilities simmered while about 25 million Russians and Russian speakers found themselves, for the first time in two centuries, outside the borders of Russia proper: in the three Baltic states of Latvia, Lithuania, and Estonia; in Moldavia; in Georgia; and in the Ukraine. In central and eastern Europe similar age-old ethnic tensions survived and were reactivated while the historic displacement of cultural identities was aggravated by the sudden and dramatic migration of millions of people to the West in search of economic security and prosperity. In Yugoslavia, where the civil war had begun with Slovenian and Croatian secession, the revival of nationalism flared into the enduring Bosnian battles which contributed a new phrase – 'ethnic cleansing' – to the public discourse of international politics.

The effects of the end of the Cold War were also felt far and wide. The euphoria which accompanied the collapse of the Berlin Wall on the continent of Europe also seemed to usher in a new era of peaceful settlements, or significant progress towards such settlements, to conflicts which had previously seemed intractable. Fresh initiatives in South Africa, the Middle

East and in the Irish imbroglio seemed to symbolize the dawning of the new age of peace and reconciliation. And the link with the new international political economy, initially obscure, soon became evident in the early 1990s as first the South East Asian 'tiger' economies and later China burgeoned with an economic growth and investment potential which threatened to dwarf those of the new Europe. Put simply, the Cold War, being essentially Euro-centric, had effectively obscured the meaning and significance of the growing power of east Asia; 1989 heralded its rise, in the form of the Pacific Rim, and consecrated the decline of Europe. The end of the Cold War marked an unequivocal shift in the global centre of gravity towards Asia, a shift only temporarily halted in the late 1990s by endemic mismanagement, corruption, a series of banking collapses, over-extended investment and rigid economic structures in the economies of South Korea, Thailand, Indonesia, the Philippines, Malaysia, Hong Kong and Japan.

It was against this convulsive background that Jacques Delors in the European Commission, Helmut Kohl, in a new unified Germany and François Mitterrand in France, together with a host of federalist forces throughout the EC – especially in Italy, Belgium and Spain, and in the European Parliament (EP) – struggled to achieve the goal of European Union first promulgated in 1972. But what was the immediate impact of 1989 upon European integration? How did Delors, Mitterrand and Kohl perceive the new European future, and how did the EC respond to the sudden and unexpected events in central and eastern Europe? In his speech of 20 October 1989 at the College of Europe in Bruges, Delors referred to the events of 1989 as 'the acceleration of history', while Mitterrand's special address to the EP in November noted the urgent need to 'forge the Europe of tomorrow'.[3] Apart from the unification (rather than the re-unification) of Germany, Kohl's priorities were spelled out to telling effect:

> We are already making preparations for the further development of the European Community beyond this date, with Political Union as our goal. For the Federal Government this large market is an important, but intermediate stage. What we want is the political unification of Europe.... We would therefore be making a bad mistake and completely misjudging the situation if we were to deprive this process of European unification of its momentum at this of all times.... And Europe – I will say again at this time – happens to be more than the Europe of the Twelve of the European Community. It is not only London, Rome, the Hague, Dublin and Paris that belong to Europe, but Warsaw, Budapest, Prague and Sofia and of course Berlin, Leipzig and Dresden as well.... The events in Central, Eastern and South-Eastern Europe in particular make it more clear to us all how the Single European Act points the way: it tells us to establish a common

foreign policy and then to implement it. ... the Federal German
Government ... is a staunch supporter of the completion of the European Union. We see no alternative to the continuation and strengthening of the process of European unification. ... we Germans are
aware of our special mission and, speaking personally, of our European vocation.... The historic events of the last few weeks and months
... have changed the face of Europe and, with it, the face of
Germany.[4]

This important speech was historic not only for being the first time that
two representatives of the European Council – the President-in-Office and
the head of government of the country closest to the events of 1989 – had
chosen to explain their views and their proposals to the EP but also
because it summarized the 'Rubic's Cube' that was 1989. Kohl's speech
had enormous implications for both the vision and the reality of Europe.
1989 had created a new *de facto* reality but it had also opened up new vistas
for European integration.

The implications of German unification were many-sided. Each member
state in the EC and each country in Europe was affected by it in some way
and perceived it in very different ways. But the country for which unification was most pertinent was France. Mitterrand, like Thatcher, was at first
lukewarm about the prospect of a new unified Germany of 80 million
people on the doorstep. And *literally* on the French doorstep. The
Germans, as West Germany, had in 30 years already served notice of their
intentions by establishing themselves as the economic giant of the EC.
Clearly one implication of 1989 was that the Franco-German equation had
changed at a stroke; unification would severely reduce Germany's political
dependence upon France. It took very little imagination to project a European future with a new unified Germany in a redefined role which would
add political leadership to its undoubted economic strength. Consequently, Mitterrand's urgent priority was to ensure that the new
Germany would be bound even tighter than its predecessor to European
integration. This urgency was what lay behind his rock-solid support for
economic and monetary union (EMU) which had originally been
included in his manifesto for the 1988 presidential election. After 1989,
Mitterrand's European policy was, therefore, constrained by one overriding purpose: to secure Germany's place in Europe. France was prepared,
albeit reluctantly, to make further concessions in both economic and
political integration in order principally to guarantee the Europeanization
of Germany.

It was Chancellor Kohl's astute awareness of and acute sensitivity to the
widespread fears and anxieties of his European partners that helped
smooth the path to German unification in 1990. Since 1982 he had con-
founded both his domestic political allies as well as his adversaries with his
remarkable political skill and strength of character in re-establishing the

Christian Democratic Union (CDU) along with its Christian Social Union (CSU) partner as the hegemonic force in German politics. The CDU–CSU partnership rekindled memories of the halcyon days of Adenauer, Erhard and Kiesinger. And 1989 furnished him with the golden opportunity to demonstrate his diplomatic finesse in linking German unification with European unification. Indeed he had already forged the link in his EP speech in November:

> the Germans who are now at last coming together in a spirit of freedom will never be a threat and are in fact a gain for the unity of Europe.... The division of Germany has always been a visible and particularly painful manifestation of the division of Europe. Conversely, Germany will be completely united only if progress is made towards the unification of our old continent. Policy on Germany and policy on Europe are completely inseparable. They are two sides of the same coin.... Germany's problems can only be solved under a European roof.[5]

This was Kohl's mission, his self-styled personal 'vocation'. In this reassuring way, continuity was preserved. The old link between Adenauer and Brandt was reaffirmed and extended to include Kohl. German unification was part of the larger process of building a federal Europe. It was the precursor to a new 'pan-European peaceful order'. What was needed for the future was 'perceptiveness, reason and political imagination'.[6]

The EC's immediate response to the events of 1989 was to send out the appropriate political signals to its new European neighbours – including, importantly, Gorbachev – and to make a variety of arrangements for economic aid and assistance. But its response was not just about cooperation. Implicit in these circumstances was the assumption, only cursorily acknowledged, that the neighbours would eventually become partners. They would become part of the common European home. The enlargement of the EC to the countries of central and eastern Europe was now firmly on the agenda and was to be formally recognised as such at the Copenhagen European Council as early as June 1993. Europe was already on the move, but it was a Europe driven not solely by intergovernmental impulses.

The role of Delors and the Commission was easily overlooked in these unique events and circumstances. What was Delors' view, and how did the Commission itself react to 1989? This was an invaluable opportunity for Delors and the Commission to seize the political initiative on behalf of the Europe which went beyond intergovernmentalism. When Delors spoke to the EP, he urged an alliance between it and the Commission to 'strengthen the Community, make it more dynamic, speed up its integration and sketch out ... the architecture of greater Europe'. This meant implementing fully the Single European Act (SEA), including its social dimension, strengthening foreign policy cooperation, finding the financial resources to demonstrate the EC's solidarity outside Europe and mapping out the design of the new Europe by 'showing imagination and coming forward with the novel ideas required to build this greater Europe'.[7] George Ross summarized the adjustment to Delors' strategy:

> He took the lead in welcoming German unification.... A Germany anchored at the centre of the EC was the *sine qua non* of the Community's future. ... the Community's destiny and the future of Europe more generally would have been bleak indeed if the Federal Republic were to become a free, newly nationalist, political electron.[8]

Here we return to the Delors–Kohl relationship which we have already mentioned in the previous chapter. Apart from their personal friendship, they each had strategic reasons for maintaining a close liaison. Delors knew that many of his achievements had depended upon the support of Kohl. In 1988, we will recall, it had been Kohl who had committed the German cash which had facilitated an agreement on the Delors package, and he had also installed Delors as chairman of the committee on economic and monetary union (EMU). But Delors also saw that 'German unity could be exploited as an argument for political union'. According to Charles Grant, Kohl too had a vested interest in the personal relationship because he 'found it handy having a friend at the head of the Commission' and he never forgot Delors' help over unification.[9]

The Commission's own self-interest was also at stake in 1989. Even before the November watershed in post-war European history, a series of events and circumstances had symbolized the enhanced influence and status of the Commission since Delors had become its President in January 1985. What had been initiated in 1985 had to be continued and completed, but the Commission had also been proactive in its relations with the non-EC members of the European Free Trade Association (EFTA) in proposing a European Economic Area (EEA). The aim was to create a new trade alignment with those countries, like Austria, Switzerland and Norway, which remained committed to freer trade in Europe but not integration. The political reality of this was that the EC held the upper hand in negotiating the conditions of this new arrangement, as was soon made clear when Austria formally applied to join the EC in July 1989. The Commission had also made considerable headway on the international stage in a different arena. At the July 1989 Paris G7 Summit, it had been given an important new foreign policy role in the coordination of G24 (OECD countries) and EC aid to Poland and Hungary. Known officially as the Poland and Hungary Assistance for Economic Restructuring Programme (PHARE), it was extended in 1990 to other east European countries, the EC negotiating its own arrangements with each of them. This was complemented by Mitterrand's own initiative in November 1989 to create the European Bank for Reconstruction and Development (EBRD) to support the economic reconstruction of central and eastern Europe. It began its operations in March 1991, under the leadership of a close associate of the French President's, Jacques Attali. Together, these developments reflected the Commission's enhanced foreign policy capacity and gave a renewed impetus to its determination to strengthen the EC's established political cooperation procedures (POCO).

We can see from this brief introductory survey of the short- and long-term implications of 1989 for European integration that both federalists and intergovernmentalists had much to be optimistic about. A detailed analysis of the events of 1989–90 would obviously support an intergovernmental interpretation of these years simply because national governments were the principal actors in the various negotiations that took place, but the political influence of the Commission and EP should not be completely dismissed. Why, after all, did both Mitterrand and Kohl decide in a manner hitherto unprecedented to explain their goals and priorities to the EP in November 1989? And why was the Commission given the political authority to implement the PHARE programme in July 1989? Moreover, it was clear to each member state and each EC institution that the turning-point of 1989 would accelerate rather than put a brake upon European integration. And the renewed impetus to far-reaching goals like EMU, political union, enlargement and institutional reform was more likely than not to push Europe closer towards a federal destination than it was further to buttress a largely intergovernmental polity.

If an aura of uncertainty persisted about the implications of 1989, there was at least a minimalist unanimity of opinion across the EC that its main goal in the immediate future was to implement the SEA. This was something that every EC member state government had ratified. Together with the single market objective, the goals of the SEA had been part of an already congested pre-1989 EC agenda. Their political implications, even had the events of 1989 not occurred, were not to be under-estimated. Let us look a little closer at them and examine how far they strengthened the position of the federalists.

## The political implications of the single market

We have already noted that the EC's commitment to what it called the internal market meant 'an area without internal frontiers in which the free movement of goods, persons, services and capital' was guaranteed.[10] This commitment reflected the Community's overriding concern in the mid-1980s for its weak position in the changing international political economy, the shifting domestic preferences of the member states and the supra-national pressures of the Commission and the EP. Mitterrand had been forced to discard his expansionary socialist economics in 1983 in order to embrace the emergent neoliberal free market agenda of Thatcher, Reagan, Kohl and Mulroney in, respectively, the United

Kingdom (UK), the United States, West Germany and Canada. Both extra- and intra-Community circumstances were propitious for a shift towards downsizing the state, privatization, deregulation and a renewed effort to promote the enterprise culture.

For Delors, as we have seen, the single market was also an integral part of his twin-pronged political strategy of first market-building and then state-building. The basic idea was that 1992 would facilitate an initial integrationist momentum out of which further qualitative progress could be made. Let us look a little closer at the economic and political assumptions which lay behind this strategy. The extent to which they underlined the interaction between politics and economics was, after all, what determined the possibilities for a federal Europe in a circuitous, almost imperceptible, route. In short, the success of the single market had enormous constitutional and political implications simply because it would require some degree of intervention from Brussels to sustain it. Constitutional and political change were, therefore, inherent in the project. What, then, did Lord Cockfield, the Commissioner for the Internal Market, mean when he referred to the completion of the internal market?

In their study entitled 'Europe's Domestic Market', published in 1988, Jacques Pelkmans and Alan Winters claimed that there was no single defi- nition of what completion of the internal market meant. Put simply it meant different things to different people. But the 'Utopian benchmark' for economists was that barriers to market access and distortions to basic economic transactions would have to be removed. A complete common market, which was the original goal of the Treaty of Rome (1957), would entail the abolition of all obstacles to the 'free movement of goods, ser- vices and factors of production' among the countries concerned.[11] Ideally this meant 'a state of market integration among member states in which no differential of economic significance attached to national frontiers or the residence and nationality of the economic agents of the member states'. But since this would have had a huge impact upon the member states' autonomy to 'follow domestic politics, and to decide on issues of economic regulation, market interventions, income redistribution meas- ures and even macroeconomic policies', the Commission's white paper, 'Completing the Internal Market', with its list of 279 detailed proposals, did not claim to pursue this ideal 'all the way'. Instead, the Commission's goal was 'to achieve the degree of market intervention' which character- ized economic transactions 'inside any of the member states'. Con- sequently the achievement of a single European market required a judicious combination of 'the dismantling of barriers to intra-EC trade with the approximation of national economic policy measures'.[12] Or as Murray Forsyth formulated it, the internal market was really about 'trans- forming the relations between several distinct state economies into rela- tions analogous to those that [pertained] within a single state economy, and to weld the external economic relations of these states with the rest of the world into a single policy'.[13]

The economic implication of this transformation did not mean that the economy of each state had simply 'ceased to exist', but it had been 'placed within a new economy – that of the Community as a whole'.[14] The simple dictum implied here was that member states should internalize their externalities. What had previously been 'external' should now be 'internal' in order to create a seamless European economy. The process involved two simultaneous activities: an opening up and an enclosing or encompassing action. The famous Cockfield white paper, therefore, involved both economic and political judgements. It constituted no more than an outline of what a real European market would require but built into the purpose – the commitment – were clear choices which could not be decided on purely functional grounds. In reality they required political judgements. The various joint measures available – approximation, dismantling, coordination and unification – had obvious political significance. Pelkmans and Winters openly acknowledged that 'in numerous cases regulation and intervention' might be necessary to 'improve the functioning of markets or to pursue other legitimate objectives'. They reasoned that 'a degree of centralization' might be required, especially as regards implementation, because 'decentralization [might] sometimes lead to inefficiency or ineffectiveness'.[15]

This brief sketch outline of the nature and meaning of the single market highlights the inescapable interaction that exists between economics and politics. In consequence, it also suggests a certain paradox in the political thought of the late twentieth-century neoliberal market enthusiasts epitomized by Thatcher. This resides in the fact that, in order for the 1992 project to work – in order for the single market to succeed on its own market terms of reference – there has to be a public recognition about the need for greater centralization of political authority in the EU. It is a fundamental irony of 1992 that the federalists were quick to detect. Let us probe a little further.

The political implications of the single market are the result of an inherent paradox, but they are not a contradiction in terms. Delors had understood the nature of the connection between market economics and political authority in the EC at the outset of the 1992 project. It was evident for all to see in the detailed provisions of the SEA. If the Community's 'big idea' could be continually focused upon market integration, it was possible to deflect the eye away from proposals which might otherwise be rejected in their own right. The Commission could, therefore, defend the need for what became known as 'economic and social cohesion' in purely market terms. Quite apart from the coincidence of enlargement of the EC to include Spain and Portugal in 1986, the introduction of cohesion policies could be justified on the grounds of counteracting market inequities, the correction of which was deemed vital to business profits. At the heart of this equation, however, was a political debate. The economic competences of the Community referred primarily to how markets functioned – the allocation of resources – rather than to the redistributive function. But, in securing a new commitment to the reform of the Structural Funds – the Regional Development Fund (ERDF), the European Social Fund (ESF) and the European Agricultural and Guidance Fund (EAGGF) – Delors and the Commission were able for the first time to establish at Community-level the principle of planned redistribution among member states. This, together with the principle of qualified majority voting (QMV) for those ten articles in the SEA which were devoted to the single market, had significant political implications for the whole 1992 project. As Delors had put it, 'We're not here just to make a single market – that doesn't interest me – but to make a political union'.[16]

In these novel circumstances, federalists were able to make the connection between the success of the single market and the need for institutional reform in the EC. They pinpointed the political incapacity of the Twelve. In other words, they were able convincingly to portray the existing Community as impotent. It did not have the political authority to fulfil even the limited requirements of the SEA. They could claim with great conviction, therefore, that the EC remained in an institutional straitjacket unable to go much beyond what already existed. Without further reform, in their view, the goal of the single market was unlikely to be achieved. The SEA actually underlined not so much the possibilities but, instead, the real limitations of the Community.

In the long-term, then, what were the likely constitutional and political implications of the single market? We will adopt a broad perspective which is confined in its sweep mainly to the foreseeable future in the decade after 1992. In this way it is possible, from the vantage point of the end of the century, to decide whether or not the implications identified can be verified. First, the ever-expanding policy jurisdiction of the Community in the 1990s would result in increasing public pressure for executive accountability. One impact of 1992 was that it would quickly expose and underline the 'accountability gap' in EC decision-making that rested primarily on the Council of Ministers and national executive authorities escaping democratic control both in the member states and in the EC itself. In contemporary parlance this came increasingly to be dubbed the 'democratic deficit', and was a criticism directed particularly at the closed nature of the Community's decision-making process. The decision to increase QMV in the Council of Ministers, albeit on only ten matters restricted to the Single Market, inevitably aggravated this problem. Looking back, we can see that this political implication – dating back arguably to Jean Monnet's conception of Europe – has been verified. The so-called 'democratic deficit' is today one of the most topical and controversial subjects of reform.

Secondly, the very success of the single market would pose the Community's future increasingly as two stark alternatives: Monnet's 'technobureaucratic' Europe versus a 'liberal democratic constitutional Europe'. In this scenario, there would inevitably be a confrontation between national governments and the elected Members of the European Parliament (MEPs) concerning the distribution of power and authority in the EC. It was here that those who wanted to 'constitutionalize' power in the EC were most vocal. And, of course, the EP as a central political institution of the Community had much to gain. Thirdly, the elements of a real crisis of political authority in the EC were also evident in the international arena because the SEA had strengthened the EP's role on issues of future enlargement and on questions of trade association agreements. In bilateral relations with the United States and, more widely, with the North American Free Trade Association (NAFTA), it could reasonably be expected that this problem would be exacerbated. Both of these continue to act as propulsive forces for reform.

Finally, the overall impact of the single market on member states and in particular on domestic policy-making suggested that the freedom of national governments to determine both macro- and micro-level economic policies would be severely curtailed. Quite apart from the ripple effect that this was likely to have on national elections, there would also be intensified pressures on member states to search for an EC-wide consensus concerning public issues about socio-economic and political priorities. After all, the single market depended upon both economic and political stability for its success. Other questions that arose indirectly from the introduction of the SEA were those concerning POCO, security issues, environmental policy, the idea of a 'people's Europe' with its obvious connotations for European citizenship, and the notion of a 'social Europe' with its recognition of social rights and implicit redistributive policies.

It was also likely that the single market would have both unforeseen and unintended consequences for the EC and its member states. They had effectively set in motion a process over which they were increasingly unlikely to exercise control. Delors himself observed famously that the Community was 'almost on the threshold of the irreversible'. If we summarize the political implications identified above, it is clear that most of them can be verified today. As we shall see, many of them were later to be treaty-based in 1992 and those, like the implications for domestic policy priorities, that were not so easily subject to this kind of yardstick remain the subject of public debate.

It is time now to leave the arguments, interpretations and insights into the political implications of 1989, the single market and the SEA and turn to what I have called 'the struggle to build political Europe'. This section concentrates upon the efforts during the late 1980s and early 1990s of the federalists across the Community arena to translate Monnet's functional Europe of concrete economic steps into Altiero Spinelli's 'political'

Europe. We will begin with a reprise of the Monnet–Spinelli conceptual confrontation that was outlined earlier in Chapter 2.

## The struggle to build political Europe

In Chapter 2 we looked at how Monnet's approach to Europe lay in the belief that, by forging specific functional links between states in a way that did not directly challenge national sovereignty, the door to federation would be gradually opened. Europe, he believed, could not be built at a stroke. It was necessary first to lay the foundations of the European federation via concrete achievements which would form, as it were, that crucial solidarity – the evolving common interest – indispensable for the removal of physical and mental barriers. Federation would emerge only out of practical experience of shared activity; only this would nurture even an incipient community of interest. Gradually, according to this reasoning, other tasks would be added to this shared activity, and other people would become subject to the same common rules and institutions. Federation would be the 'culmination' of an existing European economic and political reality, tried and tested, rather than the 'starting-point' for building Europe.

The cardinal feature of Monnet's approach to federation, we are reminded, rendered constitutionalism – the political construction of Europe – contingent upon cumulative functional achievements. The main conceptual stumbling-block was whether Europe would develop in the piecemeal, gradual, almost organic manner assumed by Monnet's method. At the end of the century, it seems clear that the building of 'political' Europe – the shift from functionalism to constitutionalism – has, at least in part, vindicated the federalist standpoint of Spinelli. This does not mean that Monnet's achievements should in any sense be either challenged or refuted. Monnet's approach to the building of Europe has been eminently successful. But the necessity for 'political' Europe arising out of Monnet's approach to federation still required, in Albertini's words, 'a much higher degree of construction'.[17] After the successful introduction of the SEA, the EC's central institutions remained weak. They did not have the capacity to go much beyond what existed. How, then, did the federalists react to the achievement of the SEA? What was their political strategy for the end of the century?

The driving force behind the federalists' search for European Union in the late 1980s and early 1990s could be reduced to a simple diagnosis of the EC's predicament: there was a fundamental contradiction between the ambitious goals of the single market and the Community's institutional capacity to achieve them. To those who wanted a stronger political Europe, the SEA was timid. Its institutional implications were extremely limited. The new cooperation procedure which had strengthened the role of the EP in decision-making and the increased QMV in the Council of

Ministers were important as small steps in the direction of enhanced procedural consensus. They could not, however, be remotely construed as significant advances in the larger quest for stronger central institutions. The Herman Report of 21 December 1988, drawn up by the Committee of Institutional Affairs of the EP, summarized the EC's continuing inadequacies:

1   In terms of power, the EC's possibilities are still inadequate, particularly in the areas of security, a common foreign policy and a single currency (central bank). In addition, there was no mention of development aid, cultural cooperation, or European citizenship.
2   In terms of decision-making efficiency, the Commission still does not have sufficient executive power and the Council still acts unanimously in areas that are vital to the EC. Its procedures are too slow and bureaucratic for it to be able to carry out its work satisfactorily.
3   In terms of democracy, the powers that the national parliaments have transferred to the EC are, for the most part, exercised by the Council which deliberates 'in camera' to adopt laws which are difficult to change subsequently and which take predence over national laws.... There is very little parliamentary democracy at the European level and, even after the Single Act, it is still possible for Community laws to be adopted after they have been rejected by the directly-elected representatives of the people.[18]

This diagnosis of the SEA sharply underlined the shortcomings of, and the limits to, the competences and powers of the EC when compared to the tasks that confronted it. If the single market was to be completed by the end of 1992, without any progress made toward monetary union and without any real strengthening of the Community's executive powers, the cherished internal market would remain fragile and vulnerable every time a member state encountered special difficulties in the adjustment process. Either the SEA would bring into being an internal market – in which case there was a real danger that the EC would be governed by a coalition of national and European bureaucracies with neither political leadership nor democratic accountability – or it would prove to be too weak to overcome the obstacles to the creation of the integrated industrial and commercial base on which the future of Europe and its people depended.

Once it had been ratified in July 1987, the SEA itself had become part of the pressure for change in the EC. It, too, was now part of the EC's inheritance, the *acquis communautaire*. It was neither a guide nor a model for the future. Instead, it was construed by the federalists as yet another milestone on the road toward European Union. The EP's political strategy, therefore, was to exploit the limits and the possibilities offered by the SEA while continuing to pursue the larger goal of European Union by transforming or replacing the Treaties and the SEA with a new treaty.

There was, of course, no Spinelli to provide that vigorous galvanizing momentum and intellectual clarity so effective during the European Union Treaty (EUT) episode between 1980 and 1984. But there was his legacy: the lessons which the EP had learned from that experience meant that both the goal and the strategy required to achieve it were well-defined. And it is worth noting that it was the EP's own EUT of 1984 which had become, and remains to this day, the 'benchmark, an aspiration and a model' at least for 'the medium term'.[19]

What lessons had the EP learned from the failure of the EUT? There were four main lessons that it took into the 1990s. First, it recognised that European Union could not be achieved by national governments alone, but that it could not be built in opposition to them either. Second, it acknowledged that the national parliaments of the member states should also be given greater involvement in the process of constitutional reform. The third lesson was related to its political strategy. This accepted that it had to have a more intensive and sustained dialogue with national governments, parliaments and citizens in a much more systematic way over a much longer timescale than that of 1984–87. Finally, it was adamant that it had to be much more fully integrated into the process of reform next time both in the 'preparatory' and the 'conference' phases based upon a legitimacy derived from its constituent and ratificatory powers. It was also noticeable that the political environment of the period 1989–90 had changed quite markedly in one particular respect. In the struggle to build political Europe, the term 'federal' was no longer taboo in political discourse about the future of Europe. Neither the Commission President, Jacques Delors nor the EP's President, Enriqué Baron Crespo, refrained from using it in the public domain. Indeed, in his speech on 8 December 1989 to the European Council in Strasbourg, Enriqué Baron urged the assembled Heads of State and Government to ensure that the future intergovernmental conference (IGC) would 'establish the constitutional basis for a European Union based on federal principles'.[20] And in the EP, the Martin Resolution of 14 March 1990 claimed that it was 'increasingly necessary rapidly to transform the European Community into a European Union of federal type' which would go 'beyond the single market and economic and monetary union'.[21]

In retrospect, there is no doubt that the year 1990 was the apogee of the Community's struggle for political Europe since its revival in the early 1980s. The Delors Report on EMU had been published in April 1989; an IGC on EMU had been agreed at the Strasbourg European Council in December 1989; German unification had been secured in October 1990; Kohl and Mitterrand had called in April 1990 for a separate IGC on political union, both of which were convened in December 1990; and the conference of the parliaments of the EC, known as the 'Assizes', met in November 1990 to formulate a common position *vis-à-vis* the two IGCs. If history had accelerated, so indeed had the pace of European integration.

The commitment to 'transform the Community from an entity mainly based on economic integration and political cooperation into a union of a political nature, including a common foreign and security policy' spoke volumes even in the guarded and sanitized language of Euro-speak.[22] Events moved swiftly; indeed, so swiftly that it was important for the Community to avoid being overtaken by them. 1990 seemed to herald the end of Monnet's Europe and the dawn of Spinelli's political construction.

Grant claims that early in 1990 Delors' self-confidence had 'soared to new – and dangerous – heights'. He believed that the Community was capable of 'a leap towards closer union and no longer thought that constitutional change could wait'.[23] His open reference to federalism and his unguarded remarks about Europe are worth more than a moment's reflection:

> My objective is that before the end of the millennium [Europe] should have a true federation. [The Commission should become] a political executive which can define essential common interests ... responsible before the European Parliament and before the nation states represented how you will, by the European Council or by a second chamber of national parliaments.... I don't see how we could build this greater Europe, the European home of Gorbachev, without a solid pier, and this solid pier is the Community of the Twelve.[24]

At this stage of the evolving Europe-wide public debate about the building of political Europe, the meaning of 'political union' remained obscure. We have already seen that the phrase had usually been confined quite narrowly in the past to different forms of POCO. By 1990, however, its meaning had widened considerably to include the following: closing the democratic deficit; strengthening subsidiarity; improving decision-making procedures; increasing Community competence; institutional reform; and developing a common foreign and security policy (CFSP).[25] An intergovernmental consensus on political union, however, was absent prior to the impending IGC. The Commission's own submission to the IGC on political union, dated 21 October 1990, included 'a single Community with a single institutional structure' which would organize a common foreign policy and 'a common security policy, including defence'. But it, nonetheless, argued against defining the 'final shape of European Union' although it did believe that it would lead ultimately to a 'federal-type organization'.[26]

Clearly the building of political Europe, even in a congested but essentially favourable political atmosphere, remained very much an intergovernmental exercise. And, as such, it suffered from competing opinions and shifting emphases which gave it a somewhat confused and incoherent appearance. Given that there were twelve distinct national perspectives on the subject, which reflected twelve different national political cultures and traditions, it was hardly surprising if member states found themselves at odds with each other over what had always been an inherently imprecise notion. To Spinelli, it had always been lucid. He had distilled its meaning to refer quite simply to institutional reform in order to build a federal Europe. To Delors and Kohl it also meant a federal rather than an inter-governmental European Union. Kohl had insisted on making EMU con-tingent upon political union; German and European unification, we will recall, had to go hand in hand. In forfeiting the Deutschmark and surren-dering control over European monetary policy which they enjoyed in the EMS to a new central bank and a single currency, the Germans clearly had the most to lose. Political union would compensate Germany for this loss. It would facilitate the resolution of difficult issues like immigration, asylum, foreign policy and defence in a more binding and regulated union with stronger central institutions like the EP in which German MEPs would be the largest national contingent. To Mitterrand, however, the meaning of political union and the idea of building political Europe – even as a federalist – brought to the surface his deeply ingrained centralist French executive prejudices and his aversion to handing power over to elected representatives in the EP and non-elected appointees in the Com-mission. EMU was one thing, but the implication of political union being spoken of in any other terms than those of a confederation with a stronger European Council, with (albeit reluctantly) a few more powers for the EP, was unthinkable. Mitterrand considered himself to be a federalist, but his federalism had always been pragmatic. He had always been somewhat ambivalent about the EP and, although a man of the Fourth Republic, his political experience of the Fifth Republic with its weak role for the French National Assembly under the Gaullist constitution did not augur well as a recommendation for a strong EP. Moreover, his concern about the size and population of the new Germany which would be entitled to a greater number of MEPs than any other member state did not endear him to a stronger EP.[27]

If we take stock of the intergovernmental balance-sheet on EMU and political union in 1990, it seems clear that Germany was close to France on EMU and close to Italy, Spain and the Benelux countries on the dyad of political union and EMU while the UK's position ranged from lukewarm at its most compromising to openly hostile at its most inflexible. Thatcher had been particularly awkward and difficult as the lone curmudgeon in resisting the integrationist momentum towards both EMU and political union throughout 1989–90. She had fought tenaciously in the French, Irish and Italian European Councils in this period either to halt or deflect the movement towards closer union. As in June 1985 at the Milan summit, however, she had been effectively ambushed and forced to go along with what the other 11 member state governments had decided. She had graced the public platform in the UK and the European stage continu-ously for 11 years when, in November 1990, she was compelled to resign over her resolute refusal to moderate her intolerable obsession with

Delors and his federalist intentions. The EC's *annus mirabulis* of 1990 turned into Thatcher's *annus horribilis.*

In the struggle to build political Europe during the late 1980s and early 1990s, the British government had become increasingly isolated in the portals of the EC. Thatcher's insistence upon old-fashioned balance of power politics rather than European integration as a way of containing Germany and the Germans received no significant support. Almost as soon as the Berlin Wall collapsed, it had been widely assumed that unification was inevitable. And the initial reservations of some member states, like France, did not develop into an advertised and persistent opposition. Thatcher's dogged resistance to 'tying the German Gulliver down within a federal European Community' was quickly rendered futile because, as she readily confessed, 'the underlying forces of federalism and bureaucracy were gaining strength as a coalition of socialists and Christian Democrat governments in France, Spain, Italy and Germany forced the pace of integration and a Commission equipped with extra powers began to manipulate them to advance its own agenda'.[28] This assertion, the particular use of language notwithstanding, was not that far from reality. In acknowledging the inherent tension and competition between the two realities of supra-nationalism and intergovernmentalism, it underlined the notion of a relative autonomy for the EC distinct from its component member state parts. Intergovernmentalism alone could not explain European integration. But, in refusing to see the obvious merits of a new European order, Thatcher had simply failed to understand the march of history.

The two IGCs on EMU and political union that opened in Rome in December 1990 ran parallel to each other and culminated, in December 1991, at the end of the Dutch presidency, in intensive intergovernmental bargaining as each member state brought its own aims and expectations to the table of negotiations in Maastricht. The conclusion, in February 1992, to what became a veritable smorgasbord of institutional, policy and procedural compromises among the Twelve, was the Treaty on European Union (TEU). As we shall see in the next section, the emergence of the TEU or Maastricht Treaty, as it was commonly known, was somewhat inauspicious as a proclamation of European Union. Indeed, it was arguably an unworthy outcome of the intensified efforts since the SEA of both federalists and intergovernmentalists to arrive at their respective destinations. Let us look at the TEU in order to assess the overall impact of these two broad schools of thought on the achievement of European Union. We will not provide a clause-by-clause account of the Maastricht Treaty because the subject has already been exhaustively analysed in many articles and books. Instead, our purpose is to examine the TEU from the particular standpoint of federalism and European Union. We will begin with a brief assessment of the impact of federalism and the federalists on the two IGCs which forged the new treaty.

## The Treaty on European Union: a curate's egg

The economic and political circumstances which surrounded the appearance of the TEU in February 1992 were very different from those which had characterized the SEA in February 1986. The influence of the federalists on the TEU was less obvious than it had been on the SEA. The Commission was present at the IGC negotiations, but the EP was not. Nonetheless, as Richard Corbett has ably demonstrated, its political influence was enhanced by the support of the Italian and Belgian parliaments which adopted resolutions stating that they would not authorize the ratification of the new treaty unless it had first been approved by the EP. A majority of parties in the German parliament also took this line so that EP approval of the outcome was necessary. Moreover, monthly interinstitutional conferences were held between the ministers and a delegation of 12 MEPs, while the President of the EP, Enriqué Baron Crespo, was invited to attend ministerial meetings, and the chairman of the IGC participated in parliamentary debates and appeared before parliamentary committees. Along with the Commission, the EP's political influence contributed to 'the momentum behind the move for an all-encompassing reform' with the agenda 'wide open'.[29] Certainly, Delors and the Commission cannot be ignored in this process. After all, the ICC on EMU had been founded upon the *Delors Report* of July 1989 and it had served as the basis for intensive Franco-German discussions about the various stages in the timetable to achieve EMU.

The preliminary discussions in the IGC on political union concerning the content of the agenda took an agonizing series of twists and turns as the Twelve struggled to arrive at some sort of consensus, however fragile. The British government, led by the new Prime Minister, John Major, was predictably as obdurate as it had been under Thatcher. As the 'odd man out' in the IGC, it served notice at the outset that it would never countenance the inclusion of any reference to federalism in the new treaty. Consequently, it led the IGC a merry dance in semantics as it persisted with its refusal to allow the 'F-word' to be incorporated even in the draft text for discussion. The revised Luxembourg draft text of June 1991 which described European integration as marking 'a new stage in the process leading gradually to a Union with a federal goal' was peremptorily rejected, as indeed was the later Dutch text which referred to the 'federal vocation'.[30] Douglas Hurd, the British Foreign Secretary, explained that the UK 'did not intend to be committed to the implications which, in the English language, the phrase "federal goal" carries'.[31] The irony of this public fuss was that the federal reference was removed and replaced by a reference to the new treaty marking 'a new stage in the process of creating an ever closer Union among the peoples of Europe in which decisions are taken as closely as possible to the citizens'. As Corbett has noted, the phrase 'an ever closer Union' logically implied a more centralized

European Union than a federal one but it satisfied the British delegation probably because it had been fossilized in the Treaty of Rome for over 30 years.[32] The 'F-word' in continental Europe, unlike in the UK, had always meant a decentralized political union and had never carried the connotations which it did for the British. Thatcher's cantankerous opposition to the word was a consequence of her fundamental misunderstanding of the thing. She wrote later that 'The European Commission, which had always had a yen for centralized power, was now led by a tough, talented European federalist whose philosophy justified centralism'.[33] Delors was typically undaunted: 'What does the word matter, as long as we have the actual thing?'[34]

The intergovernmental compromise on the federal objective, as Delors noted, did not detract at all from the structure and content of the TEU. Agreed by the European Council at Maastricht in December 1991, and signed there in February 1992, the TEU was the product of a particular set of circumstances which arose from the complex conjunction of national, European and international imperatives. Member state governments were in any case formally committed by the SEA to review the existing provisions on European political cooperation five years after its entry into force. This, and the commitment to complete the single market by 31 December 1992, provided the formal impetus to make further progress toward European Union. But in the light of this complex, convoluted background, what kind of treaty emerged at Maastricht in December 1991? Mindful of the fact that it was another logical step toward the building of Europe which stretched as far back as 1950, what conception of Europe did it presage? As we shall see, the shadows of Monnet, Schuman and Spinelli fell indelibly across the new monument to European Union.

In view of the title of this section, it is useful to begin with a reminder of the parable of the curate's egg. A nervous young curate seated at the breakfast table with his bishop was eating an egg which, unknown to the bishop, was bad. When asked by the bishop if it was to his liking he was too timid to tell him the truth and replied that 'parts of it were excellent'. I want to suggest that, from a federalist perspective, the TEU was good in parts and bad in others. We will, therefore, adopt a broad brush approach to sketch out the main features of the TEU in order to comment upon both its strengths and weaknesses from a federalist perspective. Let us begin with Title I of the Treaty, called 'Common Provisions'.

Article A confirmed that the Maastricht Treaty, unlike the SEA, had at last established 'a European Union'. But in the extent to which it identified 'the peoples of Europe' and the organization of 'relations between the Member States and between their peoples' rather than a single people, it was essentially confederal in nature. Article B committed its signatories to the following broad objectives: the creation of EMU; a common foreign and security policy (CFSP) including 'the eventual framing of a common defence policy which might in time lead to a common defence'; the introduction of a citizenship of the Union; close cooperation in justice and home affairs; the maintenance in full of the *acquis communautaire*; and the principle of subsidiarity. There was no doubt that the implications of these provisions were federal. Article C promised that the Union would be served by a 'single institutional framework' which would guarantee 'the consistency and the continuity of the activities carried out in order to attain its objectives' while at the same time respecting the *acquis communautaire*. This had been part of the Commission's submission to the IGC, but the language did not accord with the substance of what the Commission had proposed. Article D confirmed the European Council's intergovernmental role to provide the new Union with 'the necessary impetus for its development' which it would also define. This was clearly confederal in nature. Article E reconciled the various treaty obligations of the EP, Council of Ministers, Commission and Court of Justice in the light of Maastricht, while Article F sought *inter alia* to slay the mythical dragon which threatened Milward's nation state: 'The Union shall respect the national identities of its Member States whose systems of government are founded on the principles of democracy'.[35] Tilting at windmills, this was the intergovernmental version of Euro-speak.

The TEU established a 'European Union' based firmly upon the existing EC, together with two new intergovernmental arms, namely, cooperation in foreign and security policies (CFSP) and in justice and home affairs (JHA). Both of these new forms of cooperation fell outside the legal purview of the Treaty of Rome and were therefore beyond the reach of the Court of Justice, but there was to be a general review of Maastricht in 1996. The clear intention of the majority of member states was gradually to bring these areas of intergovernmental cooperation under standard Community rules so that they too would be part of an ever-expanding *acquis communautaire*. The world of Maastricht, then, was commonly represented as the 'Greek Temple' with a distinct vertical Community pillar standing alongside two separate intergovernmental pillars and each of them linked together by a common horizontal structure of institutions with varying decision-making competences and responsibilities.

The centrepiece of the TEU was the formal commitment to EMU which was to be crowned with a single currency by 1 January 1999 at the latest. Mapping out the EC's course until the end of the century, Maastricht conformed to earlier notions of a 'timetable' as witnessed by the customs union for the original EEC and the internal market programme in the SEA. Setting new goals and deadlines for the foreseeable future had been a highly successful political strategy given the vicissitudes of intergovernmental politics and personalities. If monetary union and a single currency came into existence, there was a very real likelihood that the economic power which this would bestow upon the Community would effectively equip it to become a federal European Union.[36] This, however, was a question for the future. Sufficient convergence of member states' economies might not be achieved and the evident desire for EMU in 1992 might not be sustained in later years. But this was all speculation. The financial turbulence of the markets and the currency instability which characterized the early 1990s severely tested the existing Exchange Rate Mechanism (ERM) and could equally be used to justify the pressing need for a single currency.

Articles J.1 to J.11 under Title V of the TEU endorsed the statement made at the beginning of the Treaty under Title I, 'Common Provisions', namely, that the Community would assert its external identity via the implementation of a CFSP including the eventual framing of a common defence policy which might, in time, lead to a common defence. As with EMU, the Treaty and its annexes charted the road ahead in developing a common EC defence policy through the Western European Union (WEU). The two 'Declarations' on WEU confirmed that it would be developed as the defence component of the European Union as well as a means to strengthen the European pillar of the Atlantic Alliance. Described in the Treaty as an 'integral part' of the Union's development, the WEU became the new focus for a distinctly 'European' defence arrangement which was intended to include not only those member states which were part of the European Union but also those European member states of NATO which were invited to become 'associate members'. The new defence framework was to be reviewed in 1996 pending the expiry of the WEU Treaty in 1998. The implications of Maastricht for POCO also had the potential to be significant. The Treaty reaffirmed intergovernmental consultation on foreign policy with a view to coordinated, concerted and convergent action as specified in the SEA. But the need for increased coordination on 'the political and economic aspects of security' originally identified in Title III of the SEA was more firmly underlined. The formal recognition of unanimity required for the Council to decide on the principle of joint action, which bound member states, also included the possibility simultaneously to decide how far majority voting could be used to implement the action. This had to be viewed in the overall context of enhancing the capacity of the EC to act as a single agent with a single external political identity.

Turning to the other intergovernmental pillar of Maastricht, namely, cooperation in JHA, the following areas were deemed 'matters of common interest': asylum policy; immigration and the treatment of nationals of third countries; combating drug addiction and fraud; judicial cooperation in both civil and criminal matters; and police cooperation against terrorism, drug-trafficking and other serious forms of international crime. Articles K.1 to K.9 under Title VI of the TEU determined that the Council would adopt joint decisions, promote cooperation and take joint actions which might be implemented by QMV. It was also empowered to draw up conventions for formal ratification by the member states, the implementation of which could be agreed by two-thirds of the governments of the

Council. Such conventions contemplated a role for the Court of Justice, but otherwise such matters were deemed to be beyond its jurisdiction.

The EC's capacity to make common policies and to supervise member states' policies was strengthened in two ways. First, existing competences, such as research and technology, environmental policy and cohesion policy, were enhanced but, second, a range of new competences were also incorporated in the new Treaty. These included the following: education; vocational training and youth; culture; public health; consumer protection; trans-European networks for transport, telecommunications and energy infrastructures; and industry. With the notable exception of industrial policy, it was important to recognise the stronger role that the EP was given in these and other policy fields. It was able to negotiate amendments directly with the Council, via a new procedure of codecision, on all internal market legislation, as well as those measures mentioned above. Moreover, if its amendments were not accepted, it had a veto to reject the legislation. The assent procedure, whereby the Council could not enact a measure without the EP's explicit approval, was extended to all international agreements, and its approval was also required for a uniform procedure for European elections, as well as measures concerning the citizen's right to move and reside throughout the EC and, significantly, the nomination of a new Commission.

The Commission itself emerged relatively unscathed from Maastricht. Its own pivotal position in the triangular relationship between itself, the EP and the Council was reaffirmed and the scope of its activity was widened along with that of Community competences. Clearly there was more involvement for both the Commission and the EP in standard EC business covered by the Treaty of Rome than in either EMU or immigration policy, but these kinds of deficiencies and disappointments were part of the price to be paid for intergovernmental agreement. Besides, the stronger political base which seemed likely to accrue to the Commission as a result of the EP's new power to approve its appointment was not to be dismissed lightly. Furthermore, the adoption of QMV in the Council on most of the EC's new competences indirectly strengthened both the Commission and the EP in their quest to promote further European economic and political integration.

In summary, then, what are we to make of the Maastricht Treaty? And if it was, as has been suggested above, a curate's egg, what were the bad bits? The *Financial Times* described it as 'a union with several rooms', and one of its leader writers, David Buchan, alluded to Maastricht as 'a curious hybrid' that would 'win no prizes for symmetry'.[37] But apart from being impossible to achieve in the prevailing circumstances, symmetry was not important, and its absence simply reflected the realities of hard intergovernmental bargaining. Hard negotiations and serious arguments about fundamental issues lead to compromise, but compromise is rarely conducive to symmetry. Indeed, an insistence on the goal of symmetry would have meant no treaty at all. What mattered in the early 1990s was to achieve some kind of consensus, however fragile, to enable the European project once again to move forward on the road toward European Union.

For those who wished to see the EC evolve in a federal direction, there remained much to do. The EP was still not fully integrated into the decision-making process on an equal basis with the Council. A whole battery of important competences – including foreign, security and defence policies, immigration policy and social policy – were left almost entirely in the intergovernmental arena. The principle of subsidiarity in Article 3b of Maastricht remained ambiguous in practical legal terms. The assertion in Article C of the 'Common Provisions' of the TEU that the Union would be served by a 'single institutional framework' was open to serious doubt. Social policy was divided between the commitments of the Twelve in the SEA and the stronger provisions agreed by the Eleven (with the UK outside) at Maastricht. Defence policy could also conceivably have posed a particular problem if Denmark and Ireland did not formally join the WEU. And the official protocols giving both the UK and Denmark opt-outs on the third stage of EMU might also have served ultimately to undermine both the structure and the timetable envisaged for the very jewel in the Maastricht crown. Finally, the entrenchment of intergovernmental cooperation, typically deemed by the British government to be a new avenue for future EC progress, harboured the danger of 'creeping intergovernmentalism' whereby movement might go in the opposite direction – from the EC back to intergovernmental decision-making.

These, then, were some of the shortcomings – the 'bad bits' – of the Maastricht Treaty. As the successor to the SEA, it built upon much that went before. And while certainly not a complete federal union, the EU did look increasingly like a solid monetary union en route to a single currency. Whether or not it involved what some federalists, like Spinelli, had detested, namely, a 'multi-speed' path toward European Union with 'variable geometry' was not as important to other activists whose interpretation focused upon the slow but certain emergence of a new European sovereignty. Much of what Maastricht contained had been foreshadowed in the Tindemans Report of 1976 and in the EP's own European Union Treaty (EUT) of 1984. Indeed, it is quite striking, in retrospect, how far so many elements of the wide-ranging policy content of the EUT found their way into both the SEA and the TEU. These included:

1   the principle of citizenship (Article 8–8e, TEU);
2   fundamental rights (Common Provisions, Article F, TEU);
3   the social chapter (Protocol on Social Policy, Articles 1–7, TEU);
4   health policy (included in Article 129, TEU);
5   consumer policy (first appeared as 'Consumer Protection' in Article 129a, TEU);
6   cultural policy (enshrined in Article 128, TEU);

7    environmental policy (Article 130 r–t, TEU);
8    education policy (first formally acknowledged in Articles 126 and 127, TEU); and
9    regional policy (known as 'economic and social cohesion', included in Article 130 a–e, TEU).

Significantly the EUT had also recognized the principle of subsidiarity (Common Provisions, Articles B and 3b, TEU) that became such a subject of great public attention and debate during the late 1980s and early 1990s.

If we compare the Tindemans Report, EUT, SEA and TEU it can be seen that there is an unbroken line of continuity concerning federalism and European Union which stretches back at least 20 years to the Paris Summit of October 1972. Federal ideas, influences and strategies had successfully co-mingled and competed with conventional intergovernmental conceptions of European Union to arrive at a new crossroads in 1992. But it was only a crossroads and not the final destination of European Union in either policy content or institutional architecture. For the federalists, much remained to be achieved. And, like its predecessor, the SEA, Article N of the Maastricht Treaty laid down that there would be another IGC in 1996 with the distinct possibility of a further treaty revision based, once again, on unanimity among the Twelve.


## Conclusion: appointment with history

The TEU had been conceived, as Roy Pryce noted, 'in a continent still divided into rival political and economic systems', but having been launched on 'a wave of great optimism about the EC' it would have to be 'applied in very different circumstances'.[38] Given the bewildering nature of these circumstances into which the treaty negotiations had been plunged, and out of which the TEU eventually emerged, it was small wonder that it was neither an entirely coherent nor a symmetrical treaty. The TEU was the last treaty of the Cold War.

In retrospect, we can look upon the Maastricht experience as representing yet another building block in the struggle to make the goal of European Union a 'federal union'. Although the TEU certainly did not furnish the new European Union with fully fledged federal institutions, it did add some very important procedural elements, new competences and formal commitments. While serving to entrench the intergovernmental basis of the JHA and CFSP, they nonetheless combined also to buttress the federal features that coexisted simultaneously in the evolving economic and political union. But opinion about Maastricht has not surprisingly been sharply divided. One hostile critic of the TEU has understandably described it as tantamount to a 'Europe of bits and pieces' having a 'convoluted structure' which confirmed that the intergovernmental conference method of building upon the *acquis communautaire* was hopelessly inadequate. Indeed, the intergovernmental concessions made in the form of opt-outs, protocols and various derogations reduced the Treaty to a mere 'umbrella Union' which threatened 'constitutional chaos'.[39] Doubtless many federalists concurred with this fierce rebuke, but they also recognized that the 'process' of treaty revision determined its 'substance'. They knew that the intergovernmental reality promised little and usually achieved less.

The TEU was formally ratified on 1 November 1993 but by then national, European and global circumstances had changed once again for the worse, making further European integration both difficult and unpopular with mass publics and even with some hitherto sympathetic political and economic elites. Public concern in the early 1990s had become preoccupied once again with the practical realities of economic growth and unemployment to the detriment of mega-packages of treaty revision which seemed irrelevant to an increasingly sceptical and disillusioned populace. The Danish Referendum in June 1992, in which 50.7% of the voters had rejected the TEU as against 49.3% in favour of it, had temporarily derailed the constitutional reform process in the Community. A huge chasm had opened up between European political elites and their electorates. Monnet's strategy of European integration, which had always been essentially an elite affair, was confronted for the first time by concerted public opposition which had fired a warning shot across its bows. The practical implication of the Danish rebuff was that the Europe of economic elites – of business, commerce, agriculture, industry, management and technocracy – with customarily low public interest and awareness, had been superseded by a new Europe of interested mass publics which could be effectively mobilized against elitist conceptions of spillover.[40] In what Michael Baun has called 'the new pragmatism', Monnet's strategy for building Europe seemed in consequence outmoded; the elite assumption of a 'permissive consensus' in favour of European integration no longer applied.[41] At last, it was time to engage the real public debate about the building of political Europe.

In June 1993, before the TEU had been ratified, the European Council in Copenhagen took a step which was to have huge implications for federalism and European Union. It finally broached the thorny issue of enlargement to include the countries of central and eastern Europe. By then, there was already a queue of eight national states which had applied to join the Community: Turkey (1987); Cyprus (1990); Malta (1990); and a group of EFTA countries, namely, Austria (1989); Sweden (1991); Finland (1992); Switzerland (1992); and Norway (1992). The Copenhagen declaration was, therefore, extremely ambitious in its attempt to 'absorb new members while maintaining the momentum of European integration'.[42] The so-called 'Visegrad' countries, Poland, Hungary, and the Czech and Slovak Republics, had already signed association agreements with the EC in 1991, as had both Romania and

Bulgaria shortly thereafter, while other states also interested in member-ship included Latvia, Lithuania, Estonia, Slovenia and Albania. In Article 0 (final provisions) of the TEU, the formal commitment to opening up the European Union to 'any European state' that could meet the agreed con-ditions of admission had already been established. The Copenhagen agreement specified three main economic and political conditions which, for our purposes, can be suitably summarized as the following: first, the acceptance of liberal democratic institutions based on the rule of law, respect for human rights and the protection of minorities; second, the existence of a functioning market economy; and, third, the ability to take on the obligations of membership, including political, economic and monetary union.[43]

The economic and political implications of enlargement to include the four EFTA countries – Austria, Finland, Norway and Sweden – were daunt-ing enough without contemplating the massive impact that further enlargements to include central and eastern European states would inevitably bring in their train. It required little imagination to envisage the impact that a European Union of 20, 22 or 24 member states would have upon the institutional framework and the decision-making processes of a polity that had been originally designed for only six countries. Widening and deepening were intimately connected and it was imperative that the institutional implications of these processes were given the serious atten-tion that they merited. Delors' opinion was characteristically candid: if this problem was not confronted, the European Union would be 'reduced to a mere intergovernmental organization, a paralysed talking-shop, nothing more than that'. In language which bore an uncanny resemblance to that used by Spinelli, Delors pleaded for a 'greater centralization of powers vested in the executive body and stronger democratic control'. Member states had to grasp the nettle and decide between an executive body empowered properly to fulfil its role in the Europe of tomorrow or con-tinue with the existing unwieldy collection of national ministers meeting weekly in Brussels.[44] Only by choosing the former would the European Union, in the words of ex-French President Giscard d'Estaing, be 'ready for its appointment with history'.[45]

If there were any lessons to be learned from the Maastricht experience, one of them was surely that the building of Europe also meant institution-building. But the building of political Europe – shifting from functional-ism to constitutionalism and strengthening the central institutions – meant crossing the Rubicon to a federal Europe. Had the TEU furnished the basis for such a transformation? Or did the new crossroads of 1993 really reflect a Europe at intergovernmental cross-purposes? The TEU was followed in 1995 by the enlargement of the European Union to 15 member states, including Sweden, Finland and Austria, and inevitably by hollow-sounding promises of engagement with the implications of enlargement and the need for institutional reform in the next round of treaty revision due in 1996. The intergovernmental arena, however, was once again unpredictable with numerous cross-currents ranging from concern for growth, unemployment, inflation and a new GATT agreement to further progress in matters relating to EMU, the principle of subsidiarity, the democratic deficit, and strengthened social and environmental policies. The old dichotomy between institutional and policy reform persisted, with most member states preferring the latter to the former approach. Institutional reform might open up a veritable can of worms; it might compel the EU to return to first principles and reappraise both the conceptual and the substantive basis of the Union itself. Its very *raison d'être* might conceivably be called into question in circumstances that would probably not be conducive to the sort of political imagination and innovation required to facilitate further progress in the building of political Europe. Fundamentally divergent conceptions of Europe were more likely to be exposed and underlined than any hope of a new intergovernmental consensus.

The ratification of the TEU on 1 November 1993 conveniently brings this chapter to an end. We have traversed much ground in our attempt to analyse and assess Maastricht from the particular standpoint of federalism and the federalists, and we can understand much more clearly why so many commentators and critics of both the process leading to and the substance of the TEU were pessimistic about its future prospects. After all, how could such a 'strange heterogeneous creature' effectively meet the demands of European integration in the early 1990s?[46] In the next chapter, we will attempt to answer this question as we turn to chronicle the sequence of contemporary events which led to the Treaty of Amsterdam and to investigate its significance for federalism and the building of Europe.

## NOTES

1  E. Hobsbawm, *Age of extremes: the short twentieth century, 1914–1991*, London: Michael Joseph, 1994, pp. 4–5.
2  T.G. Ash, *The uses of adversity: essays on the fate of central Europe*, Cambridge: Granta Books, 1991, p. 169.
3  Mitterrand's speech to the EP, *Debates of the European Parliament* (DEP), 3–383, p. 153, 22 November 1989.
4  Kohl's speech to the EP, *DEP*, 3–383, pp. 156–57, 22 November 1989.
5  Kohl's speech to the EP, *DEP*, 3–383, pp. 158–59, 22 November 1989.
6  Kohl's speech to the EP, *DEP*, 3–383, p. 159, 22 November 1989.
7  Delors' speech to the EP, *DEP*, 3–383, p. 171, 22 November 1989.
8  G. Ross, *Jacques Delors and European integration*, Cambridge: Polity Press, 1995, p. 49.
9  C. Grant, *Delors: inside the house that Jacques built*, London: Nicholas Brealey Publishing, 1994, pp. 140–41.
10  Article 8A, section II(I), The Single European Act (SEA), *Bulletin of the European Communities*, Supplement 2/86, (Luxembourg: Office for Official Publications, 1986, p. 11.

11  J. Pelkmans and A. Winters, *Europe's domestic market*, London: Routledge, 1988, p. 3.

12  J. Pelkmans and A. Winters, *Europe's domestic market*, p. 4.

13  M. Forsyth, *Unions of states: the theory and practice of confederation*, Leicester: Leicester University Press, 1981, p. 5.

14  M. Forsyth, *Unions of states*, p. 184.

15  J. Pelkmans and A. Winters, *Europe's domestic market*, pp. 4–5.

16  C. Grant, *Delors*, p. 70.

17  M. Albertini, 'Europe on the threshold of union', *The Federalist*, vol. XXVIII, p. 27, 1986.

18  The Herman Report, Doc. A.2–3222/88, *EP*, p. 19, 21 December 1988.

19  Explanatory statement of the Interim Report of the EP's Committee on Institutional Affairs, Martin I Report, Doc.trav/conference, *EP* 068.

20  Extract from the speech of the president of the EP to the European Council, Strasbourg, 8 December 1989. See also Delors' important speech to the EP upon the presentation of the Commission's annual programme for 1990 in which he referred to 'the future federation' and 'the federation of the Twelve', *DEP*, 3–385, p. 114, 17 January 1990.

21  Martin I resolution, *EP*, Doc. A3–47/90, 14 March 1990.

22  D. Dinan, 'The European Community, 1978–93' in Annals, *AAPSS*, 531, pp. 10–24, January 1994.

23  C. Grant, *Delors*, p. 134.

24  C. Grant, *Delors*, p. 135.

25  See Delors' speech to the EP, *DEP*, 3–385, 17 January 1990.

26  See the Commission Opinion to the IGC on 'Political Union' COM(90)600, Brussels, 3, 23 October 1990.

27  See E. Haywood, 'The European Policy of François Mitterrand', *Journal of Common Market Studies*, 31(2), pp. 269–82, June 1993.

28  M. Thatcher, *The path to power*, London: HarperCollins, 1995, p. 491 and *The Downing Street years*, London: HarperCollins, 1993, p. 536.

29  R. Corbett, 'The intergovernmental conference on political union', *Journal of Common Market Studies*, 30(3), p. 275.

30  See R. Corbett, 'The intergovernmental conference', pp. 279–81; and D. Dinan, *Ever closer union? an introduction to the European Community*, London: Macmillan, 1994, pp. 172–73.

31  Quoted in the *Financial Times*, 18 June 1991, p. 1.

32  R. Corbett, 'The intergovernmental conference', p. 281.

33  M. Thatcher, *The Downing Street years*, p. 559.

34  See *Agence Europe*, 6 December 1991, p. 4.

35  See Article F., Title I, 'Common Provisions', Treaty on European Union, *TEU*, Luxembourg: Office for Official Publications, 1992, p. 9.

36  This is the view of J. Pinder, *European Community: the building of a union*, Oxford: Oxford University Press, 1991.

37  D. Buchan, 'A Heath Robinson Design for Europe', *Financial Times*, 12 December 1991, p. 16.

38  R. Pryce, 'The Maastricht Treaty and the new Europe', in A. Duff, J. Pinder and R. Pryce (eds), *Maastricht and beyond: building the European Union*, p. 3.

39  D. Curtin, 'The constitutional structure of the union: a Europe of bits and pieces', *Common Market Law Review*, 30, pp. 17–69.

40  On this question, see M. Franklin, 'Uncorking the bottle: popular opposition to European unification in the wake of Maastricht', *Journal of Common Market Studies*, 32(4), pp. 455–72, December 1994; and M. Franklin, M. Marsh and L. McLaren, 'Referendum outcomes and trust in government: public support

for Europe in the wake of Maastricht', *West European Politics*, 18(3), pp. 101–17, 1995.

41  M.J. Baun, *An imperfect union: the Maastricht treaty and the new politics of European integration*, Boulder, CO: Westview Press, 1996, pp. 134–39.

42  Conclusions of the Presidency after the Copenhagen European Council, *Bulletin of the EC*, 6–1993, 21–22 June 1993.

43  Conclusions of the Presidency after the Copenhagen European Council, *Bulletin of the EC*, 6–1993, I.13, 21–22 June 1993.

44  Delors' speech to the EP, *DEP*, 3–383, p. 62, 21 November 1989.

45  Giscard d'Estaing's speech to the EP, *DEP*, 3–383, p. 65, 21 November 1989.

46  D. Buchan, 'A Heath Robinson design for Europe', *Financial Times*, 12 December 1991, p. 16.

# 7    From Maastricht to Amsterdam, 1994–98

In many ways we are still too close to the turbulent events of Maastricht fully to appreciate its likely constitutional and political implications. The *Financial Times*'s reference to 'A Heath Robinson design for Europe', presumably suggesting that the Treaty on European Union (TEU) was ingenious but absurdly impracticable, has so far been disproved. Whatever the institutional shortcomings and policy deficiencies of the TEU, it appears to have weathered the initial storms and continues to furnish the basis for a much more binding Europe into the next century. It reflects, we are reminded, the intergovernmental realities – the national policy preferences – of the early 1990s. But these policy preferences are not ephemeral; they are binding commitments to the future. They acknowledge the irreversible nature of European integration. In consequence, the *acquis communautaire* continues to expand. And, if the Maastricht consensus revealed certain deep-seated reservations among some member states about Economic and Monetary Union (EMU) and the Social Protocol, it is important to remember that these countries nonetheless recognised the national, European and global imperatives which combined irresistibly to push them toward further treaty commitments in pursuit of their own national interests. It is worth recalling Alan Milward's concession that there are 'other advantages of integration which suggest that once chosen it may be retained even if the dissimilarities between national policy bundles become wide'.[1] In this sense European integration at the end of the twentieth century remains a persistent search by the national state for solid guarantees about its future, based upon political judgements about the long-term national interest.

What, then, were the policy priorities of the member states and the European Union (EU) in the years between the Maastricht consensus and the Treaty of Amsterdam (TA)? First it should be noted that, like the Single European Act (SEA) before it, the TEU incorporated a commitment to convene another intergovernmental conference (IGC) in 1996 in order to decide which policies and forms of cooperation needed to be revised 'with the aim of ensuring the effectiveness of the mechanisms and the institutions of the Community'.[2] Maastricht had clearly confirmed its significance as part of the continuing quest to build Europe rather than being the terminal end-point of that process. But the years between 1994 and 1996 represented a very difficult period of consolidation and not a little stock-taking. A dark cloud seemed to hang over Europe after the political turbulence which had surrounded the ratification process of the TEU. After two damaging Danish referendums, a wafer-thin electoral majority in France and a notorious qualified approval in the German constitutional court in Karlsruhe in 1993, the atmosphere of bleakness and despondency was hardly surprising. The ratification process underlined a sea-change in the nature of European integration; EU leaders were reminded that there was nothing preordained about the progress of European integration. It was something that required unremitting effort.

In the mid-1990s, Europe experienced another economic downturn reflected in widespread anxieties about its competitive weaknesses, rising unemployment, falling investment and the impact of two bouts of currency turmoil that had swept through the continent and unhinged the Exchange Rate Mechanism (ERM). None of these pressing economic problems seemed likely to be resolved in the short-term by the EMU programme, and there was little evidence that the EU's leading member states had any remedies for Europe's economic ills. Germany was preoccupied with the costs of unification, and the United Kingdom (UK) had an opt-in on EMU and an opt-out on the Social Protocol, with its sights fixed largely upon its own strategy for national economic recovery. Meanwhile, France contemplated the structural economic reforms deemed necessary to achieve the convergence criteria for membership of EMU. On other fronts, there was also good reason for the sombre mood. The persistent obstacles to an agreement on the multilateral GATT (now World Trade Organization) negotiations strained EU–US relations which were already severely tested by the war in Bosnia. One of the new realities of the post-Cold War era was the implicit readjustment in relations between Europe and the United States, and this had major implications for one of the TEU's principal objectives, namely, the Common Foreign and Security Policy (CFSP). The Soviet threat having vanished, American proclivities in Europe and around the world suggested a major reappraisal of strategic objectives leading to a much lower international profile in the next century. This put a new gloss on the Maastricht commitment to a CFSP; if the EU was serious about this far-reaching objective, it would have to go much further than what was in the TEU. At the very least, it suggested a significant change in Germany's future role in a fully-fledged European foreign policy. This, in turn, would have important implications for an emergent defence policy and for the nature of what was to become the Paris–Berlin axis by the year 2000.

Other practical measures could be introduced immediately. These included improved cooperation between police forces and the judiciary in the EU to tackle crime; the official launching of the new Brussels-based

Committee of the Regions (CoR), giving sub-national units a direct input into EU decision-making for the first time; the location of the proposed European Monetary Institute (EMI), which would be the forerunner of the European Central Bank; and the strengthening of the European Investment Bank's lending facility to include energy, environmental and inner city projects in addition to transport-related areas. At the special summit meeting in Brussels at the end of October 1993, these decisions were taken but much remained uncertain. The EU awaited the Delors Commission's proposals for growth and unemployment, a resolution of the GATT trade talks and the outcome of discussions about streamlining EC/EU decision-making procedures in preparation for the next round of enlargement negotiations which were to be completed by 1 January 1995.

The proposed enlargement of the EU in January 1995 to include Austria, Sweden and Finland was, along with efforts to move ahead with EMU, the most pressing issue of 1994. If the unification of Germany in 1990 had pushed Europe eastwards, the inclusion of Sweden and Finland clearly propelled it in a northern direction. But the unerring movement eastwards seemed likely to continue by the turn of the century. In February 1994, Europe Agreements between the EU and Hungary and the EU and Poland entered into force, while in July Partnership and Cooperation Agreements between the EU and the Ukraine and the EU and Russia were signed, together with free trade arrangements between the EU and the Baltic states. In March and April, formal EU membership applications were lodged respectively by Hungary and Poland, and in May nine East European and Baltic states were admitted as 'associate' partners of the Western European Union (WEU) – Hungary, Poland, the Czech Republic, Slovakia, Bulgaria, Romania, Latvia, Lithuania and Estonia. Indeed, only President Yeltsin's implacable opposition prevented some of these countries from pressing ahead with full membership of the North Atlantic Treaty Organization (NATO).

The economic and political implications of these developments, and especially of a fifth enlargement of the EU in the foreseeable future, were of course colossal. Much talk was heard about the new political shape of the new Europe. Would *widening* conflict with the goal of *deepening*? What were the policy and institutional implications for the EU? Federalists saw no necessary contradiction between widening and deepening, provided that serious consideration was given to institutional reform. Changes to the decision-making process involving a reappraisal of Council and European Parliament (EP) majorities, the future of Qualified Majority Voting (QMV) and appropriate transitional arrangements were in any case deemed inevitable. But the need for institutional reform was essential. Small wonder that these contemporary developments, together with the TEU, prompted a bout of fresh terminological jousting. Rhetorical flourishes abounded. European integration would now be 'differentiated integration', reflected in phrases which included a 'multi-speed Europe', 'variable geometry' and 'Europe à la carte'. With a specific policy focus, there would now also be a 'multi-layered Europe'. Depending upon a particular set of variables which might include time, space, function(s) and territory, European integration quickly assumed a kaleidoscopic basis for all kinds of wishful thinking. Intergovernmentalists in particular could draw some comfort from this kind of largely empty rhetoric because it seemed to imply, in different ways, a looser, less binding Europe. In short, the increasing complexity of European integration might be an obstacle to a more federal Europe. But this posture was melodramatic. After all, most of these terms had already been either incorporated or suggested, without the accompanying razzmatazz, in EC treaties and reports stretching back at least to the 1970s.

The gist of the terminological debate in the mid-1990s was really about the idea of flexibility in the political evolution of the EU. If European integration was to proceed in the post-Cold War era, it had to adjust to new social, economic, political and military realities. Asymmetrical progress and asymmetrical relations would become the hallmark of integration in the 1990s, provided that they did not relegate the national interests of some member states to the sidelines of Europe's future. Consequently, the publication in September 1994 of a policy paper entitled 'Reflections on European Policy', which openly advocated the institutionalization of notions of a multi-speed Europe and of a Europe of variable geometry was a cause for considerable concern among some member state governments, largely because of its authoritative source. Emanating from the federalist portals of the German Christian Democratic Union (CDU), allied with the Christian Social Union (CSU), the report provoked a speedy and hostile response from some member state governments, like Spain and Italy, and more than a ripple of interest among established EU observers and commentators. Issued by a group which included Wolfgang Schauble and Karl Lamers (Helmut Kohl's Foreign Policy adviser), the report naturally attracted the attention of those member states which sensed that they might be excluded from the emergence of a new core group of countries forging ahead in European integration.[3]

This event, along with the advocacy of a Europe of 'concentric circles' by the French Prime Minister, Edouard Balladur, simply reflected the natural reservations and anxieties evident among political elites about Europe's uncertain future. It is best construed as part of what Brigid Laffan has called 'the battle of ideas' about the future of European integration.[4] Meanwhile, the fourth set of direct elections to the EP were held from 9–12 June 1994 – elections contested for a central institution which now had the power of co-decision. But with turnout down by two per cent compared to 1989, and little indication that the party political groups and federations had contributed very much to 'forming a European awareness' despite an increased use of common election manifestos, the elections seemed to suggest little of great political significance.[5] The end of 1994 also represented the end of the third Commission led by Jacques Delors, and marked the last year of a decade of remarkable energy, imagination and political leadership of the EU's most maligned and misunderstood institution. His political legacy, however, was indelibly stamped upon both the form and substance of the EU and of European integration. By 1995, then, two stalwarts of the European idea who had worked selflessly towards a federal Europe, Delors and Mitterrand, had departed the European stage.

In January 1995, the new Commission led by Jacques Santer assumed office following a vote of confidence by the EP of 417 votes to 104. The operation of the two new, staggered procedures introduced according to the TEU for appointing the new Commission and its President, almost provoked a crisis of legitimacy at the outset. Santer's appointment by the European Council was approved by 260 votes to 238 with 23 abstentions, and only after considerable negotiation and arm-bending in the EP.[6] Nonetheless, it was clear that these important innovations at last amounted to confirmation of an official vote of confidence by the parliamentary authority over the executive power in the EU.

Apart from the continuing discussions about EMU among the 15 EU member states, the main preoccupation of public debate during 1995 involved practical arrangements for the next IGC in 1996. At its June 1994 Corfu meeting, the European Council had agreed to establish a preparatory 'Reflection Group' to begin in June 1995 to clear some of the ground for the IGC. Chaired by the Spanish Secretary of State for European Affairs, Carlos Westendorp, the 18-strong group included the following representatives: one from each member state, two from the EP and one from the Commission. In six months the 'Reflection Group's Report' was published just in time for the European Council meeting in Madrid in early December. A fairly concise report of about 50 pages, its recommendations remained at the level of three broad generalities: making Europe more relevant to its citizens; enabling the Union to work better and preparing it for further enlargement; and giving the Union greater capacity for external action. These main areas had been distilled from the production of reports by the Commission, EP and Court of Justice which offered interim assessments of the functioning of the TEU since its ratification in 1993. With evidence of considerable division among the Reflection Group members, the more detailed recommendations and observations for the IGC included the following: a fundamental streamlining of decision-making procedures, including the strengthening of the principle of subsidiarity; an increase in QMV in the Council; improvements in aspects of the third Justice and Home Affairs (JHA) pillar; and a recognition that the second CFSP pillar was not working effectively.[7] There is no doubt that Santer's influence as a consolidator rather than an innovator determined the Commission's somewhat anaemic response. Federalists clearly wanted to see a merger of pillars two and three into the first EC pillar which would bring both CFSP and JHA formally into the *acquis communautaire* and firmly within the democratic procedural reach of the Commission, EP and Court of Justice. This would also have given reality to the Commission's much-coveted goal of a genuine 'single institutional framework' for the EU. Realistically, of course, they expected much less; more QMV and a stronger role for the Commission and EP in CFSP and JHA together with an increase in the formal powers of the EP was likely to be the most that they could hope to achieve. But it was at least clear that there was widespread discontent with the way that the TEU was working; another window of opportunity seemed to be opening.

When the IGC was formally launched in March 1996, at a special Heads of Government meeting in Turin, Italy, it was anticipated that the work would be finally completed in time for the Amsterdam European Council meeting in June 1997. Initially the quest was for 'greater efficiency, coherence and legitimacy', with a policy agenda that included a reappraisal of CFSP and institutional reform but as we shall see, the IGC did not manage to impose effective self-discipline upon its member state governments; it was not able to keep rival policy priorities and perspectives at bay. We will turn shortly to analyse and assess the Treaty of Amsterdam which surfaced from these rather unpropitious political circumstances in 1997, but it is appropriate first to look more closely than we have done so far at an aspect of federalism and European Union which has loomed large in both elite and public perceptions of European integration during the last decade, namely, the principle of subsidiarity. The relationship between federalism, subsidiarity and European Union has been both confusing in its complexity and tantalizing in its likely implications. The next section, therefore, will examine the historical and philosophical origins and the practical application of this obscure principle in the specific context of the evolution of European Union.

## Federalism, subsidiarity and European Union

Since the ratification of the SEA in July 1987, federalism and subsidiarity have become an integral part of the common language and public discourse of the EU even if both are frequently misunderstood and misrepresented. The 'F' word has been joined by the 'S' word. In one sense, subsidiarity has no obvious relevance to the political development of the EU while, in another sense, its evolving relationship to the building of European Union is perfectly understandable. In the public mind subsidiarity has surfaced gradually during the last decade as a principle which is relevant to the limits rather than to the possibilities of European integration. It has come to represent an instrument crucial to the integrity, and indeed the very survival, of the national state in Europe. Let us look first at the historical and philosophical origins of subsidiarity in order to provide our subject with its contextual background.

Subsequently, we shall examine its emergence in the late 1980s as a kind of talisman of some EU member state governments and we will also explore its wider political, legal and constitutional implications for European Union. But first let us begin with the word 'subsidiarity' itself and its original meaning.

In an essay first published in 1991, entitled 'Subsidiarity: Theory of a new Federalism?', Andrew Adonis claimed that 'In origin subsidiarity has nothing to do with the European Community, nor even with federalism as such'.[8] Yet in a subsequent collection of essays published in 1993 by the Federal Trust, subsidiarity was referred to as 'a federalist concept'.[9] How can these two seemingly contradictory assertions be reconciled? If subsidiarity in origin has little or nothing to do with federalism, how has it come today to be almost indissolubly connected to this distinctive political concept?

Subsidiarity derives from a peculiarly Catholic view of organic society given particular ecclesiastical authority in the papal encyclicals of *Rerum Novarum* (1891), *Quadragesimo Anno* (1931) and *Pacem in Terris* (1963). It is implicit in the emergent 'Social Catholicism' of the late nineteenth century which rejected both economic and political liberalism and socialism. In the first important social encyclical, *Rerum Novarum*, Pope Leo XIII tried to strike a delicate balance between the modern liberal society which produced a new individualism and undermined the inherited sense of community, and the system of unbridled laissez-faire capitalism which created a new class of selfish entrepreneurs, subjected the working class to inhuman conditions and resulted in a growing insensitivity to spiritual values. This official papal standpoint thus stood awkwardly at the crossroads between a dominant liberal individualism which advocated minimal state interference in society, and an emergent collectivist socialism which looked to class solidarity and organized class struggle to achieve social and economic justice.

In Catholic teaching, government was the promoter of the common good. It was not the agent of any particular class or vested interest in society. On the contrary, Catholic teaching defended the position that society had an objective common good which transcended the private goods of the individual members or any class. Government, therefore, must protect justice in society and this meant, in practice, some degree of central control over economic life. The Catholic critique of liberalism inevitably extended to liberal democracy itself, which was viewed as an instrument of the new propertied classes, the bourgeoisie, who would use public authority to promote and protect their own industrial and commercial interests, and gradually weaken the hold that traditional values – religion among them – had on the people. Catholic social theory presupposed a public authority superior to, and independent of, the particular entrenched interests existing in society. Those who governed did so with an authority derived from God. They represented no particular section of society, but rather its totality; they were servants of the common good. Similarly, in the specific area of economic life both liberal individualism and socialist class conflict were rejected. Instead, a primitive form of corporatism was advocated. Following the model of the medieval guilds, Catholic doctrine recommended that men organize themselves in vocational or professional groups – associations made up of owners, managers and workers involved in the same branch of production or the same branch of industry. The many different forms of primary and secondary production would give rise to groupings that represented not the interests of one single class but the concerns of an entire trade, thus enabling them to speak with a voice which cut across class conflict.

Clearly the Catholic critique of modern industrial society outlined above was worked out in the light of an idealised past, the organic society of the feudal age, when those who owned the land saw themselves as protectors of the people who lived and worked on it. They themselves were the promoters of the common good. Catholic social theory was predicated upon the notion of the organic community in which people were united by profound social bonds, like religion, inherited from the past and the continuing source of their vitality and creativity. The significance of *Rerum Novarum* lay in its formal adoption of 'Social Catholicism' and in the way that it defined the direction of Catholic social teaching. But it was also important for the assumptions which it made about the nature of man and society. These assumptions had far-reaching political implications. They coalesced in a pluralist conception of society which acknowledged man's innate propensity to enter into a multitude of relations with his fellow beings. These relations produced a veritable host of groups, associations, communities and societies extending from the family to international society. And it is also important to stress here that they were freely formed associations which existed independently of the state and owed nothing to it for their creation. In short, they constituted the very living practice of society, forming part of an immense network of complex and diverse social institutions reflective of man's multiple identities and capacities.

In 1931, Pope Pius XI published the encyclical *Quadragesimo Anno* in which he summarized previous Catholic social teaching and extended it under the impact of changing social and economic conditions. Here he outlined the changes that had occurred in both capitalism and socialism since *Rerum Novarum* in 1891, and attacked them for neglecting spiritual values. Advanced monopoly capitalism had resulted in the subservience of government to the selfish interests of the large corporations, while socialism had placed the concentration of political and economic power in the hands of the state, creating threats to the freedom of individuals and their associations. The ambiguity of papal teaching in *Rerum Novarum* concerning liberalism and socialism was carried over into *Quadragesimo Anno*. Pope Pius XI retreated from an outright condemnation of capitalism, preferring merely to use government legislation to break the power of monopolies, restore free competition and regulate the relations between capital and labour in accordance with the laws of justice. In order to limit both state power and the growth of government, while simultaneously demanding that public authority be used to regulate the economy and protect the working class by just legislation, Pius XI invoked the ancient social 'principle of subsidiarity' against excessive centralization. This principle, which was derived from the experience and vision of an essentially organic society, was defined thus:

> It is a fundamental principle of social philosophy, fixed and unchangeable, that one should not withdraw from individuals and commit to the community what they can accomplish by their own enterprise and industry. So, too, it is an injustice and at the same time a grave evil and a disturbance of right order, to transfer to the larger and higher collectivity functions which can be performed and provided for by lesser and subordinate bodies. In as much as every social activity should, by its very nature, prove a help to members of the body social, it should never destroy or absorb them.[10]

Put simply, subsidiarity was defended by the Catholic church as a moral principle. It constituted the moral barrier against the kind of centralization that Pope Pius XI saw as the inevitable consequences of socialism. But the principle of subsidiarity, which might well be translated as 'small is beautiful', was actually balanced by a counter-principle which could be called 'big whenever necessary'.[11] This counter-principle, known as the 'principle of socialisation' was first introduced by Pope John in his encyclical *Mater et Magistra* in 1961. It demanded that smaller social or economic units that were unable to provide adequately for their own needs must enter into cooperative relations with others and seek greater coordination of their activities so that together, collectively, they would be able to resolve the problems of all. The principle of socialization limited the free enterprise of economic corporations when they failed to provide for the needs of the wider community. It also empowered the government to initiate cooperation and coordination in the national economy, widen the base of participation in the decisions affecting production and distribution, and guide the economic development of the state if the needs of the people were not being met. As regulated capitalism, it suggested an early form of social market economy. In summary, the principle of socialization referred to a process in society whereby the separate concerns of subordinate groupings were coordinated through the multiplication of social relations and guided by appropriately higher authority structures. In this way the original principle of subsidiarity was accompanied by its dialectical complement, the principle of socialization: small is beautiful, but big whenever necessary.

How, then, did subsidiarity enter into federalist discourse and when did it take place? Adonis was correct to claim that it was through post-war Christian Democrats that the concept first entered the world of practical politics.[12] But this claim does not tell us precisely how this came to be so. The point is that subsidiarity was part and parcel of nineteenth-century 'political Catholicism', which itself was gradually superseded by Christian Democracy in the immediate aftermath of the Second World War.[13] Consequently, many of the core traditional political and philosophical values of Roman Catholicism were simply carried over, or woven, into the broader spectrum of Christian Democratic ideas and beliefs. The key to understanding the link between subsidiarity and federalism, then, lies in the uniquely Christian Democratic approach to power and authority. Theirs is essentially a pluralist conception which favours the dispersion of power both territorially and functionally. Taking its cue from Catholic doctrine, man is a member of certain natural groups – the family, the craftsmen, the profession, the commune, the region, the neighbourhood – which are natural law entities whose autonomy should be protected by the state. We are reminded here of the survey which we have already made of these ideas in Chapter 1 when we traced the philosophical ideas of Bullinger, Althusius and Proudhon. Since the main danger in modern society is defined as the development of an all-powerful state, the idea of federation that emerges is a political order which seeks to accommodate the greatest possible number of communities and societies, primary and intermediate, without destroying them. Accordingly, federation is construed as a living pluralist order which builds itself from the ground upwards, constructing its tiers of authority and decision-making according to the principle of subsidiarity. It is, in short, the reverse of a centralized state; it is a state based upon the territorial and functional dispersion of power with limited centralization.

We can already see from this brief sketch outline of Christian Democratic social and political thought that their conception of federalism and, by implication, European Union is both multi-dimensional and organic. It is largely a societal concept of federalism, but one which has enormous constitutional and political implications. Federation in this sense constitutes the only form of the state which can logically satisfy the requirements of the social order described above. Accordingly, if subsidiarity is to be applied to the entire social order, the federal principle of dividing powers and competences between different levels of authority is its logical complement.

Before we investigate the appearance of subsidiarity in the EU, it is important to underline the fact that both its origins and significance have been related to the role and structure of the state. It does not appear to have had any particular significance for international relations until *Pacem in Terris* was enunciated in 1963. In this papal encyclical the principle of subsidiarity was formally elevated to the discussion of international relations and world order. Here the Catholic conception of the world community, having as its fundamental objective 'the recognition, respect, safeguarding and promotion of the rights of the human person', requires that modern states acknowledge their interdependence in solving major problems. Subsidiarity applied to relations between the world community and modern states is expressed thus:

> The public authority of the world community is not intended to limit the sphere of action of the public authority of the individual political community, much less take its place. On the contrary, its purpose is to create, on a world basis, an environment in which the public authorities of each political community, its citizens and intermediate associations, can carry out their tasks, fulfil their duties and exercise their rights with greater security.[14]

There is, then, an essentially continuous, unbroken link between the citizen, associated groups, the state and the international community. Subsidiarity is a principle which is universal. Its implications for the EU, then, do not at first sight seem particularly perplexing. Indeed, the European People's Party (EPP) in the EP, which is dominated by the Christian Democratic parties of the member states, defined subsidiarity in its own draft federal constitution for Europe in 1983 in the following way:

> The principle of subsidiarity has been used in allocating the duties of state to the Union and the States of the Union, the division of powers and the allocation of financial resources. The principle is that for all state duties, the lowest appropriate level of authority shall be responsible. Duties are only assigned to the Union where this offers greater efficiency so as to conserve public resources while obtaining equally satisfactory or better results.[15]

'Greater efficiency' was 'one of the reasons for transferring powers to the Union', and these included foreign affairs, development aid, financial and monetary policy, environmental and consumer protection and the coordination of crime prevention.[16] But 'the group of the European federalists' also acknowledged that 'legislation is essentially a matter for the States of the Union': the Union was only empowered to legislate 'where the Constitution confers on it explicit legislative powers'. And powers could be transferred to the Union by the constituent states only 'under clearly defined circumstances'.[17]

These brief extracts from the EPP's draft constitution, intended as 'a model for the final stage of a European federal state', illustrate the way in which Christian Democratic social and political thought have penetrated both the debate about, and the process of, European integration.[18] Subsidiarity in the EC context first appeared in the discussions leading to the Tindemans Report of 1976, but it only entered the language and discourse of the EP's Committee on Institutional Affairs (CIA) in 1981–82. Indeed it was a British Conservative MEP, Christopher Jackson, who claimed personal responsibility for its prominent inclusion in the EP's own 'Draft Treaty establishing the European Union' in 1984.[19] Altiero Spinelli, who initiated the EP's struggle for European Union in the early 1980s, did not care much for the principle of subsidiarity and agreed to incorporate it in the draft treaty only at the insistence of the Christian Democrats.[20]

In the draft treaty, subsidiarity was elevated to a preambular principle:

> Intended to entrust common institutions, in accordance with the principle of subsidiarity, only with those powers required to complete successfully the tasks they may carry out more satisfactorily than the States acting independently.[21]

It was also more implicit in articles 10, 11, 12, 34, 54 and 66. Article 12(2) was especially interesting:

> The Union shall only act to carry out those tasks which may be undertaken more effectively in common than by the Member States acting separately, in particular those whose execution requires action by the Union because their dimension or effects extend beyond national frontiers.[22]

In practice the draft treaty (via article 38) established a complicated procedure for gradually extending the powers of the Union by a series of variable majorities and time-limits placed upon both the EP and the Council of the Union. There were, then, undeniably strong procedural pressures for a piecemeal, if almost indiscernible, accretion of powers and competences at the Union level. In this way what has since become known as the European Union Treaty (EUT) actually presupposed a decisive quality leap. Chapter 4 has already demonstrated how far the EUT contained the inherent capacity to go beyond what then existed.

In retrospect, it is difficult to view the incorporation of the subsidiarity principle in the EUT as having anything other than symbolic significance. This is not to deny the importance of symbolism in the quest for European Union, but it remains the case that subsidiarity in the EUT would not have been an effective brake upon the 'common action' of the Union. It would not have prevented the central authority from expanding. This brief discussion of subsidiarity in the EUT suggests that it had only very limited relevance to the future of European integration. Adonis was wrong to claim that subsidiarity had been 'entirely transplanted from its original context', since it did address the issues of world community and international relations, albeit relatively recently in *Pacem in Terris*.[23] Moreover, the life and meaning of a political concept cannot always be confined to its original setting. But he is surely correct to emphasize how far the principle is now used indiscriminately, even after its purported clarification in the TA in

1997. 'It has become a slogan and a debating brick-bat'.[24] How and why has this 'slogan', this symbol of national autonomy, acquired such dramatic, widespread visibility and popularity in the public debate about European Union? Let us turn our attention to the years which followed the ratification of the SEA in 1987, and explore the journey of the concept.

Subsidiarity did not loom large in the SEA. It was implicitly acknowledged in article 130r, but there was no indication in the SEA that it would soon become a watchword for a whole range of different and sometimes conflicting purposes. The sudden appearance of the word 'subsidiarity' in the public debate about European Union owed much to the Commission President, Jacques Delors. He it was who invoked it publicly in October 1988 in the EP as an official Commission response to Mrs Thatcher's misleading nightmare vision of a 'European super-state' advanced in her abrasive Bruges Speech of the previous month. According to Delors, subsidiarity was the perfect antidote to this unfounded fear:

> What can be decided at regional or local level should not be decided at national level. And under no circumstances should things decided at national level be decided at Community level.[25]

This early, simplistic definition clearly stressed the original Catholic meaning of the principle. Charles Grant claimed that Delors' attachment to subsidiarity had been 'longstanding' and that he had spoken of the need for it in his first Presidential speech to the EP in January 1985.[26] And this should not surprise us. We have already seen how Delors' firmly-held convictions about Europe were deeply rooted in the French Catholic socialist tradition – a rich intellectual tradition in which the Catholic personalist ideas of the French philosopher, Emmanuel Mounier, figured prominently. Delors' own spiritual and philosophical background had equipped him to understand subsidiarity perfectly well. In February 1989, in the EP, he emphasized another of the many faces of subsidiarity when he claimed that:

> Some undertakings can be completed better at European than at national level ... the work put in at European level is not enough to secure maximum results ... We have to do more.[27]

In November 1989, in the EP, Delors reaffirmed his faith in subsidiarity as a safeguard against 'excessive centralism' and warned against public discussion developing in 'dogmatic terms'.[28] But by the end of 1989, the most interesting trend in the evolving saga about subsidiarity lay in what Delors called 'the institutional choice' to be made concerning future EC reform. The former French President, Valéry Giscard d'Estaing, who would later be appointed by the EP to be its rapporteur on the question of subsidiarity, underlined this important shift in the public debate:

It is becoming absolutely necessary to put the principle of subsidiarity on an institutional footing. Many fears and misunderstandings would be dispelled if we drew up a clear, detailed and practical list, based on the subsidiarity principle, of the matters to be included in the future sphere of competence of the Union and those that are to remain within the Member States' competence; in other words a list defining the two levels of democratic legitimacy in the Community. Such a definition of levels of competence must be an essential part of the future European constitutional act.[29]

Giscard's comments were telling. He had placed the subsidiarity question firmly in the larger context of the future European constitution. The underlying public debate was really about the constitutional basis of the emergent European Union. To this extent, subsidiarity served as a necessary surrogate – a kind of code language – for what many participants in the European Union were reluctant fully to confront. Once again the shadow of Spinelli, who had championed the EP drive for constitutionalism in the early 1980s, continued to infuse the contemporary debate about the building of Europe.

In January 1990, in the EP, Delors pursued his quest for meaning when he told those MEPs present that 'the concept of subsidiarity will have to be clarified and reflected in the institutional and legal arrangements'. Echoing Giscard's earlier plea, he added:

Subsidiarity … must be the watchword underlying any scheme for allocating responsibilities between the Community, the national authorities and the regional authorities. And in the federation of the Twelve – which will be unusual in that the central authority's primary role will be to provide the impetus – the principle of subsidiarity will have to act as a constant counterweight to the natural tendency of the centre to accumulate power … this new step forward must be taken openly and with the question of who does what at Community, national and regional level clearly defined.[30]

Once the decision to convene a new IGC for the further revision of the treaties was taken in June 1989 in Madrid, the Commission took a leading role in the official debate about subsidiarity. And when the EC's progress towards EMU coincided with the unification of Germany and the collapse of the Soviet Union so that two IGCs – one on EMU and the other on political union – were created at the insistence of Chancellor Kohl and President Mitterrand, the Commission's formal 'Opinion on Political Union' of 21 October 1990 confirmed the link between federalism and subsidiarity:

The question of subsidiarity is closely linked to the redefinition of certain powers. The Commission considers that this common-sense principle should be written into the Treaty, as suggested by Parliament in its Draft Treaty on European Union. It should serve as a guideline for the institutions when, under a new Article 235 freed from its purely economic purpose, they have to take a unanimous decision of principle on new Community action in pursuit of general treaty objectives. Compliance with the principle could be checked by a retrospective control of the institutions' activities to ensure that there is no abuse of powers.[31]

Here the Commission construed subsidiarity in terms of the future European Union as a 'federal-type organization'.[32] The principle of subsidiarity would establish broad guidelines in the evolving federation of the Twelve concerning 'the redefinition of certain powers' rendered necessary by 'new Community action in pursuit of general treaty objectives'.[33] It was also a golden opportunity, as Andrew Duff has correctly emphasized, for the Commission to propose the simplification of EC law via a new legislative hierarchy.[34] But in the tangled web of elite bargaining between the EC's main intergovernmental and supra-national institutions, it gradually became clear that any consensus upon subsidiarity would be both limited and fragile. The conflicting objectives of the principal actors guaranteed an awkward compromise.

The TEU explicitly enshrined the subsidiarity principle in new clauses. Article A of Title I (Common Provisions) welcomed the 'new stage in the process of creating an ever closer union among the European peoples, in which decisions are taken as closely as possible to the citizen'. Article B stated that the objectives of the Union would be achieved 'while respecting the principle of subsidiarity as defined in Article 3b'. And article 3b of Title II (Provisions amending the Treaty of Rome) defined subsidiarity in the following way:

> The Community shall act within the limits of the powers conferred upon it by this Treaty and of objectives assigned to it therein.... In areas which do not fall within its exclusive competence, the Community shall take action, in accordance with the principle of subsidiarity, only if and in so far as the objectives of the proposed action cannot be sufficiently achieved by the Member States and can therefore, by reason of the scale or effects of the proposed action, be better achieved by the Community. Any action by the Community shall not go beyond what is necessary to achieve the objectives of the Treaty.[35]

Clearly the consensus about subsidiarity reflected in these clauses was possible only because it obscured significant differences in interpretation. And the ambiguity of meaning which was incorporated in them served to generate more heat than light. The competing differences of view did not end with the British and German governments. They also included the governments of the smaller EC member states, the German Länder and of course the Commission itself. The so-called consensus on subsidiarity was, in reality, a hollow consensus.

What did subsidiarity mean in the Maastricht Treaty? At first glance, the first paragraph of article 3b seemed to be a clear statement of intent. The Community could act only 'within the limits of the powers conferred upon it by this treaty'. But the rest of the paragraph – 'and of the objectives assigned to it therein' – effectively rendered the first section meaningless. By limiting the Community's area of activity to treaty objectives, the signatories had actually reaffirmed their commitment to article 235 of the Treaty of Rome – the doctrine of 'Community competence' – which empowered the Council of Ministers to identify what such objectives were. Accordingly, the Council could implement these objectives whether or not article 3b was included in the treaty.

The key to understanding the second paragraph, which dealt with those areas outside the Community's exclusive competence, lay in the interpretation of the word 'sufficiently' and the phrase 'by reason of the scale or effects'. Here the ambiguity scaled new heights. Deciding precisely what words meant depended entirely upon subjective judgements. The word 'sufficiently', as Adonis and Tyrie have argued, appeared to imply that subsidiarity should have been construed narrowly as an 'effectiveness test'.[36] But it could equally have been thought of in terms which were much wider. What, after all, was really 'sufficient'? Furthermore the words 'scale or effects' were just as problematic. They were linked to Community action in a baffling way. The qualification as to the 'scale or effects of the proposed action' literally left the question of Community action wide open to debate. Interpreted in an expansive sense, these words could have been used to justify almost any Community action. One could almost sense the lawyers rubbing their hands with glee.

The third paragraph of article 3b introduced what did appear to be a tight constraint on Community action which seemed to override the previous two paragraphs. Douglas Hurd, the British Foreign Secretary, claimed responsibility for detaching the last sentence from the previous paragraph in order to render subsidiarity 'in its fully developed form' applicable both to shared or parallel Community competence, as well as to exclusive Community competence. He called this 'the necessary test'.[37] He also referred to it as 'minimum interference'.[38] Given the studied vagueness of subsidiarity in the TEU, then, it required little thought to imagine just what a legal minefield had been left for the European Court of Justice (ECJ). It was initially feasible to argue that, in most cases, the question of subsidiarity would be decided by national political and administrative authorities. Member state governments would work it out for themselves in the early days, and would presumably want to keep decisions at the national and in some cases the regional levels to begin with. But it was also widely recognised that there would inevitably be a residue of potentially controversial legal questions which would have to be resolved by the Court in Luxembourg. In other words, there would be an active role for the Court in making judgements which might conceivably be disputed as highly 'political'. Lord Mackenzie-Stuart, the President of the ECJ between 1984 and 1988, underlined precisely this fear when he warned:

> The interpretation of subsidiarity is a political issue and not one for the Court of Justice of the European Communities. Maastricht, however, places that responsibility squarely on its shoulders. Worse … the definition of subsidiarity contained in the Treaty … is a rich and prime example of gobbledygook embracing simultaneously two opposed concepts of subsidiarity. To regard the chosen formula as a constitutional safeguard shows great optimism.[39]

The principle of subsidiarity in the Maastricht Treaty did not seem to augur well for European integration in the 1990s. It seemed to promise further confusion and more intensive intergovernmental conflict. And when the Danish electorate narrowly rejected the TEU in the June 1992 referendum, an already confused public debate degenerated further into a panic debate. The Danish voter rebellion seems in hindsight to have marked a significant turning-point in the quest to give substance to the concept of subsidiarity. Arguably the main beneficiary of the dramatic change in the political environment of the EC was the British government. Its primary objective at Maastricht had been to secure a solid line of defence against 'automaticity': the steady accretion of powers to Brussels. The Danish referendum result had provided a golden opportunity for it to obtain a revised definition of subsidiarity which would guarantee a much less intrusive EC. To this end, the British government's overriding aim at the Lisbon meeting of the European Council at the end of June 1992 was to establish a direct link between the EC's prospects of rescuing the Maastricht Treaty and the United Kingdom's (UK) determination to decentralize Community decision-making. The British Prime Minister, John Major, confirmed his goal of giving 'life' to the concept of subsidiarity, by which he meant obliging the Commission to provide more effective 'justification' for all new legislation and the abandonment of unnecessary or outdated directives. From the beginning of the UK presidency of the EC in July 1992, then, there seemed to be a distinct convergence of opinion in the EC about the need to placate the Danes by using subsidiarity to contribute to 'the harmonious development of the (European) Union over the coming years'.[40]

With the Commission on the defensive and the British government at the helm of the EC for the six months between July and December 1992, subsidiarity became a veritable buzzword. Indeed, in some British government circles it seemed to have an almost inherent talismanic quality designed to safeguard member states' interests in the Community. The emergency one-day meeting of the European Council in Birmingham in mid-October 1992 appeared to confirm this view. The centrepiece of the special summit was a discussion of how far the EC should make treaty adjustments after the Danish and French referenda on the TEU. The narrow French approval of Maastricht in the September 1992 referendum served to ease the worries of EC member state governments about the possible collapse of the Community itself, but it had also reaffirmed the fragility of the European project. At Birmingham, it was imperative not to fail. The importance of the summit meeting was as much psychological as it was political. Subsidiarity dominated the proceedings, but even as the key theme there was no real attempt to give it a more precise meaning. Delors' offer of a £140,000 reward to anybody who could produce a one-page working definition of subsidiarity that could be understood by all underlined the low expectations of the summiteers. And his own confession that subsidiarity was 'strewn with pitfalls and riddled with ulterior motives' epitomized the crisis of confidence in the EC.[41]

In its October 1992 statement on subsidiarity, the Commission moved to regain the initiative which it seemed to have lost after the Danish referendum. In a ten-page communication entitled 'The Principle of Subsidiarity', it reminded the EC that the principle should 'help to assure the citizen that decisions will be taken as closely as possible to the citizen himself, without damaging the advantage which he gains from common action at the level of the whole Community and without changing the institutional balance'. Taking into account the mounting fears and anxieties evident among EC mass publics during the convulsive ratification process of Maastricht, the Commission had promised to look into the possibility of applying subsidiarity to existing areas of competence so that its interference would be reduced and might even lead to it handing back some of these areas to the member states. The document trod carefully:

> Subsidiarity is a dynamic concept in the Community system. Far from putting Community action in a straitjacket, it allows it to be expanded where circumstances so require and, conversely, to be restricted or abandoned where it is no longer justified.[42]

This time, the test of 'comparative efficiency' was adopted in areas outside of exclusive competence. EC action should always be proportional to the dimension of the issue in question:

> In the Community context, subsidiarity means that the functions handed over to the Community are those which the Member states, at various levels of decision-making, can no longer discharge satisfactorily. Any transfer of powers must have due regard for national identity and the powers of the regions.[43]

Finally the Commission sounded a warning note about the conditions under which it was prepared to implement subsidiarity. The principle was to be used neither to obstruct the decision-making process nor deliberately to undermine the Commission's own role and powers of initiative. It repeated its right to withdraw a draft proposal if either the Council or the EP contravened the principle of subsidiarity.

The conclusions on subsidiarity reached at the Edinburgh European Council meeting during 11–12 December 1992 were modest but merit inclusion here. They can be grouped for convenience in the following way:

a   Articles A and B (Common Provisions) were confirmed as 'a basic principle of the European Union'.

b   Article 3b was confirmed as 'general principles of Community law' having 'a new legal significance'.

c   Making the principle of subsidiarity and article 3b work was an obligation 'for all the Community institutions, without affecting the balance between them'.

d   The principle of subsidiarity did not relate to, and cannot call into question, the powers conferred on the European Community by the Treaty as interpreted by the Court.

e   The application of subsidiarity will respect the general provisions of the Maastricht Treaty, including the 'maintaining in full of the *acquis communautaire*'. It will not affect the primacy of Community law nor will it call into question the principle set out in article F(3) of the Maastricht Treaty according to which the Union will provide itself with the means necessary to attain its objectives and carry through its policies.

f   Subsidiarity is a dynamic concept and should be applied in the light of the objectives set out in the Treaty. It allows Community action to be expanded where circumstances so require, and, conversely, to be 'restricted or discontinued where it is no longer justified'.

g   Where Community action is excluded, Member States are still required to respect and fulfil their obligations under the Treaty.

h   Subsidiarity will not have 'direct effect', but it will be justiciable. Interpretation of the principle, as well as a review of compliance with it by the Community institutions, are 'subject to control by the Court of Justice, as far as matters falling within the Treaty establishing the European Community are concerned'.

i   Paragraphs 2 and 3 of article 3b apply only to the extent that the Treaty gives to the institution concerned the choice whether to act and/or a choice as to the nature and extent of the action. 'The more specific the nature of a Treaty requirement, the less scope exists for applying subsidiarity'. Subsidiarity will not therefore apply where the EC has specific obligations, such as competition policy, the need to enforce EC law and to account for EC expenditure.

j   In areas of shared competence between the EC and the national level, the type of measures to apply will be decided 'on a case by case basis in the light of the relevant provisions of the Treaty'.

The Edinburgh Annex also laid down a set of guidelines for the application of article 3b. Simply stated, these involved the assurances that:

a   The proposed action is within the limits of the powers conferred by the Treaty, meets one or more of its objectives, and has the necessary legal basis.
b   Transnational aspects are involved.
c   Non-EC action will conflict with Treaty requirements or damage Member States' interests.
d   EC action will establish clear benefits according to qualitative and, wherever possible, quantitative indicators.

In addition, the EC was committed to a range of measures which were designed both to justify and legitimize its future actions. Administrative and financial burdens were to be minimized and kept in proportion to objectives. EC law was to be framework in character, leaving considerable discretion to national implementation. The amount of EC law was to be kept to a minimum and was not to apply to all member states unless all of them were affected. The Commission agreed to consult more widely before proposing legislation and this included a more systematic use of consultation documents in the form of green papers. It also reaffirmed its commitment, originally made at the Lisbon European Council, to 'justify in a recital the relevance of its initiative with regard to the principle of subsidiarity'. Furthermore it acknowledged the importance of monitoring 'the observance of the provisions of article 3b', including the submission of an annual report on subsidiarity. And, finally, it produced a list of over 20 measures of EC law which it used to demonstrate what the Community should seek to avoid in the future. This list accompanied a declaration of intent to withdraw, amend and re-examine certain EC measures which were either not warranted or went into excessive detail. It did not, however, imply a wholesale repatriation of EC law for which many inter-governmentalists had doubtless hoped.

Turning to the intergovernmental machinery of the EC, the Edinburgh Annex confirmed that conventional Council voting and rules of procedure would apply to the application of article 3b and this included the EP's opinion along with the Council's reaction. Of particular importance was the statement that 'Care should be taken not to impede decision-making in the Council and to avoid a system of preliminary or parallel decision-making'. This was crucial if the EC integration process was not to be hijacked by new intergovernmental intrusions in the future.[44]

The Commission paper of October 1992 clearly influenced the

Edinburgh Council proceedings and its overall institutional and legislative position remained intact. In true Community fashion, the Edinburgh Annex appeared to represent the compromise which satisfied all of the vested interests involved. Consequently it was, and remains, open to many interpretations. Broadly speaking, the maximalist interpretation of subsidiarity, which was represented by the British government, viewed the agreement as having confirmed the limits to European integration. In the future, so-called 'automaticity' would be effectively curbed and replaced by the rule of 'minimum interference'. In contrast, the minimalist view of subsidiarity, which was reflected in the position of the Commission and of several small member states, regarded the agreement as having established procedural clarity and legal entrenchment to what, in effect, already existed in practice. Their main concern was to prevent the 'watering-down' of European integration. Within this broad spectrum, of course, there were many nuances and gradations of interest. But in hindsight, probably the most significant implication of the whole Edinburgh Council episode was the impact that the new accord was likely to have upon the future role of the ECJ.

Even after the Edinburgh revisions, much doubt and uncertainty continued to surround the meaning of the principle of subsidiarity. How far would the application of the principle affect the existing balance (or imbalance) between the EU's central institutions, between the EU and its member states, and between the various sub-national authorities within each member state? In other words, what would be its horizontal and vertical implications? These questions and others explained why the issue resurfaced during the IGC negotiations in 1996. In response to the Maastricht legacy of legal and political ambiguity and the resulting level of disquiet, a new 'Protocol on the Application of the Principles of Subsidiarity and Proportionality' was inserted into the new Amsterdam treaty in 1997. Close analysis of the new protocol reveals that it is really only a summation and clarification of the Edinburgh Annex. Nonetheless, the loose ends which it has finally tied up mark it out as 'the definitive statement about the principle of subsidiarity, what it is and how it should be applied'.[45] According to Andrew Duff, the Amsterdam Protocol had two main consequences: first, that both elements of article 3b, that is subsidiarity and proportionality, must be taken together; and, second, that it weakens the ability of the ECJ to claim that, although the interpretation of subsidiarity falls within its jurisdiction, it is not in practice justiciable.[46] The latter conclusion would seem to suggest that the ECJ might in future find itself embroiled in matters of a political or quasi-political nature which it would construe as singularly inappropriate for such an institution. Duff's final assertion that the new Protocol would serve to 'deepen the federal character of the European Union' was somewhat tarnished by his parting remark that it was also a 'useful compromise' that would depend upon 'political will' to exploit it – a statement that does not seem to augur well either for intergovernmental or legal harmony in the future.[47]

What, then, does this short survey of the life and times of the principle of subsidiarity tell us about the nature of the relationship between federalism and subsidiarity? Is it correct to claim that 'subsidiarity is a federalist concept'? Duff certainly supported this view in 1993, while also acknowledging that 'it sits uneasily in a European federal system that is not comprehensive, not fully democratic and still not working very well'. The application of 'the federalist principle of subsidiarity', he added, was 'only possible within a federal system'.[48] This bald assertion, though undeniable, was clearly unhelpful because it amounted to a truism. Certainly subsidiarity, despite its origins, could be defended as 'a federalist principle' in the general sense that it favoured the building of a union from the bottom upwards, constructing tiers of authority without destroying the integrity of lower bodies. In this rather weak sense, it was little more than a declaration of support for what we might call 'reciprocal autonomy'. But the real problem arose when attempts were made to translate it into practical legal action in the EC. As Anthony Cary has noted, it was because the Community was not a classic federal system that the Commission and the Council had not opted to apply the principle of subsidiarity 'by drawing up lists of subjects to be dealt with at different levels of Government'.[49] This would, in effect, have meant the establishment of a European constitution. In the case of the Community, of course, the point of departure has been very different from previous federal unions. The building of Europe has been the result of Monnet's Europe – a Europe of piecemeal, incremental and cumulative steps, rather than a single constitutional act.

The contemporary controversy about subsidiarity is partly the result of Monnet's Europe. It is Monnet's troublesome legacy. Consequently, we might question how far the Amsterdam Protocol will provide a clear guide as to how 'areas for which the Community does not have exclusive competence' might be exercised at the Community level.[50] In the absence of a federal constitution for the EU, subsidiarity will remain something of an oddity. It is marooned in a Europe which is still only partly built. Its uncertain destination is the result of an integration process which remains incomplete. But it is here to stay and the EU must find ways of living with it that do not result in zero-sum conflicts which are notoriously difficult to resolve. In short, the principle of subsidiarity might introduce new problems which the treaties are currently ill-equipped to handle. In this sense it is an argument, once again, for a European constitution.

Having briefly explored the shifting relationship between federalism, subsidiarity and European Union, it is time to return to the intergovernmental and supra-national politics of the Treaty of Amsterdam (TA). We will not examine every clause of the treaty because it has already been thoroughly investigated in the mainstream literature on the evolution of the EU.[51] Instead, we shall adopt an approach which is intended to throw some light upon the increasing federalization of the European project. Let us begin with some background information and contextual comments which will help to put the TA into its proper perspective.

## The Treaty of Amsterdam: the Holy Roman Empire revisited

The emerging academic literature on the TA seemed to arrive at a consensus bonded by deep disappointment and not a little despair. The EU had reached another crossroads in its overall evolution, but it was yet another difficult destination. The conclusions about both the process of constitution-building and the substance of the treaty were gloomy and despondent. It did not seem to matter that we had been here before in 1990–92; the air of disillusionment and pessimism remained pervasive.[52]

Why did the TA produce so much discontent among federalists and intergovernmentalists alike? How do we explain the huge discrepancy between its goals and its achievements? Let us consider first the legacy of Maastricht, and then look more closely at the political environment out of which the TA emerged. We have already noted the commitment made in the TEU to hold another IGC in 1996. The EU created at Maastricht had been, in a sense, an unfulfilled union. There remained much unfinished business. Important matters regarding CFSP in pillar two and JHA in pillar three, questions concerning a common defence policy linked to the future role of the WEU and issues surrounding citizenship and the legitimacy of the EU's overall political authority, furnished ample justification for another IGC. But these imperatives would not be addressed in the same political context as others had been at Maastricht. Nobody could have foreseen the political environment in which they would be discussed and negotiated. Nobody, therefore, could have anticipated what the vicissitudes of the fragile, unpredictable world of intergovernmentalism would allow. It was always important to keep up the momentum established by previous bargains and commitments, but even irreversible agreements could still be temporarily delayed, diverted and even diluted in policy content by sudden changes in the political atmosphere. A series of intra-EU events and circumstances occurred in 1996–97 which served to darken and obscure the political atmosphere surrounding the treaty negotiations. Most member state governments, for a variety of mainly domestic reasons, were not emboldened in their respective commitments to further European integration. Political tensions in Germany and France in particular deflected the energies of Kohl and Chirac towards overriding domestic concerns. EMU and its socio-economic implications suddenly and unexpectedly cast a dark shadow over domestic public affairs and reduced the possibilities of yet another qualitative move forward in the building of Europe. In Germany, a massive row broke out between the federal government in Bonn and the Bavarian government in Munich over the vexed question of whether EMU should be allowed to proceed with some member states showing an estimated budget deficit slightly above the Maastricht benchmark of three per cent of gross domestic product. One consequence of this political skirmish in the summer of 1997 was Kohl's stiffened resolve to see the EMU timetable through to its Maastricht conclusion. This meant that he subordinated all other domestic, foreign and European policy considerations to the unstinting push for EMU. But his room for manoeuvre had, in any case, been severely restricted by a dynamic combination of self-assertive Länder and an ever-vigilant German public, increasingly sensitized to EU affairs by a seemingly omnipresent constitutional court in Karlsruhe.

In France, the surprise electoral victory of the socialists led by the lugubrious Lionel Jospin, knocked the French President, Jacques Chirac, temporarily off balance as both he and the French people contemplated a significant shift in the country's national agenda. With Kohl concentrating all of his personal energies on EMU, anticipating national elections due in September 1998 and constantly looking over his shoulder at party political concerns, and Chirac handcuffed to the domestic issues which an uneasy cohabitation with the socialists required, it was small wonder that the Paris–Bonn axis struggled to find common ground during the Amsterdam IGC. Elsewhere, uncertainties abounded in this period. In the UK, the long-awaited electoral contest between John Major and Tony Blair resulted in a new Labour government which was much more warmly disposed than the Conservatives had been to the EU's Social Protocol, and clearly in favour, like Jospin, of a shift towards European policies that would tackle unemployment and poverty. But the new British government was as attached to the transatlantic alliance and the continuation of NATO as its predecessor had been. Italian efforts to support the more ambitious and progressive policies at the IGC, meanwhile, had become typically subdued after the electoral and political convulsions of the early 1990s, while the Spanish government prepared itself for a veritable war of attrition in Amsterdam in its pursuit of equality of voting rights along with the four largest member states in the Council of Ministers. None of this augured well for an ambitious treaty reform in 1997. Indeed, with both the script and the priorities having changed so dramatically during the IGC 'it came as no surprise that meeting deadlines and keeping to timetables gradually assumed more importance than the actual substance of the reform'.[53]

Given this sort of bleak intergovernmental background context to the IGC, a certain level-headed, pragmatic sobriety based upon low expectations was accorded to both the proceedings and the ultimate outcome. Federalists braced themselves for more high-sounding rhetorical flourishes backed up by underwhelming institutional and policy achievements. Let us flag up some of the most politically-salient features of the TA and comment upon their significance for the building of a federal Europe. To the extent that the EU had been constructed in 1992 via three pillars supporting one roof at Maastricht, there was clearly more basic continuity than fundamental change. In this sense, the assumptions which under-pinned Maastricht had been reinforced. But there were some important policy gains and institutional improvements made.

The TA modified the TEU pillar structure without altering its shape in a fundamental way by moving common visa, immigration and asylum policy from the intergovernmental third pillar to the first pillar of the European Community (EC) and renamed the former 'Police and Judicial Coopera-tion in Criminal Matters'. The significance of this for federalists was that it had moved important elements of primarily intergovernmental policy away from member state governments and into the *acquis communautaire* where they would subsequently fall within the embrace of the Commis-sion, EP and ECJ. This development was related indirectly to the Schen-gen Agreement which was bolted on to the TA in order that, within five years of its ratification, the free movement of persons as well as goods, ser-vices and capital could be established in an area without internal frontiers. The British Labour government, however, balked at the idea of a new 'area of freedom, security and justice' and insisted, as John Major had done previously, on a UK opt-out from both this and the Schengen *acquis*.

The confirmation of fundamental human rights and freedoms, together with the institutional capacity to combat discrimination based on sex, racial or ethnic origin, religion or belief, disability, age or sexual orientation and the inclusion of gender equality in pay and employment strengthened the EU's relevance to the direct and immediate concerns of its mass publics. And the addition of a whole chapter on employment policy not only enhanced the status of the goal as a formal EU objective, but it also sig-nalled a modest centre-left shift back towards traditional social democratic values and away from the narrow neoliberal assumptions implicit in the Maastricht model of EMU. Other additions to the policy content of the TA included environment, public health and consumer protection, social policy, citizenship, fraud and transparency (that is, the right of public access to EU documents). Modesty was also the word which can be con-sidered to have characterized progress in CFSP. A policy planning and early warning unit was created which facilitated Commission participation and a shared right of initiative, but the WEU was not formally subsumed into the EU. Instead its Petersburg Tasks – humanitarian and rescue, crisis management and peace-keeping – were incorporated in the TA and the future role of the WEU, and its relationship to the EU, were left undefined.

Turning to institutional matters, the federalists could take some comfort from the strengthening of the powers of the EP. According to Duff, in securing co-decision with the Council, albeit acting by unanimity in 8 new policy areas, the EP was 'the main beneficiary of Amsterdam'. These new powers were situated somewhat strangely alongside the existing 15 old competences which operated with the Council acting by QMV. But given that one of the IGC's aims had been to simplify and clarify the EU's complicated legislative procedures, their reduction to just three, namely, consultation, assent and co-decision could reasonably be construed as goal-attainment. In this way the EP was 'the big winner of Amsterdam'.[54] The Commission suffered some setbacks regarding competition and trade policies, but its right of initiative in legislative matters remained intact. Its role in matters of internal security was modestly extended, and the role of its President-elect was strengthened *vis-à-vis* the choice of other Commission members. Santer the consolidator could at least be satisfied that his own presidency would not be remembered solely for the almost embarrassing *de facto* investiture by the EP in 1995.

The role of the ECJ was also indirectly strengthened in two ways. First, provision was made for a potential widening of its jurisdiction under the third pillar (Police and Judicial Cooperation) so that it could give preliminary rulings in those references made to it by national courts, subject to member state governments agreeing to it. Second, the possibilities of judicial review were automatically extended to include the fundamental rights, civil proceedings and common policy areas concerning visas, refugees and asylum issues located in the first EC pillar.

Four remaining areas merit brief discussion before we attempt to assess the overall significance of the TA for federalism and the federalists. Regarding the thorny question of subsidiarity, we have already noted the persistence of studied ambiguity in the TA. The 'S'-word seemed to have emerged from the IGC as both a legal norm and a political principle. It was not, and is still not clear, precisely how and upon what grounds the principle of subsidiarity will be implemented. Indeed, if the Commission's position is taken at face value, the EU appears to have adopted a contradictory position with regard to the implementation of subsidiarity. If it relies wholly upon the ECJ for a legal interpretation to resolve EC competences, this might suggest an emphasis upon the limitation of central powers to act; whereas if the operating principle is essentially political, the scope for expanding these competences might be much more feasible. For students of federalism and federation, the conundrum of the impact of European integration upon established federations – like Germany, Austria and Belgium – as themselves constituent units of a larger evolving federal union, was underlined in an interesting way by the 'Declaration on Subsidiarity' incorporated in the general 'Protocol on the Application of the Principles of Subsidiarity and Proportionality' of the TA. Here it was formally acknowledged that action taken by the EC in accordance with the principle of subsidiarity concerned not only the member states themselves, but also 'their entities' to the extent that they had their own 'law-making powers conferred on them under national constitutional law'.[55] This added spice to the already contentious question about the vertical impact of subsidiarity upon the distribution of territorial power within national states, and raised important empirical questions about the territorial dispersion of power in federations.

The second issue which has continued to raise more than an eyebrow when the TA is analysed, refers to the question of enlargement. The 'Protocol on the Institutions with the Prospect of Enlargement of the EU' aptly underlined the fragility of the intergovernmental compromise that had produced the TA. The brevity of the protocol was related inversely to its potential significance. It asserted that another IGC would be convened at least one year before the membership of the EU exceeded 20 in order to conduct a comprehensive review of the composition and functioning of the central institutions.[56] This really referred to the abject failure of the member states to address the question of institutional reform. Clearly any attempt to refashion the existing institutional imbalance between national and supra-national interests on the one hand, and between the concerns of smaller and larger member states on the other, was always going to be fraught with difficulty. The search for an agreement on the number of votes each country should wield in the Council of Ministers remains a battle that will have to be fought again early in the next century when the next enlargement is addressed. Conceivably, this could constitute another of those crucial steps in the building of a federal Europe because, in some respects, the task would involve the member states returning almost to first principles.

The third area concerns EMU. We should recall that the IGC had no official mandate to revisit the EMU articles in the TEU. But the significance of the project and the manner of its gradual implementation by fixed stages, with the third stage beginning in January 1999, ensured that the shadow of EMU would fall obtrusively across the deliberations of the IGC. Consequently, the European Council passed three resolutions concerning EMU at Amsterdam. The first of these reaffirmed what had first been agreed by the European Council in Dublin in December 1996, namely, the commitment of the member states to avoid excessive government deficits so that sound national budgetary policies would strengthen the conditions for general price stability. In Dublin the main elements of a Stability and Growth Pact, involving the surveillance of budgetary positions and the coordination of economic policies, had been agreed. The second resolution linked the general convergence criteria to a common approach to employment, while the third dealt with revisions to the ERM which meant linking the currencies of those within and without the new Euro zone. In these circumstances, Kohl's single-minded determination to solidify the intergovernmental commitment to the Stability and Growth Pact at least had the merit of maintaining the Maastricht momentum towards the goal of EMU. After Amsterdam, few could have seriously questioned the political will of the member states to introduce the euro in January 1999. Moreover, the achievement of EMU, as Pinder has already demonstrated, would clearly complete the process whereby the EU would have acquired, in step-by-step fashion, 'the essential economic powers of a federation'.[57] And as Duff has already observed, the strict adherence to both the content and the timetable of EMU suggests that it might not be long before a new impetus might develop behind moves for a stronger system of economic governance for the EU and, perhaps, even a 'political counterweight' to the European Central Bank.[58]

Finally, the elusive concept of 'flexibility' merits more than a passing reference in this chapter. We have already referred briefly to the fashionable analytical perspectives subsumed within the umbrella phrase 'differentiated integration', to which many commentators have recently had the temptation to resort. The general thrust of these contemporary conceptual categories – like 'multi-speed Europe' and 'variable geometry' – is to suggest an EU which, in future, will be much more complex and variegated with a corresponding need for increasingly asymmetrical relations at both institutional and policy levels. The new Article 5A in the TA was a response to precisely this problem. Initially it was the direct outcome of an extremely difficult set of circumstances brought about chiefly by the rigid and uncompromising attitude of the British Conservative government led by Major, but it might also be viewed in another, less pessimistic, light. The growing prospect of an increased range of opt-outs for individual member states through the use of the new flexibility principle could conceivably be construed as the logical consequence of the deepening and widening processes of European integration which will undoubtedly continue into the twenty-first century. Indeed, this practice might come to be regarded as a regrettable but necessary development if the building of Europe is to proceed at all.

What, then, did Article 5A stipulate? In short, it allowed any member state to block the QMV vote to trigger closer cooperation if its national interests justified it and it restricted the application of so-called 'flexibility' to the powers already attributed to the Community, thereby making it extremely difficult in the future for a core group of member states to forge ahead alone towards further integration. The gist of the new article, therefore, protected the cherished *acquis communautaire* but still harboured many dangers for the building of Europe, not least the incorporation of a kind of legal version of the infamous Luxembourg Compromise. This clause in the treaty furnished the legal basis for a reassertion of the powers of member state governments in terms of national rather than supra-national interests. It will certainly have implications for the future of European integration and would seem to indicate something of a watershed in inter-institutional relations in the EU. But if Maastricht was a curate's egg, what sort of treaty emerged from Amsterdam? What are its strengths and weaknesses, and what remains to be done?

In October 1997, 18 months after the launch of the IGC in Turin, 15 EU foreign ministers signed the TA which confirmed an intergovernmental consensus of sorts on the future of the EU and European integration. In consequence, the Maastricht process was continued, a door had been opened which allowed the next enlargement negotiations to begin in 1998. The EU had at last given substance to what it called an area of 'freedom, justice and security' for its 370 million citizens. Moreover the UK seemed finally to have reconciled itself, EMU, NATO, Schengen and immigration notwithstanding, to much of what had passed for a more democratic, flexible, transparent and efficient EU. For federalists there were, of course, many disappointments, including the absence of institutional reform; anaemic changes to EU defence arrangements; the UK, Danish and Irish derogations concerning free movement in Schengen; the persistent limitations of both QMV and co-decision; the prevalence of the unanimity rule in the new communitarized fields of immigration and asylum policy; the failure adequately to make the treaty comprehensible to EC citizens; the lack of a real obligation on member states to convert the lofty statements about employment into practical policy proposals; a loosening of the Commission's grip on competition policy; and no further progress made in the policy fields of energy, tourism and civil protection.

Federalists, however, had some reasons to be cheerful. Progress in EMU continued apace, the EP's powers had been strengthened and its competences extended, the Commission had escaped a mauling by both Kohl and Chirac in the field of competition policy, citizenship linkages via Schengen, immigration, asylum, and human and social rights had been confirmed, enlargement was still on course for the next century, and another IGC for the Year 2000 seemed unavoidable. In other words, more federalist pieces in the jigsaw of a federal Europe had been put in place. In the difficult circumstances which had surrounded the evolution of the TA, these were not inconsiderable achievements. Indeed some of them, like 'freedom, justice and security', were quite remarkable innovations. But even for federalists, the Europe which emerged from Amsterdam was a veritable institutional, procedural and policy labyrinth buttressed by opaque language and terminology which had mind-boggling legal implications. Speaking for international lawyers, horrified by the legal non-uniformity of the outcome, Philip Allot described the TA as 'a sort of nightmare resurrection of the Holy Roman Empire'.[59] Flexibility was clearly not a virtue for lawyers.

In summary, the TA had enshrined key areas of EU policy in the hands of the member state governments, and its so-called 'flexibility' principles had furnished further opportunities to promote a checkerboard Europe in the next century, but it had also strengthened European integration in significant ways. And if the TA resembled a revamped version of the Holy Roman Empire, it is important to remember that this imperial union, founded upon loose confederal elements, endured for about one thousand years. Mindful of this mixed verdict, it is time to conclude the chapter with some reflections on the vision and reality of the EU in the years between Maastricht and Amsterdam.

## Conclusion: vision and reality

In many ways it was quite remarkable for any treaty to have emerged in 1997. The circumstances which characterized the four years between the ratification of the TEU in November 1993 and the agreement on the TA in October 1997 were not conducive to the sort of major breakthrough in European integration which Maastricht had witnessed with EMU. If public controversy had been the hallmark of Maastricht, disappointment and despair had been the watchwords of Amsterdam. But how should we assess these years, and would it be accurate to regard the TA as a counsel of despair?

In a recent commentary on the TA, two American scholars, Andrew Moravcsik and Kalypso Nicolaidis, have rejected what they call the 'near widespread negative assessment of the outcome'; because it is 'misleading' and because the standards against which the results have been judged are 'unrealistic'. Their contention is that the sense of doom and gloom which continues to surround the TA is based upon a fundamentally-flawed assumption, namely, 'a teleological understanding of European integration as moving inexorably, if at an uneven pace, toward greater substantive scope, universal participation by expanding numbers of participants, and greater uniformity in the application of institutional and legal procedures'.[60] Consequently, if the TA is judged according to 'a teleological mode of evaluating progress toward European integration' which requires that its successes and failures be set against 'an ideal federal standard', it is hardly surprising if it yields pessimistic conclusions. On this reckoning, the purported failure of Amsterdam becomes something of a self-fulfilling prophecy. In reality, they claim, the failure of the TA to make more progress than it did was due to 'the lack of any compelling substantive reason to deepen cooperation'. Member state governments simply did not agree on overriding objectives.[61] But far from being 'the last of its kind', Amsterdam was actually 'the harbinger of the future'. Reflecting upon what the TA represents and assessing its implications for European integration, Moravcsik and Nicolaidis conclude paradoxically in a strong federalist vein: Amsterdam marks 'the beginning of a new phase of flexible, pragmatic constitution-building in order to accommodate the diversity of a continent-wide polity'.[62] This is a Europe of federal and confederal elements.

What are we to make of this impressive, cogently argued but unequivocally intergovernmental assessment of the TA's past, present and future? There is no space here to conduct a detailed analysis of this assessment. Instead, we shall focus briefly upon those arguments and interpretations which have particular resonance for federalism and the federalists. There is clearly much in this analysis with which federalists can concur. Indeed, in some important respects there is very little intellectual distance between the federalists and the intergovernmentalists. Moravcsik and Nicolaidis concede that member state governments continue to move forward towards 'centralized federal institutions in some areas', notably EMU, while searching for conventional intergovernmental cooperation in others.[63] But it is nonetheless important to question the assumptions upon which these two critics of so-called 'federal ideals' base their arguments. Put simply, it is misleading to saddle all federalists with the burden of a 'venerable federalist vision' which incorporates an 'expanding, undifferentiated and uniform Europe': 'a teleological ideal – a United States of Europe – characterized by centralized, uniform, universal and undifferentiated institutions'.[64] This blanket assumption, rather like Milward's sweeping use of the term 'rescue' of the nation-state, is over-simplified. As we have already noted above, federalism is rooted in the accommodation of diversity rather than the suffocating centralization and drab uniformity that a unitary model of Europe would undoubtedly portend. There is certainly something to be said for taking historical evolution into account. This suggests that, since the building of Europe for the last half century has gone beyond the pioneering era of the 1950s and 1960s to reach a much more advanced stage of development in the late 1980s and 1990s, further integration will encounter many new obstacles unknown to the early federalists. In short, the era of Monnet and Spinelli is now over. But this is far from accepting the misrepresentation of so-called 'federalist visions' as if they were rigid, uncompromising and ultimately Utopian. Federalists have always had to contend with critics who have repeatedly accused them of looking at Europe through rose-tinted spectacles. The determination of the federalists to build Europe, however, has always been founded firmly upon the changing needs of reality. As the federalist Commission President, Jacques Santer, observed recently, 'What was not done in Amsterdam will be done in the near future. Reality will force us'.[65] Where the federalist vision coincides with reality, it is capable of being translated into practice. There is, then, much to admire in the perceptive intergovernmental analysis of Moravcsik and Nicolaidis but in their scathing attack upon federalism and the federalists, and their somewhat predictable verdict, they are really tilting at windmills.

One of the main purposes of this book has been to demonstrate the resilience of federal ideas, influences and strategies for the building of Europe during the last half century. It has emphasized the continuity of these ideas and underlined the consistent pragmatic influence that federal economic, political and bureaucratic elites and federal political leadership have had upon the evolution of European integration. During that long period, federalist ideas and strategies have been adapted and adjusted to suit changing conditions and circumstances. It is indeed a particular strength and virtue of federalism that it has the inherent capacity to accommodate difference and diversity at all levels of democratic decision-making. This is its very *raison d'être*. Consequently, federalists do not fear 'flexibility'. On the contrary, it is itself a federal attribute, but not if it is deliberately designed by a small minority to prevent further progress in European integration.

It is time to bring this chapter to a convenient close. We have arrived at a point on the threshold of the twenty-first century where the broad contours of a federal Europe are evident for all to see. This does not mean that a federal polity is either imminent or inevitable. Far from it. But if EMU is achieved, it does suggest that the European Union will approximate to a federal union, though admittedly not a federation in the near future. CFSP and defence policy are approaching the reach but still outside the grasp of the central institutions. And the central institutional framework of the EU retains linkages to governments and citizens which lack legitimation and make it incomplete. Much remains to be done. What, then, do these contemporary features of the EU suggest about the nature of the 'ever closer union' in the new millennium? What criteria should we use to reach a novel understanding of both the 'idea' and the 'thing'? There are neither signposts pointing the way nor footprints to follow. Nobody has been here before. In order to extend and enrich our understanding of the federal and confederal principles at work in the EU, it is necessary for us to turn and look at the building of Europe from a completely different perspective. We need to explore the EU from the standpoint of the American federal experience in order to see what fresh insights might be gained from the interaction of federal and confederal principles in a different historical setting. The reasoning behind this logic lies in the attempt to locate the intellectual puzzle that is the contemporary EU in the controversy surrounding the transformation of the United States from a confederation to a federation in 1789. The focus is upon conceptual *legerdemain*. Let us, therefore, turn in the next chapter to investigate the EU as an intellectual puzzle.

## NOTES

1  A.S. Milward, *The frontier of national sovereignty: history and theory 1945–1992*, London: Routledge, 1993, p. 16.
2  Article B, title I (common provisions), *Treaty on European Union* (TEU), Luxembourg: Office for Official Publications of the EC, 1992.
3  Reflection Group's Report, 'Reflections on European Policy', Brussels: General Secretariat of the Council, 1995; and *European Access*, October 1994, 5, pp. 11–15.
4  B. Laffan, 'Developments in the member states' in The European Union 1994: Annual Review of Activities, *Journal of Common Market Studies*, 33, p. 127, August 1995.
5  See N. Nugent, 'Redefining Europe' in The European Union 1994: Annual Review of Activities, *Journal of Common Market Studies*, pp. 9–11; and R. Corbett, 'Governance and institutional developments', pp. 47–48 in the same issue.
6  Corbett, 'Governance and institutional developments', pp. 39–42.
7  See the Reflection Group's Report and N. Nugent, 'Building Europe – A need

for more leadership?', The European Union 1995: Annual Review of Activities, *Journal of Common Market Studies*, 34, pp. 6–8, August 1996.

8  A. Adonis, 'Subsidiarity: theory of a new federalism?', in P. King and A. Bosco (eds), *A constitution for Europe: a comparative study of federal constitutions and plans for the united states of Europe*, p. 64, London: Lothian Foundation Press, 1991.

9  A. Duff, 'Towards a definition of subsidiarity', in A. Duff (ed.), *Subsidiarity within the European Community*, p. 11, London: Federal Trust, 1993.

10  A. Freemantle (ed.), *The papal encyclicals in their historical context*, London: Mentor-Omega, 1963, p. 342.

11  For this argument, see G. Baum, *Catholics and Canadian socialism: political thought in the thirties and forties*, Toronto: James Lorimer & Co., 1980, p. 290.

12  Adonis, 'Subsidiarity', p. 65.

13  See M. Burgess, 'Political catholicism, European unity and the rise of christian democracy', in M.L. Smith and P.M.R. Stirk (eds), *Making the new Europe: European unity and the Second World War*, pp. 142–55, London: Pinter Publishers, 1990.

14  Fremantle (ed.), *The papal encyclicals*, p. 420.

15  ' "Europe: the challenge", the principles, achievements and objectives of the EPP Group from 1979 to 1984', Luxembourg: General Secretariat of the EPP Group, December 1985, p. 235.

16  'Europe: the challenge', p. 236.

17  'Europe: the challenge', p. 236.

18  'Europe: the challenge', p. 234.

19  Interview with Christopher Jackson, MEP, 17 May 1985, European Parliament (EP), Strasbourg. See M. Burgess, *Federalism and European union: political ideas, influences and strategies in the European Community, 1972–1987*, London: Routledge, 1989, p. 166.

20  Interview with Spinelli, 15 September 1983, *EP*, Strasbourg.

21  Draft treaty establishing the European union, *EP*, February 1984, p. 9.

22  Draft treaty, p. 16.

23  Adonis, 'Subsidiarity', p. 66.

24  Adonis, 'Subsidiarity', p. 66.

25  Delors' speech to the EP, 26 October 1988, *OJ*, Annex No. 2–370, pp. 155–56.

26  C. Grant, *Delors: inside the house that Jacques built*, London: Nicholas Brealey Publishing, 1994, p. 218.

27  Delors' speech to the EP, 15 February 1989, *OJ*, Annex No. 2–374, p. 143.

28  Delors' speech to the EP, 21 November 1989, *OJ*, Annex No. 3–383, p. 61.

29  Giscard's statement to the EP, 21 November 1989, Annex No. 3–383, p. 66.

30  Delors' speech to the EP, 17 January 1990, *OJ*, Annex No. 3–385, p. 114.

31  EC Bulletin, 2/91, p. 81.

32  This was the language used by the Commission in its *Official Opinion of 21 October 1990 to the IGC on 'Political Union'*, COM(90), 600, Brussels: European Commission, 23 October 1990, p. 3.

33  *EC Bulletin*, 2/91, p. 81.

34  Duff, 'Towards a definition of subsidiarity', p. 9.

35  *TEU*, articles A and B (common provisions) and article 3b, pp. 7–8 and pp. 13–14.

36  A. Adonis and A. Tyrie, 'Subsidiarity: no panacea', London: European Policy Forum, 1992, p. 20.

37  Hurd's speech to the House of Commons, 2 July 1992, H.C. Debates, pp. 210, 986, in Duff, 'Towards a definition of subsidiarity', p. 9.

38  Interview with Douglas Hurd, 'Europe: the state of the union', *Financial Times*, 1 July 1992, p. 12.

39  Quoted in Adonis and Tyrie, 'Subsidiarity', p. 22.

40  D. Buchan and D. Gardner, 'A state of limbo in Lisbon', *Financial Times*, 29 June 1992, p. 12.

41  'Bad omens for Birmingham Summit', the *Independent*, 15 October 1992, p. 2. Delors claimed that the offer was made in jest.

42  EC Bulletin, 10/92, 2.2.1.

43  EC Bulletin, 10/92, 2.2.1.

44  The whole Edinburgh Annex is reprinted in full as Appendix One in Duff (ed.), *Subsidiarity within the European Community*, pp. 117–30.

45  A. Duff, *The treaty of Amsterdam: text and commentary*, London: Federal Trust, 1997, p. 100.

46  Duff, *The treaty of Amsterdam*, p. 106.

47  Duff, *The treaty of Amsterdam*, p. 106.

48  Duff, 'Towards a definition of subsidiarity', pp. 11 and 30.

49  A. Cary, 'Subsidiarity – essence or antidote to European Union?', in A. Duff (ed.), *Subsidiarity within the European Community*, p. 47.

50  'Subsidiarity Protocol', in A. Duff (ed.), *The treaty of Amsterdam*, p. 96.

51  See G. Edwards and A. Pijpers (eds), *The politics of European treaty reform: the intergovernmental conference and beyond*, London: Pinter, 1997; A. Duff (ed.), *The treaty of Amsterdam: text and commentary*; A. Duff (ed.), *Reforming the European union*, London: Federal Trust, 1997; and G. Edwards and G. Wiessala (eds), The European union 1997: annual review of activities, *Journal of Common Market Studies*, 36, September 1998.

52  The pessimistic background to the IGC is sketched out in the pages of volume 3, nos. 23–27 of *European Voice: the weekly view of the EU*.

53  The *European Voice*, 3, 25, 26 June–2 July 1997, p. 13.

54  Duff, *The treaty of Amsterdam*, pp. xxxv and 143.

55  'Declaration by Germany, Austria and Belgium on Subsidiarity', in Duff, *The treaty of Amsterdam*, p. 99.

56  'Protocol on the institutions with the prospect of enlargement of the European Union', in Duff, *The treaty of Amsterdam*, p. 300.

57  J. Pinder, 'Economic and monetary union: pillar of a federal polity', *Publius: The Journal of Federalism*, (special edition), M. Burgess (ed.), 'Federalism and European union', 26(4), p. 135, Fall 1996.

58  Duff, *The treaty of Amsterdam*, p. 207.

59  Quoted in A. Moravcsik and K. Nicolaidis, 'Federal Ideals and Constitutional Realities', *Journal of Common Market Studies*, 36, p. 15, September 1998.

60  Moravcsik and Nicolaidis, 'Federal Ideals', p. 16.

61  Moravcsik and Nicolaidis, 'Federal Ideals', p. 33.

62  Moravcsik and Nicolaidis, 'Federal Ideals', pp. 34 and 36.

63  Moravcsik and Nicolaidis, 'Federal Ideals', p. 17.

64  Moravcsik and Nicolaidis, 'Federal Ideals', p. 16.

65  *Financial Times*, 11 September 1997, p. 2.

# 8 The European Union as an intellectual puzzle

## Federal and confederal elements in European integration

In his classic 'The Development of European Polity', a series of lectures delivered in the University of Cambridge during the closing years of the nineteenth century, Henry Sidgwick remarked that 'much learning and subtlety' had been applied to distinguishing the conception of a 'federal state' (*Bundestaat*) from that of a 'confederation of states' (*Staatenbund*). He also claimed that perhaps 'undue importance' had been attached to the 'aim of getting a clear and sharp distinction' between these two discrete concepts. 'The two notions – confederation of states, federal state – represent', he argued, 'two stages in the development of federality'.[1] In this chapter, I intend to utilize Sidgwick's notion of 'federality' as a convenient route into the study of European integration and the European Union (EU) in order to explore both the 'federal' and the 'confederal' elements which have characterized post-war European economic and political integration.

We have already discussed the Treaty on European Union (TEU) signed on 7 February 1992 by the Europe of the Twelve at Maastricht and ratified shortly after on 1 November 1993. We have also briefly surveyed the Treaty of Amsterdam (TA) agreed by the Europe of the Fifteen on 2 October 1997, which was finally ratified in 1999. The TEU, as we have seen, represented yet another significant step forward in the long journey towards 'European Union' first projected at the Paris Summit in October 1972. It formally established the EU – identified as 'the Union' – and claimed that it marked 'a new stage in the process of creating an ever closer union among the peoples of Europe'.[2] The TA can be construed as the logical corollary to the TEU in the extent to which it added yet more institutional, procedural and policy substance to the evolving EU. While not the product of 'automaticity' – the purported ratchet effect of integration – it was, nonetheless, a joint intergovernmental and supra-national response to what was viewed by many political elites as unfinished business.

In this book we have seen that the Single European Act (SEA), the TEU and the TA are inextricably intertwined and, together, represent the outcome of Monnet's Europe. It is a Europe, we are reminded, that has been built on the firm basis of reason, peace and cooperation. It has endured for half a century and has evolved to a level of complexity and sophistication where the broad contours of a federal Europe are clearly visible. The complex interaction of economic and political integration has yielded a voluntary union which is an international reality with unique institutions, extraordinary decision-making processes and conspicuous policy outputs. But it is also a conceptual enigma. And, since political scientists are called upon to explain and clarify the world of states and citizens, the EU presents them with a particularly difficult conundrum. After all, it does not conform precisely to the well-established theories of international relations. Nor does it fit neatly into the various categories and models of political integration advanced by conventional federalists, confederalists, neofunctionalists and intergovernmentalists. Indeed, it continues to confound the received wisdom about unions of states and citizens. It is, in short, an intellectual puzzle.

As we witnessed in Chapter 2, the EU continues to defy conventional political science definition and classification. But this should not surprise us at all. A detailed analysis of the post-war evolution of the European construction suggests that it has always been construed by its advocates – and its opponents – in many different and competing ways. To some national governments, as Milward has argued, it meant little more than short-term economic benefits with no pronounced long-term commitments; while to others it offered the prospect of a much more favourable long-term security environment. This referred especially to economic trade and interdependence but it clearly had military implications as part of a secure union. Still others regarded the EU as having the capacity ultimately to create a new distinct European identity in world affairs – a dangerous post-war world of superpower rivalries. Whatever the motivations – and there were many – the building of Europe has always been about the organization of power rather than about any idealistic conception of Europe for its own sake. And as we have seen, the European construction itself is not static even when it appears so. Impasses are temporary, disagreements eventually produce agreements, vetoes yield compromises and complexity furnishes the basis for asymmetry. The EU moves and changes; it acts and reacts. Consequently, the combination of elites which have consistently championed the cause of closer union – public men and women, national governments, military leaders, farmers, industrialists, business men and women, and an assortment of other interest group activists – cannot easily be forced into a neat and tidy theory of European integration. There is no handy Procrustean bed.

But the conceptual enigma that is the EU today should not become a counsel of despair. After all, it was Alexis de Tocqueville who once remarked that human beings more easily invent new things than new words to describe them. And no better example of this awkward predicament exists than that of 'The Federalist' which, under the heading of

'Publius', sought to persuade New Yorkers to vote in favour of the new constitution drawn up in the summer of 1787 at the Philadelphia Convention in Pennsylvania. Like the TEU signed at Maastricht nearly two centuries later, the new constitution promoted by Alexander Hamilton, John Jay and James Madison was the result of a series of difficult compromises at the constitutional convention between vested interests 'compelled to sacrifice theoretical propriety to the force of extraneous considerations'.[3]

Accordingly, political scientists seeking accurately to define the EU today on the threshold of the twenty-first century find themselves in precisely the same quandary as 'Publius' a little over two centuries ago. The use of words – of terminology – to express basic ideas and concepts with clarity and precision continues to perplex us. It is at this juncture, therefore, that we can return to Sidgwick's notion of 'federality', introduced at the beginning of the chapter. Here Sidgwick suggested that the term 'federality' embraced a wide divergence of views about federal principles, akin almost to a spectrum of federality. And his phrase 'federal polity' can be conveniently reduced to two main types, namely, a federal state (or federation) and a confederation (or league of independent states). But as he observed, 'in neither case is the distinction simple and sharp since the balanced combination of "unity of the whole aggregate" with "separateness of parts", which constitutes federality, may be realised in very various modes and degrees'.[4]

This particular interpretation of 'federality' is useful because it does not compel us prematurely to construe the EU in the conventional terms of international relations theory which invariably makes its classification a foregone conclusion. According to this view, the EU is either a federation or a confederation. But since it is clearly not a federation, it must be the latter. However, the notion of 'federality' helps us to avoid just this sort of simple preconception. Instead, it enables us to examine in detail both the federal and confederal elements which have come increasingly to characterize the EU without first having to classify it in conventional terms. In short, it is an essentially heuristic approach which allows for nuance and complexity, whereas the conventional international relations approaches construe the EU in terms of confederation, regime theory or a rather vacuous theory of interdependence – or are simply unable to classify it at all.[5] Instead, we shall not predicate our analysis upon some terminal endpoint. Rather, we shall regard the EU as part of a journey rather than a destination. It has no destiny – no preordained teleology – other than what human agency can achieve. In order to buttress this argument, we shall use the historical precedent of the American federal experience – and the controversies which continue to surround it – as our preliminary background context. As we shall see, the public discord which informed the pages of 'The Federalist' can serve as a useful entrance into the European debate post-Maastricht. Let us look briefly at the American experience.

## The triumph of experience: from confederation to federation

> The use of words is to express ideas. Perspicuity therefore requires not only that the ideas should be distinctly formed, but that they should be expressed by words distinctly and exclusively appropriate to them. But no language is so copious as to supply words and phrases for every complex idea, or so correct as not to include many unequivocally denoting different ideas.[6]

The Philadelphia Convention was called into existence by the Continental Congress – a meeting of the constituent states of the American Confederation – 'for the sole and express purpose of revising the Articles of Confederation'.[7] But as is now well-known, the 55 delegates from twelve states who met in secret deliberation to revise the Articles exceeded their formal brief and constructed a new constitution. The proposed constitution which 'The Federalist' strove so fiercely to defend was, as Madison famously put it, 'in strictness, neither a national nor a federal Constitution, but a composition of both'.[8] Since it contained a mixture of republican, federal and national elements, there was no single word to describe it.

In hindsight, it is clear that the great American debate of 1787–89, especially as we follow it in the pages of 'The Federalist', was more than just a loud war of words. Words convey meaning but they can also be used deliberately to mislead and deceive political opponents. One of the great ironies of the late eighteenth-century American debate surrounding the ratification of the new constitution was the way in which its formidable proponents virtually commandeered the term 'federal'. It was certainly no accident that they chose 'The Federalist' as the title of the essays published in 1788. We are reminded that the Founding Fathers of the American constitution had a very different understanding than we do today of what 'federalism' meant. The conventional late-eighteenth-century American understanding of federalism was what existed according to the Articles of Confederation during 1781–89 rather than what succeeded them. The prevailing conceptual distinction was between confederal (or federal) government and unitary (or national) government. There was no separate and distinct category for what later became known as 'federal government'. In an elegantly written essay, Martin Diamond put it thus:

> We now give the single word federal to the system the framers regarded as possessing both federal and national features. This means we now deem as a unique principle what 'The Federalist' regarded as a mere compound.... The men we have come to call the 'anti-federalists' regarded themselves as the true federalists. ... the opponents of the Constitution fought as the true defenders of the federal principle. Everything that 'The Federalist' says about the federal aspects of the

Constitution must be understood ... in the light of its great necessity: the demonstration that the Constitution should not be rejected on the grounds of inadequate regard for the federal principle.[9]

It is important to remember that one purpose of 'The Federalist' was to attack the traditional understanding of federalism. It sought deliberately and (some would say) desperately to muddy the waters so that much less was required for a new political system to be deemed fully federal. Hamilton in particular was determined to create a federal test which the proposed new constitution could easily pass.

If we summarize this section of the chapter, it is clear in retrospect that, after the ratification of the constitution in 1789, there had been a significant substantive change in the nature of the American union. This represented an empirical shift away from confederation to a much more consolidated form of union – what was often referred to as a 'compound republic' – in which the national characteristics were expected ultimately to predominate. And it was precisely this move away from the Articles of Confederation which later gave rise to a new conceptual distinction in political science between confederation and federation. It was, however, a gradual rather than an abrupt change.[10] As Diamond astutely observed:

'The Federalist' had no novel understanding of what is federal, it only departed from others in regarding the simply federal as radically inadequate for the purposes of the Union it had in mind. It did have a novel understanding of a new thing, not simply a federal thing but a compound which it was happy to have men call by the old name federal. ... the Convention ... avoided past confederal errors by creating a Union which was radically less federal.... What was wrong with the Articles and other confederacies were the essential federal principles themselves. The great teaching of 'The Federalist' is not how to be federal in a better way, but how to be better by being less federal.[11]

This conclusion remains contentious. In a nutshell, it claims that, in reality, the new American constitution actually departed from the established and accepted understanding of federalism. Hamilton confessed that there was 'an absolute necessity for an entire change in the first principles of the system'; it was so 'radically vicious and unsound' that it required not mere amendment but 'an entire change in its leading features and characters'.[12] Consequently, the new constitution altered the conventional federal form by 'subtracting from it certain decisively federal features and adding to it certain decisively national features'. In other words, the significant contribution of 'The Federalist' was 'the presentation and justification of a new form of government, neither federal nor national, but an admixture of both characters'.[13] And this interpretation had the authority of none other than Tocqueville to recommend it:

> Evidently this is no longer a federal government, but an incomplete
> national government, which is neither exactly national nor exactly
> federal, but the new word which ought to express this novel thing
> does not yet exist.[14]

Tocqueville's remarks – written in 1835 – bring us back once again to the
conceptual enigma that is the contemporary EU. They remind us that the
problem of its definition and classification in political science is far from
unique. And they also enable us to underline some significant parallels
and similarities between the building of Europe and the making of the
American constitution. One of the most important observations to make
in this respect is that the early American constitutional experience – like
the current European adventure – was a journey rather than a destination.
Americans were not agreed about their precise destination; they were
uncertain about their future. There is, then, a real danger while interpreting American state-building and national integration of reading history
backwards, with the advantage of hindsight, from a national perspective.
To do this is to misinterpret and misunderstand the American experience.
In practice, it would lead to the over-simplification and distortion of
history.

Equally, the danger for Europeans is to assume in unthinking fashion
that the evolution of the American national experience has any necessary
implications for the contemporary construction and reconstruction of
Europe. After all, the TEU refers to 'an ever closer union among the
peoples of Europe', while the American constitution asserts the existence
of 'one people'. The former phrase is confederal while the latter is
federal. Moreover, the building of an American union founded upon
a single people or nation took at least 70 years, from 1789 to the end of
the Civil War in 1865. As Murray Forsyth has emphasized, it developed
only gradually 'under the aegis of a confederal political structure and
then burst through and beyond this structure' in order to assert the new
unity, that of a fully-fledged federation.[15] In other words, the so-called
'consolidation' of 1787–89 was itself not fully consolidated until the mid-
nineteenth century.

We have just seen that one important legacy of this remarkable American journey – the processes of state-building and national integration –
was the conceptual displacement of the confederal category. But this was
not all. There was also a concomitant legacy of considerable intellectual
significance. This was that the new conceptual distinction between confederation and federation had an entirely unexpected consequence. Put
simply, the practical weaknesses of the American Confederation were both
undeniable and evident for all to see, but few could have foreseen the
stigma that would eventually be attached to the label 'confederation'. In
launching a fierce attack upon the Articles of Confederation, which he was
compelled to do, Hamilton's critique had a far-reaching, if unintended,

intellectual impact. It helped subsequently to tarnish the reputation of confederations in general and it encouraged some historians and political scientists to dismiss them as hopelessly inadequate forms of union. Not for the first time was history written by those who had triumphed. Let us look briefly at this unfortunate legacy.

## The stigma of confederation

The term 'confederation' has often been used in a pejorative sense. Political scientists and historians have frequently dismissed confederal government as both weak and transient. Indeed, there has been a general tendency to regard it as a mere transition on the road towards federation – that more perfect union. The American experience has been held as the defining model. Confederations will either drift apart or they will form a new state. This conveys the sense that they can exist only in a conceptual limbo. They have been marooned in history. In his study of the theory and practice of confederation, Forsyth has acknowledged that the German *Bund* of 1815–66, the Swiss Confederation established in 1814 and 'perhaps above all' the American Confederation of 1781 have 'all suffered harsh treatment' at the hands of academics and publicists.[16] He was certainly correct to emphasize the American example. In his classic study of the continental congress, Edmund Cody Burnett confirmed that 'it has been much the practice to heap criticisms' upon the Articles and 'even to treat it with a measure of scorn'.[17] Unlike Burnett, however, Forsyth concluded that there was 'an understandable basis for the scorn which is conventionally heaped on confederations'. This was because, once a community had achieved the lofty goal of statehood, it tended to 'look back with almost amused disdain on the efforts at unity that fell short of statehood'.[18]

For Hamilton, of course, the first federal constitution – the Articles of Confederation – was simply inadequate to its purposes. His assertion that the government of the United States was palpably 'destitute of energy' enabled him to identify what he saw as the real lacuna in confederation:

> The great and radical vice in the construction of the existing Confederation is in the principle of LEGISLATION for STATES or GOVERNMENTS, in their CORPORATE or COLLECTIVE CAPACITIES, and as contradistinguished from the INDIVIDUALS of whom they consist.... But if ... we still will adhere to the design of a national government, ... we must extend the authority of the Union to the persons of the citizens – the only proper objects of governments.[19]

In this famous passage from 'The Federalist' 15, Hamilton struck a savage blow at the Confederation by revealing the underlying impotence of the union. He believed that such polities had been 'the cause of incurable disorder and imbecility'.[20] Accordingly what was needed to remedy this condition of affairs was 'energetic government' which meant the 'augmentation of federal authority' at the expense of the constituent state governments. And in order further to condemn existing federal principles as deficient, both Hamilton and Madison used 'The Federalist' 16–22 to conduct an extensive historical analysis of all earlier confederations (called 'confederacies').

The result of their brief historical examination of previous confederacies – which included the ancient Greek and the German, Swiss and Dutch cases – was far from surprising. They had a vested interest in deliberately maligning confederative experiments and produced a damning indictment of existing federal principles and assumptions. Their conclusion was unequivocal: confederacies in general either survived to live contemptibly or perished miserably precisely because of their fidelity to federal principles, which were deemed erroneous:

> The important truth ... is that a sovereignty over sovereigns, a government over governments, a legislation for communities, as contradistinguished from individuals, as it is a solecism in theory, so in practice it is subversive of the order and ends of civil polity.[21]

Small wonder, in this light, that modern confederation – as a union of states – has been the victim of rough justice. The prosecution was vindictive. In turn, confederal government has acquired the reputation of being weak, anarchic and highly unstable – a danger to internal order and external security. These images seem to have been passed down from one generation to the next so that the stigma of confederation has become part of an almost unquestioning conventional wisdom.

Mindful of these two important preliminary considerations – the peculiar American federal experience and the stigma of confederation – let us return to the intellectual puzzle that is the contemporary EU. We will now look at how far these considerations help us to understand the complex reality that exists in Europe today. It is here – both in the process that led to the Maastricht Treaty and in the post-Maastricht EU itself – that the public debate about a 'federal' Europe has been so confusing and confused. But as we will see, the EU exhibits both federal and confederal elements as part of the process of European economic and political integration.

## Federal and confederal elements in the European union

Since the EU is obviously not a federation, it has been common practice, in the absence of a new word to define it, to refer to it in general terms as a confederal public power. Forsyth has been more precise in describing the European Community (as it was up until 1993) as 'an economic confederation'. He used familiar language in defining it as 'a subspecies of the genus confederation ... a distinct branch of confederation'.[22] As far as it went, his analysis in 1981 was both accurate and insightful, and few would have quibbled with his definition of confederation which is worth revisiting from Chapter 2:

> It is not a state, it is not a union of individuals in a body politic, but a union of states in a body politic.... It is based on a treaty between states, ... but it is a treaty the content of which goes well beyond that of the normal treaty.... Thus a treaty of union founds a body that possesses personality.... The 'personality' formed by union is an original capacity to act akin to that possessed by the states themselves. It is a 'real' personality. ... the permanence accorded to a confederation is ... a profound locking together of states themselves as regards the exercise of fundamental powers. ... a confederation manifests itself as a constituted unity capable of making laws for its members, however it is not the constituted unity of one 'people' or 'nation', but a unity constituted by 'states'.[23]

Both the first and last sections of this definition can be traced back directly to the views of Montesquieu, which were used by Hamilton in 'The Federalist' 9 in an attempt to confuse his opponents. Together, these two sections amount to a key defining feature of confederation because it is the 'bodies politic' rather than 'individual persons' which become the 'citizens' of the confederation. In short, the Union governs not over 'individuals' but rather over 'collectivities' or 'states'.[24] But as we have already noted in Chapter 2, Forsyth's views were adjusted and adapted to reflect the changes which had characterized European integration after 1981, and these led him to identify what he called 'the federal–constitutional spirit'. This was not 'a mere fiction or aspiration for the future' but a concrete reality: a federal union.[25]

To what extent, then, does the EU exhibit both confederal and federal features? We shall confine ourselves to the accepted modern conceptual distinction, already identified above in the American federal experience, between what is deemed 'federal' and what is deemed 'confederal'. The designation of these terms, however, is not always clear. Indeed, in some circumstances, the conceptual distinction is inevitably blurred and indistinct. We are reminded of Sidgwick's remarks almost exactly a century ago. And this is as it should be. After all, basic federal and confederal principles – like voluntary union and self-rule and shared rule – inhere in both categories. Another reason for this ambiguity is that confederations have often been interpreted in the way appropriate for federations. They have been expected either to fall apart or to mature into federations. It has been common practice even for many informed observers to regard as historically successful only those confederations which followed the path towards federation. They have not usually been judged according to their own terms of reference as a particular form of union in their own right.

Given the post-war origins of the EU in Monnet's conception of Europe, we have already established in this book that the goal of many of the pioneers of European integration was a federal Europe. Federal ideas, influences and strategies have always been part and parcel of the European construction. But it is also true that, in establishing the European Economic Community (EEC) in 1957, the basic structure of the union resembled more an 'economic confederation' than anything else. In order to preserve and secure their economic statehood, each participating member state, as we have noted, internalized their externalities. In other words, their external economic relations were gradually transformed into an internal market, a seamless web akin to that of a national political economy. The confederal context of the EEC, then, suggested that it was primarily an economic confederation, but one with some significant institutional features which normally characterize classic confederation: the political union of states concerned mainly with defence and security.

Up until the ratification of the SEA in 1987, the European Community (EC) maintained its identity as largely an economic confederation. Its member state governments retained the primary political authority to resolve conflicting interests and to hammer out common policies, albeit with intermittent supra-national influence. And the EC's institutional framework was predominantly intergovernmental. The Council of Ministers and, after 1975, the European Council were the principal policy- and decision-making arenas dominated by the national leaders of the member state governments. And, although both of these central political institutions remained essentially fragmented and incoherent as bases for consistent policy outputs, the Committee of Permanent Representatives (COREPER) located in Brussels provided the real policy continuity and, in protecting established national state interests, strengthened what might be called 'confederal practice'. The European Court of Justice (ECJ) in Luxembourg was also 'fully within the logic of a confederal system'.[26] Its dual role as arbiter of disputes between the member states and interpreter of the constitutive treaty of union facilitating the uniform application of all EC laws gave it a pivotal position in the institutional framework.

The essentially confederal character of the EC up until 1987 had never really been disputed. But the confederal elements, though conspicuous, did not by themselves adequately define the EC. They did not explain everything that it did. These elements in practice coexisted with distinctly federal features. Even Forsyth was compelled to acknowledge that it was always more than just confederal. The special position occupied by the Commission in the EC's institutional structure, the emergent fiscal basis of the union, the implications of a directly elected European Parliament (EP) and the 'uncertain character' of the Council of Ministers combined seriously to 'obscure the Community's status as an economic confederation'.[27]

In other words, these institutional features served to contaminate the confederal nature of the EC. Looked at from a different perspective – that of the contemporary federalists – the EC also exhibited emergent federal elements. Parallel with but not identicial to the position of Hamilton in 'The Federalist', the goal of the federalists *inter alia* was to strengthen the central political institutions of the European construction.[28] For them, the ECJ conformed to a federal character in its judicial capacity as overseer of laws which were superior to the national laws of the member states and binding upon their citizens. And the EP, directly elected by the people of the member states akin to European citizens since 1979, also fitted into a conventional federal category. Though entitled to speak in the name of the European people, the EP, as we have already noted, could hardly claim that one European people existed. The question of the European Demos in the European construction was, and remains, conceptually problematic. But the crucial political link between the individual as a citizen of the national state and, simultaneously, as a member of the EC had been formally established. For federalists, this was what really mattered.

Since the SEA, we have witnessed the continuing evolution of the EC into the EU in 1993 and its further policy and institutional enhancement in the subsequent TA in 1997. From the standpoint of our survey of the EU as a new kind of confederation, this reflects the success of the European experiment as well as signifying the growing confidence and maturity of the European construction. But it also represents the shift from economic confederation towards a much more complete federal union of states, what Forsyth called a 'classic confederation'. If we return to our earlier conceptual distinction between confederation and federation, the problem with this kind of analysis is that, logically, federal and/or confederal principles can be identified in both perspectives. This means that if the ultimate goal is federation, understood in its post-1789 sense, the European super-state would require all of the conventional attributes of what we take to be state sovereignty, such as territorial integrity, the monopoly of the legitimate use of coercion, exclusive control of foreign and defence policies, a national economy and control of a common currency. And if it is confederation that is sought, the competences required by the new European confederal authority today would probably include common foreign and defence policies, an internal market, a common currency, limited taxation powers and a range of other common policies designed to strengthen the union such as uniform weights and measures and integrated transport and communication infrastructures. But there can be no hard and fast rule about this. On the contrary, the character of confederations has never been absolute and eternal. Rather, they have been relative and contingent. Sidgwick's observations once again loom large. Historically, the jurisdictional powers and competences of confederations like those of America, Switzerland and the Netherlands have varied according to different circumstances. Some have had stronger central authorities than others. The Dutch Confederation – the United Provinces of the Netherlands (1579–1795) – was much more developed as a substantive union than the later Swiss Confederation (1814–48). And in enduring for over two centuries, the Dutch confederal model effectively refuted Hamilton's somewhat sweeping accusation of impermanence.

Bearing these contrasts in mind, the essential point here is that the powers and competences associated with both confederal and federal authorities today could virtually be identical; it is the way in which these powers are structured and located that matters. In a federation, the central government is for some purposes the government of a single people, while in a confederation it is, strictly speaking, only ever a government of governments. It is not a union of individuals, we are reminded, but a union of states. That said, there is still plenty of room for quite wide variations in the quality and scope of confederal powers and competences. For example, if we return to Hamilton's earlier observation that governments must be able to legislate for individuals *qua* individuals, rather than indirectly for individuals in their collective capacities, we can see that he meant the passage of laws that were directly binding on the people living in the states rather than upon the states themselves. The implication was that, for some purposes, 'energetic government' should have direct effect rather than having to rely on the state legislatures to validate and implement policies. But Madison, in *The Federalist* 40, had already acknowledged the capacity of the existing confederation to do just this:

> In cases of capture; of piracy; of the post office; of coins, weights, and measures; of trade with the Indians; of claims under grants of lands by different states; and, above all, in the case of trials by courts-martial in the army and navy, by which death may be inflicted without the intervention of a jury, or even of a civil magistrate – in all these cases the powers of the Confederation operate immediately on the persons and interests of individual citizens.[29]

This important statement confirmed that the conceptual distinction between federation and confederation in this respect was actually more a question of degree than principle. Indeed, in his quest to legitimize the proposed new 'national' government, Madison confessed that its 'great principles' were not novel at all. They should be considered 'less as absolutely new than as the expansion of principles which are found in the Articles of Confederation'.[30] Confederations, then, did pass a limited range of laws that were binding on the individual citizens of constituent states in those spheres where they already had the agreed competence to do so.

Quite apart from the empirical significance of this concession made by Madison for the new American constitution, it also has a crucial conceptual significance for our purpose in this chapter. This is that the blurred conceptual boundary between federation and confederation in this important respect enables us to reinforce our position with regard to the European case. The EU contains both federal and confederal features in respect of the capacity of Brussels to act 'directly' upon both the governments and the citizens of the union. Consequently, if, conceptually, confederations never reach the dignified status of being 'the government of a single people', their capacity to have a direct policy impact upon the people cannot be gainsaid.

Given the conceptual complexities identified above, it is small wonder that problems arise when national elites and mass publics confuse the two categories. After all, the EU is moving in the general direction of both classic confederation – a federal union of states – and federation – a union of states and citizens. Part of the public confusion and misunderstanding about the European adventure since the SEA has been due to the intensified struggle to shift from Monnet's Europe of 'functionalism' to Spinelli's Europe of 'constitutionalism'. It is an inevitable function of the building of 'political' Europe. However, it is not always clear even to political scientists whether the imperatives to strengthen the central institutions and enhance the policy content of the EU march towards a confederal or a federal destination. The empirical reality on the threshold of the twenty-first century seems to suggest that the conceptual enigma that is the EU will never be resolved by posing the question in such stark terms. To use existing terminology, it is what we might call the 'confederal–federal' conundrum. In other words, the EU works in practice but not in theory. Theoretical explanations remain patchy.

If we now take stock of the confederal–federal conundrum, it becomes clear once again why political scientists have signally failed to attach a convincing label to the complexity that is the EU. Both its post-war origins and its historical evolution have meant that it has always been subject to anomalies, fluctuations of pace and even occasional movements in the opposite direction. And there has never been a formal act of confederation as there was in 1781. The most accurate description of the contemporary EU remains that of a confederation but it is certainly more than a mere 'economic confederation'. Here we return to the argument briefly sketched out in Chapter 2, namely, that the contemporary EU represents a distinctly new type of confederation. It is the harbinger of the 'new' confederations which Daniel Elazar has so grandiloquently portrayed in the pages of *Publius*. We will now conclude this short survey of federal and confederal elements in European integration by reflecting upon this possibility and then look ahead at what might be the shape of things to come.

## The rehabilitation and revitalization of confederation

We have already seen that the TEU, even with significant modifications in the TA, has become the mainstay of the EU and that it was the product of a particular set of circumstances which arose in the wake of the end of the Cold War. It is much too soon to tell whether or not the establishment in 1999 of EMU and its subsequent consolidation, together with progress in the Common Foreign and Security Policy (CFSP), will finally convert the EU, to all intents and purposes, into a federation in the post-1789 sense. But there are already indications that the modest progress on security and defence issues in the TA has pushed it in these respects much closer toward the old confederal-type unions which we have observed in the United States, the United Provinces of the Netherlands, Switzerland and the German *Bund*. It is abundantly clear, however, that the 'confederal–federal' EU of the late twentieth century, although it may stand partly in this line of descent, cannot be reduced realistically to this classical conceptual category. The EU represents a distinctly new type of confederation. Indeed, it is as much a new political invention as was the new compound republic created by the Founding Fathers of the United States in 1789. If their invention of federal government is usually regarded as their greatest contribution to the art of government, then the peculiar 'community method' of combining economic and political integration in the late modern epoch should also be credited to both Monnet and Spinelli as pioneers of a new treaty-based constitutional technique for building unions of states and citizens.

In a recent essay on the subject of confederal governance, Frederick Lister has claimed that this form of 'special order' might be 'coming back into the limelight', and that the features which characterize its 'modern reincarnation' need to be examined more closely.[31] To this end, he has identified 15 defining features which enable us to clarify precisely what governmental order is at issue in this intellectual debate about a federal Europe. We will use his list of characteristics as a convenient route into our own examination of the rehabilitation and revitalization of confederation. They are reproduced in the following way:

1  Confederation unites states without depriving them of their statehood;
2  Confederation unites states whose populations are too heterogeneous to form viable federal-type unions;
3  Confederation requires a written basic law in the form of treaty-constitutions that are legally binding upon the various confederal allies;
4  Confederation presupposes a *raison d'être* of overriding importance such as a powerful common economic interest or the need of all the confederating states for protection against a great power that threatens them all;
5  Confederation provides for a minimalist mandate that leaves most governmental powers to be exercised independently by its member states;
6  Confederation provides for two quite different types of mandate

involving collective security and/or economic union. The security mandate always includes the same functions (foreign affairs, war and peace, military integration or coordination). The economic mandate also always includes the same functions (e.g. regulation of external trade and internal commerce, standardization of such things as weights and measures, and the establishment of common or single markets);

7 Confederations require a wide measure of support among the peoples of their member states based on the belief that such ties will enhance their country's security and/or its economic growth and prosperity;

8 Confederations need to promote relations between the member states that will engender the gradual growth of popular support for, and allegiance to, the confederal union;

9 The popular support and allegiance engendered are subordinate to peoples' primary allegiance to their own national states;

10 In confederations all member states must be ready to settle their disputes through arbitration or adjudication rather than force;

11 In a confederation member state governments exercise the powers to be confederated in a joint council that meets regularly and operates under mutually agreed rules of procedure;

12 The confederal council has (i) a voting system in which state representatives vote on behalf of their countries; (ii) a decision-making system whose decisions are legally binding on its member states and are usually based on consensus or broad support rather than simple majorities of those member states; and (iii) a decision-implementing system that delegates the major burden of implementation to its member state governments;

13 Confederation presupposes a willingness on the part of the member states to furnish the funds that enable the union to carry out the tasks assigned to it;

14 Confederation also provides for the conduct of the executive and judicial functions of government in ways that are not threatening to the sovereignty of its member states; and finally

15 Confederation embodies mutually acceptable working solutions to hegemonic and other problems that may emanate from any inequalities of power and resources among its larger and smaller member states.[32]

This is a fairly exhaustive list of the defining features of confederation, and it provides a useful yardstick with which to illuminate and underline the confederal elements in the EU. But in order finally to contradistinguish between these confederal elements and the federal features of the EU, it is appropriate to identify the defining characteristics of federation too. I have, therefore, provided a brief thumbnail sketch outline of six main features of federation.

1   A federation is a state with a single people which is characterized by the accommodation of the constituent units of the union in the decision-making procedure of the central government on some constitutionally-entrenched basis.

2   Federation is based on unity and diversity which are formally recognised by the combination of 'self-rule and shared rule' in a written and supreme constitution.

3   Self-rule and shared rule are combined in at least two orders of government/governance, each acting directly upon its citizens, in which the constituent units enjoy significant autonomy in matters of local concern but have voluntarily agreed to pool their sovereignty in matters of common concern.

4   The federal constitution incorporates a formal allocation of powers and competences between the central and constituent units with a firm basis in sources of revenue and expenditure which provide the framework for fiscal federalism.

5   The constitution of the federation is not unilaterally amendable by any single order of government. It can be amended only by an overwhelming majority of both the central legislative institutions and the legislative institutions of the constituent units of the federation.

6   The federation has an umpire in the form of a supreme court to regulate the relations between the central authority and the constituent units, and between the constituent units themselves. It has the unchallengeable legal authority to adjudicate on disputes regarding the constitutionality of respective actions.[33]

If we compare and contrast these defining confederal and federal features, it reinforces the thrust of our argument in this chapter. This is that, while there are obviously significant differences between confederation and federation, they also share several common ideas, values and institutional and procedural characteristics. Lister has confirmed what we have already argued when looking closely at the EU: 'the spheres of responsibility allocated to the central authorities and to the member states are surprisingly similar in federal and confederal unions'.[34] Clearly, more powers – and more *exclusive* powers – are usually allocated to federal central authorities, than to confederal authorities, but the unique mix of these in the EU is once again a consequence of the building of Europe via the peculiar Community method of Monnet.

Where, then, does this conceptual analysis of the confederal and federal elements in European integration leave us? What does it tell us about the EU as an intellectual puzzle? This chapter has not explored every conceptual avenue in the intellectual debate about Europe's present and future, but it has at least released us from the old, over-simplified duality of 'either federation or confederation' bequeathed by realist international relations theories. The complex reality suggested here is that there will always be anomalies and odd variations to the general rule in history and political science. Certain hallmarks in the distinction between confederation and federation will, of course, remain valid. They are indelible. But conventional definitions need, periodically, to be adapted and adjusted to suit changing empirical realities. We also need to be reminded that the old confederations were creatures of an era which had either not yet entered or was about to enter the the age of mass (liberal) democracy. If the EU is a new confederation in the sense that we have identified it in this chapter, both the constitutional and political assumptions of the late twentieth century need to be taken into account when we quite correctly resort to historical precedents.

## Conclusion: the shape of things to come

In the unique circumstances of post-1989 Europe, the familiar terms 'confederal' and 'federal' are likely to endure in the public discourse about European integration, but there is already a sense that their meaning on the threshold of the twenty-first century has changed. The current emphasis upon the incomparable admixture of confederal and federal principles evident in the EU reflects an empirical shift away from the sort of 'energetic government' that Hamilton so revered, but it also goes beyond the classic confederations identified above. In short, it is time to carve out a new conceptual space for this new type of 'confederal–federal' union. This is where the new confederations can be located. Contemporary trends, reflected in bodies like the EU, would seem to suggest that in late modernity we are moving toward a new age of looser, more limited, forms of governance. The new European model of confederal union has replaced the classic American model of federation. And as we indicated in Chapter 2 the paradigm shift referred to by Elazar would also seem to suggest that the conventional term 'federation' is now far too constricting a label to encapsulate the new complex realities that exist in the world today. Elazar is surely correct to argue that we must now expand our concepts to accommodate this broad shift or we will simply fail to take account of the new complexities of integration and association.[35]

If this is the case, it is likely that the next century will witness both the rehabilitation and the revitalization of confederation. A double paradox is evident here. Our practical experience of federation has led us to rethink confederation, just as our reappraisal of confederation has inspired a recent reassessment of federalism. And it is the EU experience that has compelled us to reappraise and recycle our old familiar categories. But familiarity can be misleading. The new confederations must not be confused with their aged predecessors. They constitute a different type of union from those much-maligned confederations, more muscular and integrated in some respects, but less centralized than many modern federations. And the evolution of new varieties of confederal unions modelled in some cases on the EU, like the contemporary *Mercosur* in South America, should not surprise us. It is merely reflective of the changing character of international relations. We are reminded, once again, that human beings more easily invent new things than new words to describe them. It is, therefore, in many ways reassuring to note that the conceptual problem of the federal–confederal distinction that was recognised a century ago by Sidgwick has at last – like this book – come full circle. We may interpret Elazar's 'post-modern' paradigm shift in terms of Sidgwick's own notion of 'the development of federality'. In a statement of remarkable prescience a century ago, Sidgwick reflected – as we have here – upon the future evolution of the European idea:

> I ... think it not beyond the limits of sober forecast to conjecture that some further integration may take place in the West European states: and if it should take place, it seems probable that the example of America will be followed, and that the new political aggregate will be formed on the basis of a federal polity. When we turn our gaze from the past to the future, an extension of federalism seems to me the most probable of the political prophecies relative to the form of government.[36]

Sidgwick's reflections remain instructive. The American model may have been superseded but the EU is already a federal polity in the extent to which its values, institutions, policies and procedures conform to an unprecedented interlacing of basic federal and confederal principles. And it will remain an intellectual puzzle only to the extent that we have failed adequately to rethink and reappraise our basic conceptual categories in order to match the new realities.

We have almost reached the point where it is necessary to look back on and assess 50 years of European integration from the particular standpoint of federalism and the federalists. But before we turn to conclude these matters, it is worth pausing to reflect upon the central focus of this chapter. We have been trying to identify and classify the EU as a distinct confederal polity of a new kind, rather than seeking to explain how and why European integration occurs. This is because our revisionist analysis of the historical evolution of the European idea has been the dominant thrust of the book. In the conclusion, therefore, we will return to some of the unresolved controversies which continue to surround the theories of European integration. We will also explore the nature and significance of the building of Europe during the last half-century with a view to reinstating federalism as an important influence upon Europe's past, present and future.

# NOTES

1 H. Sidgwick, *The development of European polity*, London: Macmillan & Co. Ltd, 1903, p. 433.

2 Article A., Title I., (Common Provisions), *Treaty on European Union*, (TEU), Luxembourg: Office for Official Publications of the European Communities, 1992, p. 7.

3 C. Rossiter (ed.), *The federalist papers, Madison 37*, New York: The New York American Library, 1961, p. 230.

4 H. Sidgwick, *The elements of politics*, 4th edn, London: Macmillan & Co. Ltd., 1919, p. 532.

5 See, for example, R.O. Keohane and S. Hoffmann, 'Institutional change in Europe in the 1980s', in R.O. Keohane and S. Hoffmann (eds), *The new European Community: decision-making and institutional change*, pp. 1–39, Oxford: Westview Press, 1991.

6 Rossiter (ed.), *The federalist papers, Madison 37*, p. 229.

7 Rossiter (ed.), *The federalist papers, Madison 40*, pp. 247–48.

8 Rossiter (ed.), *The federalist papers, Madison 39*, p. 246.

9 M. Diamond, 'The federalist's view of federalism', in *Essays in federalism*, (no author), pp. 23–24, Claremont: Institute for Studies in Federalism, 1961.

10 For two contending views of the status of the new American union in 1789 as 'a federal union of states rather than … a federal state', see M. Forsyth, *Unions of states: the theory and practice of confederation*, Leicester: Leicester University Press, 1981, pp. 60–72; and S.H. Beer, *To make a nation: the rediscovery of American federalism*, Cambridge, MA: Harvard University Press, 1993.

11 Diamond, 'The federalist's view of federalism', pp. 38–40.

12 Rossiter (ed.), *The federalist papers, Hamilton 22 & 23*, pp. 151 and 154.

13 Diamond, 'The federalist's view of federalism', p. 41.

14 Phillips Bradley (ed.), *Democracy in America*, vol. I, New York: Knopf, 1951, pp. 158–59.

15 Forsyth, *Unions of states*, p. 72.

16 Forsyth, *Unions of states*, p. 4.

17 E.C. Burnett, *The continental congress*, New York: The Macmillan Co., 1941, p. 257. See also D. Lutz, 'The articles of confederation as the background to the federal republic', *Publius: The Journal of Federalism*, 20(Winter), pp. 55–70, 1990 for further information about the misrepresentation of the so-called 'Antifederalists'.

18 Forsyth, *Unions of states*, p. 4.

19 Rossiter (ed.), *The federalist papers, Hamilton 15*, p. 108.

20 Rossiter (ed.), *The federalist papers, Hamilton 9*, p. 76.

21 Rossiter (ed.), *The federalist papers, Hamilton 20*, p. 138.

22 Forsyth, *Unions of states*, pp. 5, 161 and 183.

23 Forsyth, *Unions of states*, pp. 7 and 15.

24 Rossiter (ed.), *The federalist papers, Hamilton 9*, pp. 74–76.

25 M. Forsyth, 'The political theory of federalism: the relevance of classical approaches', in J.J. Hesse and V. Wright (eds), *Federalizing Europe? the costs, benefits, and preconditions of federal political systems*, p. 40, Oxford: Oxford University Press, 1996.

26 Forsyth, *Unions of states*, p. 186.

27 Forsyth, *Unions of states*, p. 185.

28 J. Pinder, 'European community and nation state: a case for a neo-federalism', *International Affairs*, I, p. 53, 1986.

29 Rossiter (ed.), *The federalist papers, Madison 40*, p. 250.

30 Rossiter (ed.), *The federalist papers, Madison 40*, p. 251.
31 F.K. Lister, *The European union, the united nations and the revival of confederal governance*, London: Greenwood Press, 1996, p. 33.
32 Lister, *The European union*, pp. 33–34.
33 I have drawn on P. King, *Federalism and federation*, London: Croom Helm, 1982; D.J. Elazar, *Exploring federalism*, Tuscaloosa, AL: University of Alabama Press, 1987; and M. Burgess and A.-G. Gagnon (eds), *Comparative federalism and federation: competing traditions and future directions*, Hemel Hempstead: Harvester Wheatsheaf, 1993 for this short profile.
34 Lister, *The European union*, p. 23.
35 D.J. Elazar, 'From statism to federalism: a paradigm shift', *Publius: The Journal of Federalism*, 25(2), pp. 5–18, 1995.
36 Sidgwick, *The development of European polity*, p. 439.

# 9 Federalism and European Union

*Fin de siècle*

This study has confirmed the significance of federalism in the piecemeal, incremental development of post-war West European economic and political integration. It has demonstrated a fundamental continuity of federal ideas, influences and strategies in the evolution of the European idea, from the European Coal and Steel Community (ECSC) in 1951 to the European Economic Community (EEC) and the European Atomic Energy Community (Euratom) in 1957, all of which gradually came to be identified collectively as the European Community (EC) in the years up until the establishment of the European Union (EU) in 1993. Throughout this long, arduous and often convulsive period in post-war West European history, the continuing relevance and resilience of federalism has served as a constant reminder of the existence of a conception of Europe going well beyond mere intergovernmental cooperation.

Federal ideas have seeped into every central institution of the EU, whether supra-national or intergovernmental, significantly affecting inter-institutional relations and flowing through a wide variety of channels both within and without the formal institutional and policy frameworks of the EU. A veritable network of European organizations exists, including political parties, a myriad of interest groups and assorted professional bodies. They promote the federal cause in many ways, using different strategies and tactics, enabling them in effect to alter the political environment in a manner much more conducive to ambitious goals. Our analytical survey of the historical period 1950–2000 has already shown just how far the combination of political leadership, procedural consensus and institutional context can be employed to remarkable effect in the pursuit of a federal Europe. The very fact that the EU represents the application of federal and confederal principles to European integration underlines just how receptive institutional and policy arenas have been to alternative visions of Europe's future. This is precisely how visions become realities. When federalism connects directly with reality, it ceases to be just another alternative vision and can be put into practice. This is why today's unthinkable is frequently tomorrow's convention.

In attempting to reinstate federal ideas, influences and strategies in the

evolution of European integration since 1950, we have perforce challenged the conventional intergovernmental explanation which draws its
strength from the realist school of thought in international relations (IR)
theory and presented a revisionist history of the post-war development of
the European idea. Our purpose has not been to completely remove and
replace what is the dominant intergovernmental or realist model of European integration, but rather to supplement it by taking into account
federal thought and practice. It is no longer acceptable to subsume federalism within the overall theoretical category of neofunctionalism, where it
conveniently disappears from view. Instead, it is necessary to construe the
federal idea as a model in its own right. Fortunately we may be running
with the tide because it is now possible to detect something of a convergence of intellectual opinion about the European experiment. This is that
in order the better to understand the EU, we need a model which effectively combines IR theory, European-level analyses and national domestic
concerns. Federalism as an organizing principle would sit comfortably in
each of these broad interconnected and overlapping approaches to the
study of the EU.

But is the rehabilitation of federalism and confederalism likely in the
current theoretical debate about European integration? The indications
are not promising. IR theory remains largely obsessed with the intricacies
of neorealism versus neoliberal institutionalism which have led to important reassessments and reappraisals of the very foundations of some of the
most influential theories of international politics, but which often seem
largely introverted and of little relevance to the student of European
integration.[1] Neofunctionalism has been revived but not completely reha-
bilitated. Many of its old assumptions have had to be either revised or
replaced in the era of the Single European Market (SEM).[2] The arena of
domestic politics has become increasingly fashionable as a kind of
'bottom-up' policy-making approach to understanding the goals and
behaviour of national state governments in the EU arena, but it suffers
*inter alia* from the need to bridge the national–EU divide more effectively
to explain the strategic interaction of governmental behaviour.[3]

In the extent to which there has been a genuine effort to integrate these
three separate approaches to the study of the EU in one composite model,
the recent contribution of Andrew Moravcsik has probably been the most
instructive. The appearance in the early 1990s of what he has called
'liberal intergovernmentalism' (LI) was a valiant attempt to build a theoretical edifice upon realist IR assumptions, domestic liberal pluralist pressures and the institutional framework of the EU.[4] What emerged was more
an approach to European integration than a new theory.[5] But Moravcsik's
model left very little room for federal ideas, influences and strategies. In
summary, it presented EU decision-making and, by implication, integration as the overall result of a number of interrelated processes and interactions: domestic coalitions, national preferences, rational inter-state

bargaining and negotiations, relative power positions and the image of heads of states and governments avidly pursuing elevated but exclusively domestic concerns in the intergovernmental arena of the Council of Ministers and the European Council. The implication of this composite model of European integration was irresistible: national state actors controlled the process of integration so that its main explanation was a 'liberal intergovernmentalism'. He never seems to have engaged the debate about federalism and the federalists in any systematic way.

A fresh approach to European integration in the 1990s was certainly long overdue, and Moravcsik's LI contribution was welcome. It has stimulated much debate and controversy among interested observers of the EU and European integration, and it has encouraged informed commentators to rethink, re-examine and reappraise their own conceptions of Europe. Nonetheless, it remains a flawed approach to the understanding of European integration, and searching critiques of its basic assumptions have already begun to appear. For federalists, the main targets of attack have been institutional context, linkage politics and political leadership. LI can be criticized first for downgrading and sometimes even ignoring the role played by the central institutions of the EU. On this reckoning, the Council of Minsters plays a passive role: it merely provides a token framework for the efficient conduct of national bargaining and negotiations. Moreover the European Court of Justice (ECJ), the European Parliament (EP) and the Commission are almost invisible. They are in effect relegated to the sidelines of progress in European integration. Moravcsik's LI model, therefore, excludes the possibility of a relative autonomy for the EU institutions and overlooks the existence of an EU agenda – distinct from its constituent parts – with a likely impact upon national policy agendas. And to rely upon a simple 'demand–supply' model of decision-making to explain the EU is trite. It reduces what is a complicated process to an over-simplified cause and effect model which is incapable of explaining the complex conjunction of episodic events, new political contexts and changing leadership personnel.

Linkage politics is also unexplained. Moravcsik's model certainly helps to explain the genesis of national policy preferences, but it fails to make the crucial final link with the EU level of policy outputs. For this argument to be convincing, we would need to bridge the palpable gap between the national and the European levels of decision-making much more effectively than Moravcsik does. Finally, the LI model does not adequately conceptualize the notion of EU elite political leadership. It has conveniently overlooked, and sometimes deliberately ignored, the pivotal roles played by leading federalists in helping to steer integration towards the federal goal. To ignore or to downgrade the significance of Delors, Kohl and Mitterrand in the achievement of a closer federal union in the late 1980s and early 1990s is to run the risk of distorting the very empirical reality that Moravcsik is so keen to verify. And, in refusing to incorporate the active role of the EP, Commission and ECJ into his LI model, he merely compounds the error of underestimating the practical impact of federal ideas, influences and strategies in the building of Europe.

One consequence of Moravcsik's important contribution to the theoretical debate about European integration in the 1990s has been unintentional. This is that it confirms the absurdity of attempting to construct an all-embracing, comprehensive theory of European integration. The days of grand-theorizing along the lines of the old neofunctionalists are clearly over. Instead, we appear to have arrived at a new reality, namely, the recognition that new concepts, approaches and models of European integration are likely to be restricted to episodic events or case studies in the evolution of the European project. Examples of this recent intellectual departure are case studies of the SEM and Economic and Monetary Union (EMU), but a closer investigation of legal integration has also been evident.[6]

For federalists and confederalists alike, the role of the ECJ has always been of crucial importance. Until recently, however, it has been consistently overlooked by political scientists. Lawyers have understandably had the field almost entirely to themselves. When dealing with national courts, this is only to be expected, but in the institutional context of the EU, the role of the ECJ operates in a very different set of circumstances. In its interpretation of EC law, its pivotal position in resolving conflicts between Community law and national law, and in its role as arbiter in legal disputes between member states, the ECJ has a uniquely quasi-political duty to make judgements which enhance and promote European integration. And lawyers have never had any serious reservations or real anxieties in construing the EC as federal in legal terms.

In legal terms, the EC in the EU operates in many ways much as established federations operate. And a solid corpus of EC law independent of the national laws of member states has evolved as the result of a series of celebrated cases which have combined to make the EC literally a 'Community of law'. The famous cases of *van Gend & Loos* (C-26/62), *Costa/ENEL* (C-6/64), and the *Simmenthal judgement* (C-106/77), for example, were the means by which the principles of direct and immediate applicability, uniform interpretation and the primacy of EC law over national law have been firmly established. Clearly, the EU, even with its EC *acquis communautaire*-based pillar, is neither a 'state' nor a 'federal state' but this has not prevented the ECJ from introducing federal and/or confederal elements which have treated the EU, at least by implication, as a confederal union. In effect, the ECJ has created a new legal order, coexisting with the national legal systems of the member states.

One outstanding legal anomaly which will eventually have to be addressed in the next century is the question of granting the EU a distinct legal personality. Currently the EC and the EU are distinct legal entities, but only the former has a concrete legal personality. As Mathew Heim has succinctly demonstrated, this is a crucial ingredient which enables an international organization to enter into agreements with other legal bodies, and to acquire both rights and obligations. Legal personality is not reliant on 'an express statement by the constituent members, but is the result of the actual ability of an organization to bind and be bound'. The body which does this is, therefore, a coherent whole, a totality in its own right. At present, it is unclear which institution can function in the name of the EU or, indeed, whether it can act on its own at all. Heim's view is that a fundamental contradiction exists between the primary objectives of the EU, established by the TEU, and its legal capacity to fulfil these aims. For example, if it is to assert the Union's identity on the international scene and reinforce the protection of the rights and interests of nationals of the member states, it has to be capable of entering into international agreements. But it first has to have legal personality if it is to act in the international community. His argument is incontrovertible: if the EU is impotent in Common Foreign and Security Policy (CFSP) because it is founded upon intergovernmental agreements rather than having been communitarized, this is 'an odd position to be in when the EU is increasingly required to take a role on the world-wide stage'.[7] Legal logic coincides with federalist logic: the EU as a totality should be subject to the rule of law, merge with the EC and fall within the jurisdiction of the ECJ.

Where, then, can we expect federalist pressures to come from in the future, and what are the prospects for further progress towards converting the EU into the 'new confederation' which we have already identified in this book? In a nutshell, the pressures for a federal Europe will derive from the existing *acquis communautaire*, elite political leadership, institutional context and the logic of diversity inherent in federal principles which can accommodate various forms of asymmetrical policy positions and institutional capacity and representation. EMU is of critical importance, but it is not the only game in town. There are other imperatives. The progressive evolution of the CFSP and the new departures in defence policy, recently agreed by the British and French member state governments, to promote a distinct European defence identity with an enhanced defence capability linked to but separate from the established American-dominated North Atlantic Treaty Organization (NATO) are also urgent. There are already strong indications that Washington's interest in European security has declined. The EU must look increasingly to its own resources for future defence requirements in view of the intensified American retreat from European military affairs that now seems likely. There need be no intention purposively to undermine the western alliance, but the development of an EU capacity to intervene in European trouble spots when the United States is either unable or unwilling to do so seems now to be a self-evident necessity.

But, if there might soon be a much closer relationship between the CFSP and an emergent if selective European defence policy, it is in the

areas of enlargement and institutional reform that federalists face probably the two most challenging adjustments necessary for the new confederal Europe to function effectively. And, of course, these two areas are
intimately intertwined. The Commission's 'Agenda 2000: for a stronger
and wider union', published in July 1997, has already acknowledged this
interconnectedness and has identified and outlined a vision capable of
reality for the next century. But while many of the issues included in Parts
I and III of Agenda 2000 – particularly those dealing with the policies of
the Union and the new financial framework 2000–06 – have already begun
to be addressed, the Commission's latest official document on the future
of the EU on the threshold of the twenty-first century remains anaemic
about the precise implications for institutional reform of the most significant enlargement in its history. The Luxembourg European Council in
December 1997 preserved the original distinction made by the Commission between the six fast-track applicants most likely to be able to accommodate the requirements of membership and the remaining five
countries which might have real problems in so doing. In underlining this
distinction, however, it also acknowledged a certain degree of diplomatic
flexibility in order to avoid building a new wall between the two groups of
applicant states.

In November 1998, the first substantive talks on enlargement with the
representatives of Hungary, Poland, the Czech Republic, Slovenia, Estonia
and Cyprus began by screening their existing national policies with EU
regulations. Initially these were in the seven areas of: science and research;
telecommunications and information technologies; education and training; culture and audio-visual policy; industrial policy; small- and medium-
sized undertakings; and the CFSP. This was the beginning of what
promises to be a long and difficult process of adjustment and adaptation
which will create, in the first instance, an EU of at least 21 member states.
Federalists are, therefore, keen to see a much stronger link established
between the current negotiations, together with the much harder policy
bargaining that lies ahead, and the inescapable need for streamlining the
decision-making process, combined with overall institutional reform.
Indeed, it is not too early to begin to conceptualize and contemplate a
new EU confederation of 25 member states. Consequently the federalists'
strategy would be to adopt a major institutional reform – probably going
back in certain respects to first principles – which would be tailor-made for
the next century. If the crucial linkage between enlargement and institutional reform is not addressed, the danger of policy- and decision-making
overload and its attendant economic and political consequences in the
face of the huge adjustments required will simply grow exponentially. The
EU is unlikely to fall apart but it is in danger of being severely disabled.

Agenda 2000, then, is not by itself the answer to what the EU needs in
order to be adequately equipped for the new century. The European
experiment has reached another one of those critical watersheds in its

50-year evolution. It is time to confront some very elemental questions if it is not to risk being crippled from within. Not for nothing did the Commission include a salutary plea in the introduction to its latest ambitious project:

> The Commission ... suggests that a new Intergovernmental Conference be convened as soon as possible after 2000 to produce a thorough reform of the provisions of the Treaty concerning the composition and functioning of the institutions. This would, in any event, have to involve the introduction of qualified majority voting across the board.... With the help from a new Treaty, the support from a strong euro and a vast internal market and the driving force from the dynamics of enlargement, the Union should enter the next century in conditions which are better than those which it faces today.[8]

With these reflections from the Commission's Agenda 2000, it is time to bring our conclusion to a close. We have briefly addressed the major conceptual dimensions to a federal Europe and we have revisited the recent theoretical trends about European integration. We have also looked at the urgent and weighty challenges which lie ahead for the EU and we have underlined their complex interrelationships. It is clear from our own ruminations in this chapter that the EU on the threshold of the twenty-first century has enormous strengths and achievements to its credit, but that these merits coexist alongside serious weaknesses and failures. The building of Europe will continue apace and our conclusion is that its construction will continue in a federal vein with it constituting the first of the new confederations. This development is, as yet, only dimly perceived, and evidence for both its conceptual and empirical emergence is only just beginning to appear. But with sufficient effort and awareness, the signs can already be detected. When Carlo Azeglio Ciampi, Italy's current Treasury minister, recently threw his weight behind calls for a flexible interpretation of the EU's Growth and Stability Pact in the EMU project, he also mused about the future configuration of Europe. In calling for 'an economic government' for Europe once the Euro was launched in January 1999, he opined: 'I don't think we will have a federal government, but something between a federal state and a federation of states'.[9] This is the new confederation.

In 1999–2000, we can expect the publication of a veritable avalanche of historical surveys looking back and assessing the twentieth century, but there will also be studies whose main purpose will be to take stock of the last thousand years as well as those which will consider the multifaceted implications of the new millennium. It is with these thoughts in mind that we should contemplate our first opportunity to be able to look back and attempt to assess what is, after all, only half a century of European integration from the visionary Schuman Declaration of May 1950 to the perceptive remarks of Carlo Ciampi in November 1998. These vistas correspond to the conversion of vision into reality. We must remember that Europe could not have been built by national states alone, but that it could not have been built without them either. Spinelli was right: the EU in the year 2000 is the product of the interaction between what exists and what must exist. And it reinforces what is, perhaps, the main lesson to be learned from this remarkable venture into the building of a federal Europe, namely, the indispensable role played by political ideas about the future of Europe without which no ambitious project can ever have any realistic chance of coming to fruition.

## NOTES

1 See, for example, R. Powell, 'Anarchy in international relations theory: the neorealist–neoliberal debate', *International Organization* (IO), 48(2), pp. 313–44, Spring 1994.
2 See, for example, W. Sandholtz and J. Zysman, '1992: recasting the European bargain', *World Politics*, 42(1), pp. 95–128, October 1989; D. Mutimer, '1992 and the political integration of Europe: neofunctionalism reconsidered', *Journal of European Integration*, 13, pp. 75–101, 1989.
3 See S. Bulmer, 'Domestic politics and European Community policy-making', *Journal of Common Market Studies*, 21, pp. 349–63, 1983 and the arguments advanced by A.S. Milward, F.M.B. Lynch, F. Romero, R. Ranieri and V. Sorensen, *The frontier of national sovereignty: history and theory 1945–1992*, London: Routledge, 1993.
4 A. Moravcsik, 'Preferences and power in the European Community: a liberal intergovernmentalist approach', *Journal of Common Market Studies*, 31(4), pp. 473–524, 1993.
5 See D. Wincott, 'Institutional interaction and European integration: towards an everyday critique of liberal intergovernmentalism', *Journal of Common Market Studies*, 33(4), pp. 597–609; and A. Moravcsik, 'Liberal intergovernmentalism and integration: a rejoinder', *Journal of Common Market Studies*, 33(4), pp. 611–28.
6 See, for example, A.-M. Burley and W. Mattli, 'Europe before the court: a political theory of legal integration', *International Organization*, 47(1), pp. 41–76, Winter 1993; and G. Garrett, 'The politics of legal integration in the European Union', *International Organization*, 49(1), pp. 171–81, Winter 1995.
7 M. Heim, 'See EU in court', *Viewpoint, European Voice: a weekly review of the union*, 3(22), p. 14, 5–11 June 1997.
8 Commission of the European Communities (1997), Agenda 2000: for a stronger and wider union, *Bulletin of the European Union*, supplement 5/97, Luxembourg: Office for Official Publications of the EC, 1997, p. 13.
9 Ciampi quoted in the *Financial Times*, 13 November 1998, p. 1.

# Index